SPY×FAMILY

STORY AND ART BY
TATSUYA ENDO

4

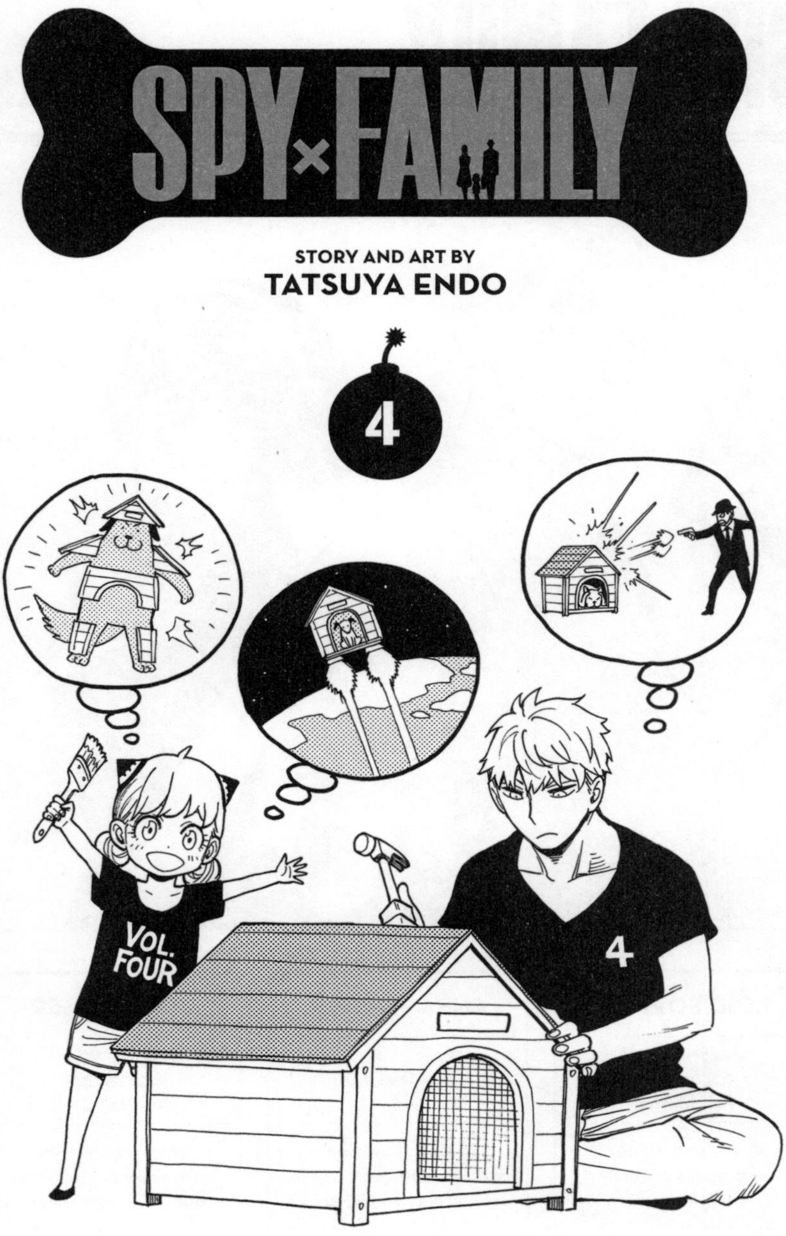
VOL.
FOUR
4

SPY×FAMILY CHARACTERS

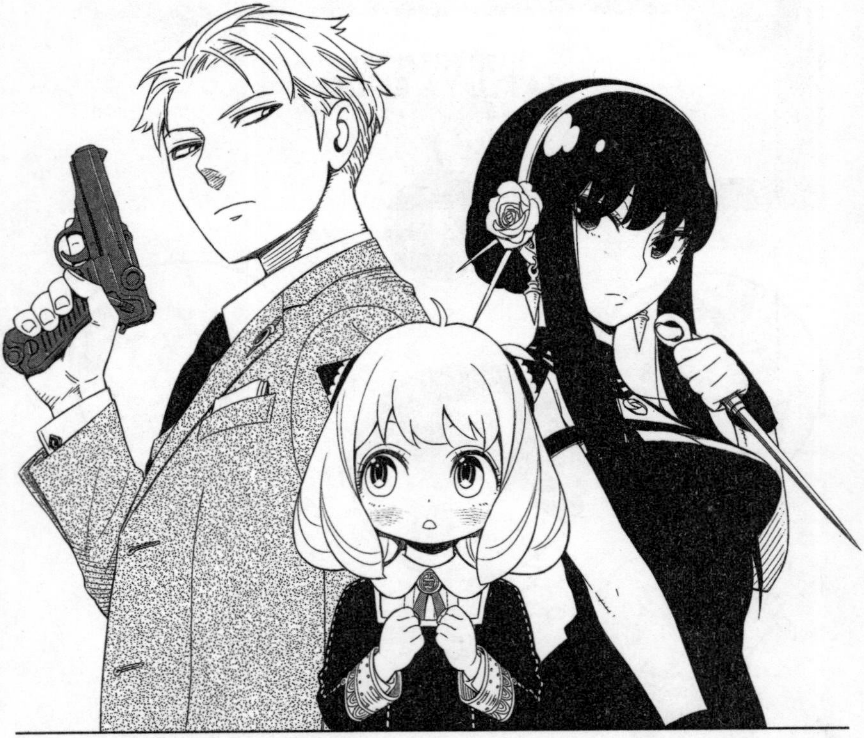

LOID FORGER

ROLE: Husband
OCCUPATION:
Psychiatrist

A spy and master of disguise covertly serving the nation of Westalis. His code name is "Twilight."

ANYA FORGER

ROLE: Daughter

A telepath whose abilities were created in an experiment conducted by a certain organization. She can read the minds of others.

YOR FORGER

ROLE: Wife
OCCUPATION:
City Hall Clerk

Lives a secret life as an assassin. Her code name is "Thorn Princess."

MISSION

OPERATION STRIX

Spy on Donovan Desmond, a dangerous figure who threatens to disrupt peace between the East and West. Must gain entry into the prestigious Eden Academy to breach the target's inner circle.

TARGET

DONOVAN DESMOND

The focus of Operation Strix. Chairman of Ostania's National Unity Party.

KEY PEOPLE

FRANKY

Intelligence asset who works with Twilight.

Handler for Westalis's intelligence agency.

BECKY BLACKWELL

Anya's friend.

DAMIAN DESMOND

Second son of Donovan Desmond.

YURI BRIAR

Yor's younger brother, a secret police officer.

STORY

Westalis secret agent Twilight receives orders to uncover the plans of Donovan Desmond, the warmongering chairman of Ostania's National Unity Party. To do so, Twilight must pose as Loid Forger, create a fake family and enroll his child at the prestigious Eden Academy. However, by sheer coincidence, the daughter he selects from an orphanage is secretly a telepath! Also, the woman who agrees to be in a sham marriage with him is secretly an assassin!

While concealing their true identities from one another, the three now find themselves living together as a family. Yor's brother Yuri harbors doubts about the authenticity of his sister's marriage, but Twilight manages to protect their secret with a brazen display of affection toward Yor. The mission for world peace continues as Anya tries to earn a *stella* star through community service...but fails. However, after reading a drowning boy's desperate thoughts and saving his life, she is awarded a star after all! As a reward, her family agrees to get her a dog. What could possibly go wrong...?

CONTENTS

SPY×FAMILY (4)

MISSION 18

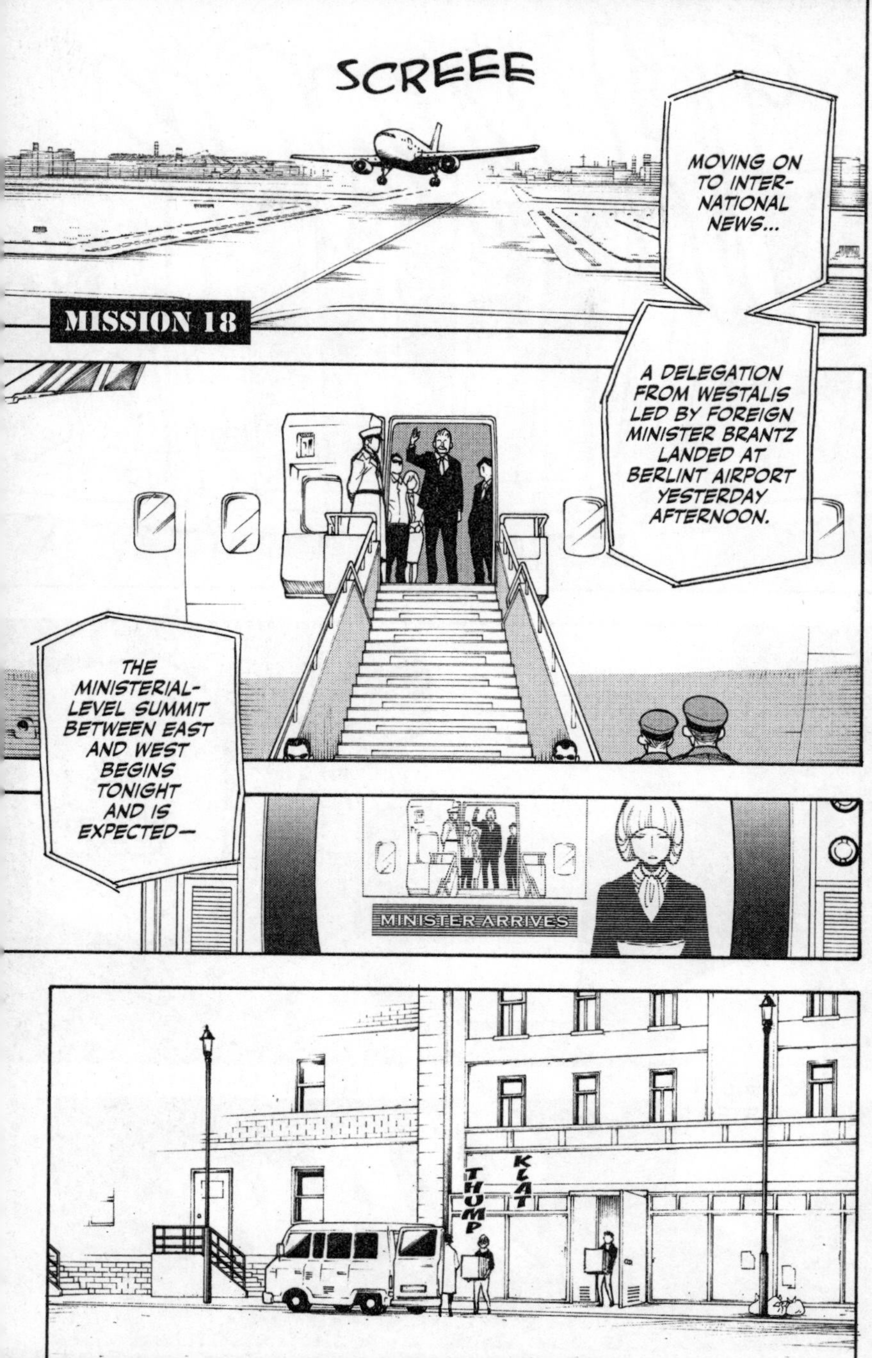
SCREEE
MOVING ON TO INTERNATIONAL NEWS...
A DELEGATION FROM WESTALIS LED BY FOREIGN MINISTER BRANTZ LANDED AT BERLINT AIRPORT YESTERDAY AFTERNOON.
THE MINISTERIAL-LEVEL SUMMIT BETWEEN EAST AND WEST BEGINS TONIGHT AND IS EXPECTED—
MINISTER ARRIVES
KLAT
THUMP

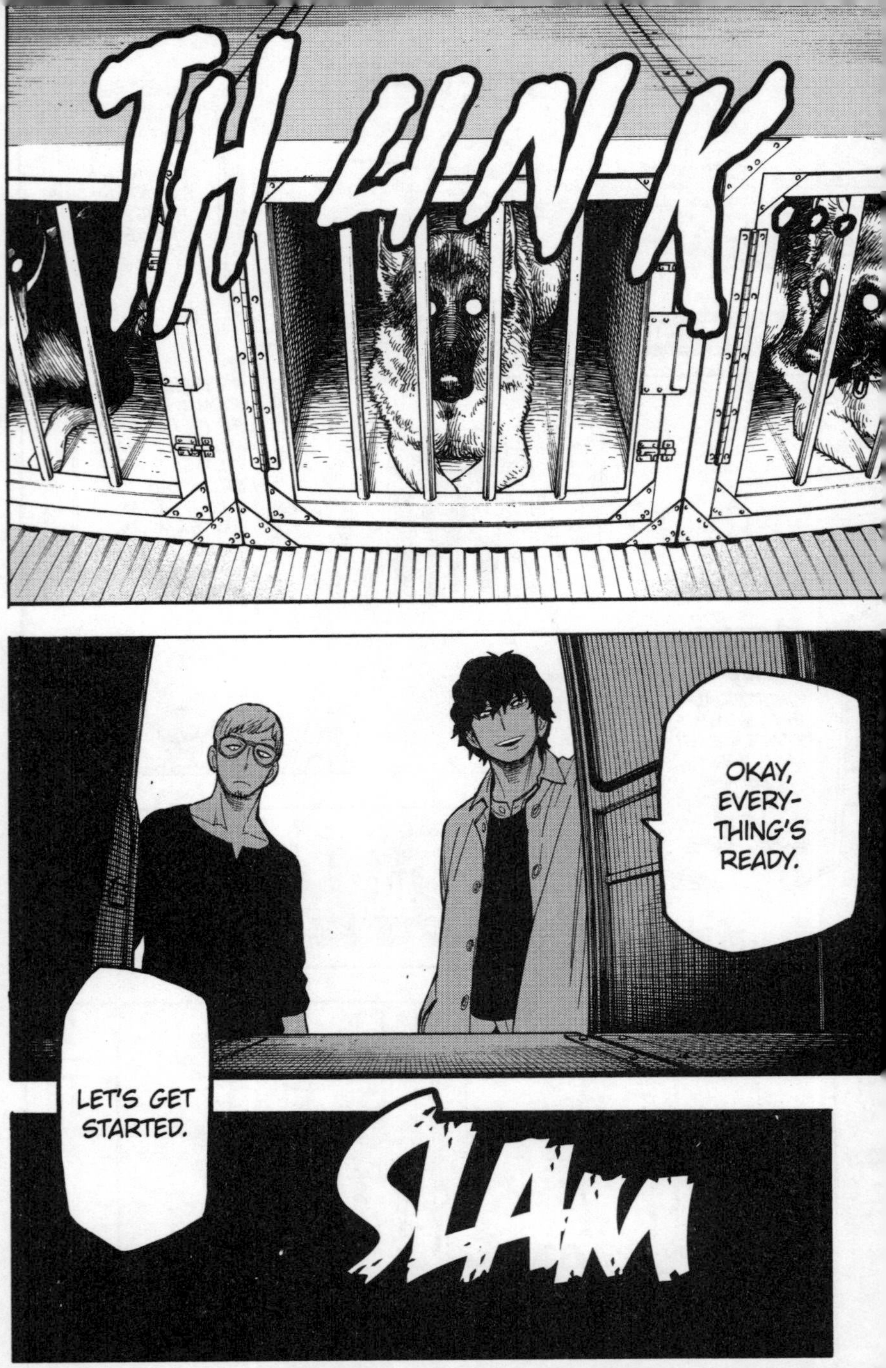
THUNK...
OKAY, EVERY-THING'S READY.
LET'S GET STARTED.
SLAM

SPY×FAMILY

MISSION 18

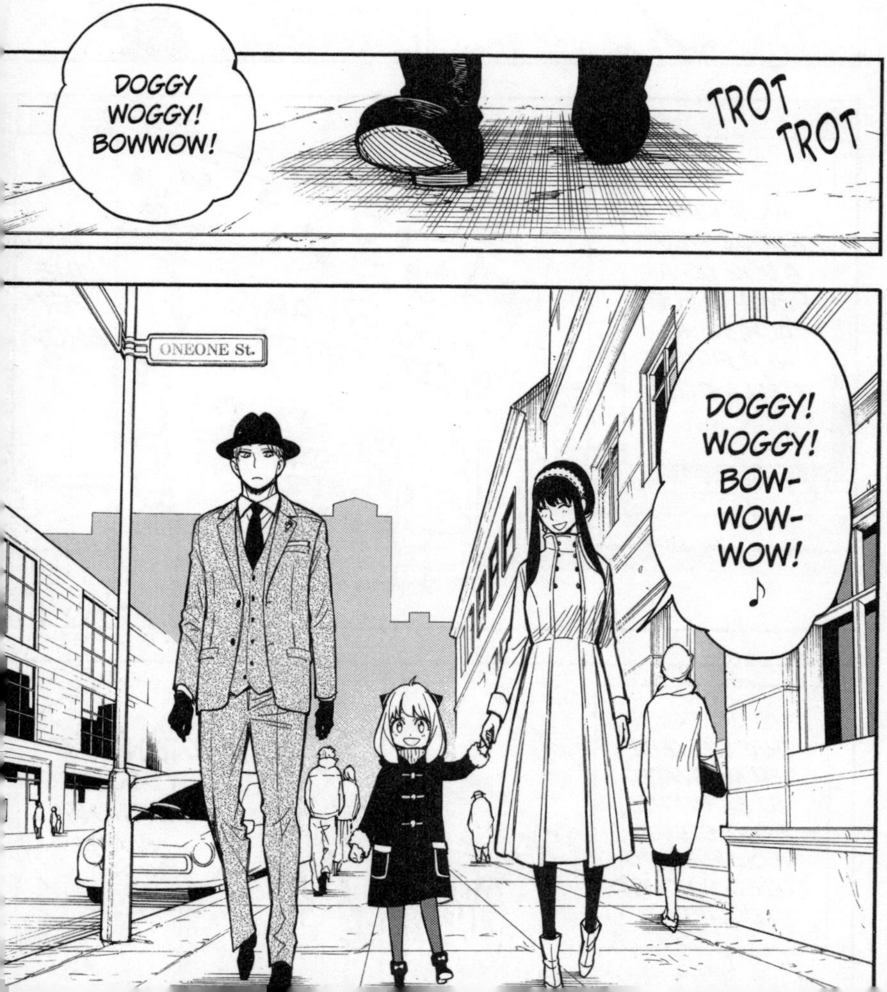
TROT TROT
DOGGY WOGGY! BOWWOW!
DOGGY! WOGGY! BOW-WOW-WOW! ♪
ONEONE St.

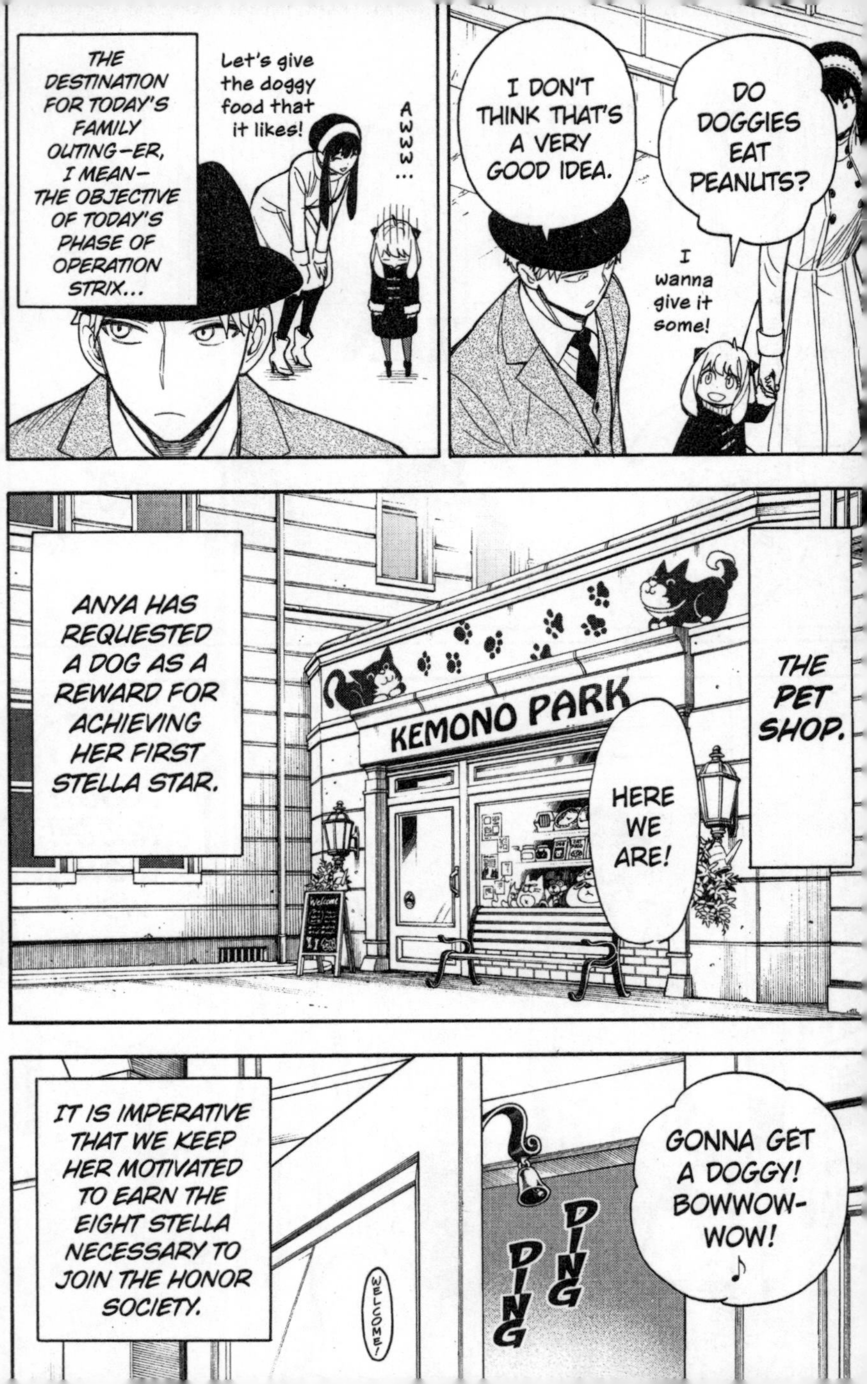
DO DOGGIES EAT PEANUTS?
I wanna give it some!
I DON'T THINK THAT'S A VERY GOOD IDEA.
AWWW...
Let's give the doggy food that it likes!
THE DESTINATION FOR TODAY'S FAMILY OUTING—ER, I MEAN— THE OBJECTIVE OF TODAY'S PHASE OF OPERATION STRIX...
THE PET SHOP.
HERE WE ARE!
KEMONO PARK
ANYA HAS REQUESTED A DOG AS A REWARD FOR ACHIEVING HER FIRST STELLA STAR.
GONNA GET A DOGGY! BOWWOW-WOW! ♪
DING DING
WELCOME!
IT IS IMPERATIVE THAT WE KEEP HER MOTIVATED TO EARN THE EIGHT STELLA NECESSARY TO JOIN THE HONOR SOCIETY.

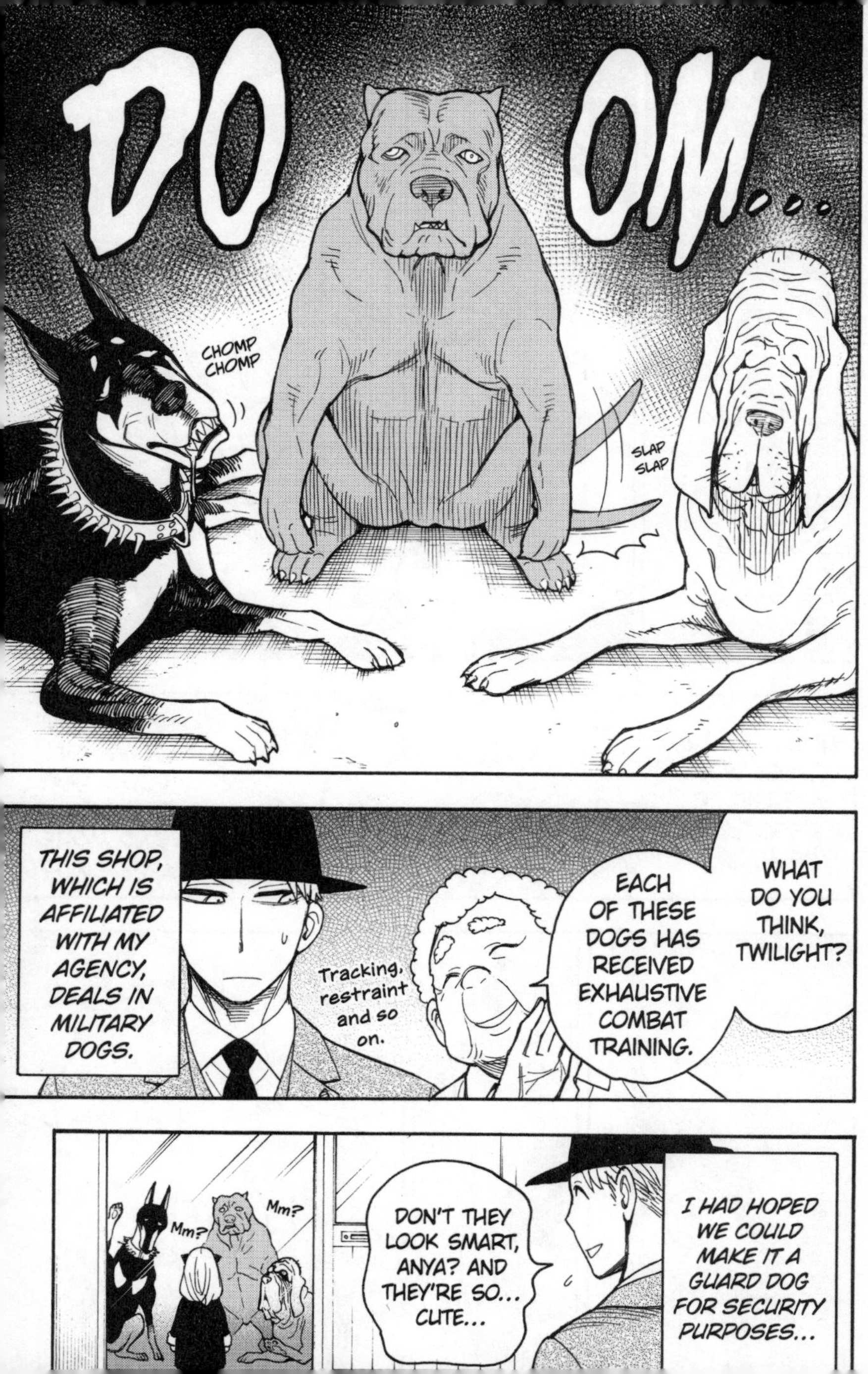
DO OM...
SLAP SLAP
CHOMP CHOMP
WHAT DO YOU THINK, TWILIGHT?
EACH OF THESE DOGS HAS RECEIVED EXHAUSTIVE COMBAT TRAINING.
Tracking, restraint and so on.
THIS SHOP, WHICH IS AFFILIATED WITH MY AGENCY, DEALS IN MILITARY DOGS.
I HAD HOPED WE COULD MAKE IT A GUARD DOG FOR SECURITY PURPOSES...
DON'T THEY LOOK SMART, ANYA? AND THEY'RE SO... CUTE...
Mm?
Mm?

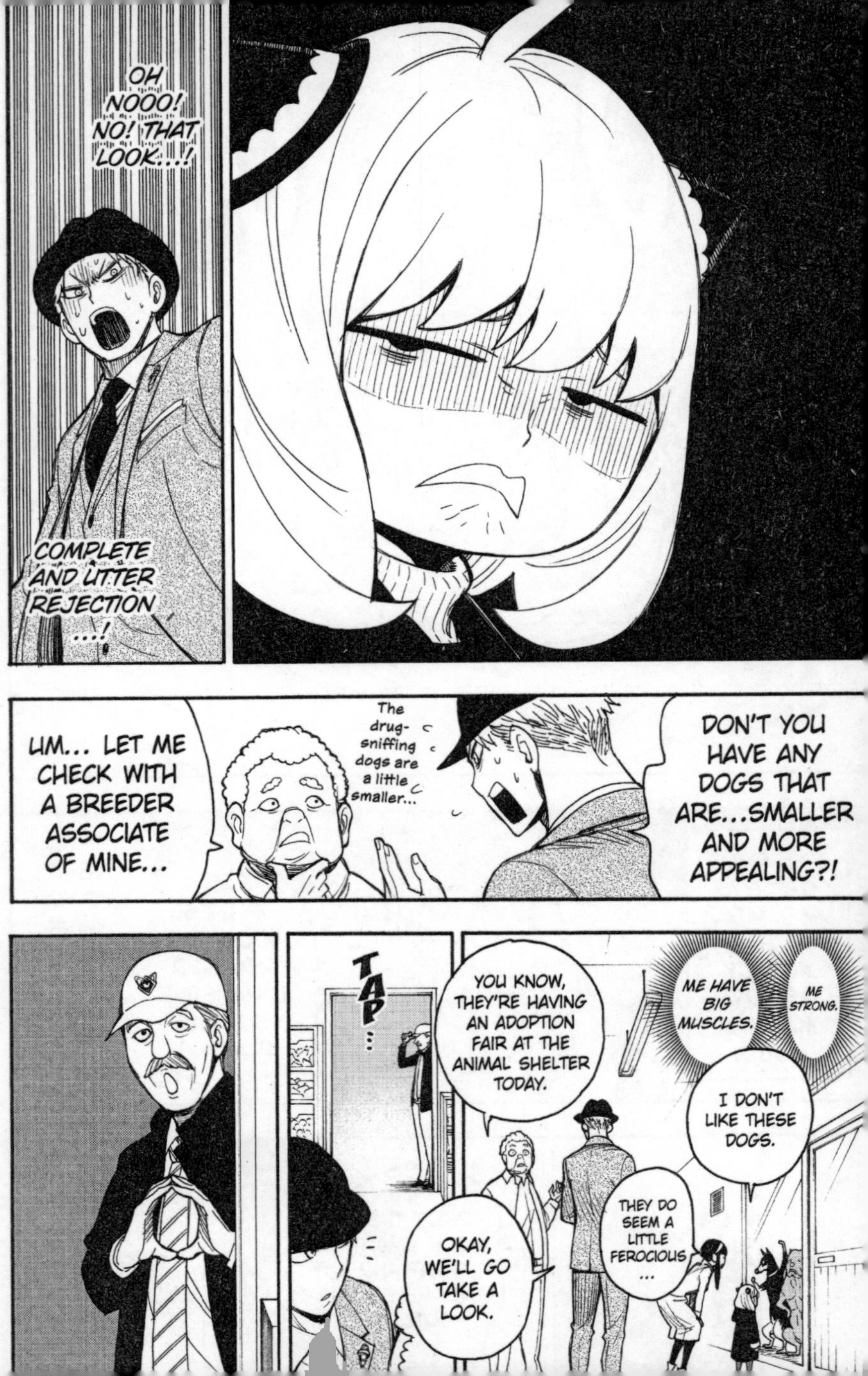
OH NOOO! NO! THAT LOOK...!
COMPLETE AND UTTER REJECTION ...!
DON'T YOU HAVE ANY DOGS THAT ARE...SMALLER AND MORE APPEALING?!
The drug-sniffing dogs are a little smaller...
UM... LET ME CHECK WITH A BREEDER ASSOCIATE OF MINE...
ME STRONG.
ME HAVE BIG MUSCLES.
I DON'T LIKE THESE DOGS.
THEY DO SEEM A LITTLE FEROCIOUS ...
YOU KNOW, THEY'RE HAVING AN ADOPTION FAIR AT THE ANIMAL SHELTER TODAY.
OKAY, WE'LL GO TAKE A LOOK.
TAP...

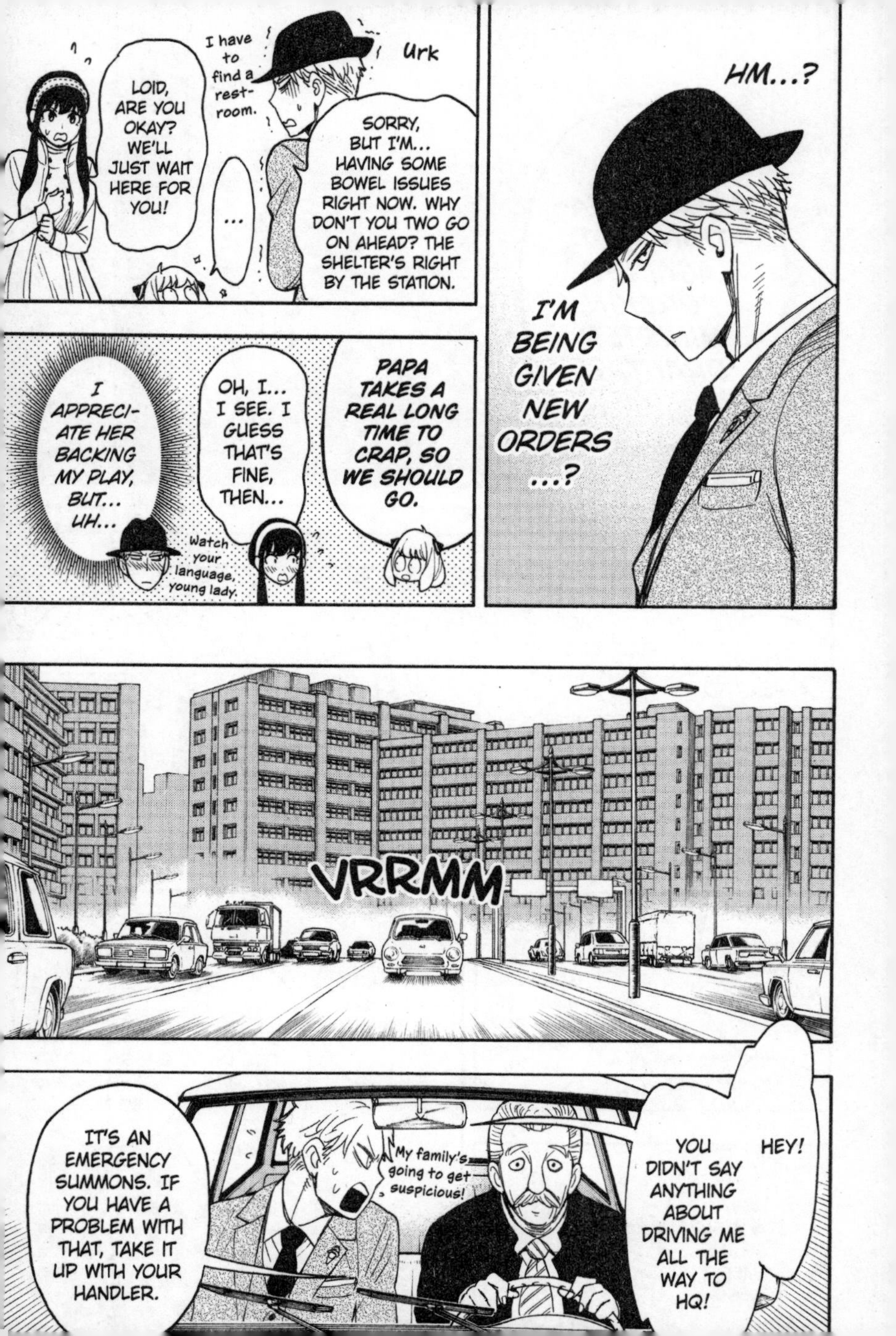
HM...?
I'M BEING GIVEN NEW ORDERS ...?
Urk
SORRY, BUT I'M... HAVING SOME BOWEL ISSUES RIGHT NOW. WHY DON'T YOU TWO GO ON AHEAD? THE SHELTER'S RIGHT BY THE STATION.
I have to find a rest-room.
LOID, ARE YOU OKAY? WE'LL JUST WAIT HERE FOR YOU!
...
PAPA TAKES A REAL LONG TIME TO CRAP, SO WE SHOULD GO.
OH, I... I SEE. I GUESS THAT'S FINE, THEN...
Watch your language, young lady.
I APPRECI-ATE HER BACKING MY PLAY, BUT... UH...
VRRMM
HEY!
YOU DIDN'T SAY ANYTHING ABOUT DRIVING ME ALL THE WAY TO HQ!
My family's going to get suspicious!
IT'S AN EMERGENCY SUMMONS. IF YOU HAVE A PROBLEM WITH THAT, TAKE IT UP WITH YOUR HANDLER.

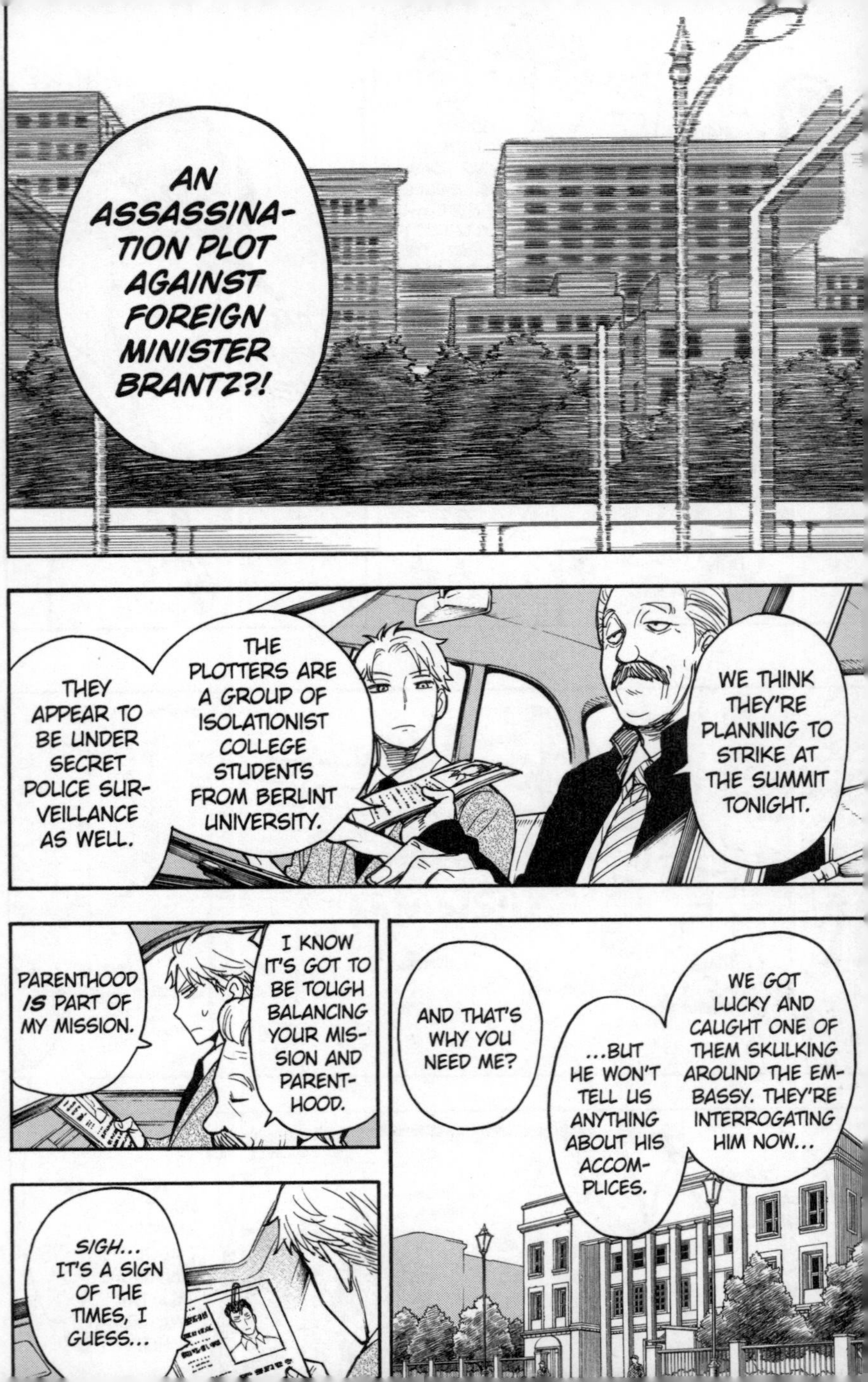
AN ASSASSINATION PLOT AGAINST FOREIGN MINISTER BRANTZ?!
WE THINK THEY'RE PLANNING TO STRIKE AT THE SUMMIT TONIGHT.
THE PLOTTERS ARE A GROUP OF ISOLATIONIST COLLEGE STUDENTS FROM BERLINT UNIVERSITY.
THEY APPEAR TO BE UNDER SECRET POLICE SURVEILLANCE AS WELL.
WE GOT LUCKY AND CAUGHT ONE OF THEM SKULKING AROUND THE EMBASSY. THEY'RE INTERROGATING HIM NOW...
...BUT HE WON'T TELL US ANYTHING ABOUT HIS ACCOMPLICES.
AND THAT'S WHY YOU NEED ME?
I KNOW IT'S GOT TO BE TOUGH BALANCING YOUR MISSION AND PARENTHOOD.
PARENTHOOD *IS* PART OF MY MISSION.
SIGH... IT'S A SIGN OF THE TIMES, I GUESS...

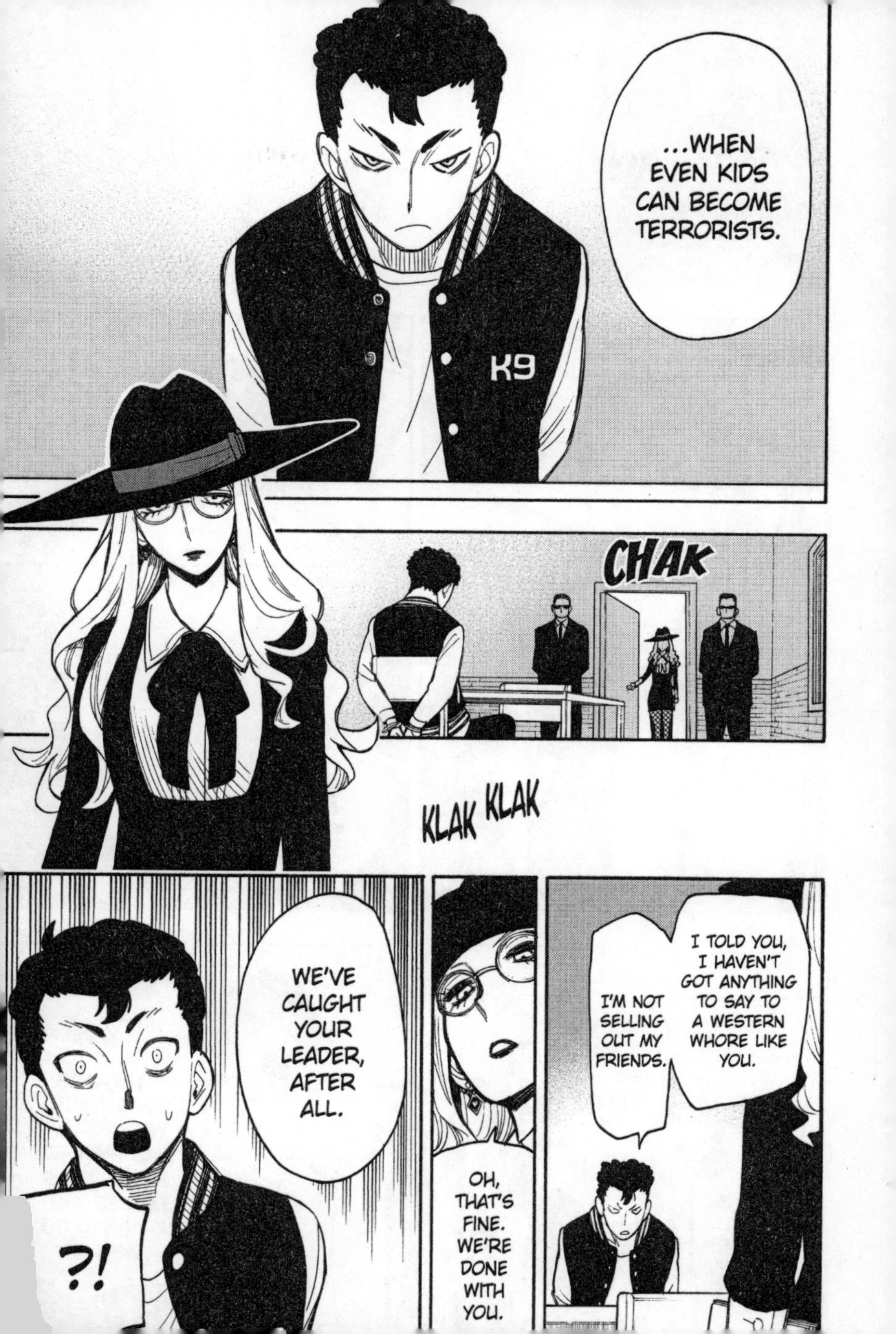
...WHEN EVEN KIDS CAN BECOME TERRORISTS.
CHAK
KLAK KLAK
I TOLD YOU, I HAVEN'T GOT ANYTHING TO SAY TO A WESTERN WHORE LIKE YOU.
I'M NOT SELLING OUT MY FRIENDS.
OH, THAT'S FINE. WE'RE DONE WITH YOU.
WE'VE CAUGHT YOUR LEADER, AFTER ALL.
?!

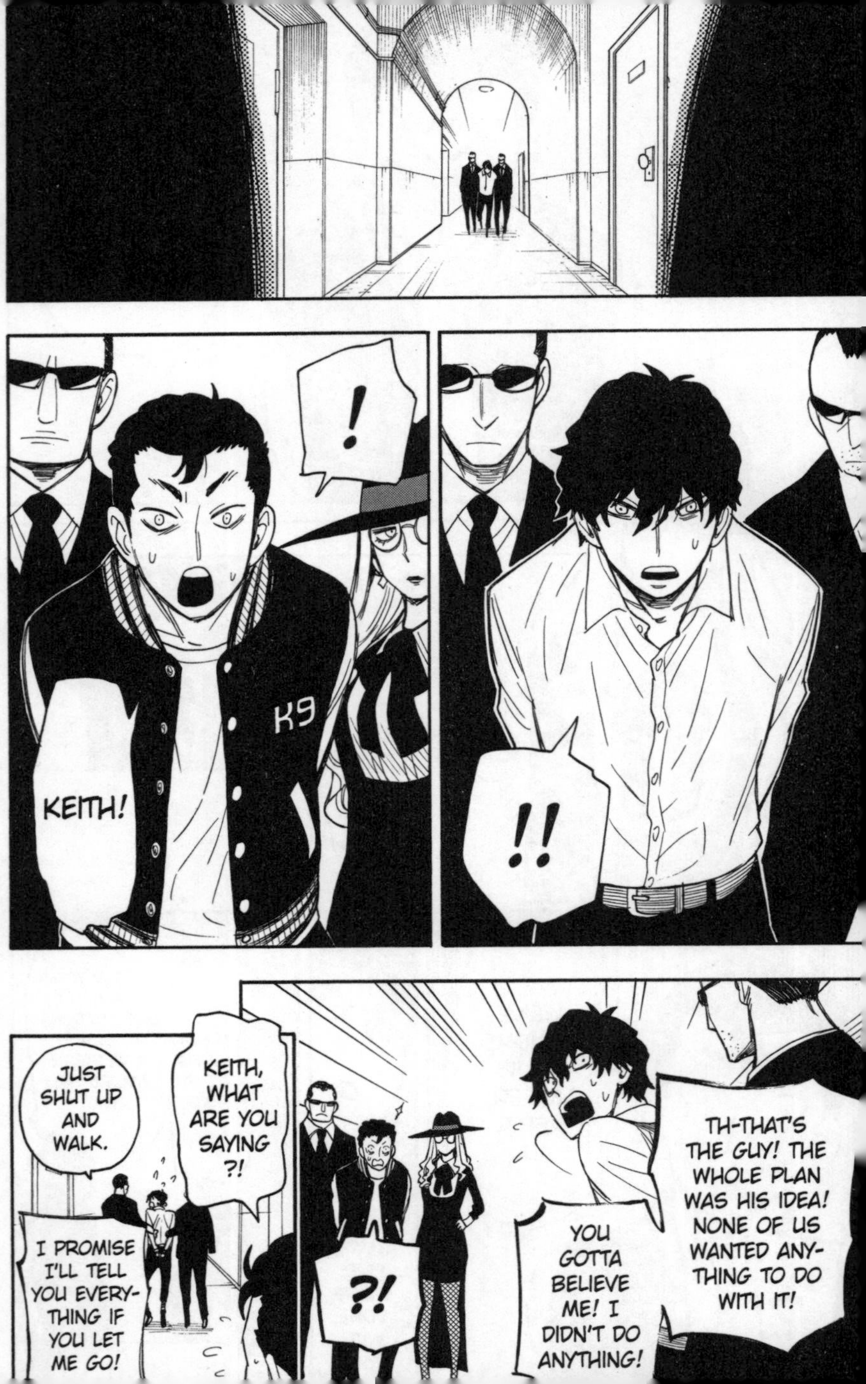
!!
!
KEITH!
TH-THAT'S THE GUY! THE WHOLE PLAN WAS HIS IDEA! NONE OF US WANTED ANY-THING TO DO WITH IT!
YOU GOTTA BELIEVE ME! I DIDN'T DO ANYTHING!
KEITH, WHAT ARE YOU SAYING ?!
?!
JUST SHUT UP AND WALK.
I PROMISE I'LL TELL YOU EVERY-THING IF YOU LET ME GO!

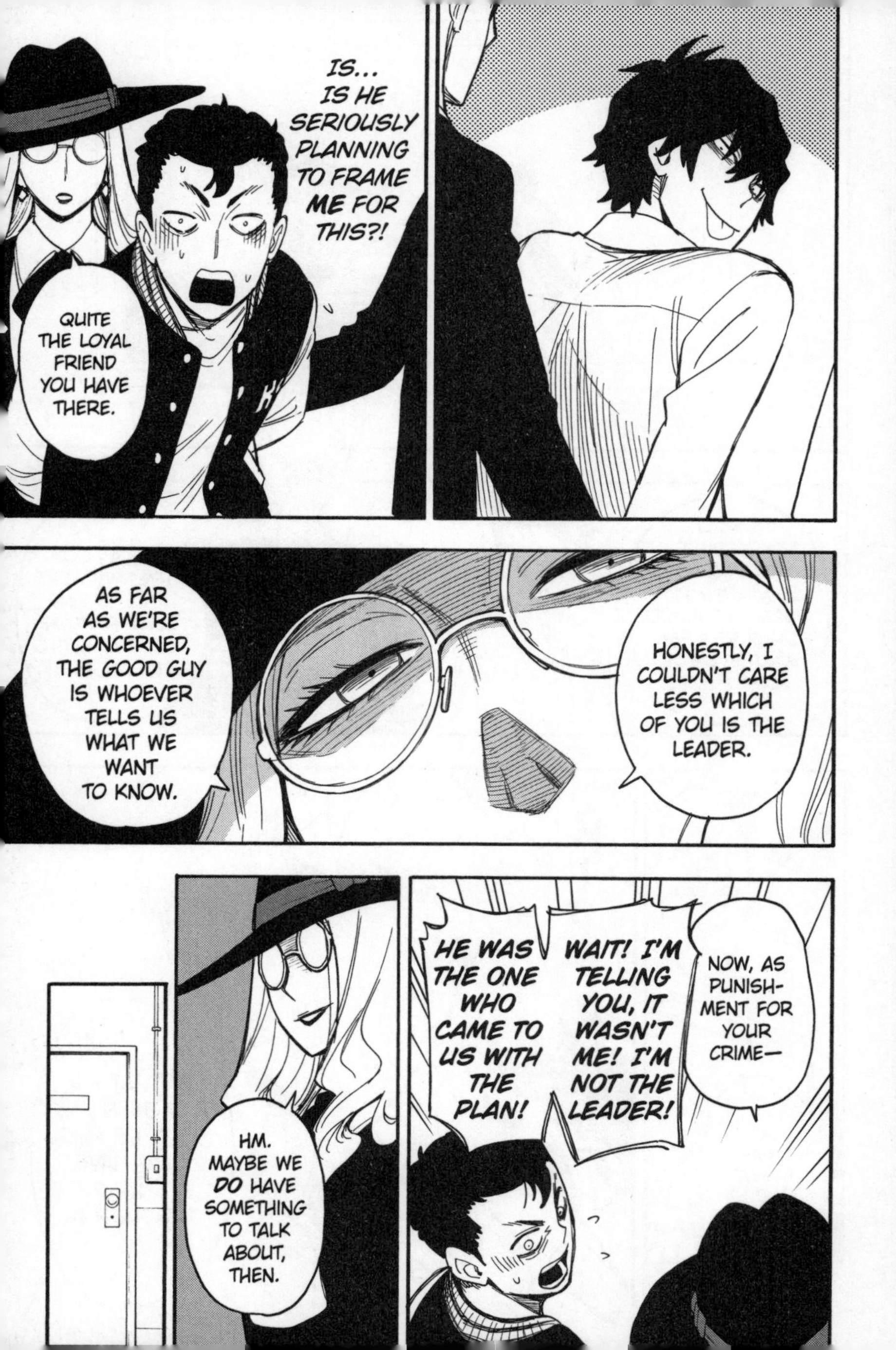
IS... IS HE SERIOUSLY PLANNING TO FRAME ME FOR THIS?!
QUITE THE LOYAL FRIEND YOU HAVE THERE.
HONESTLY, I COULDN'T CARE LESS WHICH OF YOU IS THE LEADER.
AS FAR AS WE'RE CONCERNED, THE GOOD GUY IS WHOEVER TELLS US WHAT WE WANT TO KNOW.
NOW, AS PUNISHMENT FOR YOUR CRIME—
WAIT! I'M TELLING YOU, IT WASN'T ME! I'M NOT THE LEADER!
HE WAS THE ONE WHO CAME TO US WITH THE PLAN!
HM. MAYBE WE DO HAVE SOMETHING TO TALK ABOUT, THEN.

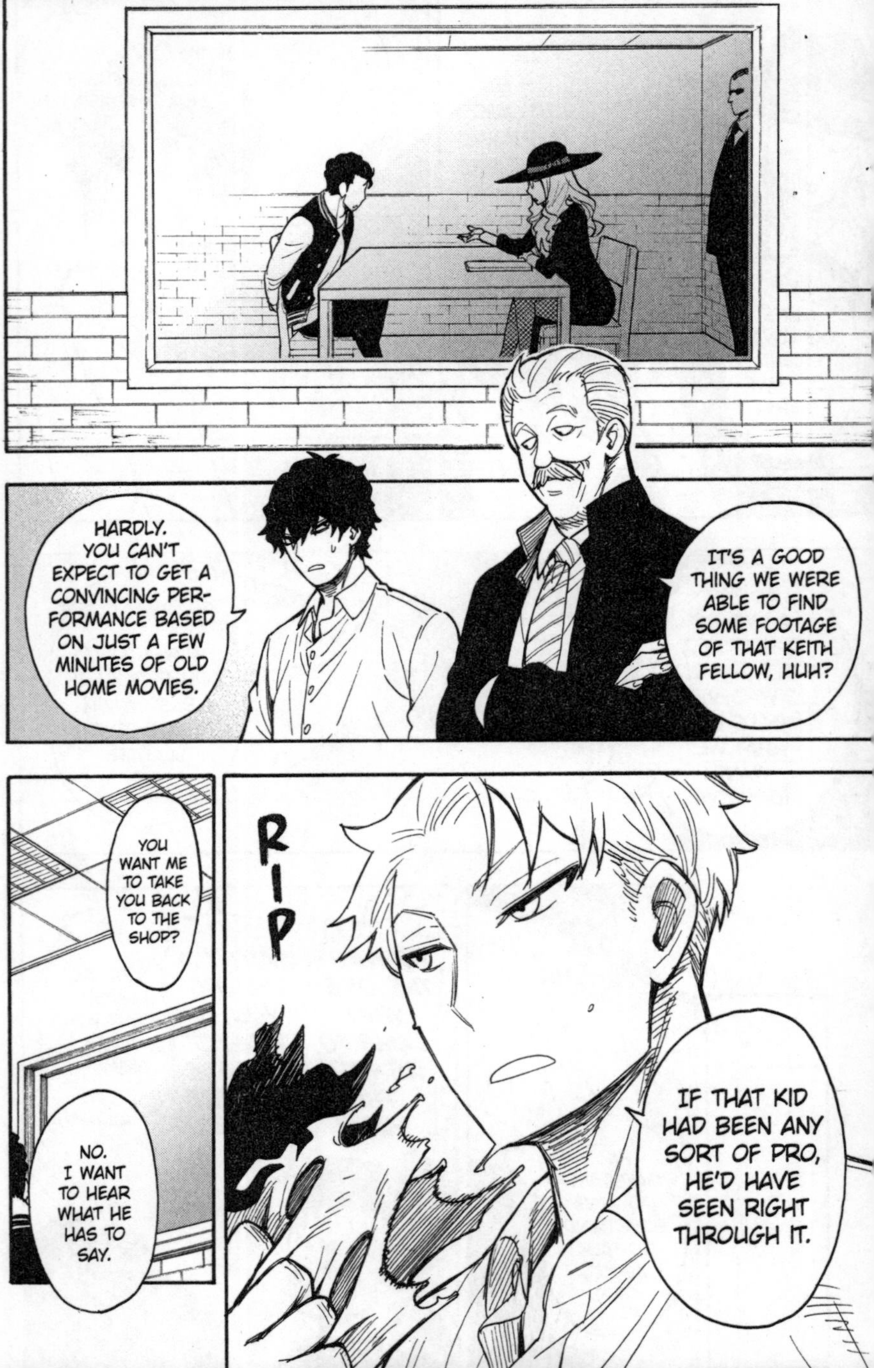
IT'S A GOOD THING WE WERE ABLE TO FIND SOME FOOTAGE OF THAT KEITH FELLOW, HUH?
HARDLY. YOU CAN'T EXPECT TO GET A CONVINCING PER-FORMANCE BASED ON JUST A FEW MINUTES OF OLD HOME MOVIES.
RIP
IF THAT KID HAD BEEN ANY SORT OF PRO, HE'D HAVE SEEN RIGHT THROUGH IT.
YOU WANT ME TO TAKE YOU BACK TO THE SHOP?
NO. I WANT TO HEAR WHAT HE HAS TO SAY.

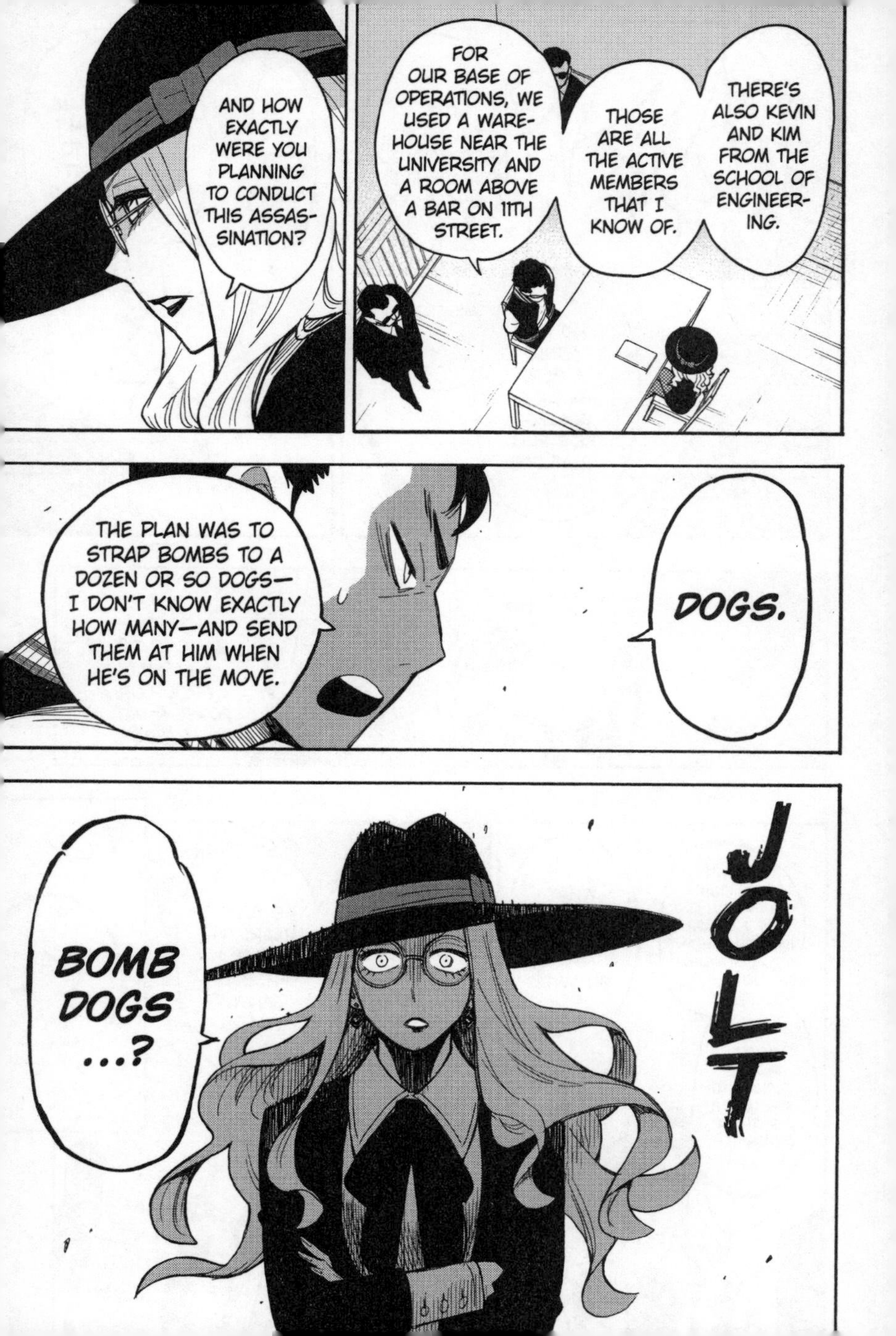
THERE'S ALSO KEVIN AND KIM FROM THE SCHOOL OF ENGINEER-ING.
THOSE ARE ALL THE ACTIVE MEMBERS THAT I KNOW OF.
FOR OUR BASE OF OPERATIONS, WE USED A WARE-HOUSE NEAR THE UNIVERSITY AND A ROOM ABOVE A BAR ON 11TH STREET.
AND HOW EXACTLY WERE YOU PLANNING TO CONDUCT THIS ASSAS-SINATION?
THE PLAN WAS TO STRAP BOMBS TO A DOZEN OR SO DOGS—I DON'T KNOW EXACTLY HOW MANY—AND SEND THEM AT HIM WHEN HE'S ON THE MOVE.
DOGS.
JOLT
BOMB DOGS ...?

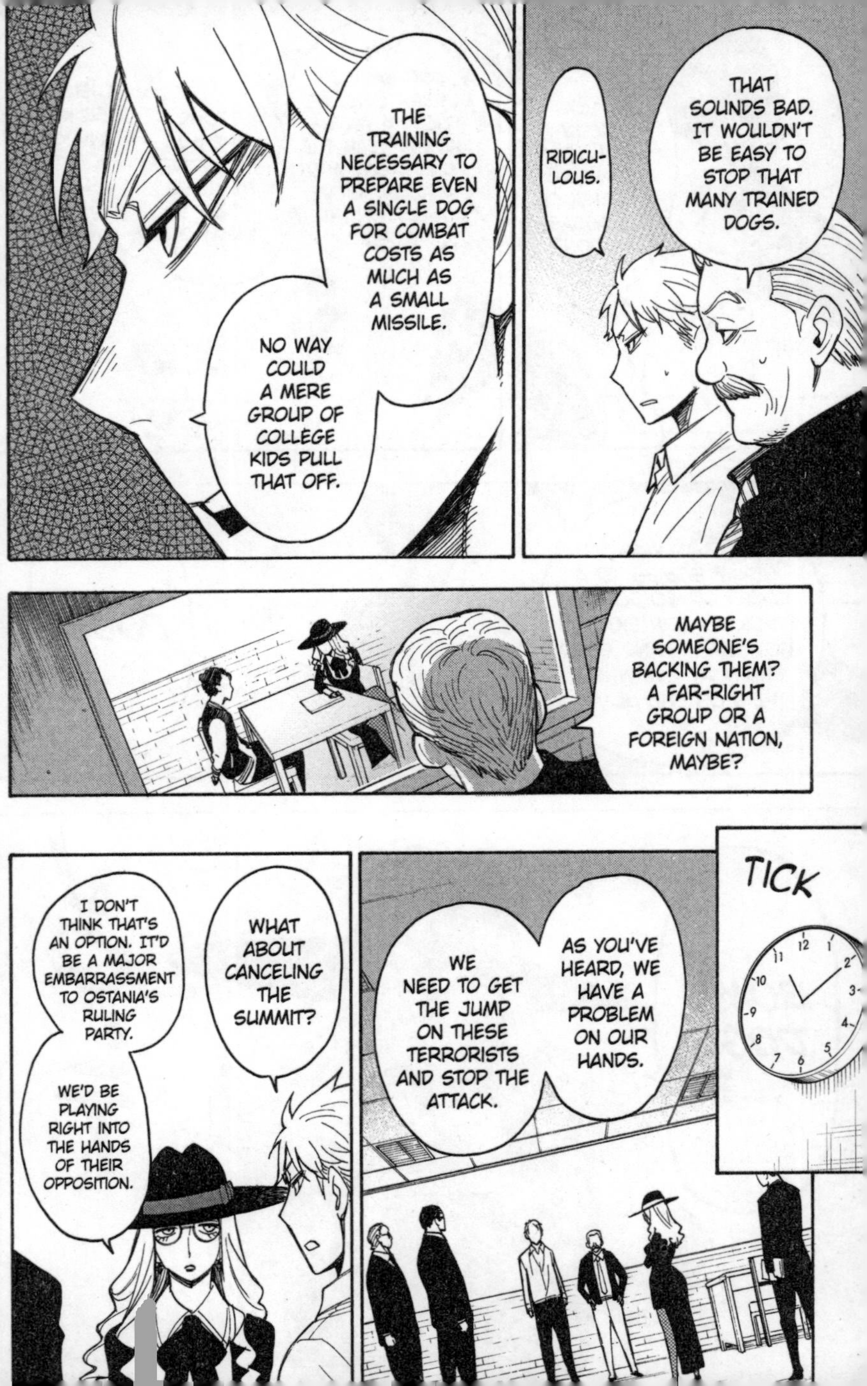
THAT SOUNDS BAD. IT WOULDN'T BE EASY TO STOP THAT MANY TRAINED DOGS.
RIDICU-LOUS.
THE TRAINING NECESSARY TO PREPARE EVEN A SINGLE DOG FOR COMBAT COSTS AS MUCH AS A SMALL MISSILE.
NO WAY COULD A MERE GROUP OF COLLEGE KIDS PULL THAT OFF.
MAYBE SOMEONE'S BACKING THEM? A FAR-RIGHT GROUP OR A FOREIGN NATION, MAYBE?
TICK
AS YOU'VE HEARD, WE HAVE A PROBLEM ON OUR HANDS.
WE NEED TO GET THE JUMP ON THESE TERRORISTS AND STOP THE ATTACK.
WHAT ABOUT CANCELING THE SUMMIT?
I DON'T THINK THAT'S AN OPTION. IT'D BE A MAJOR EMBARRASSMENT TO OSTANIA'S RULING PARTY.
WE'D BE PLAYING RIGHT INTO THE HANDS OF THEIR OPPOSITION.

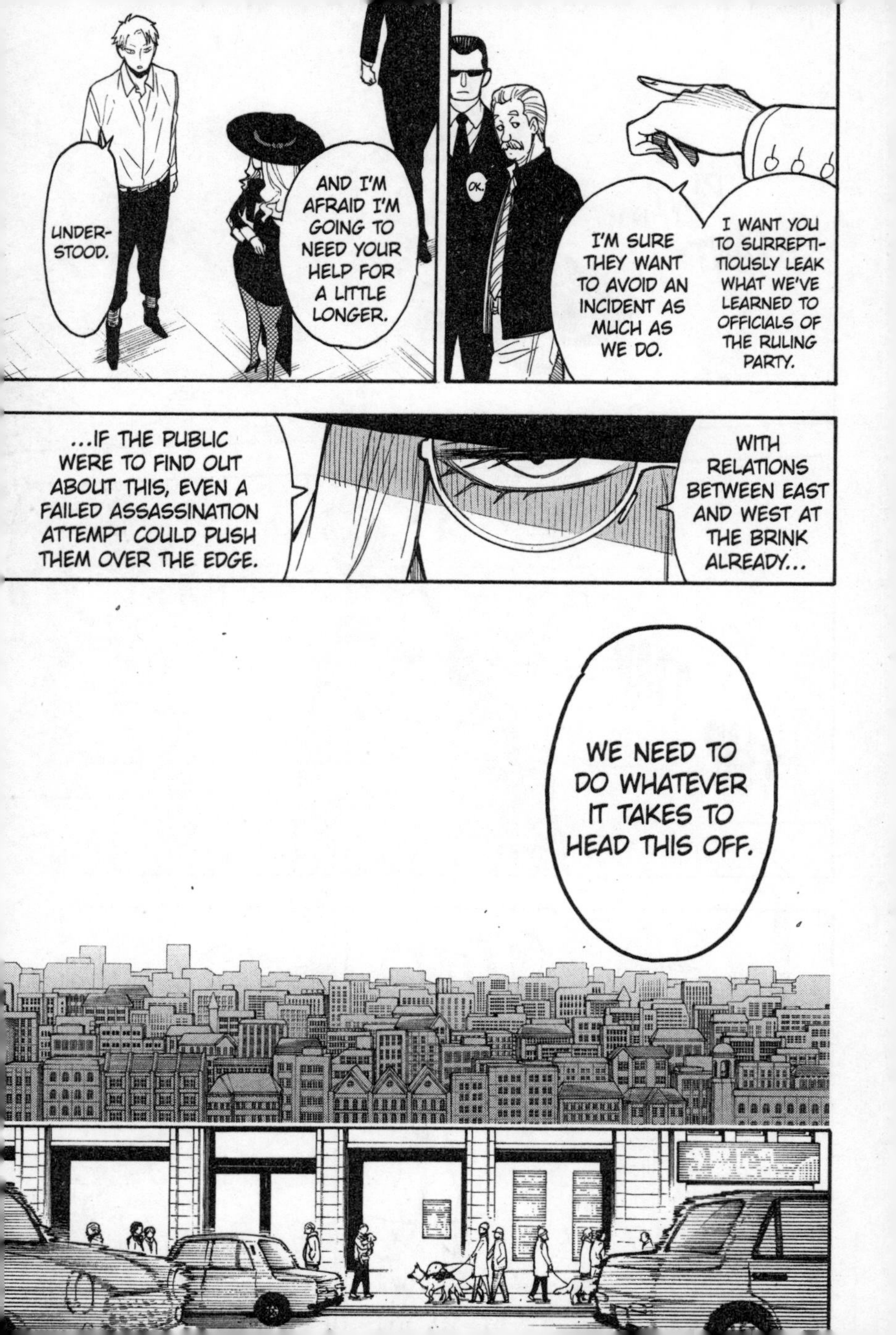
I WANT YOU TO SURREPTITIOUSLY LEAK WHAT WE'VE LEARNED TO OFFICIALS OF THE RULING PARTY.
I'M SURE THEY WANT TO AVOID AN INCIDENT AS MUCH AS WE DO.
OK.
AND I'M AFRAID I'M GOING TO NEED YOUR HELP FOR A LITTLE LONGER.
UNDERSTOOD.
WITH RELATIONS BETWEEN EAST AND WEST AT THE BRINK ALREADY...
...IF THE PUBLIC WERE TO FIND OUT ABOUT THIS, EVEN A FAILED ASSASSINATION ATTEMPT COULD PUSH THEM OVER THE EDGE.
WE NEED TO DO WHATEVER IT TAKES TO HEAD THIS OFF.

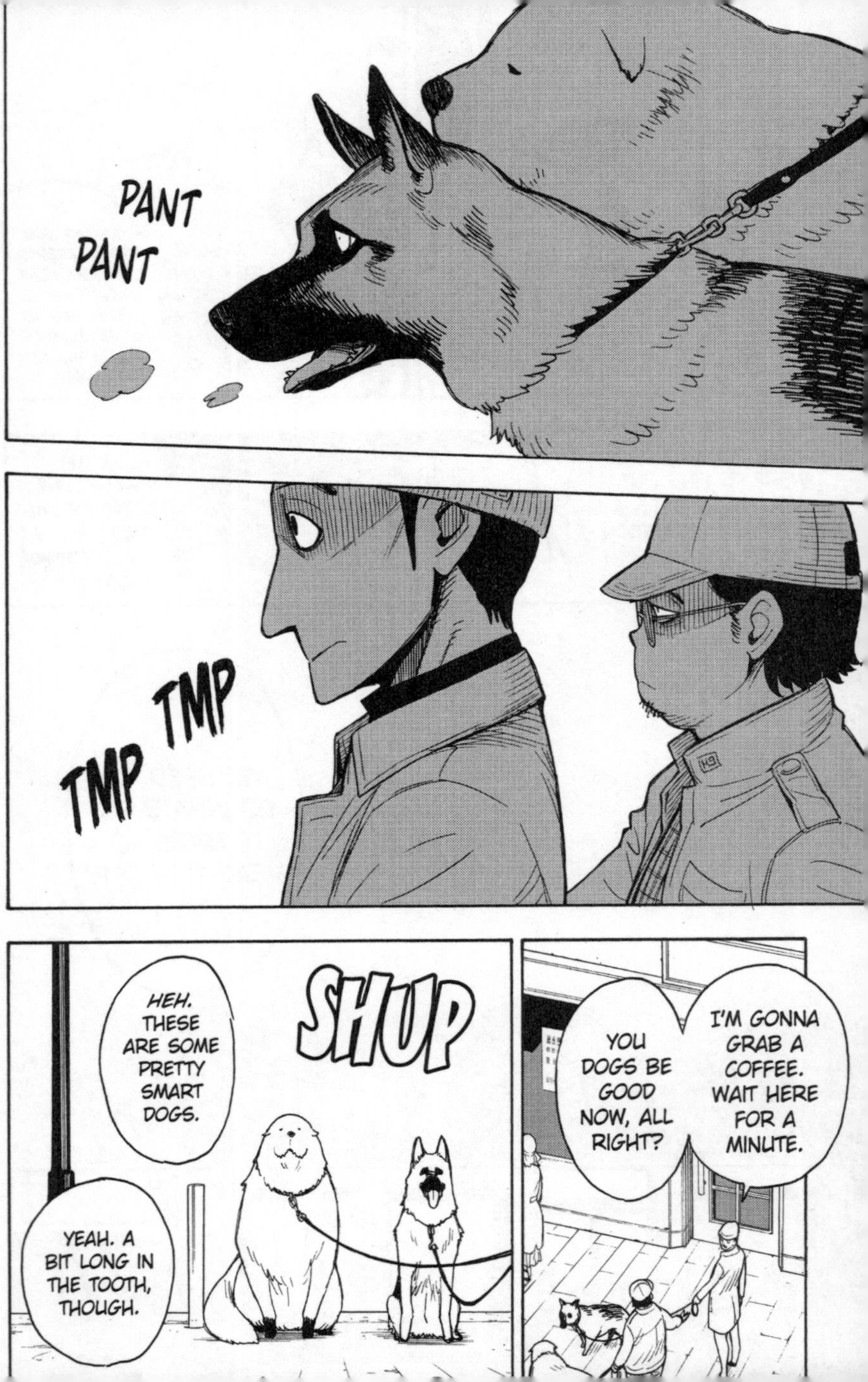
PANT
PANT
TMP TMP
I'M GONNA GRAB A COFFEE. WAIT HERE FOR A MINUTE.
YOU DOGS BE GOOD NOW, ALL RIGHT?
SHUP
HEH. THESE ARE SOME PRETTY SMART DOGS.
YEAH. A BIT LONG IN THE TOOTH, THOUGH.

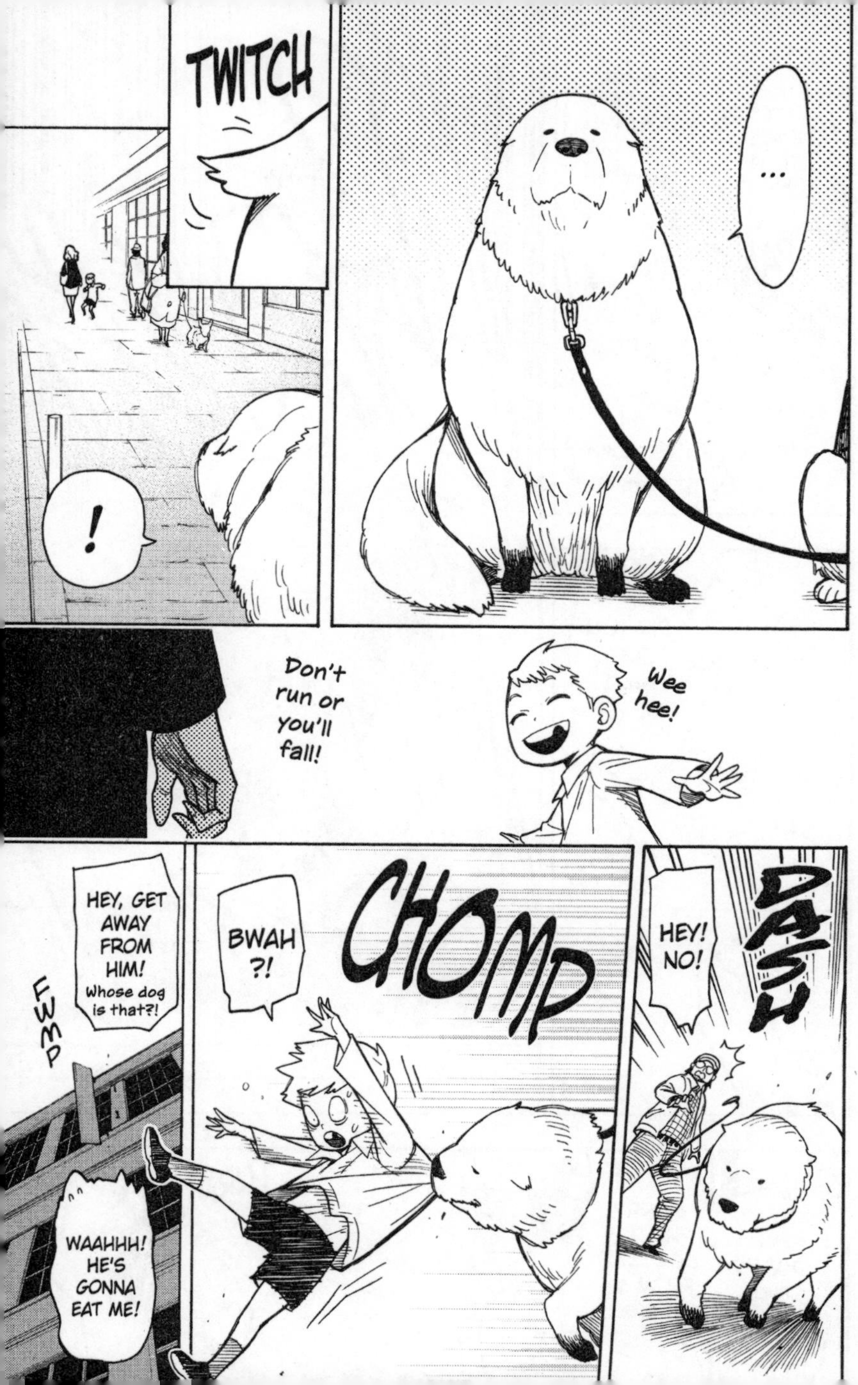
...
TWITCH
!
Wee hee!
Don't run or you'll fall!
DASH
HEY! NO!
CHOMP
BWAH?!
HEY, GET AWAY FROM HIM! Whose dog is that?!
FWMP
WAAHHH! HE'S GONNA EAT ME!

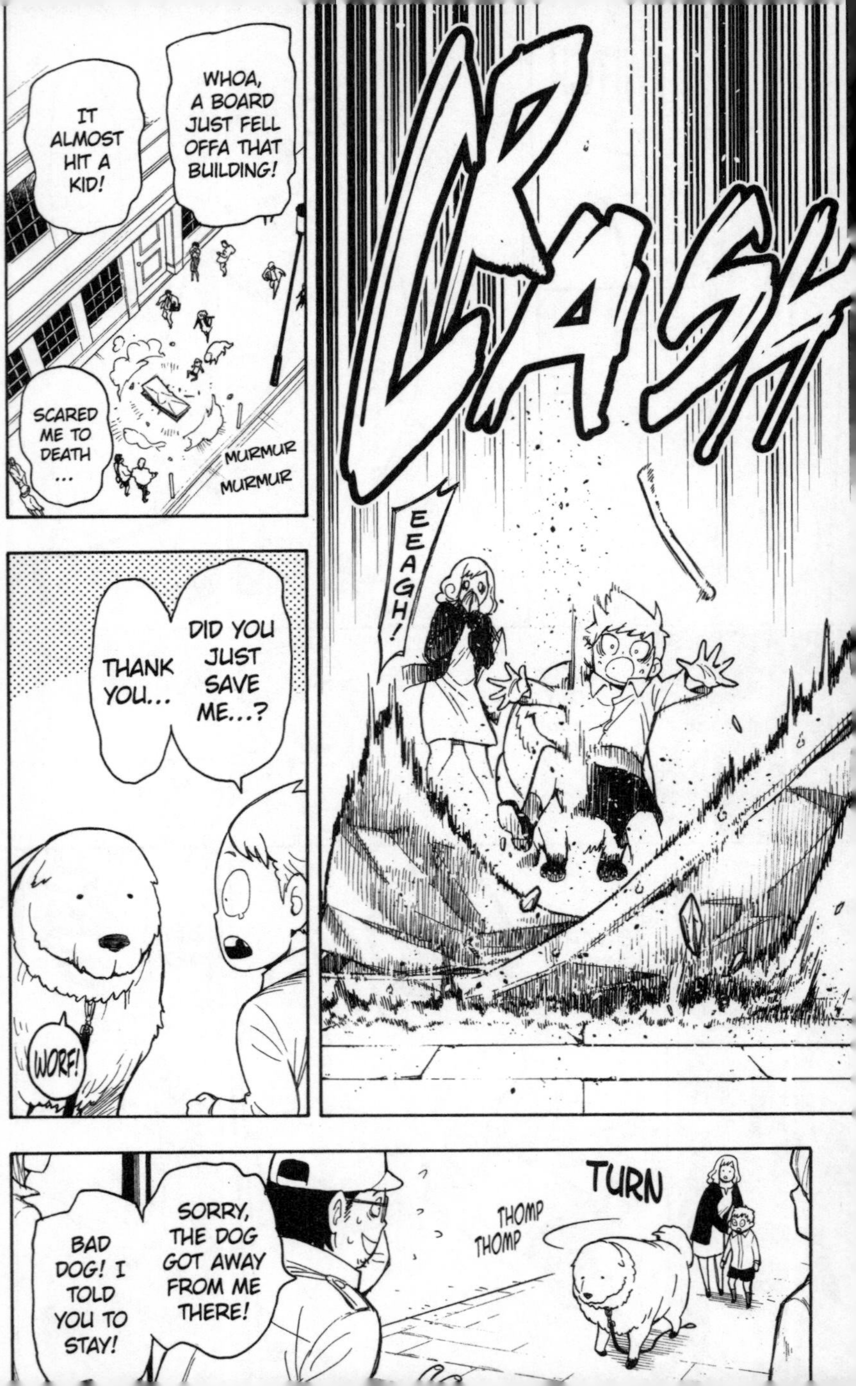
CRASH
EEAGH!
WHOA, A BOARD JUST FELL OFFA THAT BUILDING!
IT ALMOST HIT A KID!
MURMUR MURMUR
SCARED ME TO DEATH...
DID YOU JUST SAVE ME...?
THANK YOU...
WORF!
TURN
THOMP THOMP
SORRY, THE DOG GOT AWAY FROM ME THERE!
BAD DOG! I TOLD YOU TO STAY!

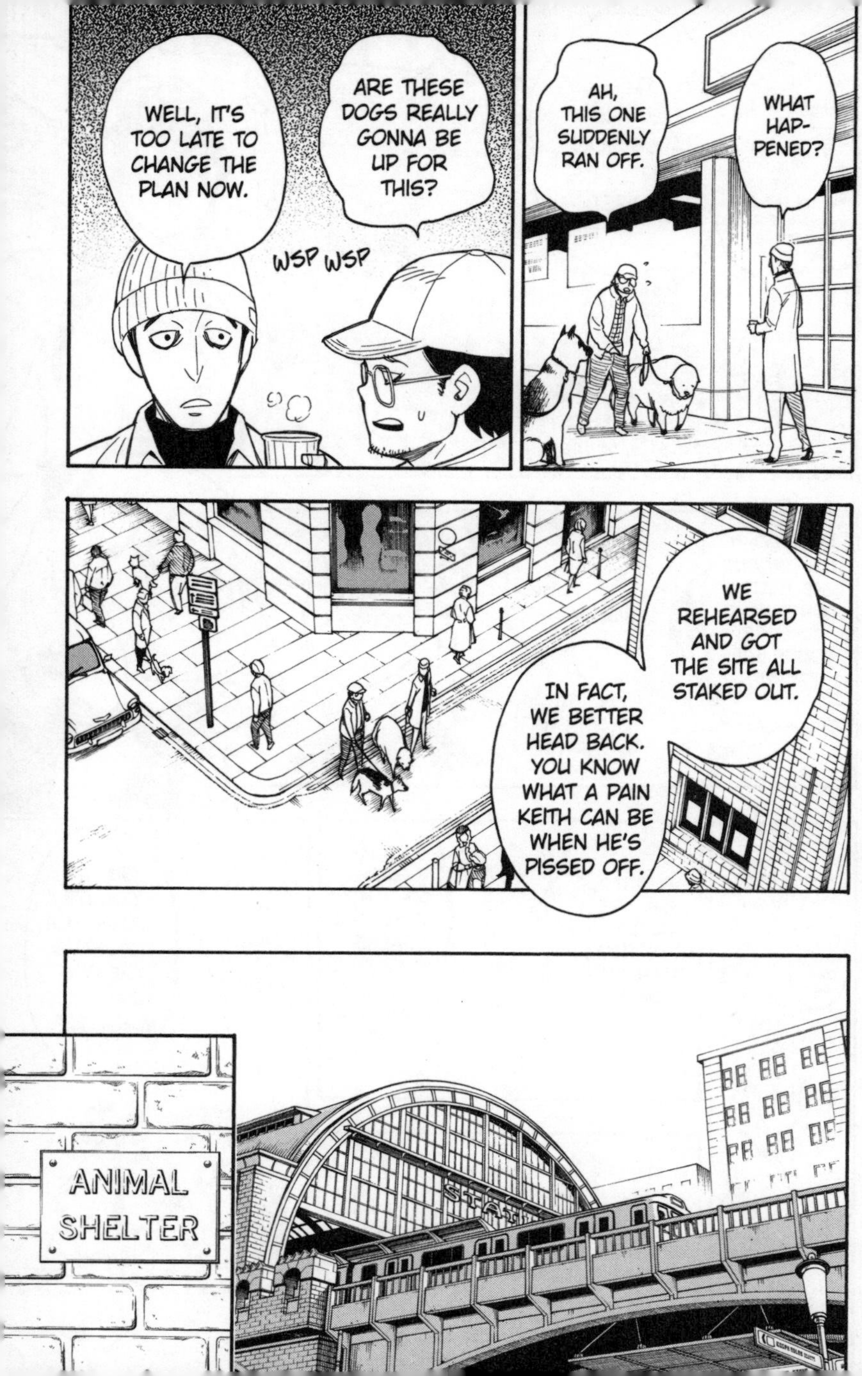
WHAT HAP-PENED?
AH, THIS ONE SUDDENLY RAN OFF.
ARE THESE DOGS REALLY GONNA BE UP FOR THIS?
WELL, IT'S TOO LATE TO CHANGE THE PLAN NOW.
WSP WSP
WE REHEARSED AND GOT THE SITE ALL STAKED OUT.
IN FACT, WE BETTER HEAD BACK. YOU KNOW WHAT A PAIN KEITH CAN BE WHEN HE'S PISSED OFF.
ANIMAL SHELTER

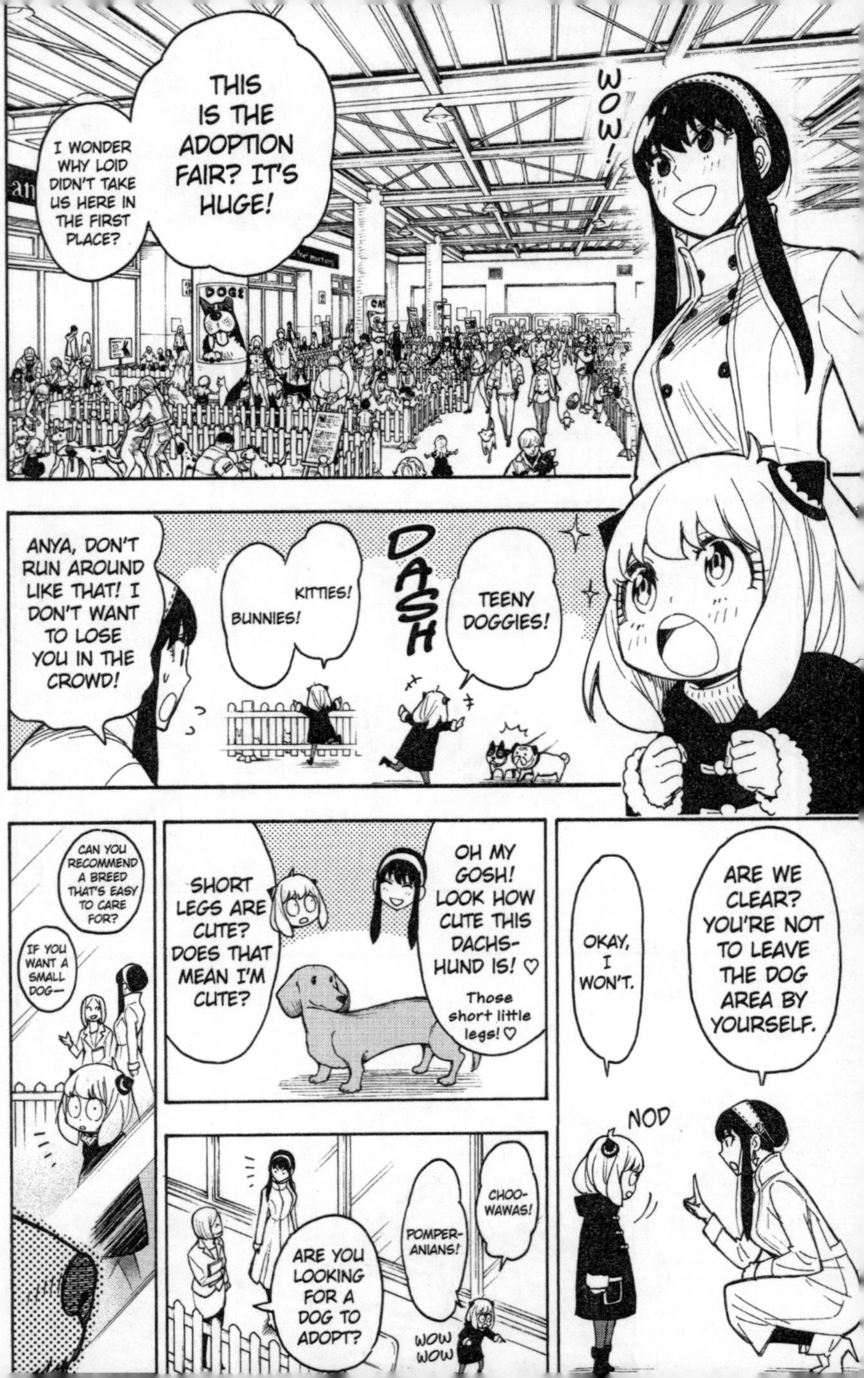
WOW!
THIS IS THE ADOPTION FAIR? IT'S HUGE!
I WONDER WHY LOID DIDN'T TAKE US HERE IN THE FIRST PLACE?
TEENY DOGGIES!
DASH
KITTIES!
BUNNIES!
ANYA, DON'T RUN AROUND LIKE THAT! I DON'T WANT TO LOSE YOU IN THE CROWD!
ARE WE CLEAR? YOU'RE NOT TO LEAVE THE DOG AREA BY YOURSELF.
OKAY, I WON'T.
NOD
OH MY GOSH! LOOK HOW CUTE THIS DACHS-HUND IS! ♡
Those short little legs! ♡
SHORT LEGS ARE CUTE? DOES THAT MEAN I'M CUTE?
CHOO-WAWAS!
POMPER-ANIANS!
WOW WOW
ARE YOU LOOKING FOR A DOG TO ADOPT?
CAN YOU RECOMMEND A BREED THAT'S EASY TO CARE FOR?
IF YOU WANT A SMALL DOG—

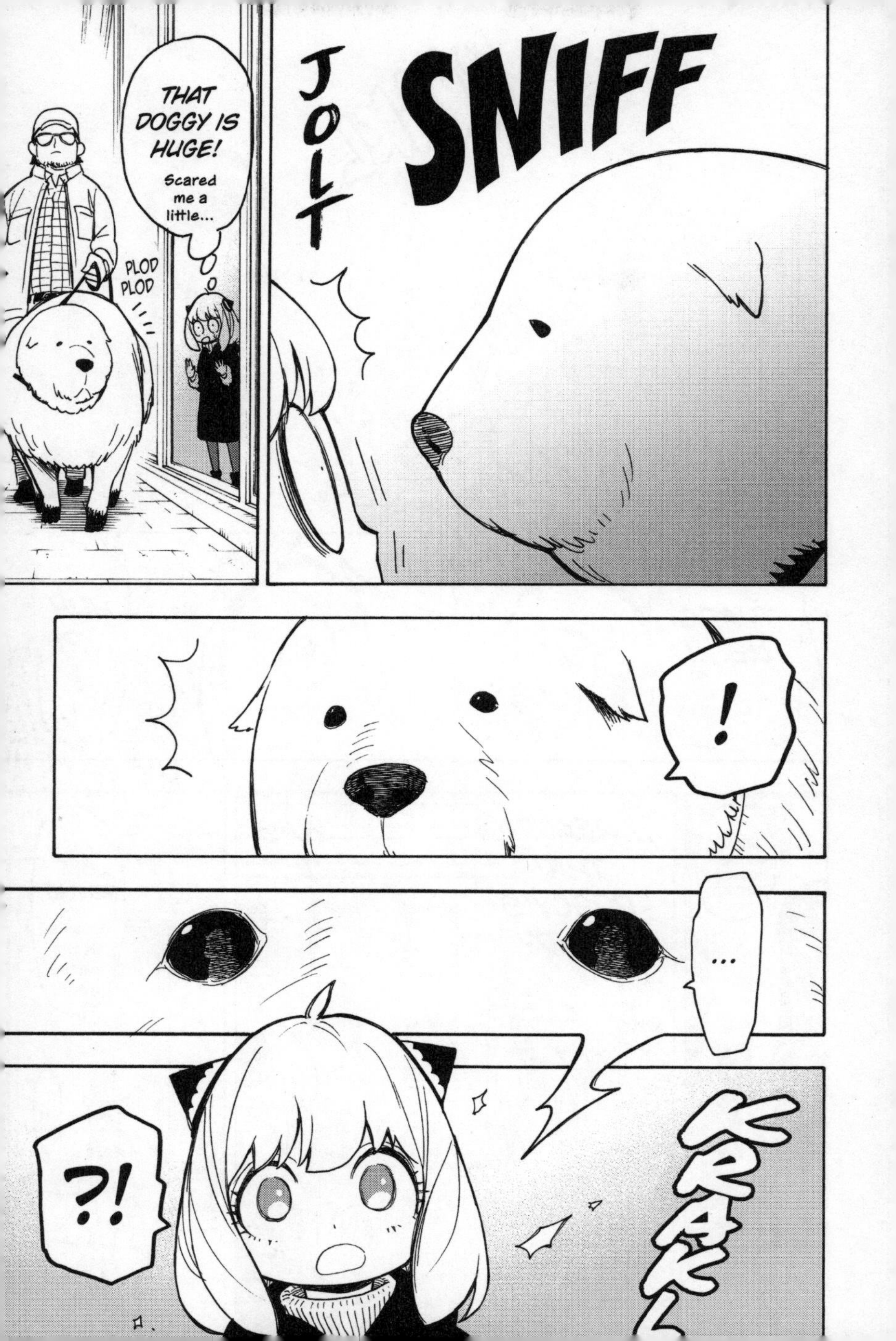
JOLT
SNIFF
THAT DOGGY IS HUGE!
Scared me a little...
PLOD PLOD
!
...
KRAK
?!

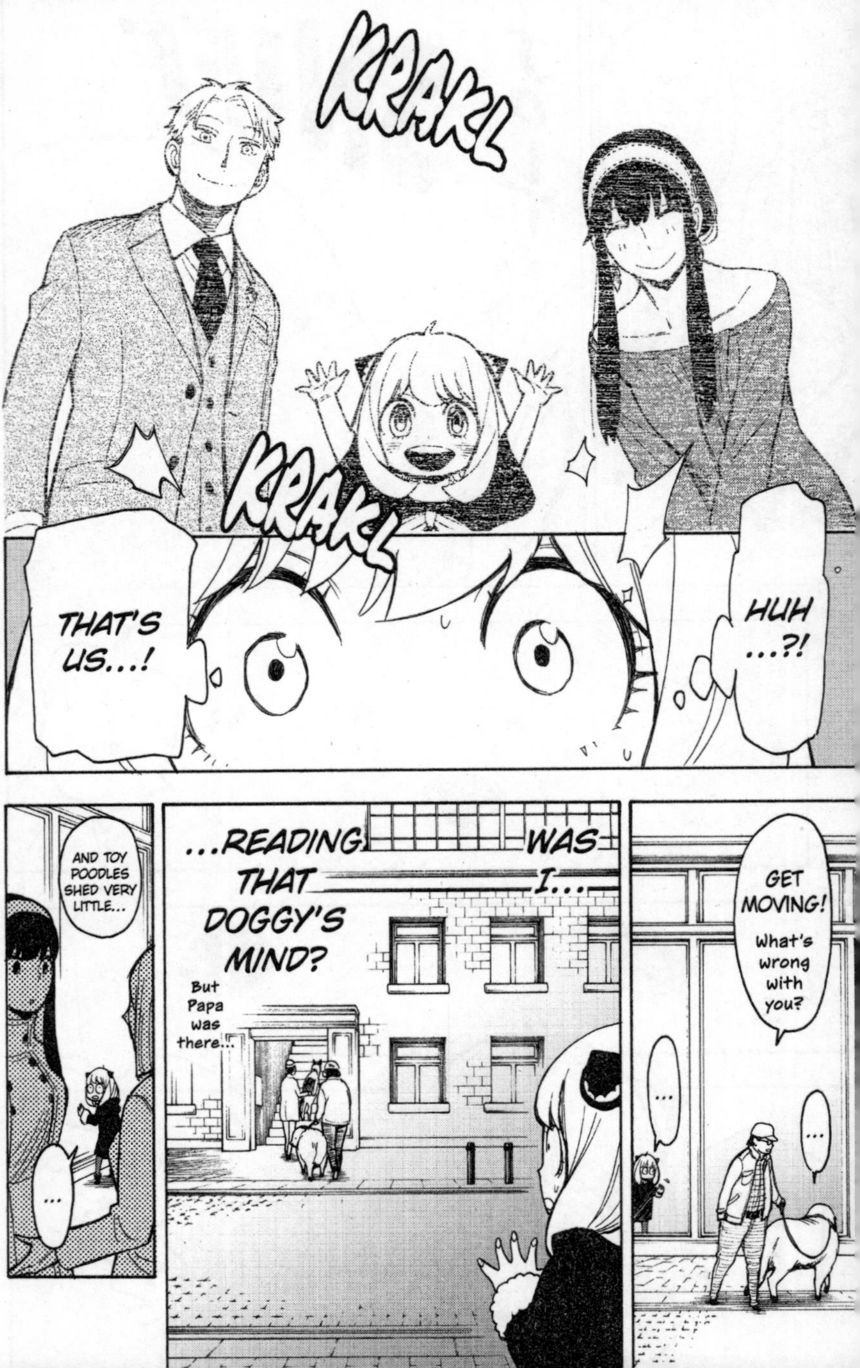
KRAKL
KRAKL
HUH ...?!
THAT'S US...!
GET MOVING!
What's wrong with you?
...
...
WAS I...
...READING THAT DOGGY'S MIND?
But Papa was there...
AND TOY POODLES SHED VERY LITTLE...
...

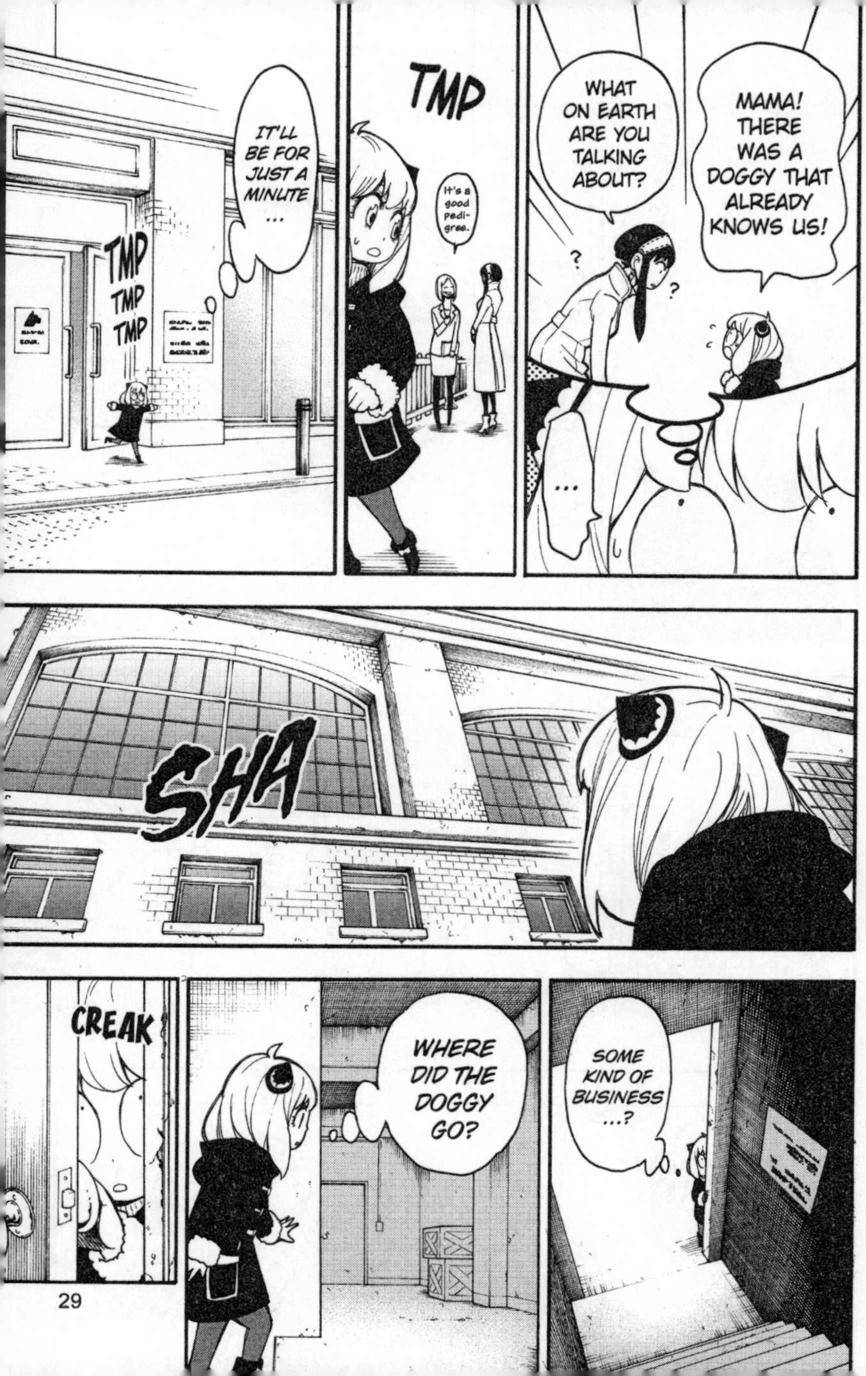
MAMA! THERE WAS A DOGGY THAT ALREADY KNOWS US!
WHAT ON EARTH ARE YOU TALKING ABOUT?
...
TMP
It's a good pedigree.
IT'LL BE FOR JUST A MINUTE ...
TMP TMP TMP
SHA
SOME KIND OF BUSINESS ...?
WHERE DID THE DOGGY GO?
CREAK

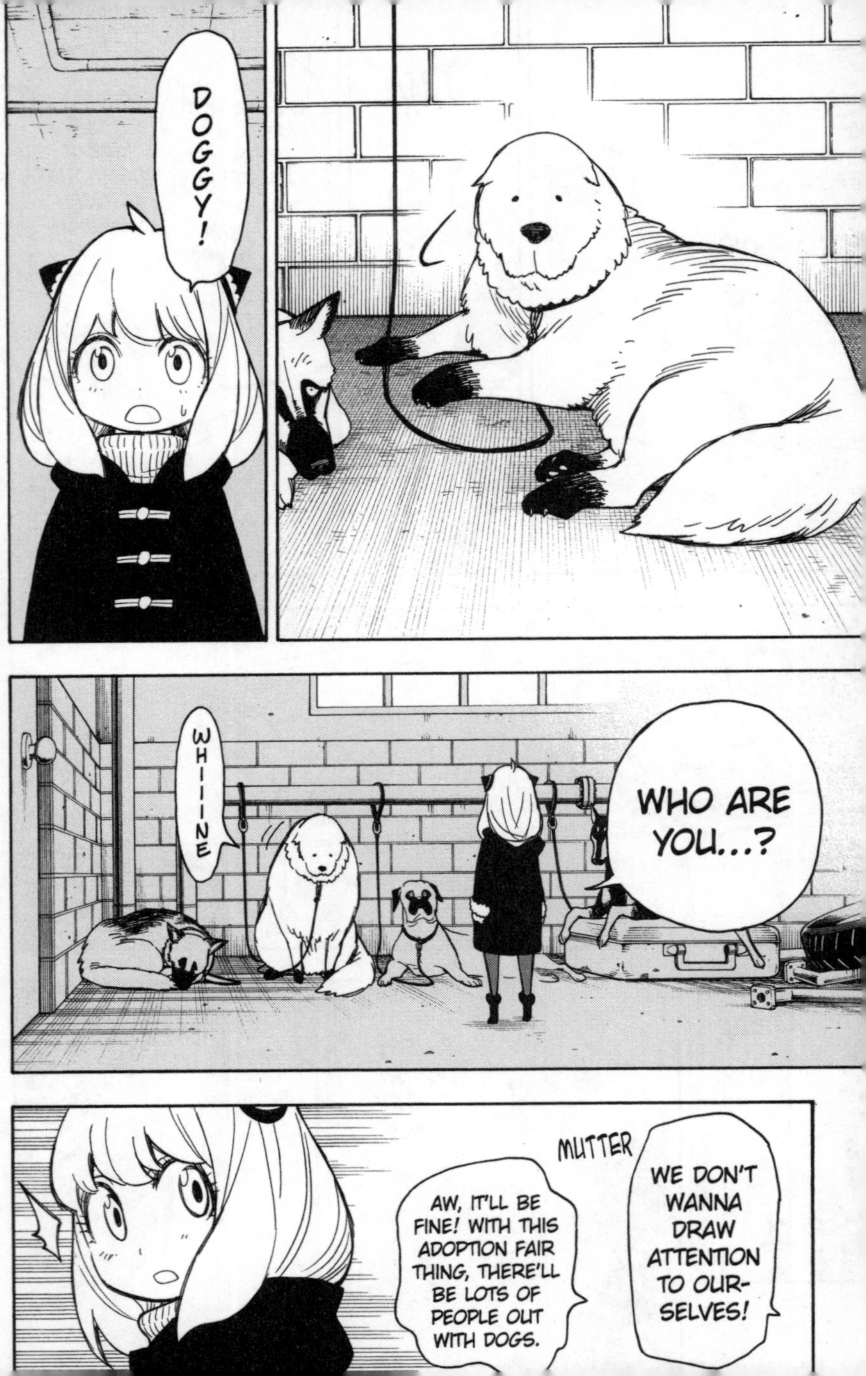
DOGGY!
WHO ARE YOU...?
WHIIINE
WE DON'T WANNA DRAW ATTENTION TO OUR-SELVES!
MUTTER
AW, IT'LL BE FINE! WITH THIS ADOPTION FAIR THING, THERE'LL BE LOTS OF PEOPLE OUT WITH DOGS.

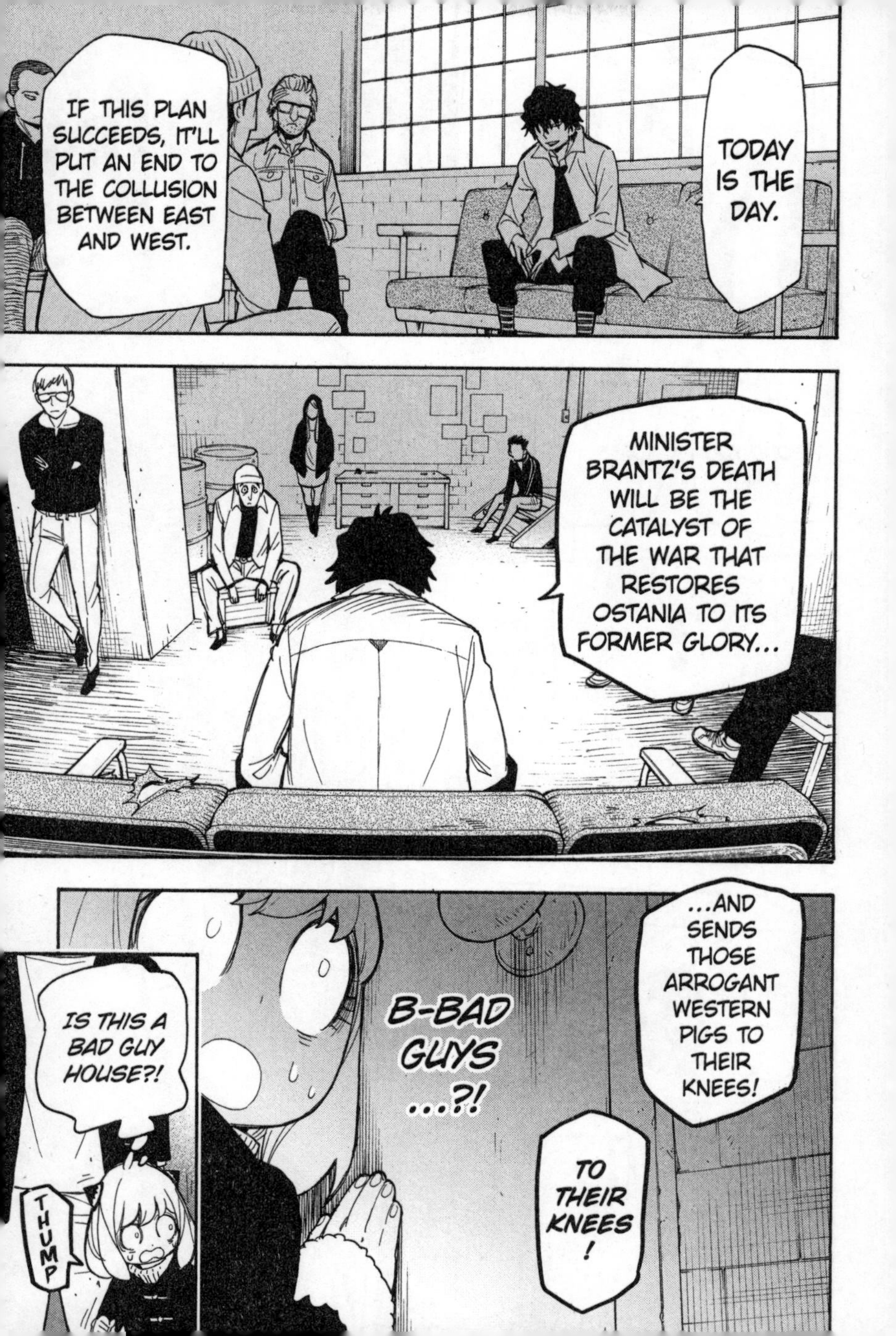
TODAY IS THE DAY.
IF THIS PLAN SUCCEEDS, IT'LL PUT AN END TO THE COLLUSION BETWEEN EAST AND WEST.
MINISTER BRANTZ'S DEATH WILL BE THE CATALYST OF THE WAR THAT RESTORES OSTANIA TO ITS FORMER GLORY...
...AND SENDS THOSE ARROGANT WESTERN PIGS TO THEIR KNEES!
TO THEIR KNEES!
B-BAD GUYS...?!
IS THIS A BAD GUY HOUSE?!
THUMP

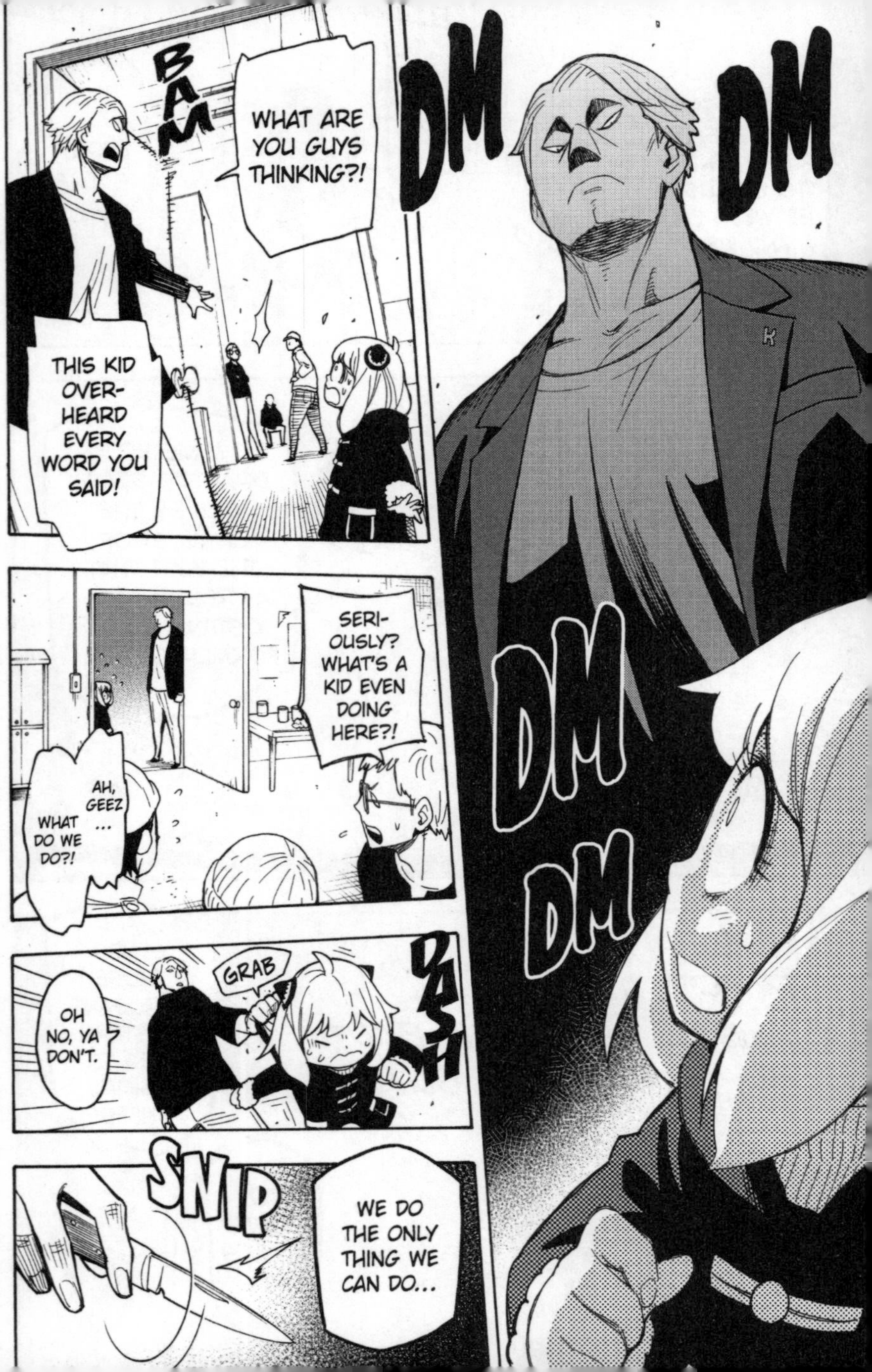
DM
DM
DM
DM
BAM
WHAT ARE YOU GUYS THINKING?!
THIS KID OVER-HEARD EVERY WORD YOU SAID!
SERI-OUSLY? WHAT'S A KID EVEN DOING HERE?!
AH, GEEZ...
WHAT DO WE DO?!
DASH
GRAB
OH NO, YA DON'T.
SNIP
WE DO THE ONLY THING WE CAN DO...

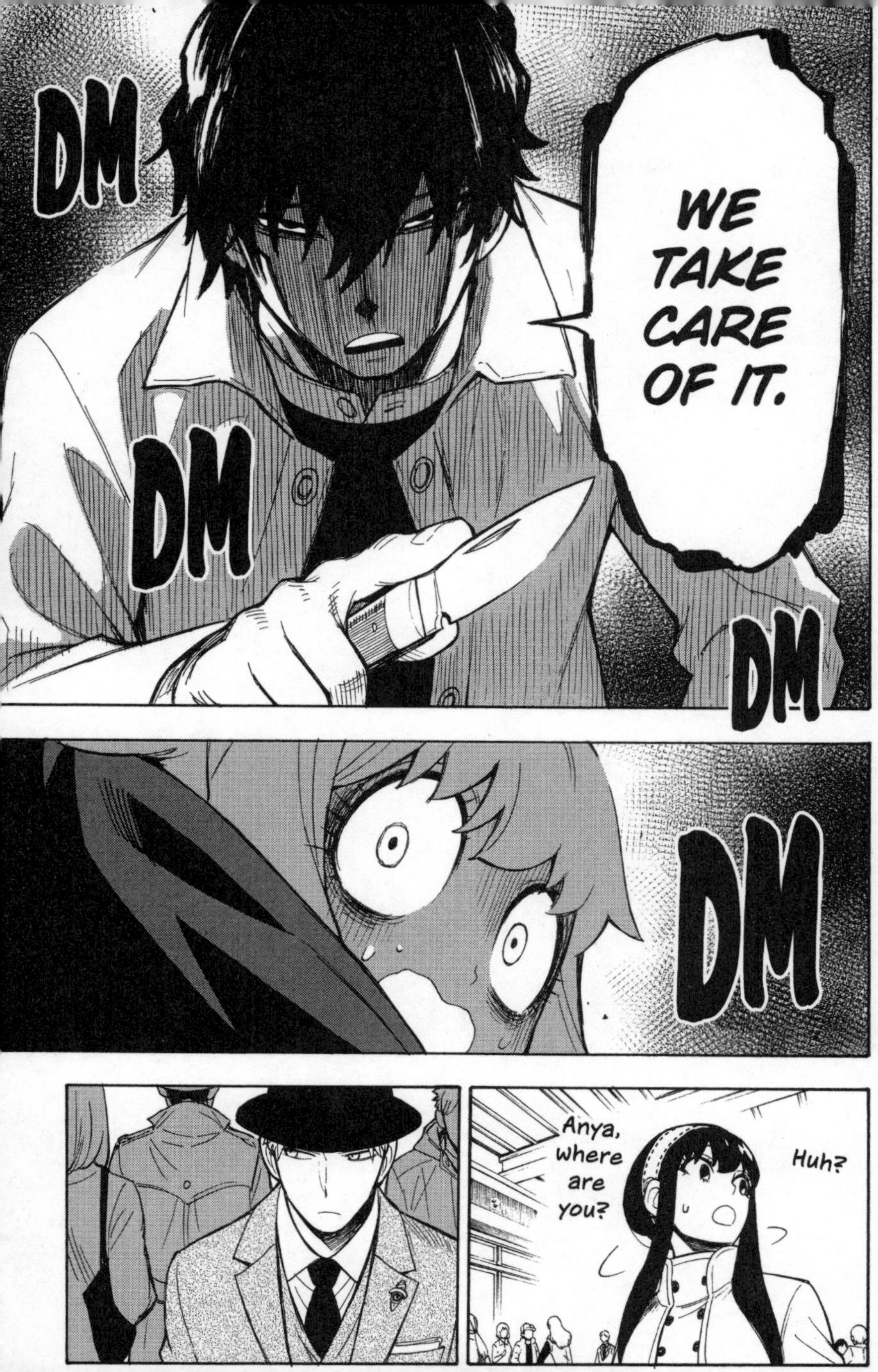
WE TAKE CARE OF IT.
DM
DM
DM
DM
Huh?
Anya, where are you?

SPY×FAMILY

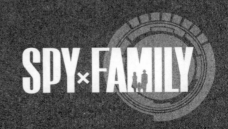

MISSION 19

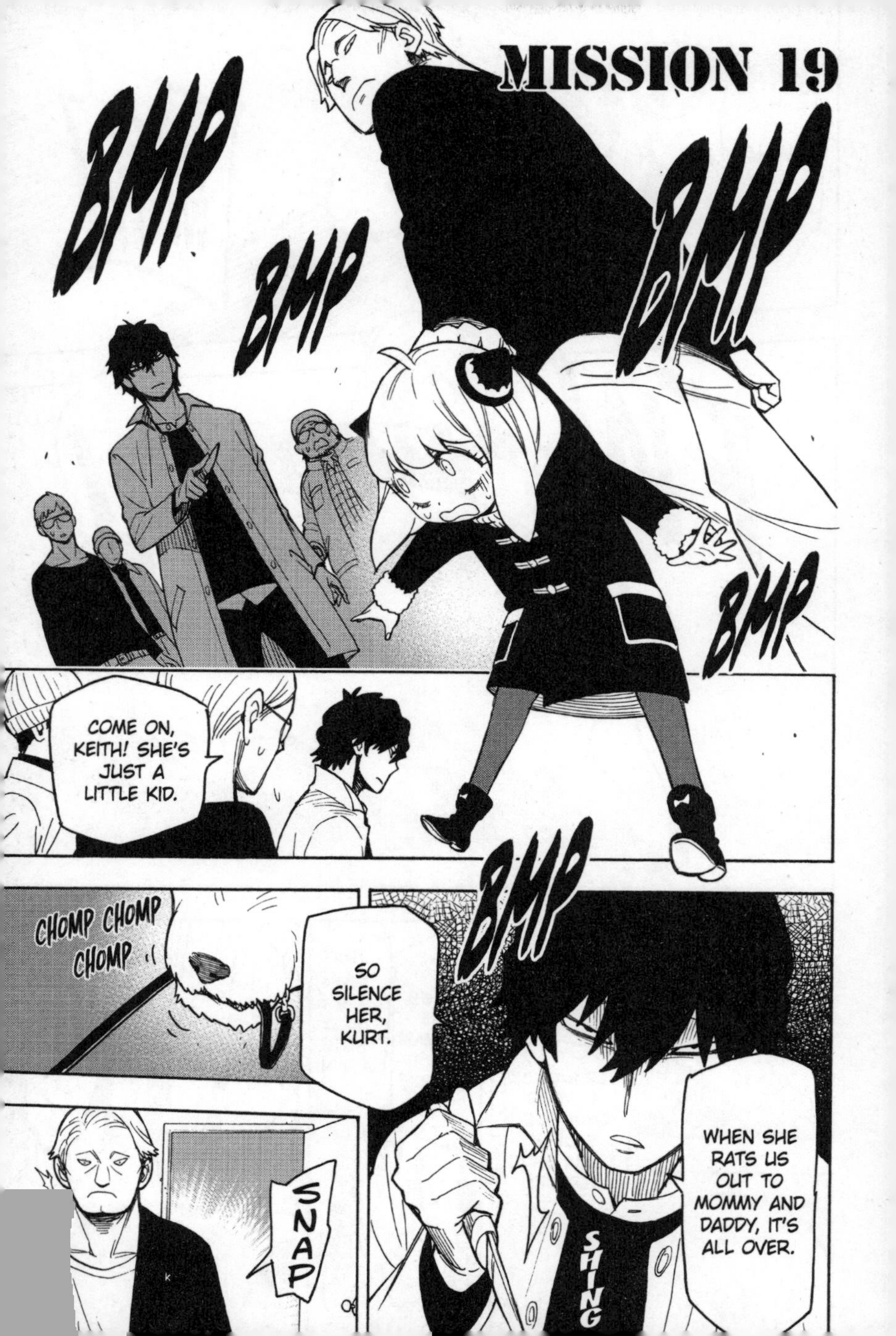
BMP
BMP
BMP
BMP
COME ON, KEITH! SHE'S JUST A LITTLE KID.
BMP
WHEN SHE RATS US OUT TO MOMMY AND DADDY, IT'S ALL OVER.
SHING
CHOMP CHOMP CHOMP
SO SILENCE HER, KURT.
SNAP

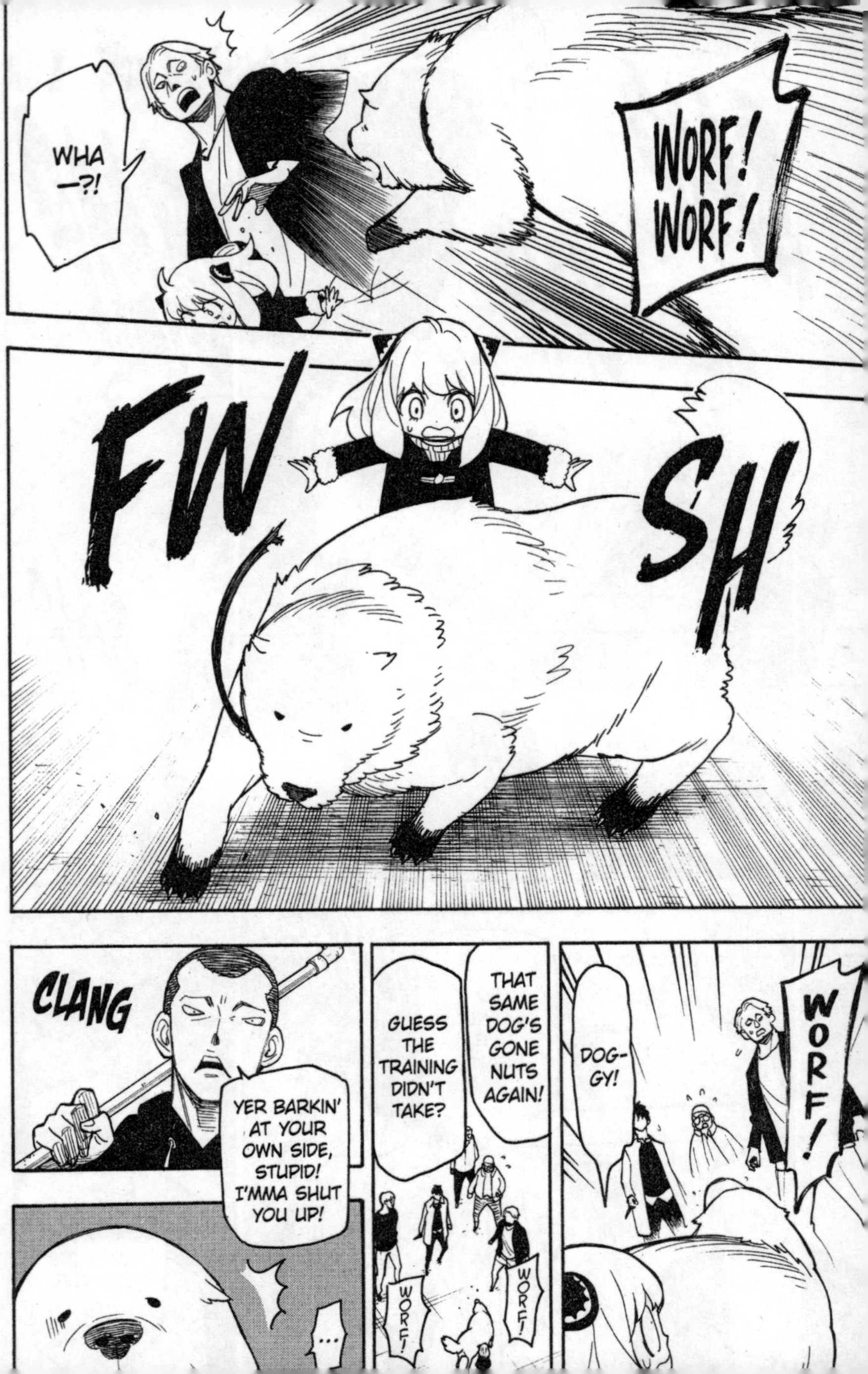
WORF! WORF!
WHA—?!
FWSH
WORF!
DOG-GY!
THAT SAME DOG'S GONE NUTS AGAIN!
GUESS THE TRAINING DIDN'T TAKE?
WORF!
WORF!
CLANG
YER BARKIN' AT YOUR OWN SIDE, STUPID! I'MMA SHUT YOU UP!
...

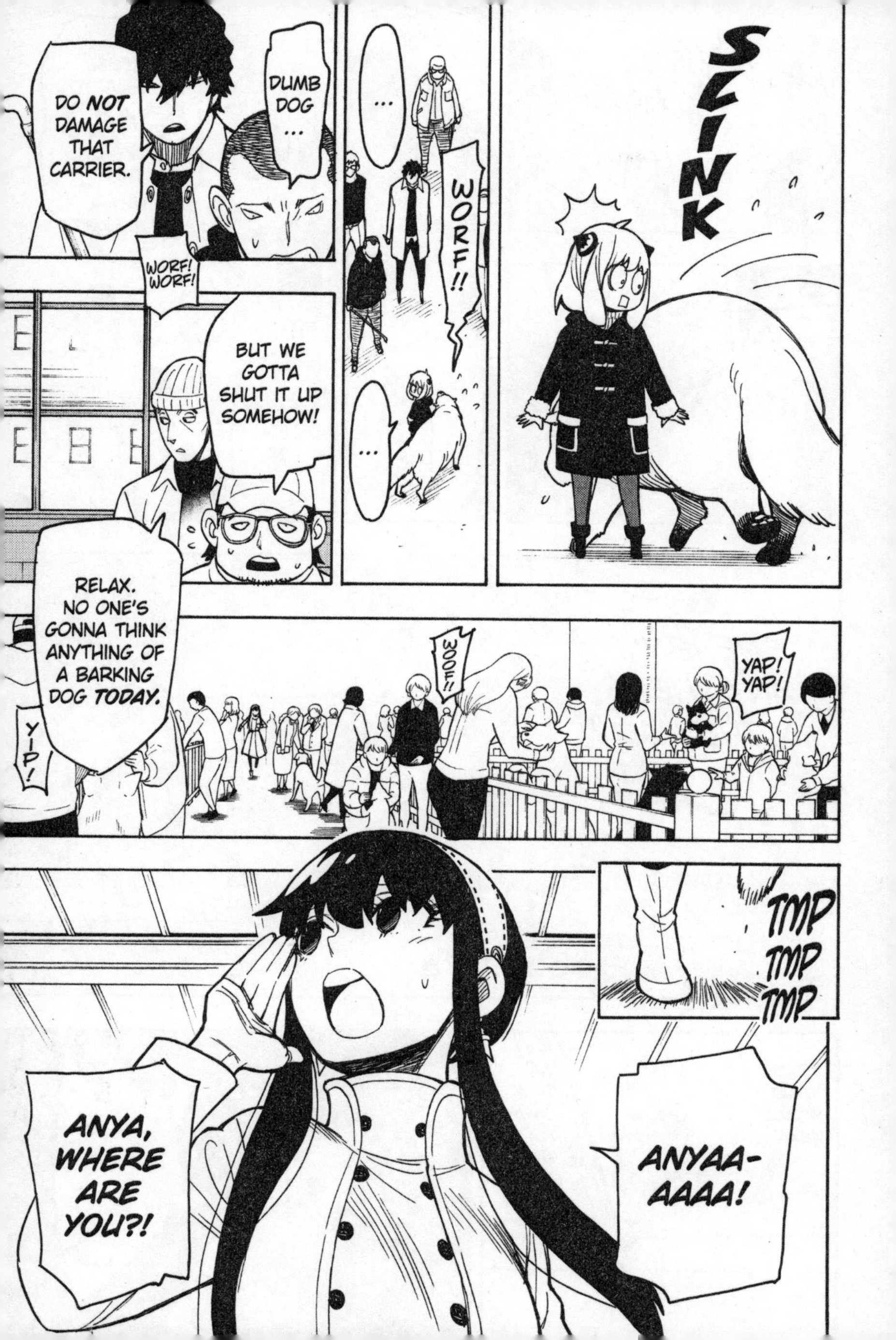
SLINK
...
WORF!!
...
DUMB DOG ...
DO NOT DAMAGE THAT CARRIER.
WORF! WORF!
BUT WE GOTTA SHUT IT UP SOMEHOW!
RELAX. NO ONE'S GONNA THINK ANYTHING OF A BARKING DOG TODAY.
YAP! YAP!
WOOF!!
YIP!
TMP TMP TMP
ANYAA-AAAA!
ANYA, WHERE ARE YOU?!

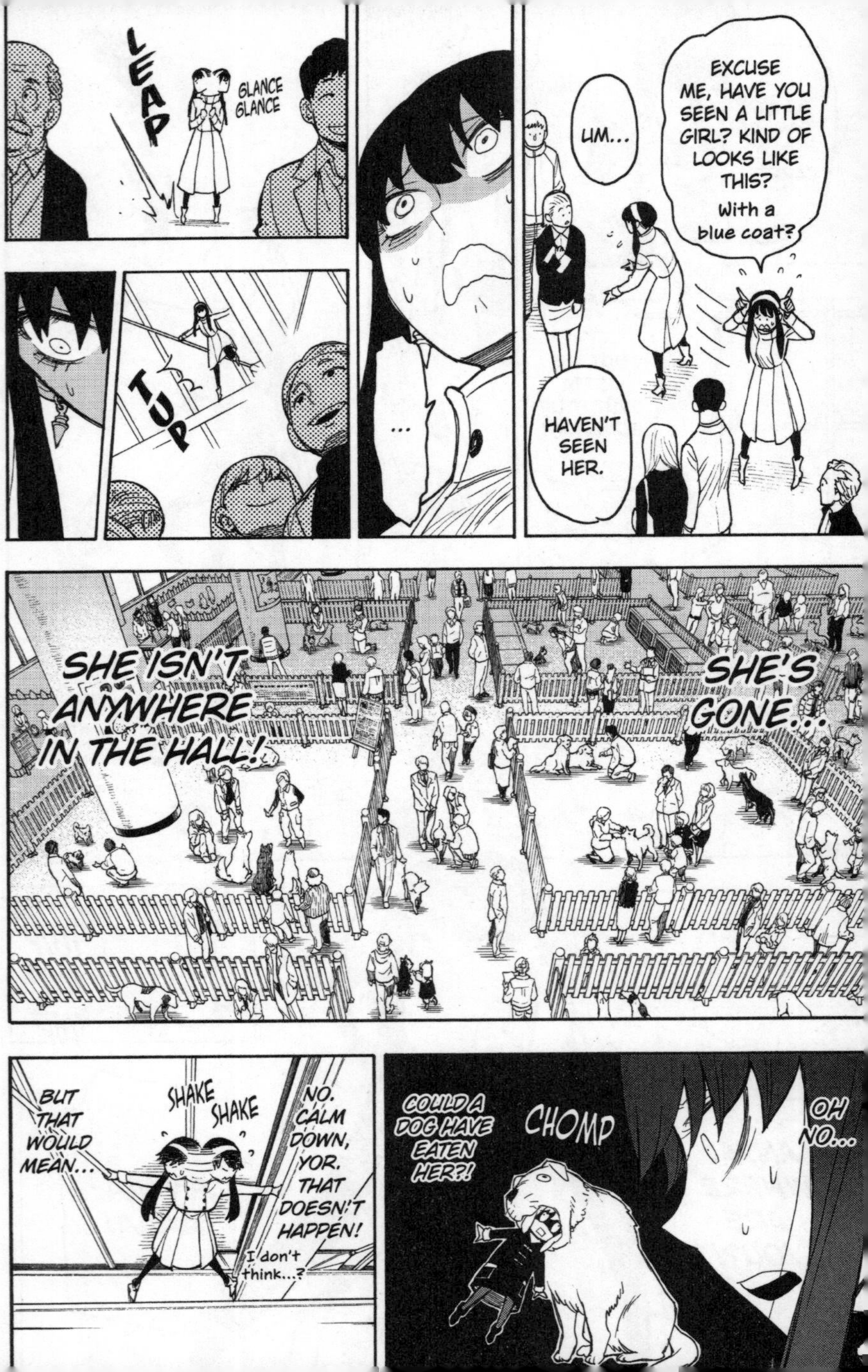
EXCUSE ME, HAVE YOU SEEN A LITTLE GIRL? KIND OF LOOKS LIKE THIS?
With a blue coat?
UM...
HAVEN'T SEEN HER.
...
LEAP
GLANCE GLANCE
TUP
SHE'S GONE...
SHE ISN'T ANYWHERE IN THE HALL!
OH NO...
CHOMP
COULD A DOG HAVE EATEN HER?!
NO. CALM DOWN, YOR. THAT DOESN'T HAPPEN!
SHAKE SHAKE
BUT THAT WOULD MEAN...
I don't think...?

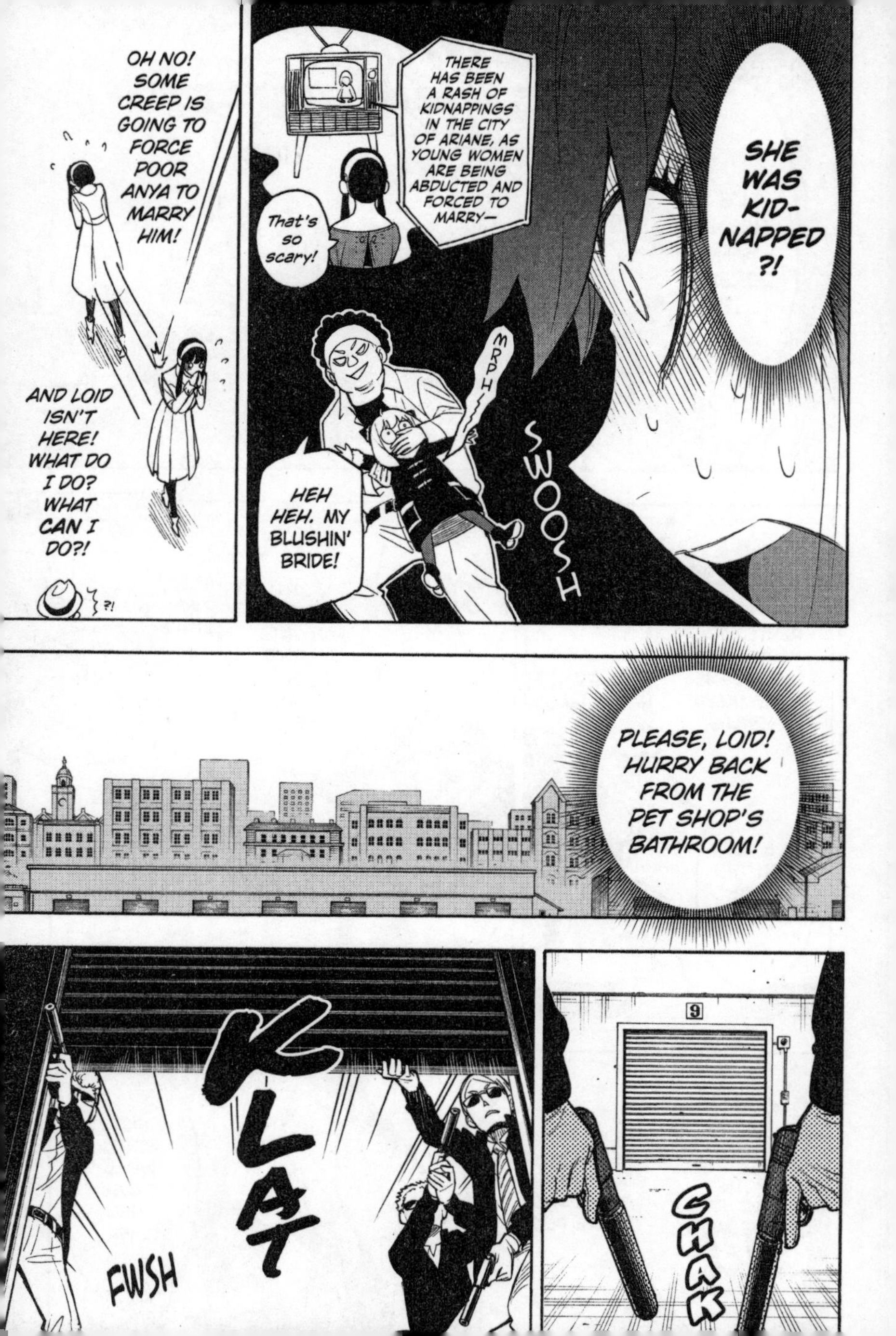
SHE WAS KID-NAPPED?!
THERE HAS BEEN A RASH OF KIDNAPPINGS IN THE CITY OF ARIANE, AS YOUNG WOMEN ARE BEING ABDUCTED AND FORCED TO MARRY—
That's so scary!
SWOOSH
MRPH
HEH HEH. MY BLUSHIN' BRIDE!
OH NO! SOME CREEP IS GOING TO FORCE POOR ANYA TO MARRY HIM!
AND LOID ISN'T HERE! WHAT DO I DO? WHAT CAN I DO?!
?!
PLEASE, LOID! HURRY BACK FROM THE PET SHOP'S BATHROOM!
CHAK
KLAT
FWSH

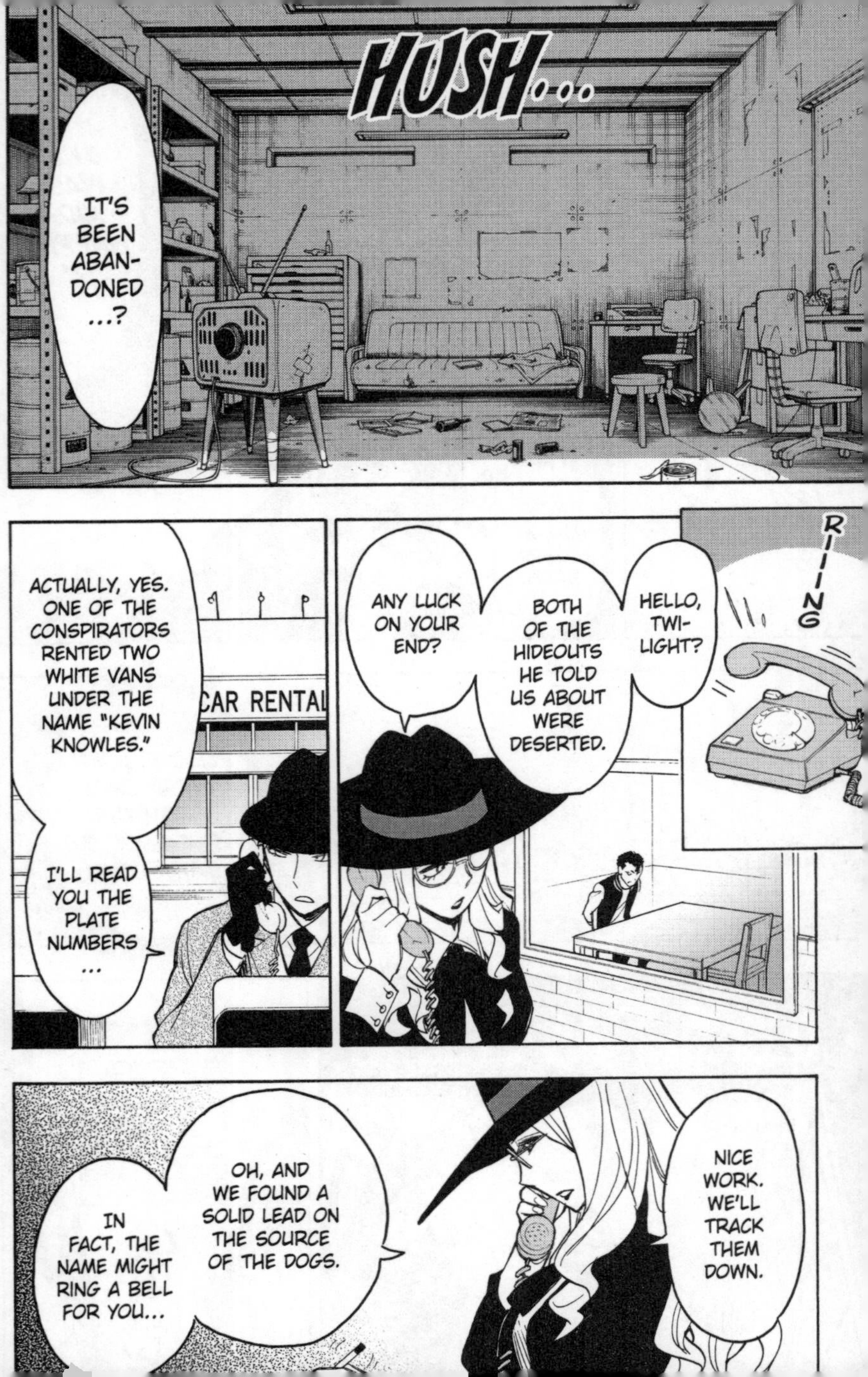
HUSH...
IT'S BEEN ABANDONED...?
RIIING
HELLO, TWILIGHT?
BOTH OF THE HIDEOUTS HE TOLD US ABOUT WERE DESERTED.
ANY LUCK ON YOUR END?
ACTUALLY, YES. ONE OF THE CONSPIRATORS RENTED TWO WHITE VANS UNDER THE NAME "KEVIN KNOWLES."
CAR RENTAL
I'LL READ YOU THE PLATE NUMBERS...
NICE WORK. WE'LL TRACK THEM DOWN.
OH, AND WE FOUND A SOLID LEAD ON THE SOURCE OF THE DOGS.
IN FACT, THE NAME MIGHT RING A BELL FOR YOU...

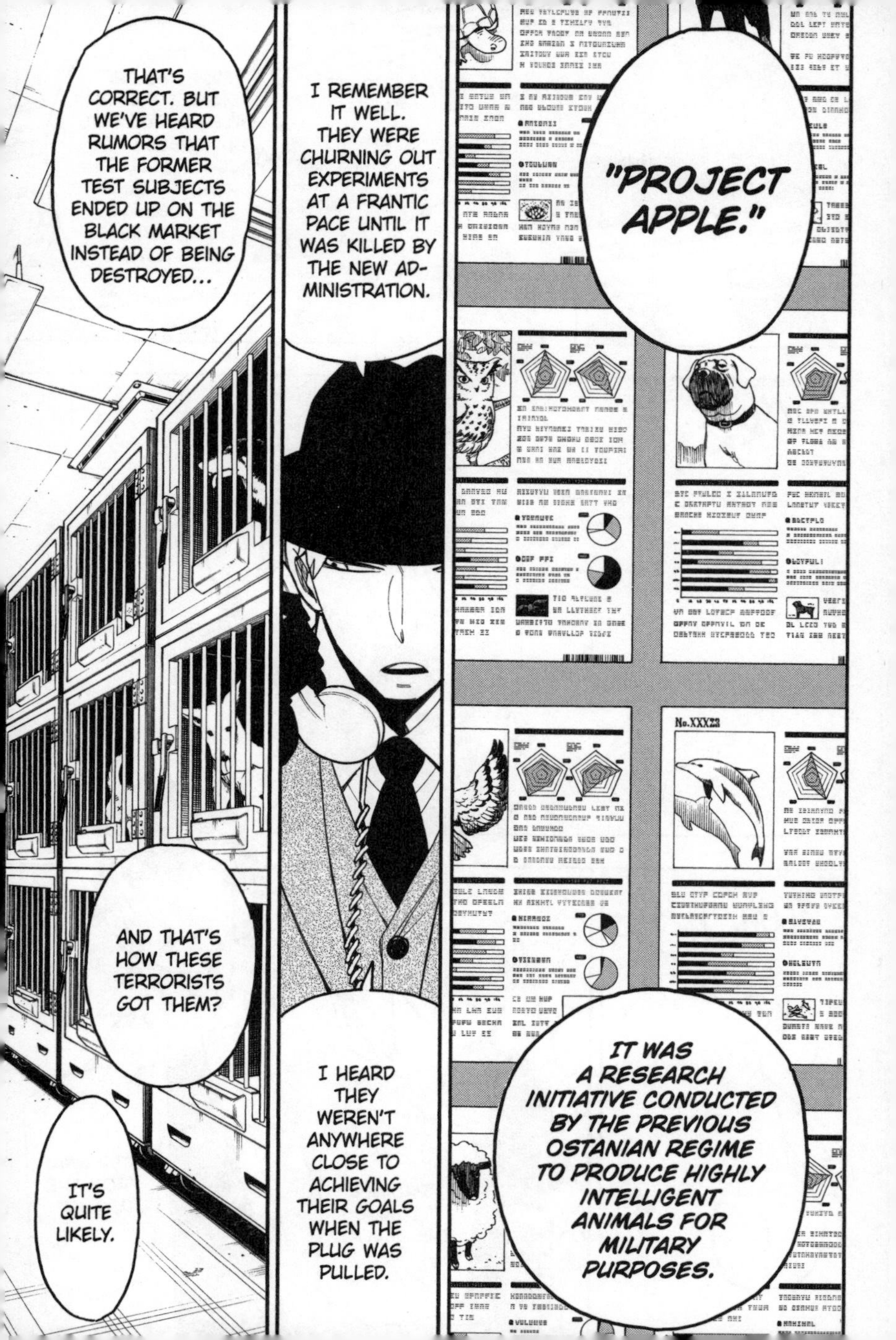
"PROJECT APPLE."
No.XXX23
IT WAS A RESEARCH INITIATIVE CONDUCTED BY THE PREVIOUS OSTANIAN REGIME TO PRODUCE HIGHLY INTELLIGENT ANIMALS FOR MILITARY PURPOSES.
I REMEMBER IT WELL. THEY WERE CHURNING OUT EXPERIMENTS AT A FRANTIC PACE UNTIL IT WAS KILLED BY THE NEW AD-MINISTRATION.
I HEARD THEY WEREN'T ANYWHERE CLOSE TO ACHIEVING THEIR GOALS WHEN THE PLUG WAS PULLED.
THAT'S CORRECT. BUT WE'VE HEARD RUMORS THAT THE FORMER TEST SUBJECTS ENDED UP ON THE BLACK MARKET INSTEAD OF BEING DESTROYED...
AND THAT'S HOW THESE TERRORISTS GOT THEM?
IT'S QUITE LIKELY.

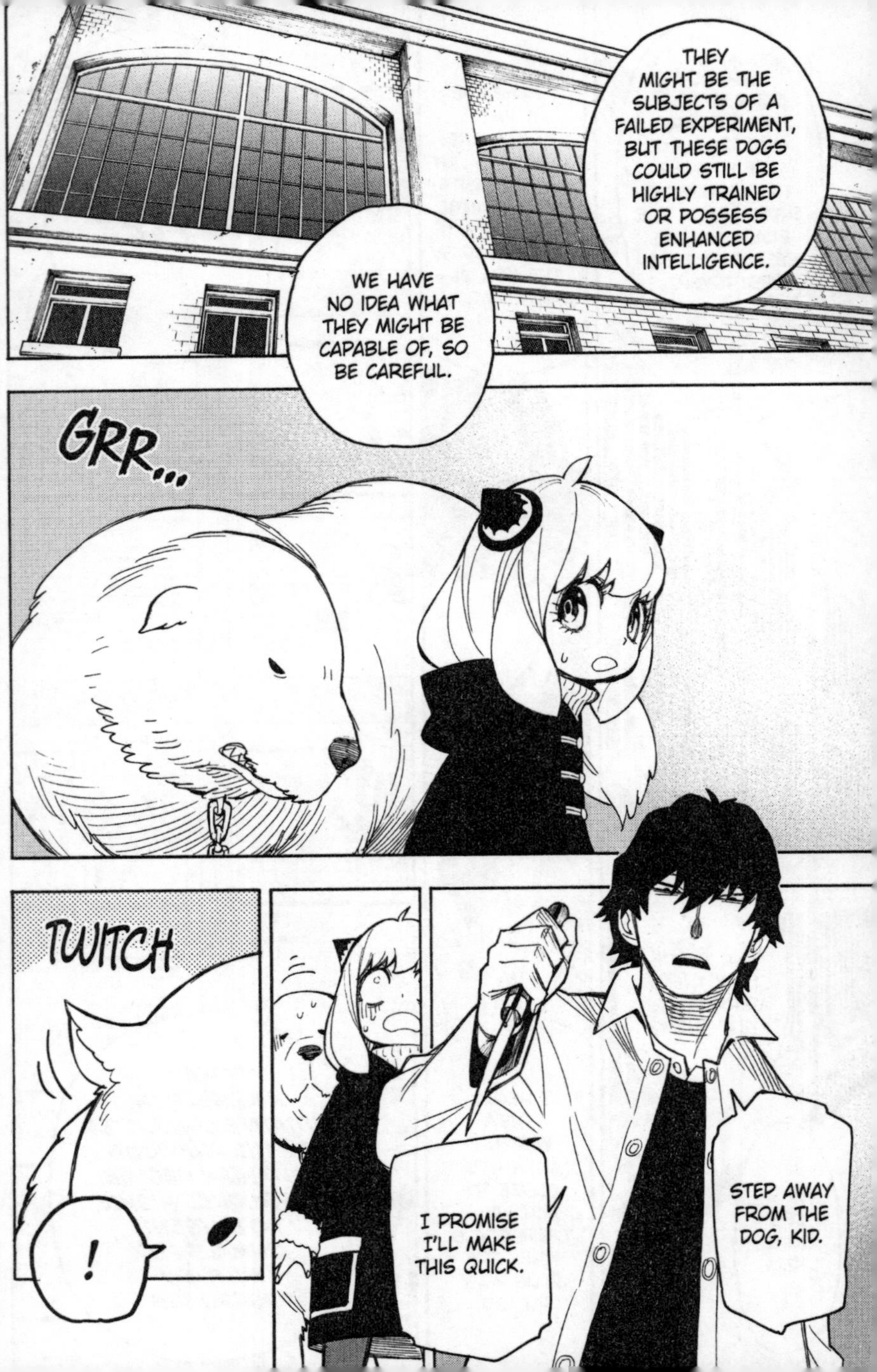
THEY MIGHT BE THE SUBJECTS OF A FAILED EXPERIMENT, BUT THESE DOGS COULD STILL BE HIGHLY TRAINED OR POSSESS ENHANCED INTELLIGENCE.
WE HAVE NO IDEA WHAT THEY MIGHT BE CAPABLE OF, SO BE CAREFUL.
GRR...
STEP AWAY FROM THE DOG, KID.
I PROMISE I'LL MAKE THIS QUICK.
TWITCH
!

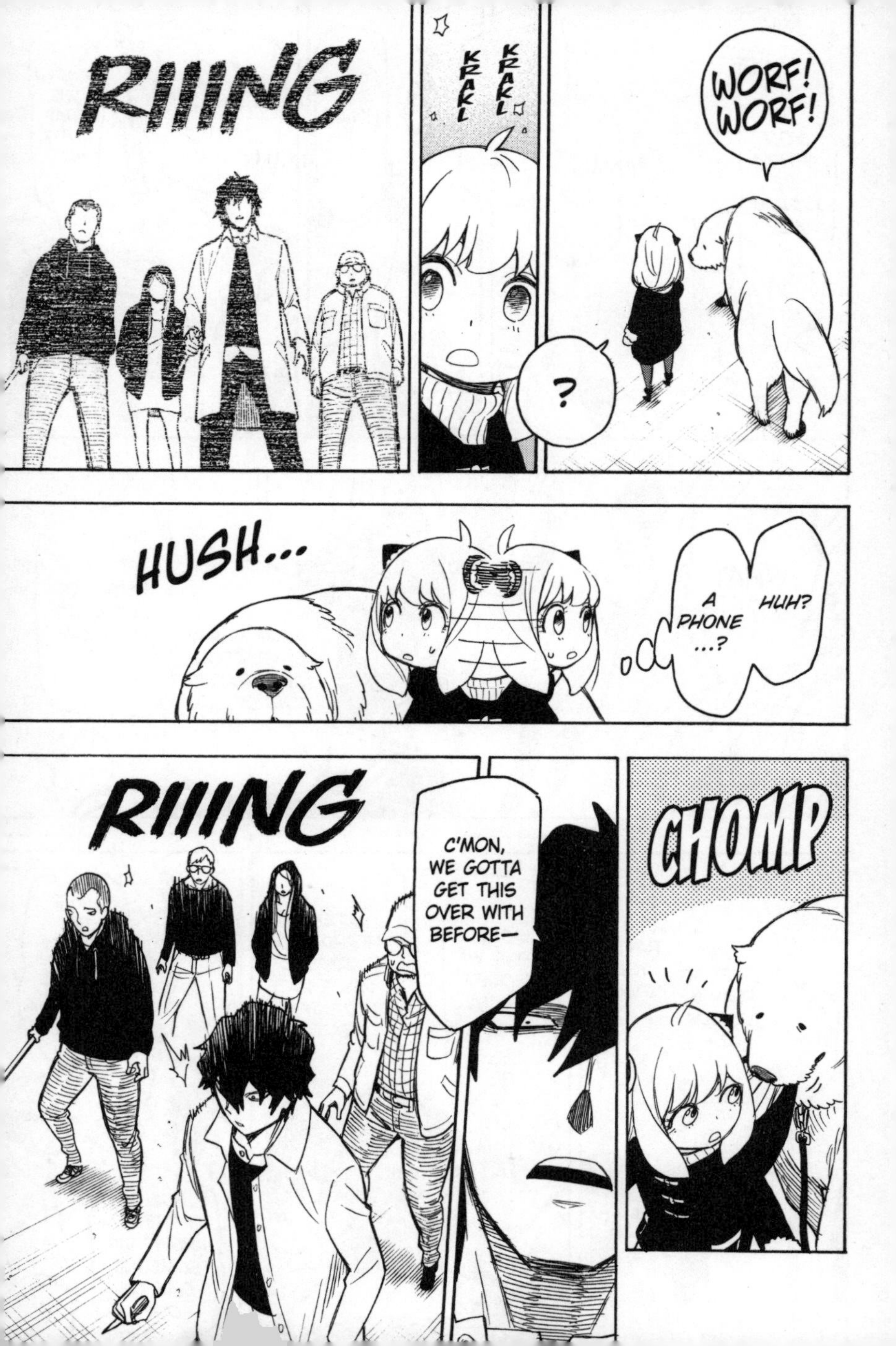
WORF! WORF!
KRAKL
KRAKL
?
RIIING
HUH?
A PHONE ...?
HUSH...
CHOMP
C'MON, WE GOTTA GET THIS OVER WITH BEFORE—
RIIING

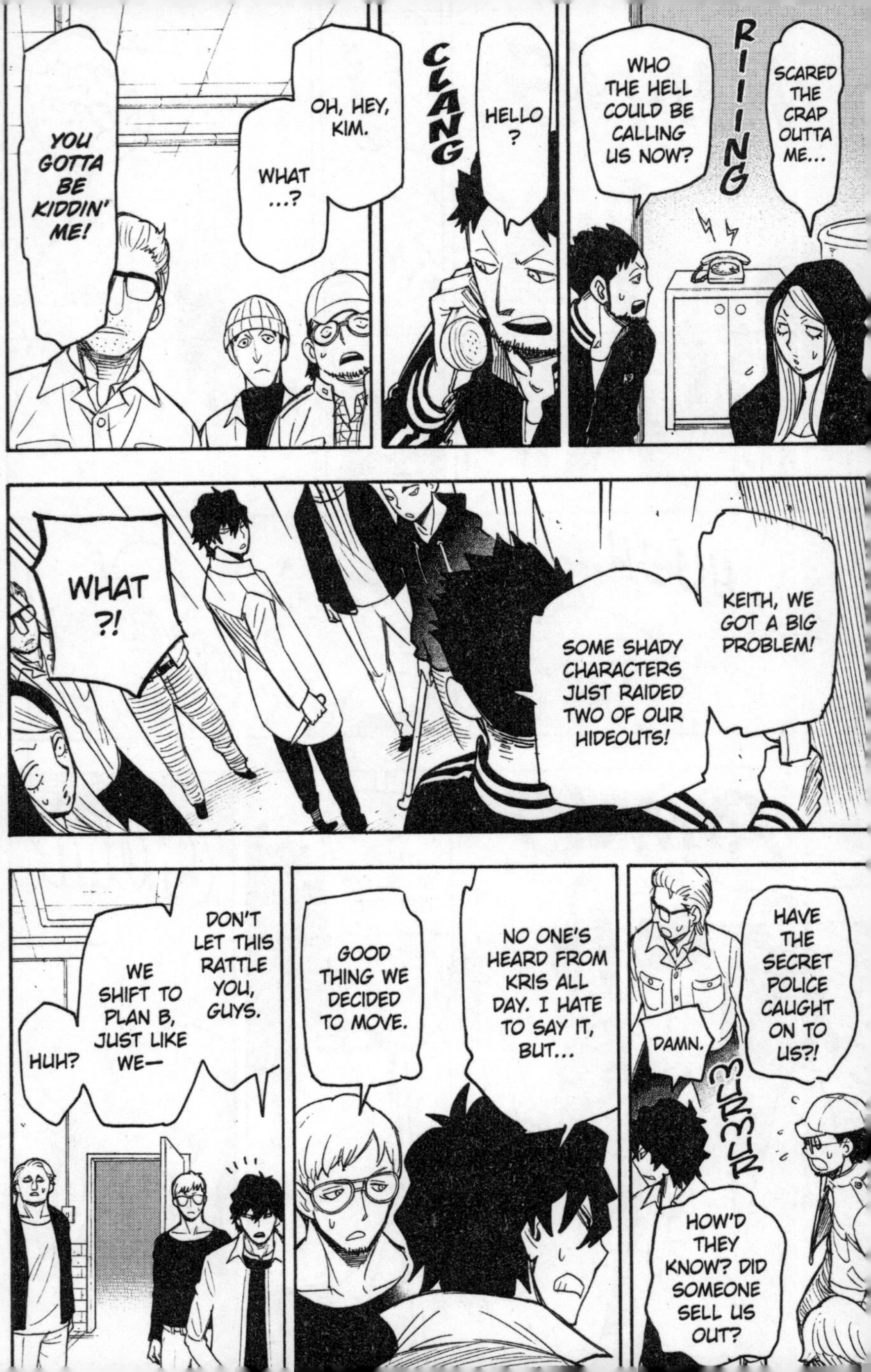
SCARED THE CRAP OUTTA ME...
RIIING
WHO THE HELL COULD BE CALLING US NOW?
HELLO?
CLANG
OH, HEY, KIM.
WHAT...?
YOU GOTTA BE KIDDIN' ME!
KEITH, WE GOT A BIG PROBLEM!
SOME SHADY CHARACTERS JUST RAIDED TWO OF OUR HIDEOUTS!
WHAT?!
HAVE THE SECRET POLICE CAUGHT ON TO US?!
MURMUR
DAMN.
HOW'D THEY KNOW? DID SOMEONE SELL US OUT?
NO ONE'S HEARD FROM KRIS ALL DAY. I HATE TO SAY IT, BUT...
GOOD THING WE DECIDED TO MOVE.
DON'T LET THIS RATTLE YOU, GUYS.
WE SHIFT TO PLAN B, JUST LIKE WE—
HUH?

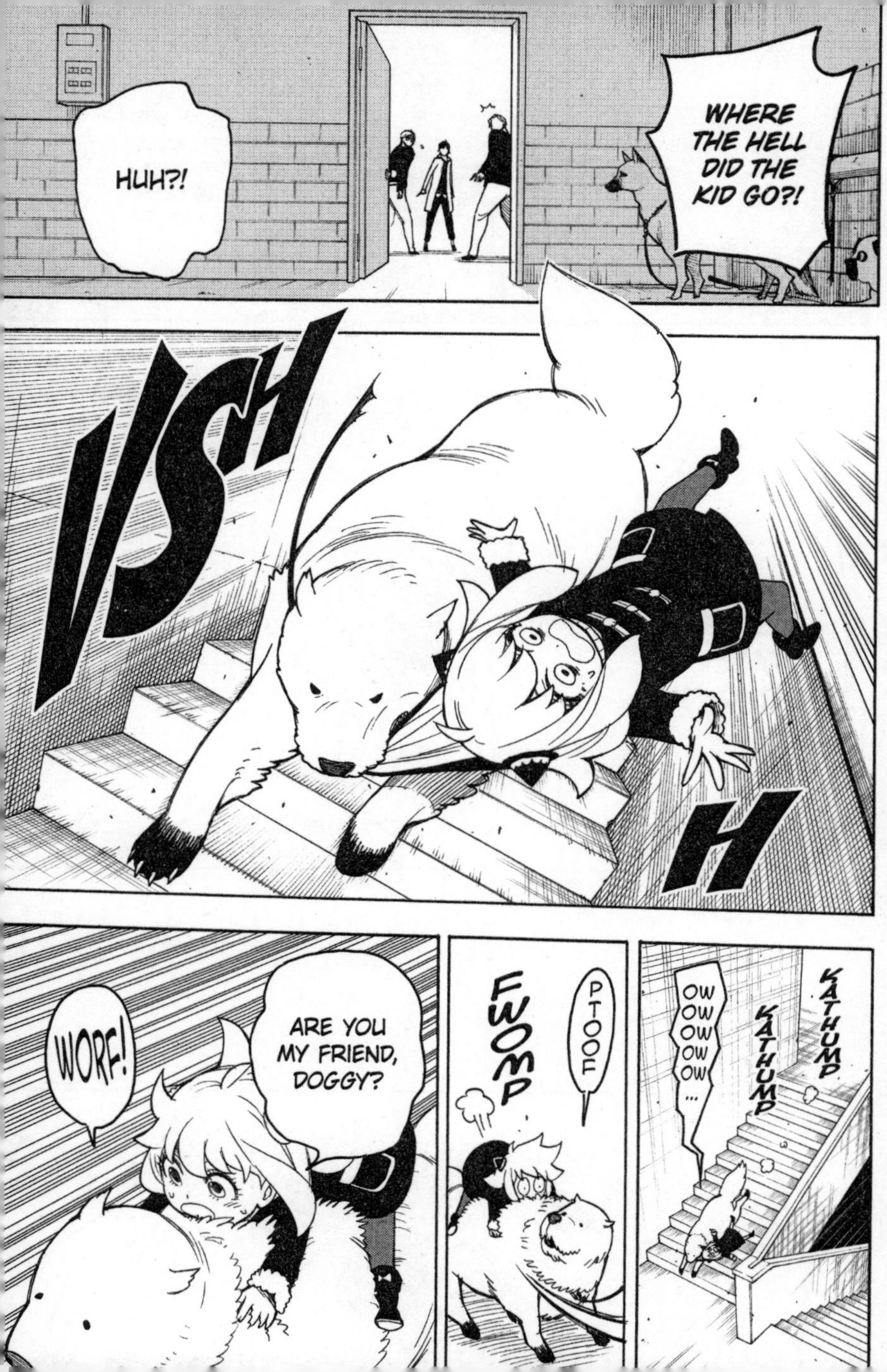
WHERE THE HELL DID THE KID GO?!
HUH?!
VISH
H
KATHUMP
KATHUMP
OW OW OW OW OW ...
PTOOF
FWOMP
ARE YOU MY FRIEND, DOGGY?
WORF!

HOW DID YOU KNOW THE PHONE WAS GOING TO RING?

CAN YOU...

...SEE THE FUTURE?

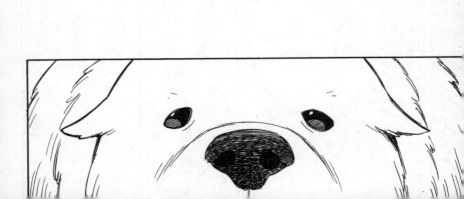

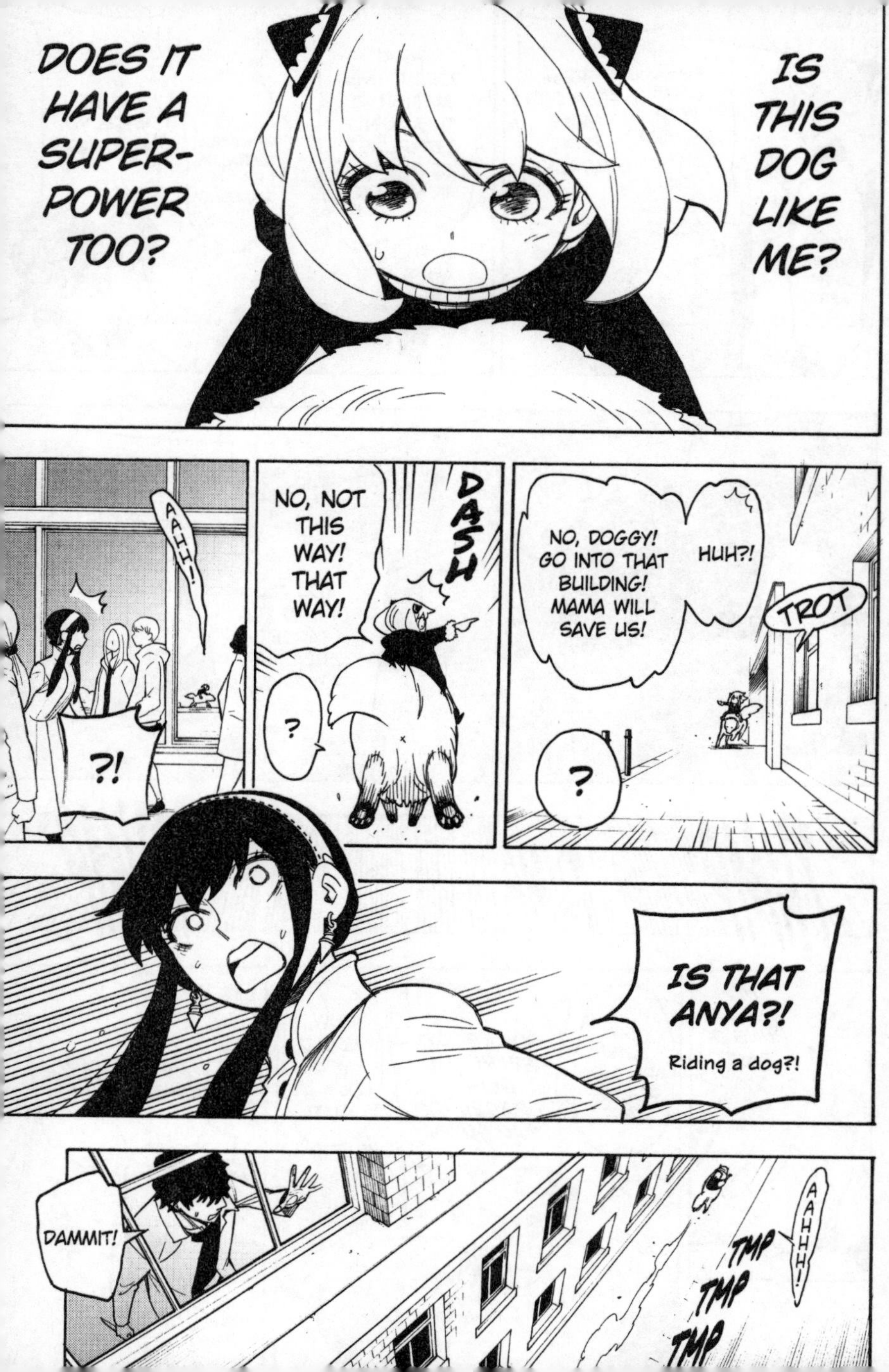
IS THIS DOG LIKE ME?
DOES IT HAVE A SUPER-POWER TOO?
HUH?!
TROT
NO, DOGGY! GO INTO THAT BUILDING! MAMA WILL SAVE US!
?
DASH
NO, NOT THIS WAY! THAT WAY!
?
AAHH!
?!
IS THAT ANYA?!
Riding a dog?!
AAHHH!
TMP TMP TMP TMP
DAMMIT!

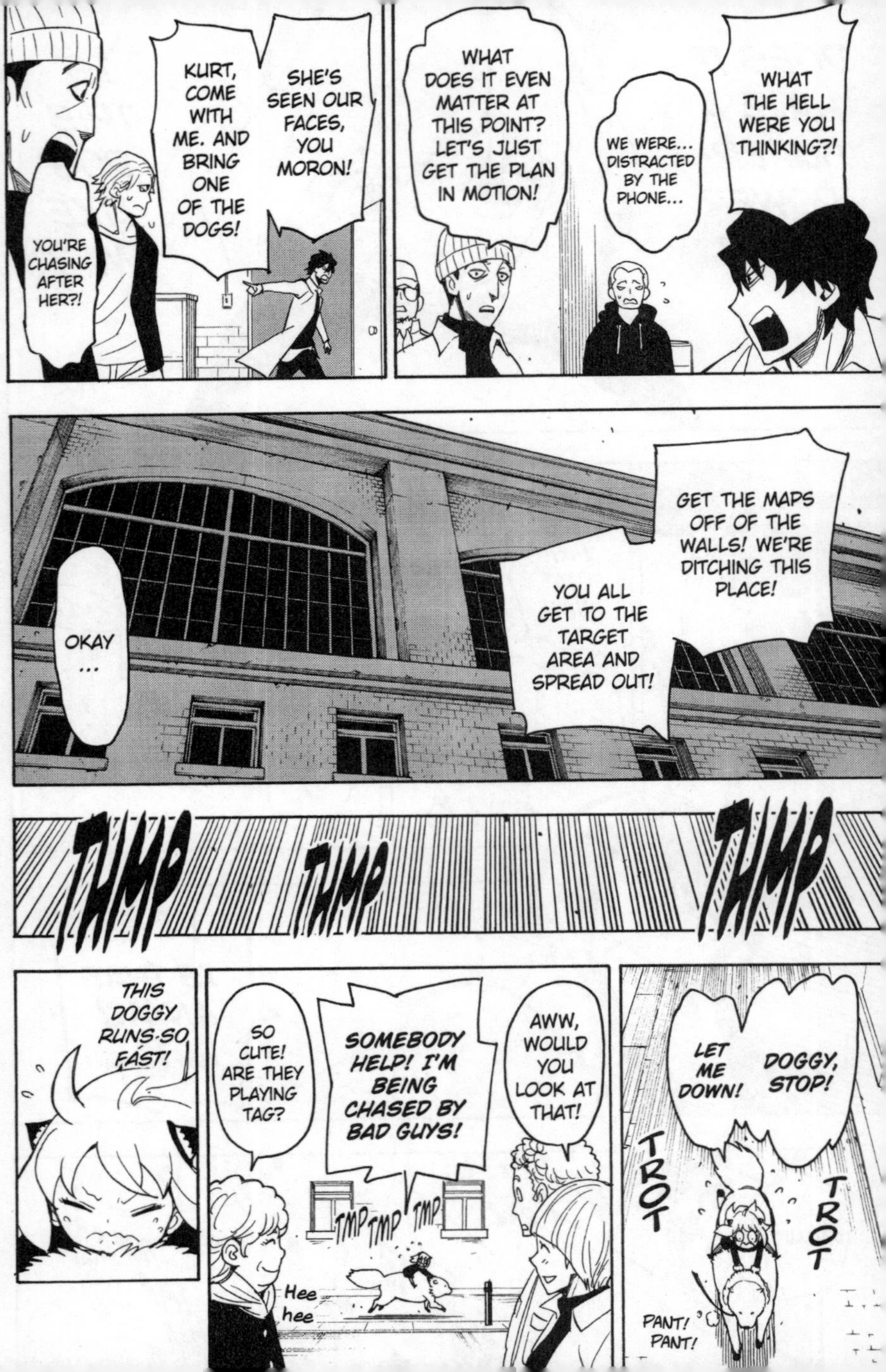
WHAT THE HELL WERE YOU THINKING?!
WE WERE... DISTRACTED BY THE PHONE...
WHAT DOES IT EVEN MATTER AT THIS POINT? LET'S JUST GET THE PLAN IN MOTION!
SHE'S SEEN OUR FACES, YOU MORON!
KURT, COME WITH ME. AND BRING ONE OF THE DOGS!
YOU'RE CHASING AFTER HER?!
GET THE MAPS OFF OF THE WALLS! WE'RE DITCHING THIS PLACE!
YOU ALL GET TO THE TARGET AREA AND SPREAD OUT!
OKAY ...
THUMP
THUMP
THUMP
DOGGY, STOP!
LET ME DOWN!
TROT
TROT
PANT! PANT!
AWW, WOULD YOU LOOK AT THAT!
SOMEBODY HELP! I'M BEING CHASED BY BAD GUYS!
SO CUTE! ARE THEY PLAYING TAG?
TMP TMP TMP
Hee hee
THIS DOGGY RUNS SO FAST!

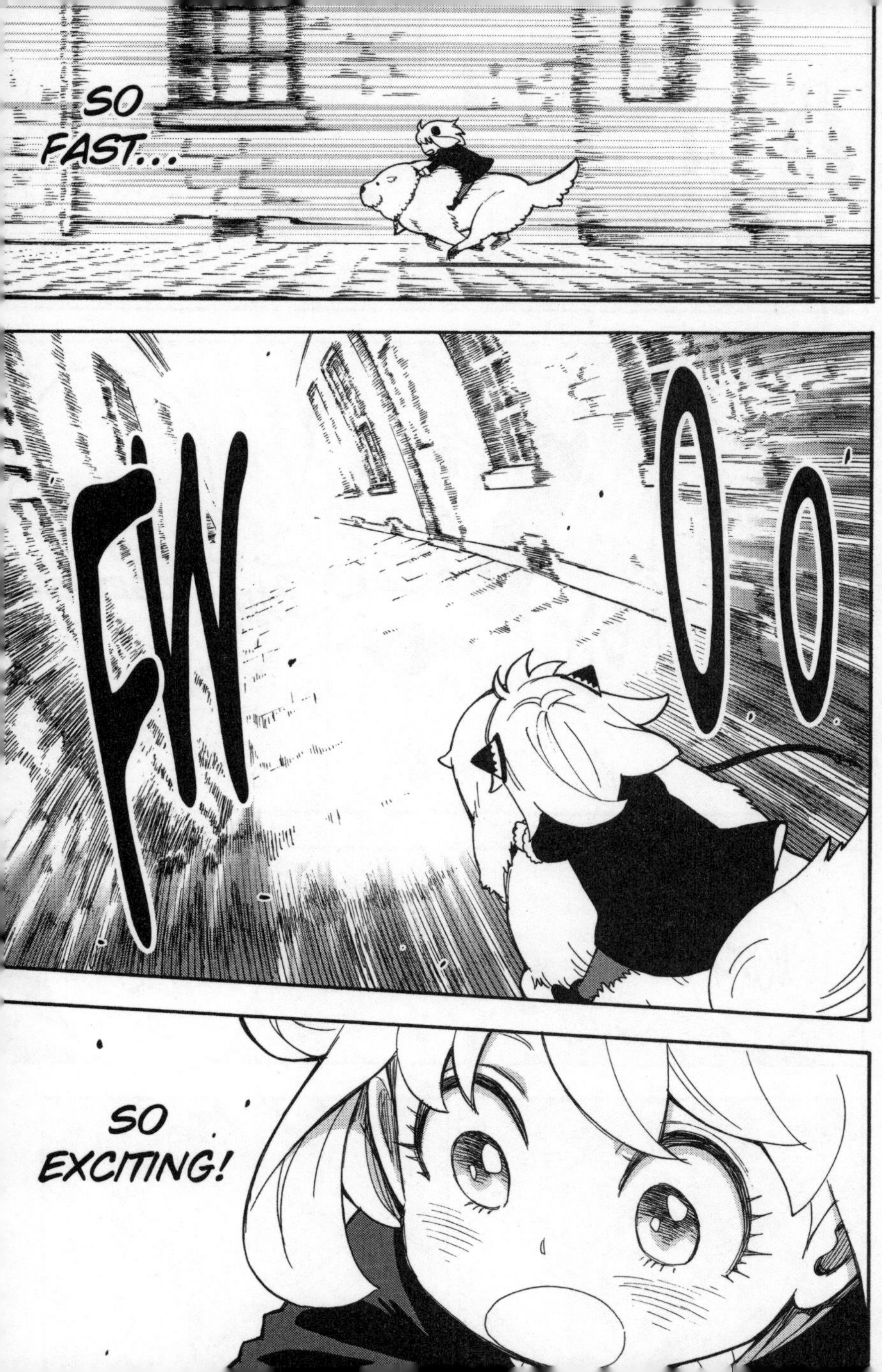
SO FAST...
FWOOO
SO EXCITING!

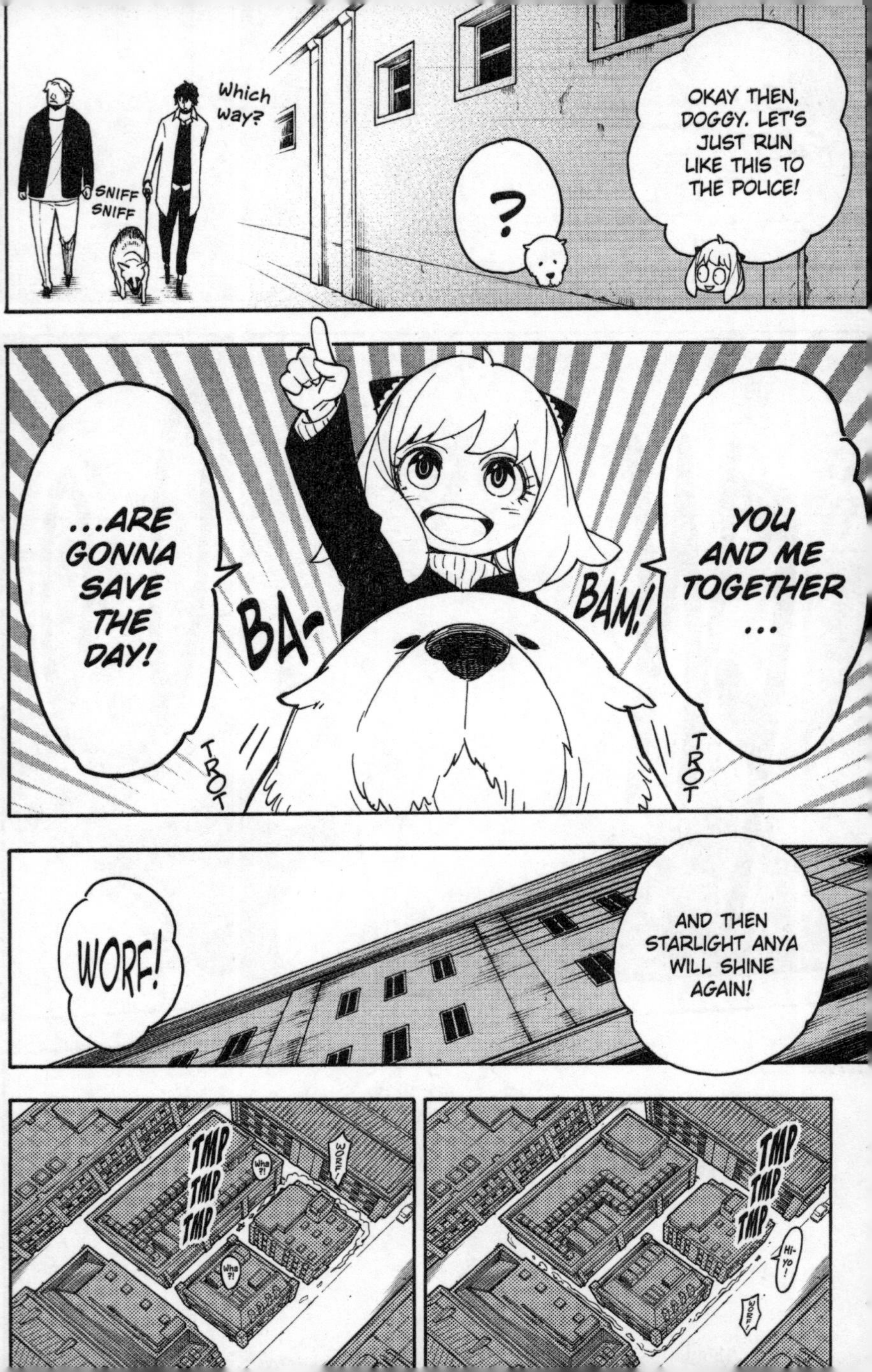

OKAY THEN, DOGGY. LET'S JUST RUN LIKE THIS TO THE POLICE!
?
Which way?
SNIFF SNIFF
YOU AND ME TOGETHER ...
BA-
BAM!
...ARE GONNA SAVE THE DAY!
TROT
TROT
AND THEN STARLIGHT ANYA WILL SHINE AGAIN!
WORF!
TMP TMP TMP
Hi-yo!
WORF!
WORF!
Wha?!
TMP TMP TMP
Wha?!

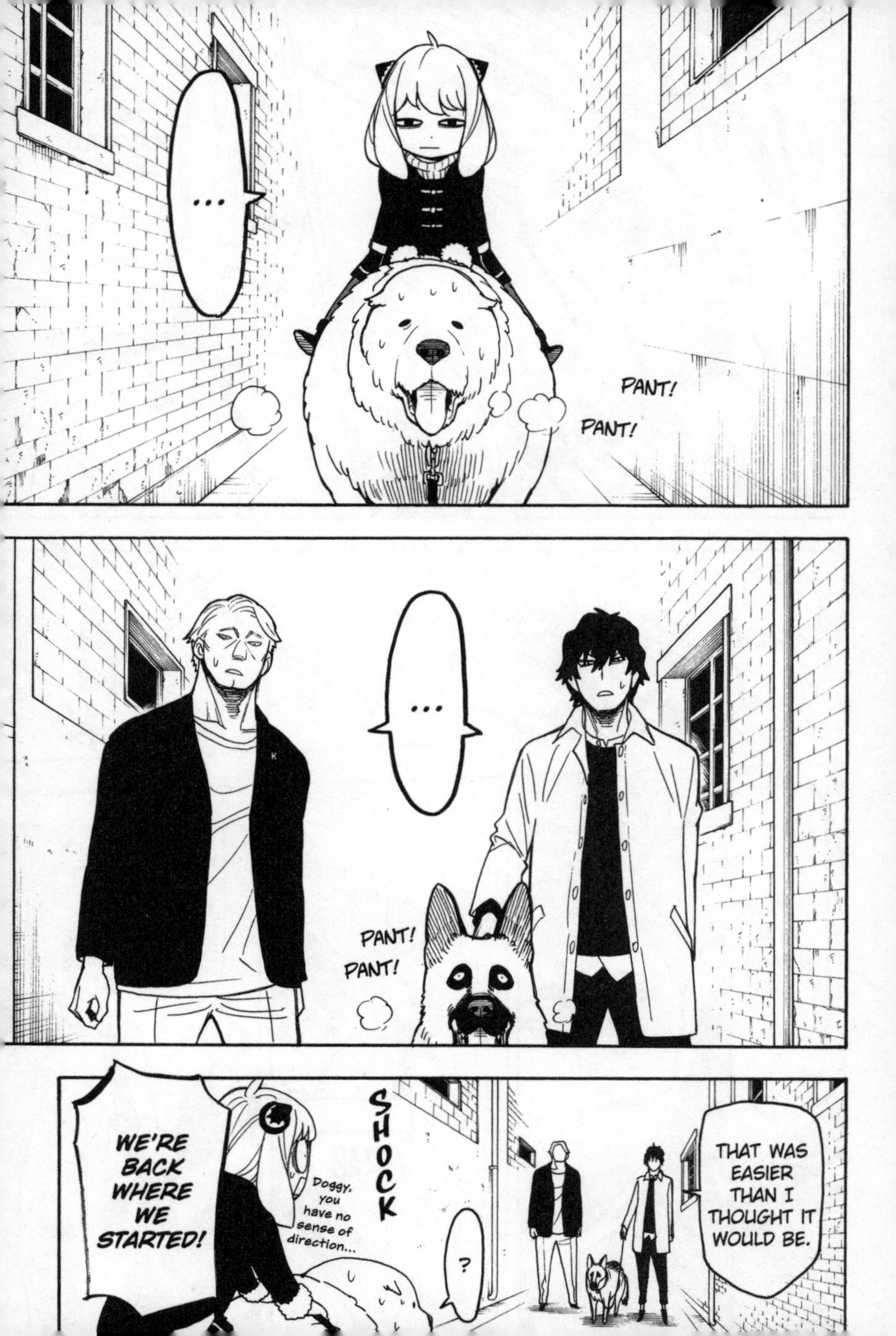
...
PANT!
PANT!
...
PANT!
PANT!
THAT WAS EASIER THAN I THOUGHT IT WOULD BE.
?
SHOCK
Doggy, you have no sense of direction...
WE'RE BACK WHERE WE STARTED!

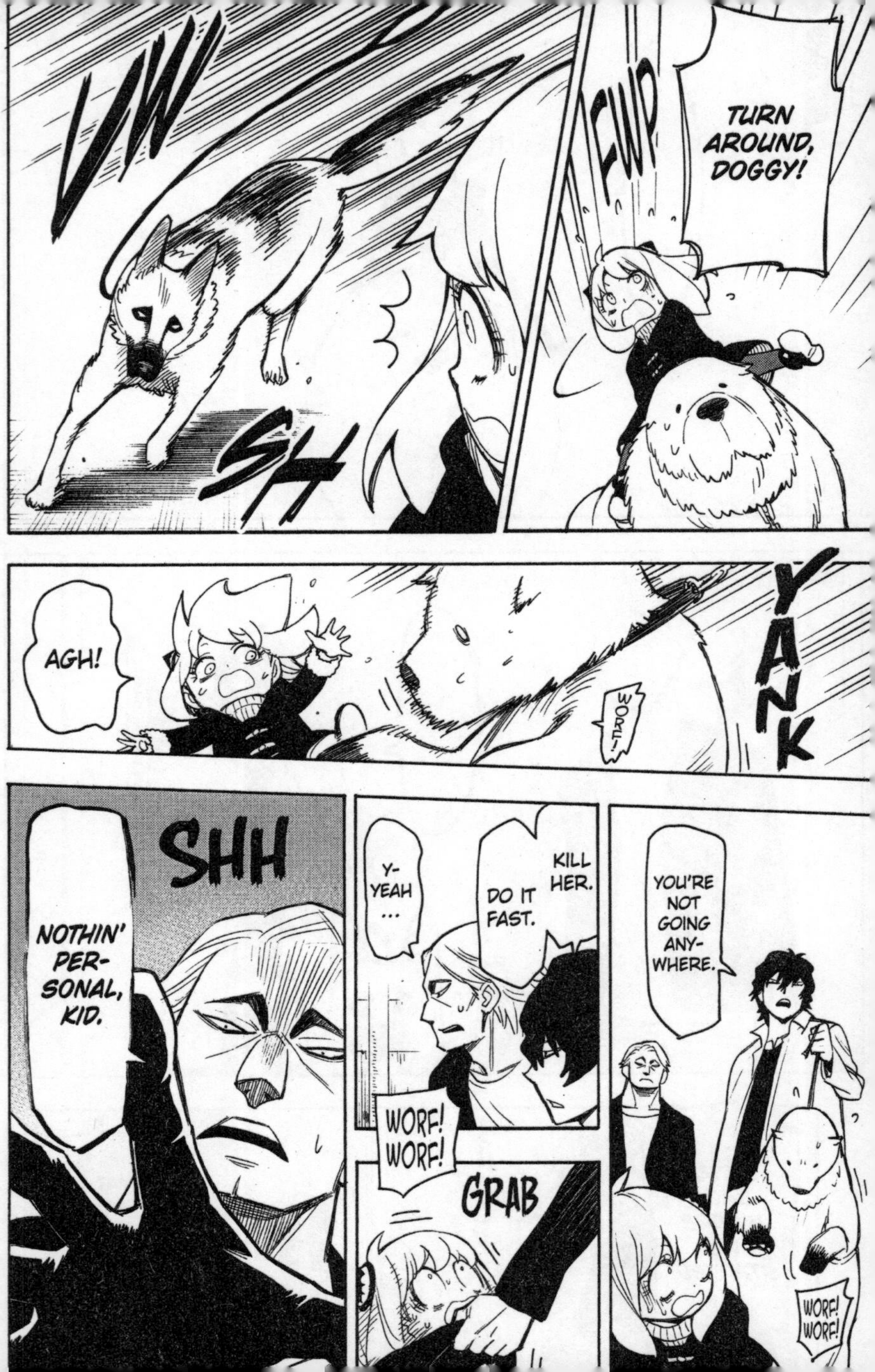
FWP
TURN AROUND, DOGGY!
VW
SH
YANK
WORF!
AGH!
YOU'RE NOT GOING ANY-WHERE.
WORF! WORF!
KILL HER.
DO IT FAST.
Y-YEAH ...
WORF! WORF!
GRAB
SHH
NOTHIN' PER-SONAL, KID.

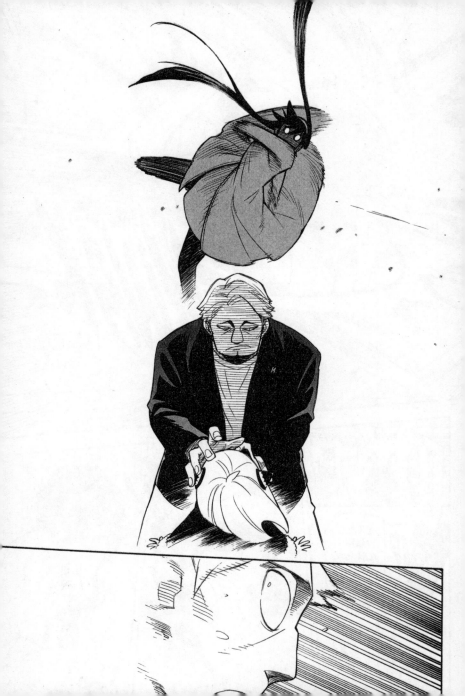

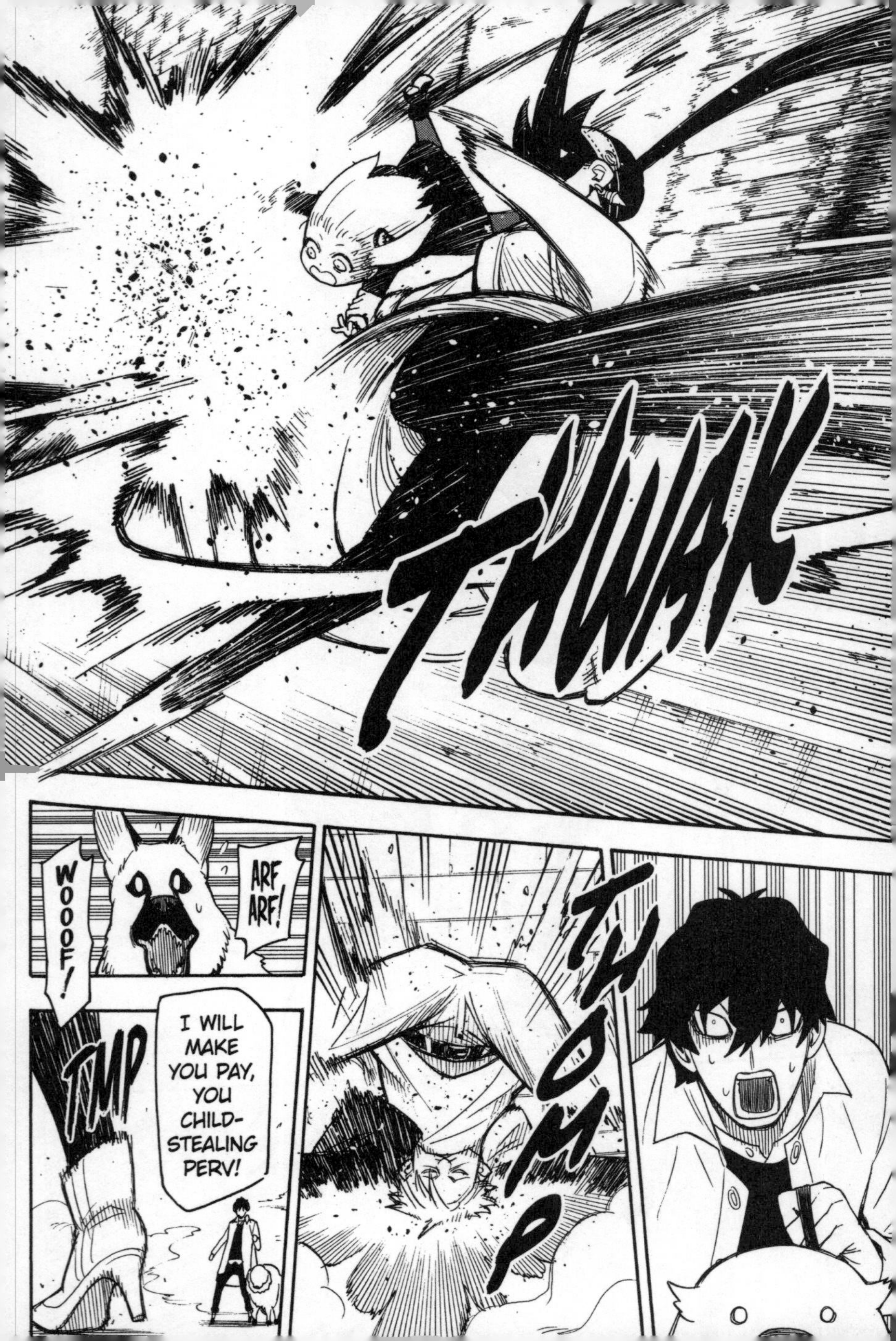
THWAK
THOMP
ARF ARF!
WOOOOF!
TMP
I WILL MAKE YOU PAY, YOU CHILD-STEALING PERV!

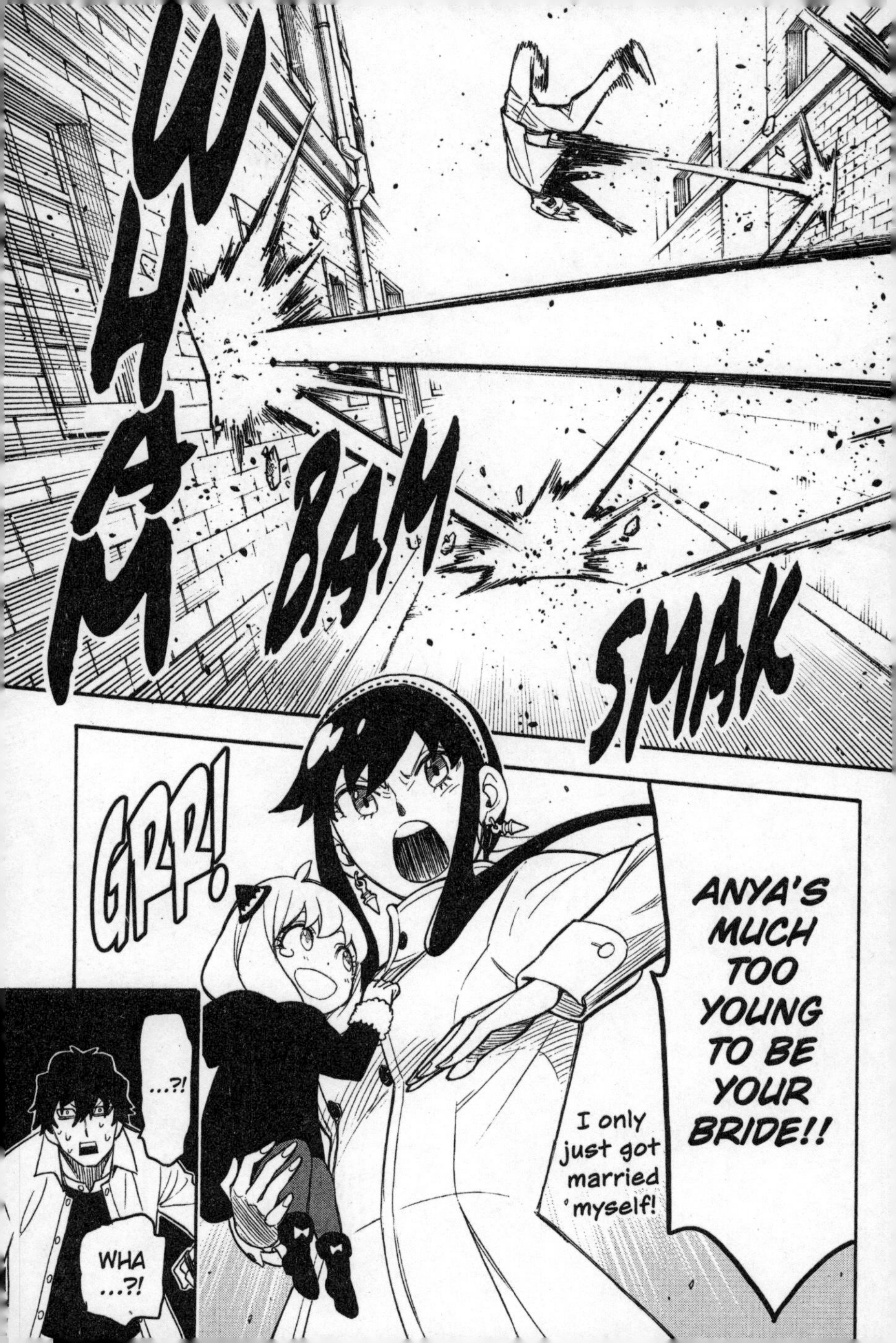
WHAM
BAM
SMAK
ANYA'S MUCH TOO YOUNG TO BE YOUR BRIDE!!
I only just got married myself!
GRP!
...?!
WHA ...?!

SPY×FAMILY

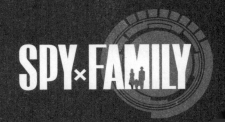

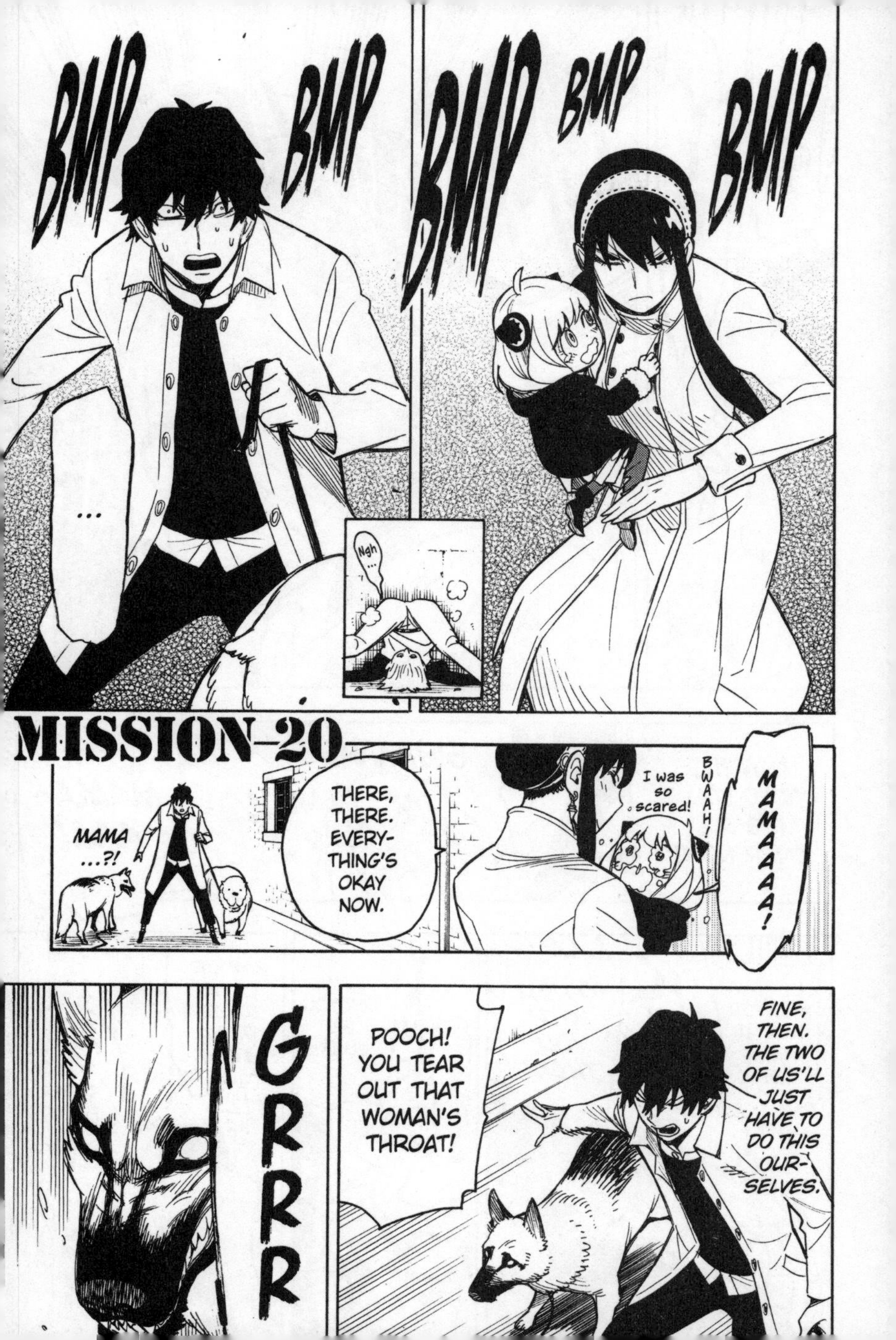
BMP
BMP
BMP
Ngh...
BMP
BMP
...
MISSION-20
MAMAAAAA!
BWAAAH!
I was so scared!
THERE, THERE. EVERYTHING'S OKAY NOW.
MAMA ...?!
FINE, THEN. THE TWO OF US'LL JUST HAVE TO DO THIS OURSELVES.
POOCH! YOU TEAR OUT THAT WOMAN'S THROAT!
GRRR

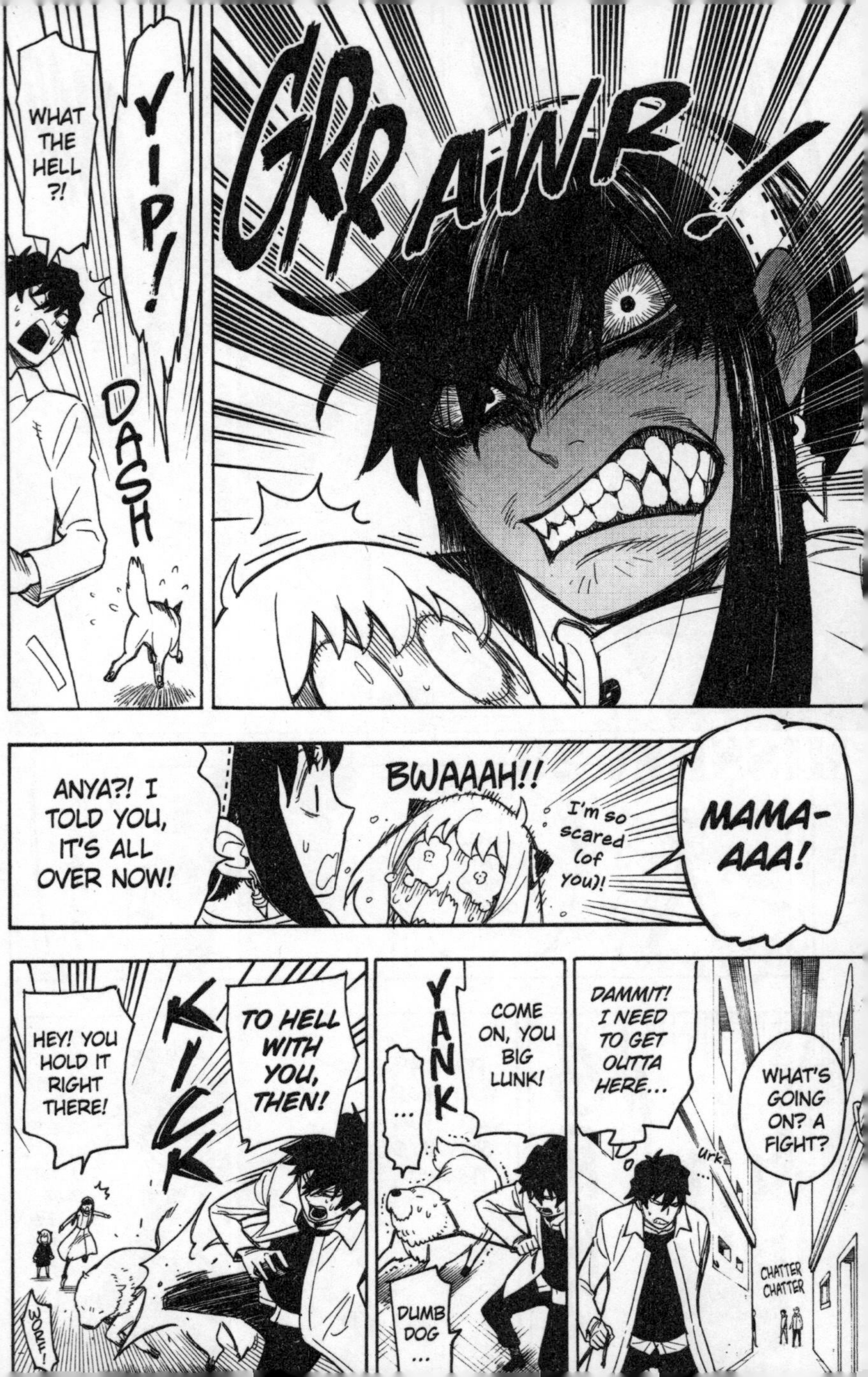
GRRAWR...!
YIP!
WHAT THE HELL?!
DASH
MAMA-AAA!
I'm so scared (of you)!
BWAAAH!!
ANYA?! I TOLD YOU, IT'S ALL OVER NOW!
WHAT'S GOING ON? A FIGHT?
DAMMIT! I NEED TO GET OUTTA HERE...
Urk
CHATTER CHATTER
COME ON, YOU BIG LUNK!
YANK
...
DUMB DOG...
TO HELL WITH YOU, THEN!
KICK
HEY! YOU HOLD IT RIGHT THERE!
WOOF!

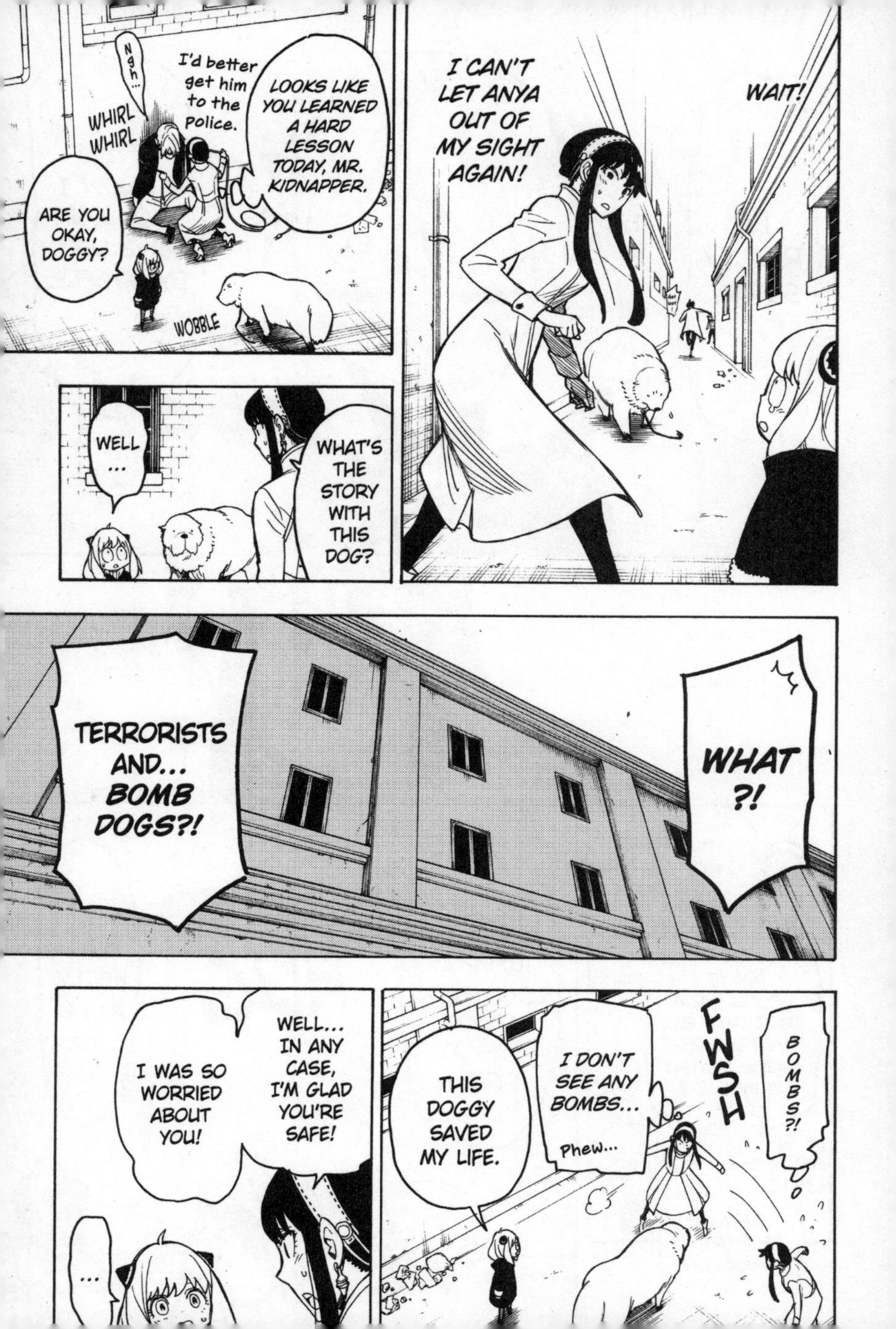
WAIT!
I CAN'T LET ANYA OUT OF MY SIGHT AGAIN!
Ngh...
LOOKS LIKE YOU LEARNED A HARD LESSON TODAY, MR. KIDNAPPER.
I'd better get him to the Police.
WHIRL WHIRL
ARE YOU OKAY, DOGGY?
WOBBLE
WHAT'S THE STORY WITH THIS DOG?
WELL ...
WHAT ?!
TERRORISTS AND... BOMB DOGS?!
BOMBS?!
FWSH
I DON'T SEE ANY BOMBS...
Phew...
THIS DOGGY SAVED MY LIFE.
WELL... IN ANY CASE, I'M GLAD YOU'RE SAFE!
I WAS SO WORRIED ABOUT YOU!
...

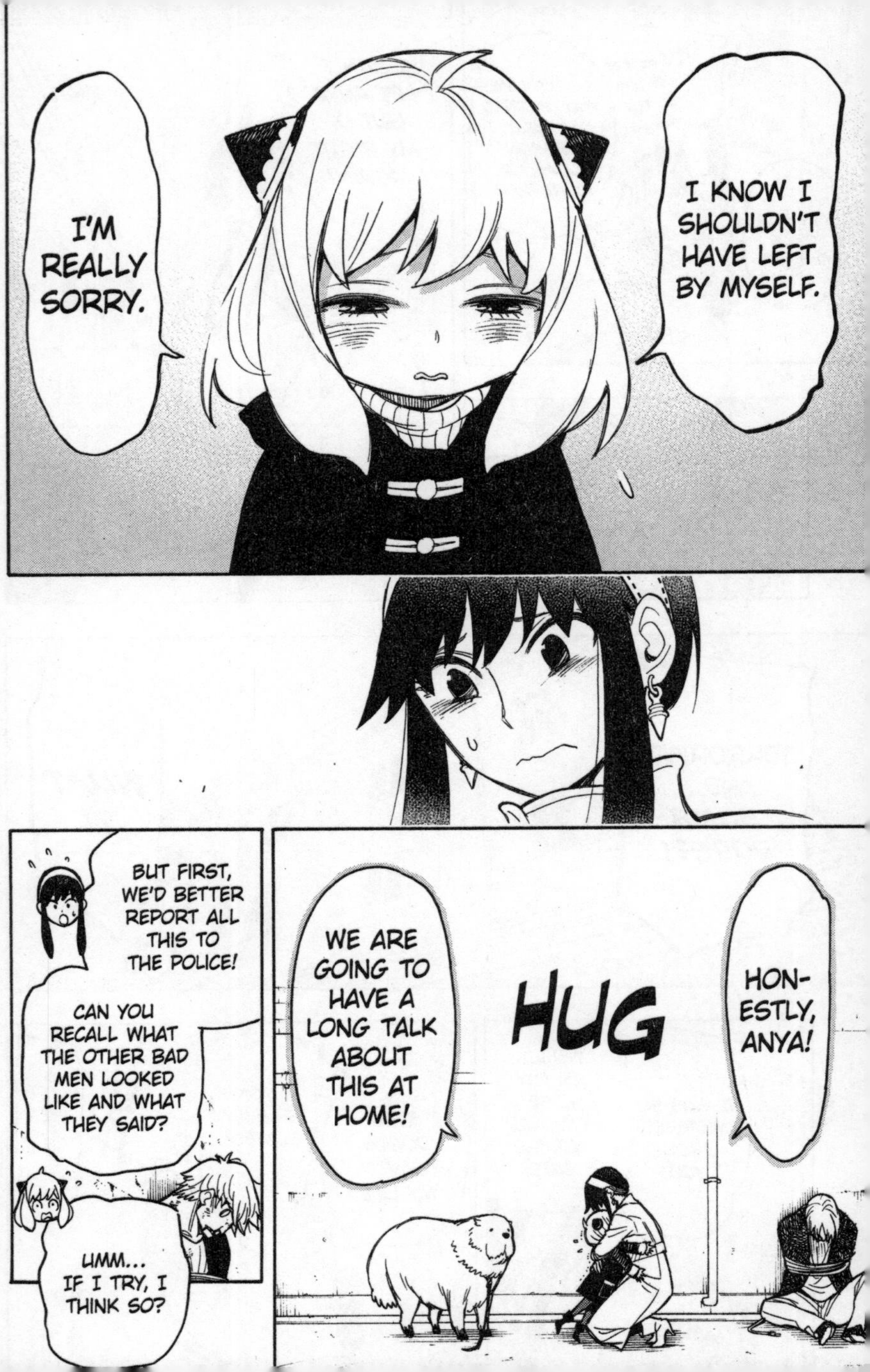
I KNOW I SHOULDN'T HAVE LEFT BY MYSELF.
I'M REALLY SORRY.
HON-ESTLY, ANYA!
HUG
WE ARE GOING TO HAVE A LONG TALK ABOUT THIS AT HOME!
BUT FIRST, WE'D BETTER REPORT ALL THIS TO THE POLICE!
CAN YOU RECALL WHAT THE OTHER BAD MEN LOOKED LIKE AND WHAT THEY SAID?
UMM... IF I TRY, I THINK SO?

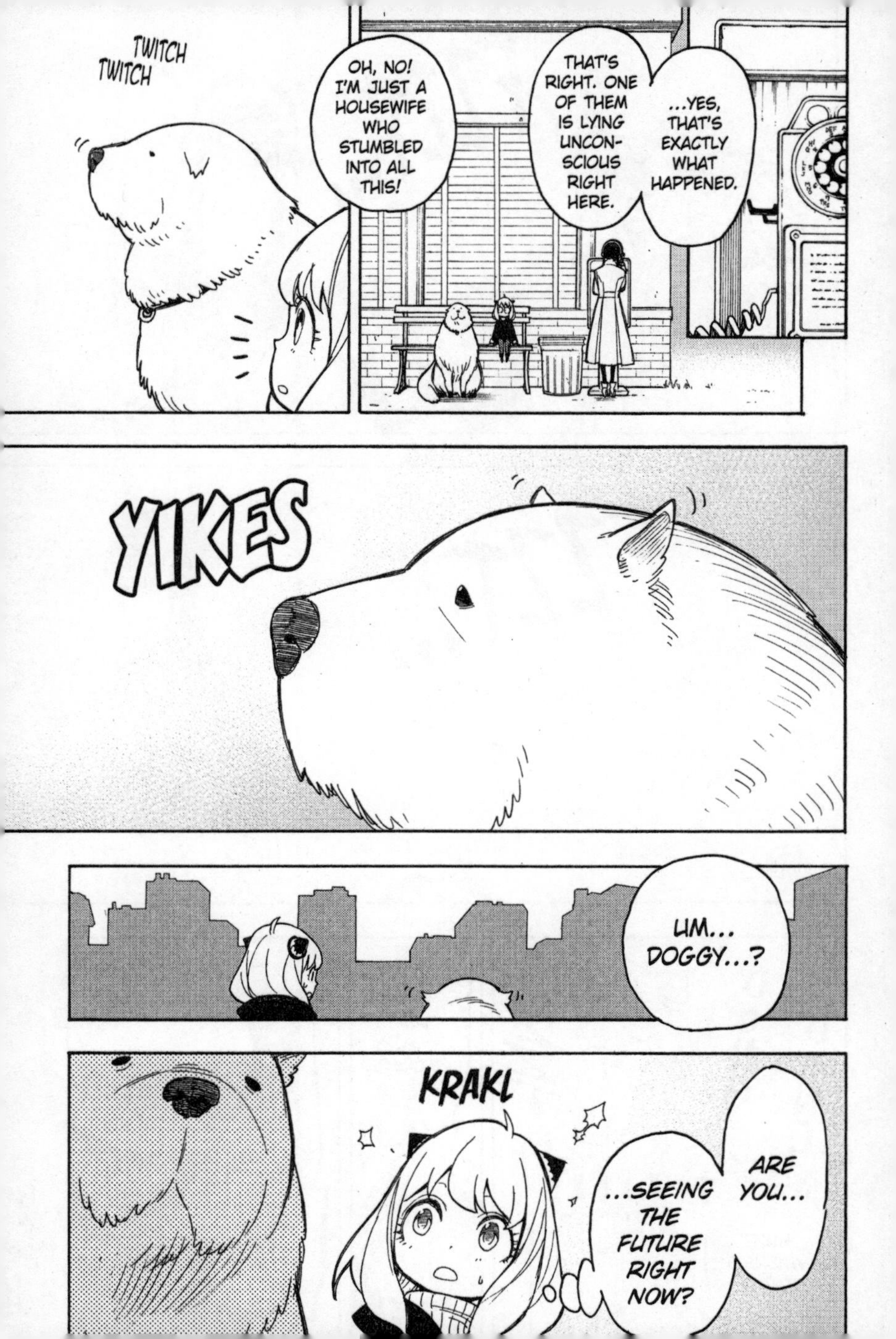
...YES, THAT'S EXACTLY WHAT HAPPENED.
THAT'S RIGHT. ONE OF THEM IS LYING UNCON-SCIOUS RIGHT HERE.
OH, NO! I'M JUST A HOUSEWIFE WHO STUMBLED INTO ALL THIS!
TWITCH TWITCH
YIKES
UM... DOGGY...?
KRAKL
ARE YOU...
...SEEING THE FUTURE RIGHT NOW?

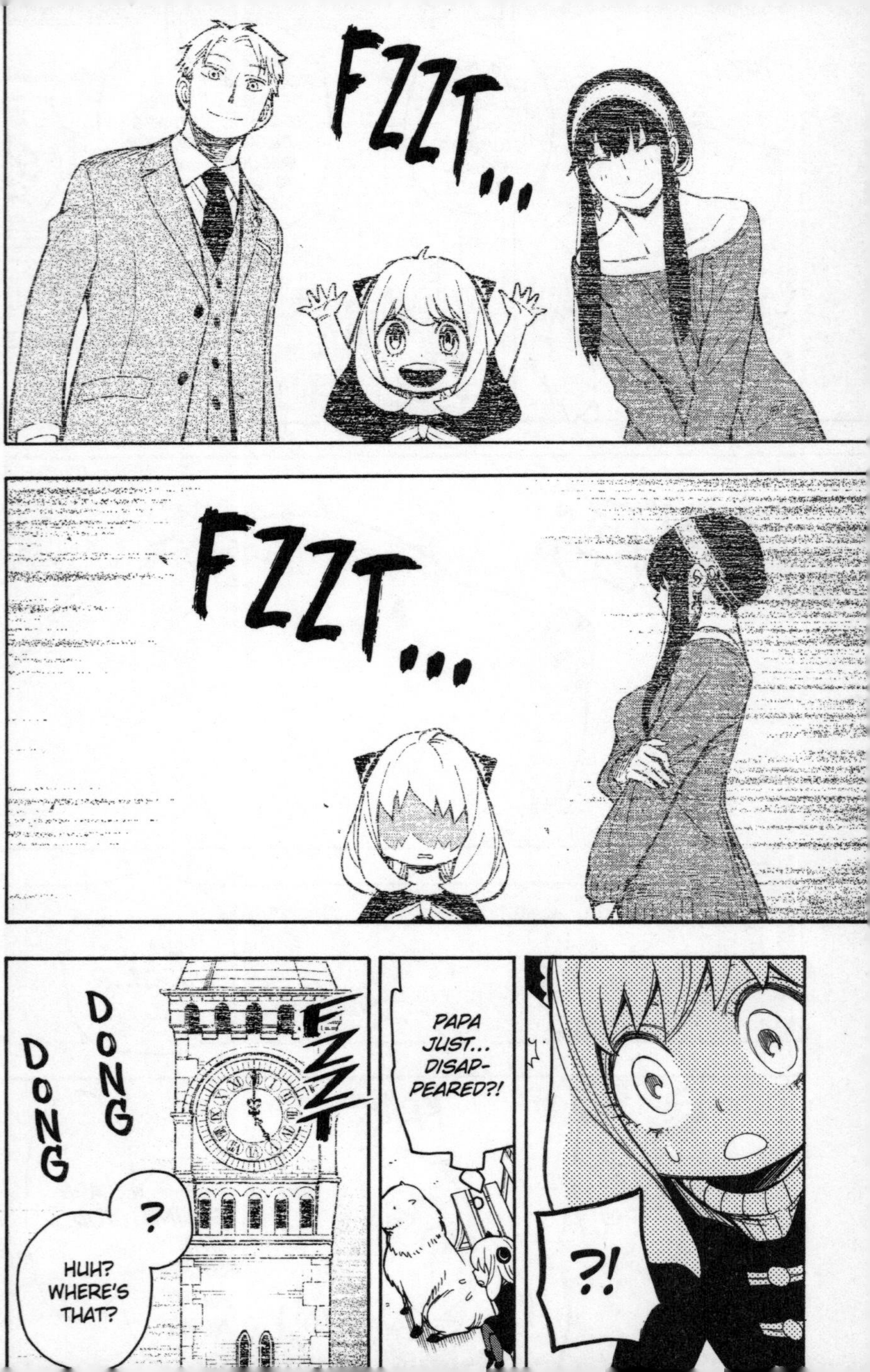
FZZT...
FZZT...
?!
PAPA JUST... DISAP-PEARED?!
FZZT
DONG
DONG
?
HUH? WHERE'S THAT?

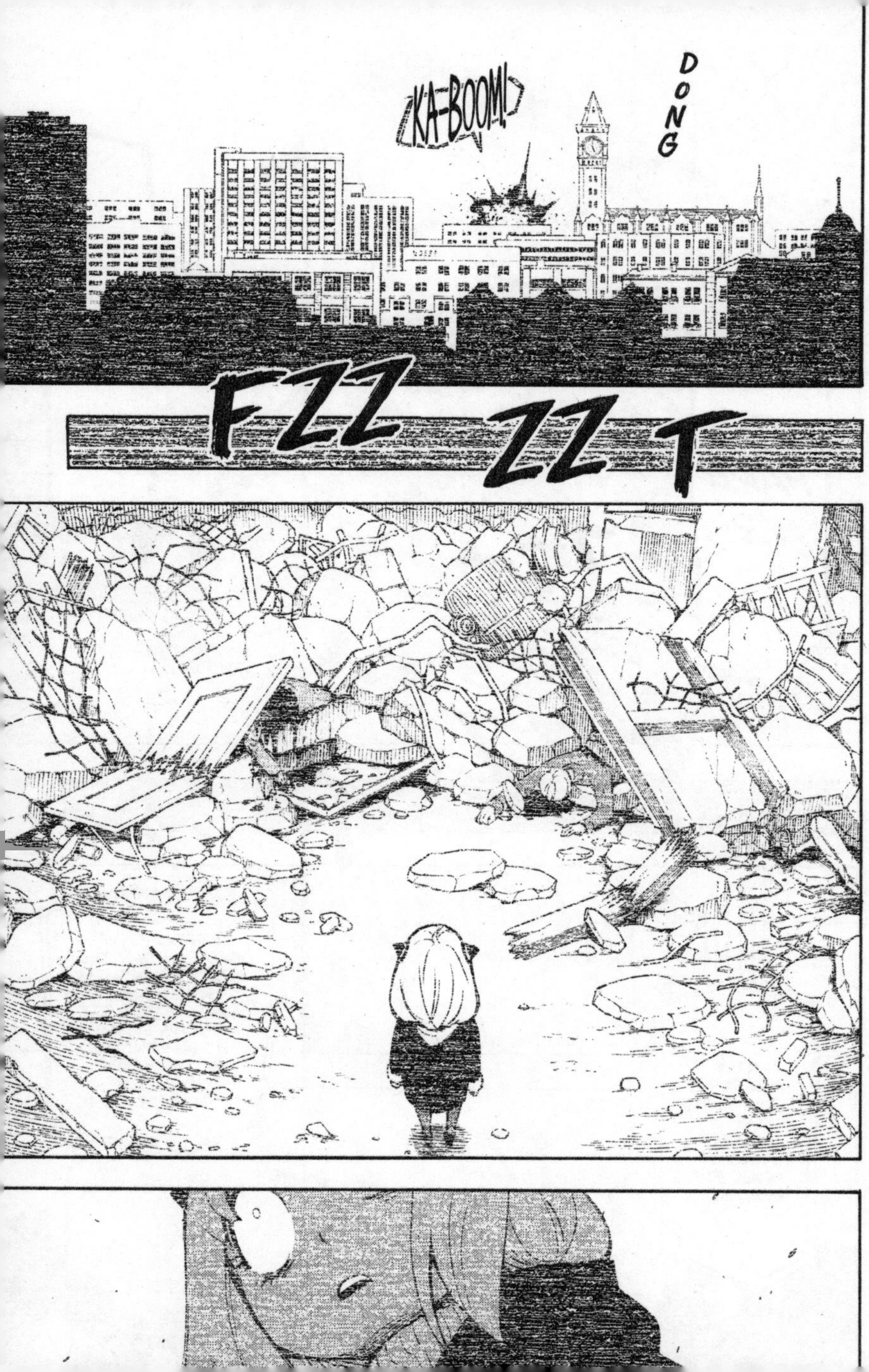
DONG
KA-BOOM!
FZZ ZZT

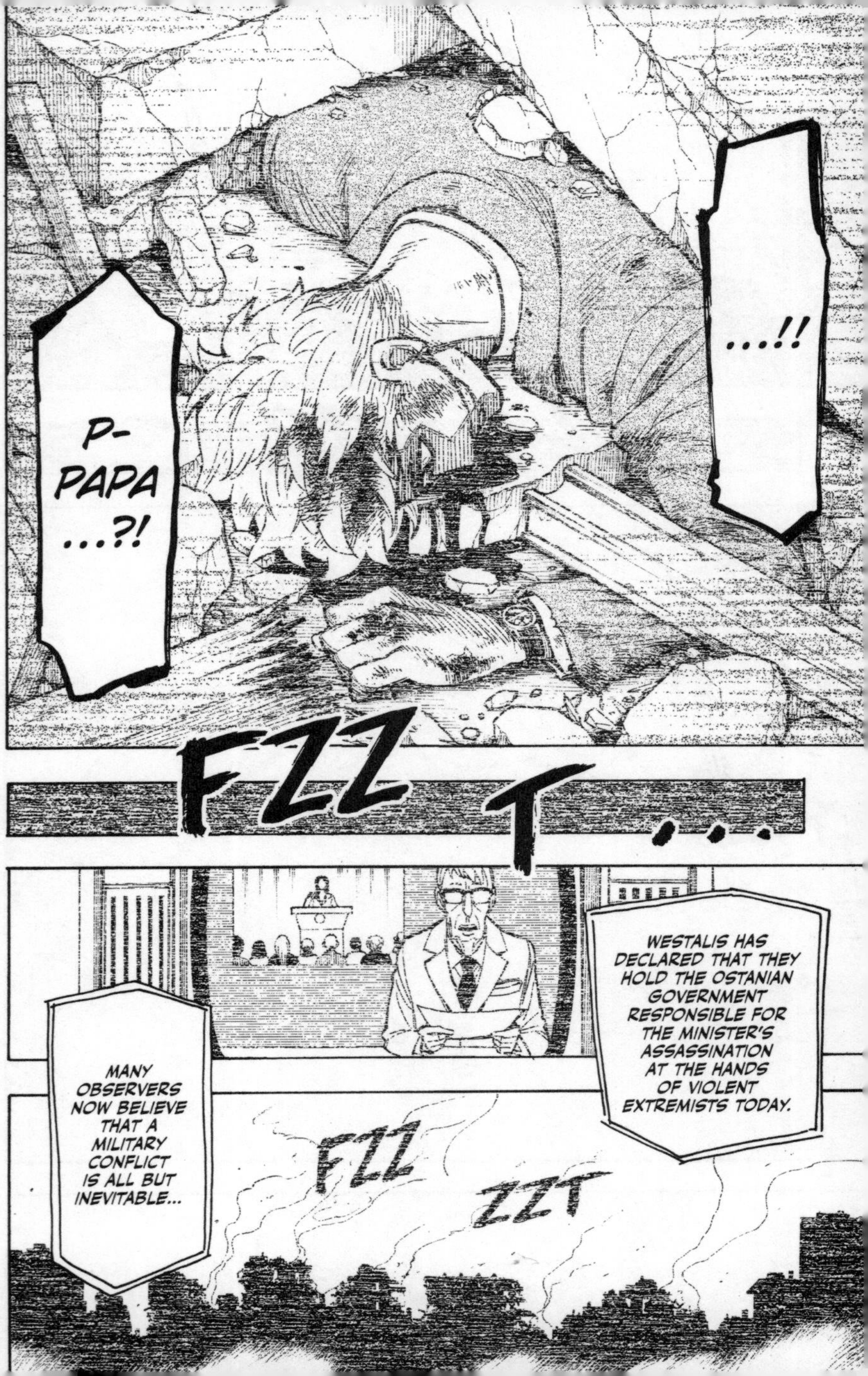
...!!
P-PAPA...?!
FZZ T...
WESTALIS HAS DECLARED THAT THEY HOLD THE OSTANIAN GOVERNMENT RESPONSIBLE FOR THE MINISTER'S ASSASSINATION AT THE HANDS OF VIOLENT EXTREMISTS TODAY.
MANY OBSERVERS NOW BELIEVE THAT A MILITARY CONFLICT IS ALL BUT INEVITABLE...
FZZ
ZZT

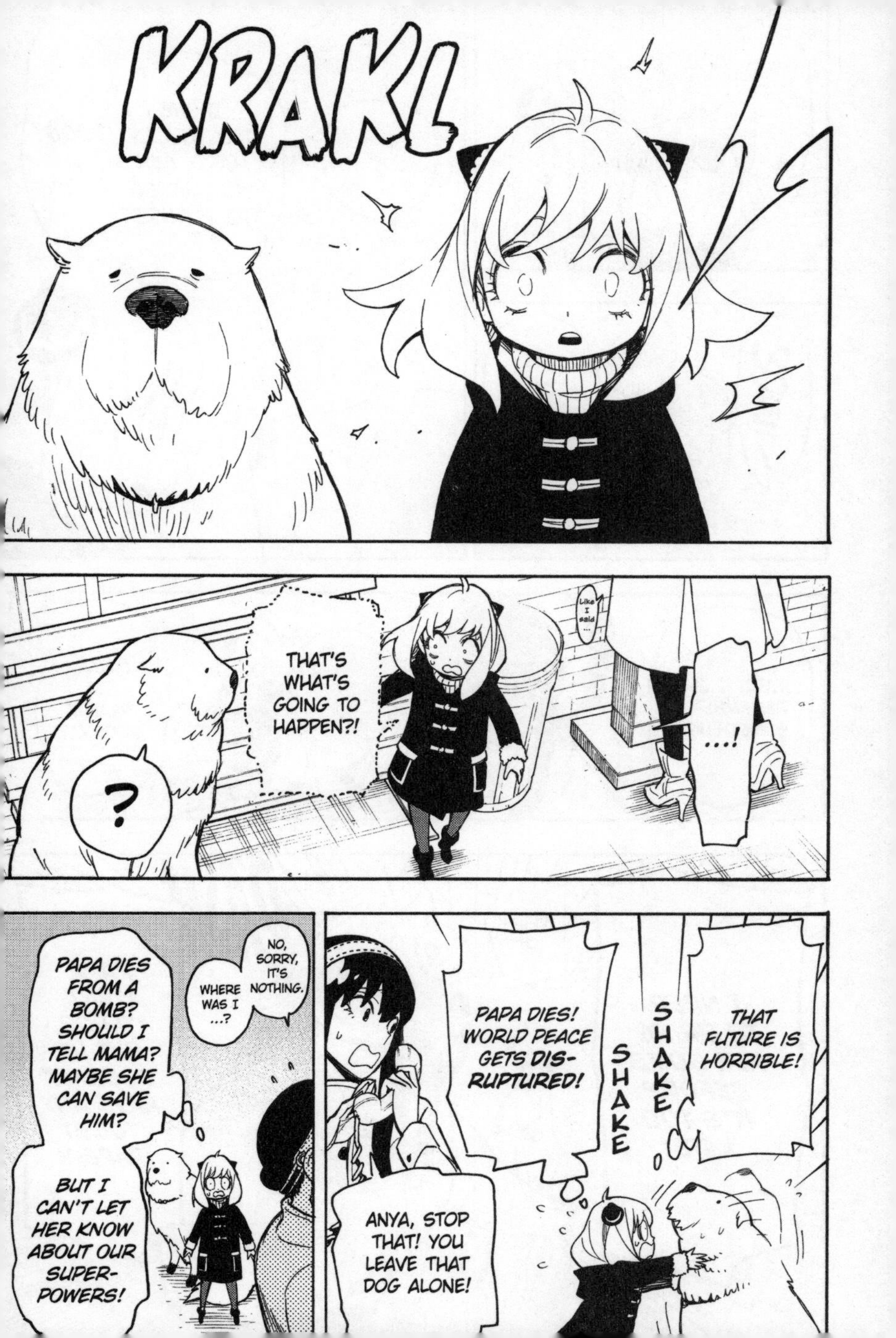
KRAKL
Like I said ...
...!
THAT'S WHAT'S GOING TO HAPPEN?!
?
THAT FUTURE IS HORRIBLE!
SHAKE
SHAKE
PAPA DIES! WORLD PEACE GETS DIS-RUPTURED!
ANYA, STOP THAT! YOU LEAVE THAT DOG ALONE!
NO, SORRY, IT'S NOTHING.
WHERE WAS I ...?
PAPA DIES FROM A BOMB? SHOULD I TELL MAMA? MAYBE SHE CAN SAVE HIM?
BUT I CAN'T LET HER KNOW ABOUT OUR SUPER-POWERS!

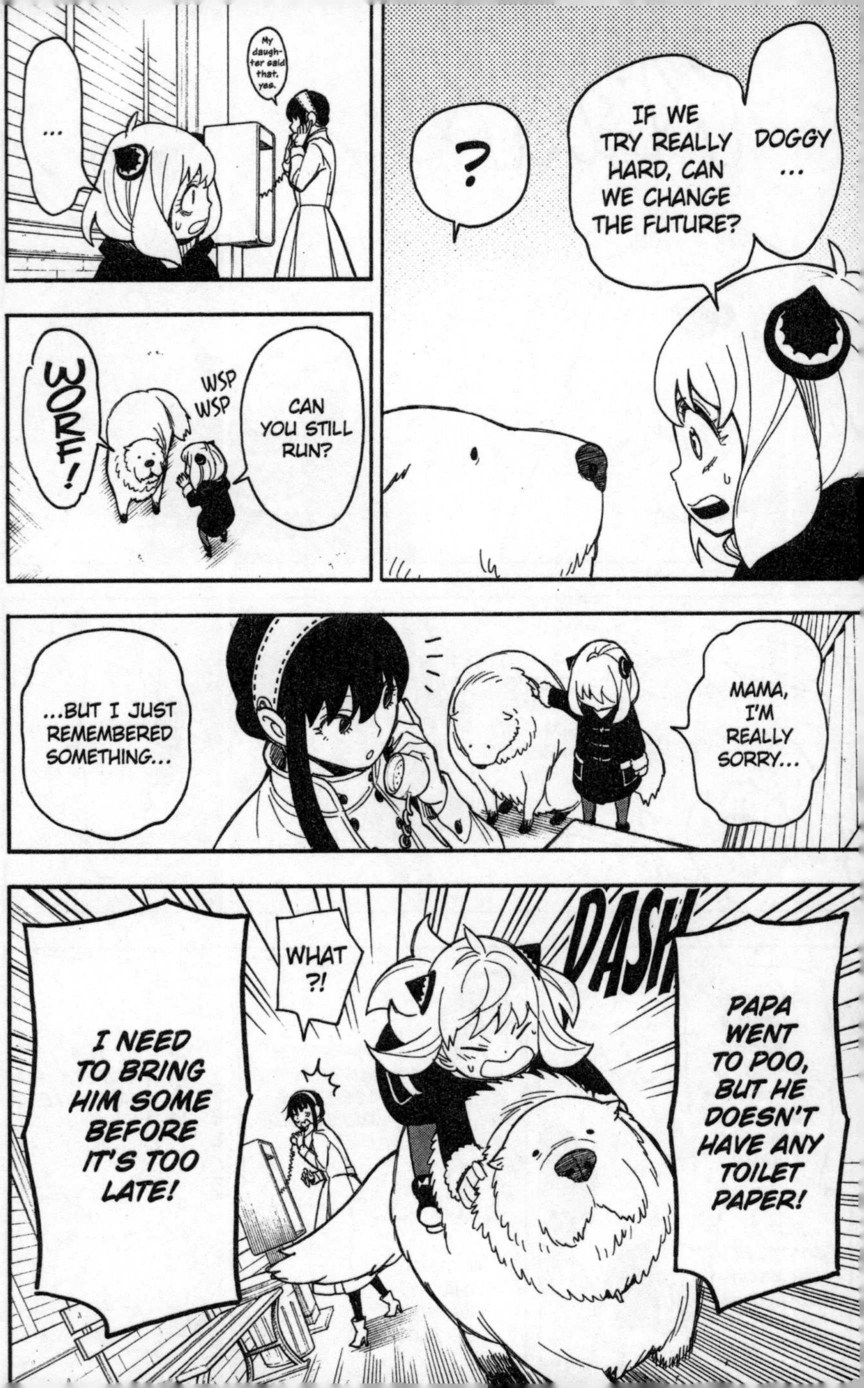
DOGGY ...
IF WE TRY REALLY HARD, CAN WE CHANGE THE FUTURE?
?
My daughter said that, yes.
...
CAN YOU STILL RUN?
WSP WSP
WORF!
MAMA, I'M REALLY SORRY...
...BUT I JUST REMEMBERED SOMETHING...
PAPA WENT TO POO, BUT HE DOESN'T HAVE ANY TOILET PAPER!
DASH
WHAT ?!
I NEED TO BRING HIM SOME BEFORE IT'S TOO LATE!

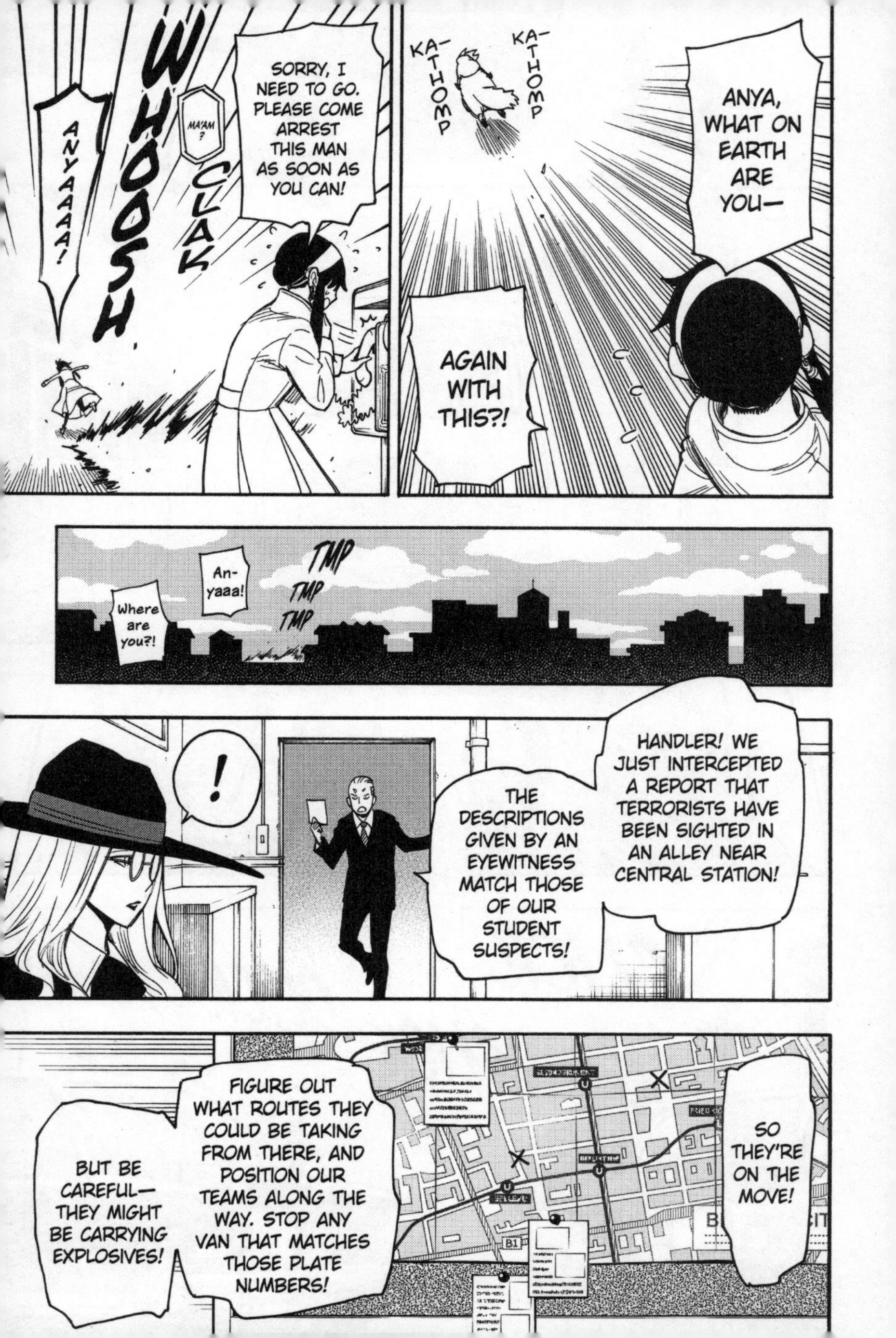
ANYA, WHAT ON EARTH ARE YOU—
KA-THOMP
KA-THOMP
AGAIN WITH THIS?!
SORRY, I NEED TO GO. PLEASE COME ARREST THIS MAN AS SOON AS YOU CAN!
MA'AM?
CLAK
WHOOOSH
ANYAAAA!
TMP TMP TMP
An-yaaa!
Where are you?!
HANDLER! WE JUST INTERCEPTED A REPORT THAT TERRORISTS HAVE BEEN SIGHTED IN AN ALLEY NEAR CENTRAL STATION!
THE DESCRIPTIONS GIVEN BY AN EYEWITNESS MATCH THOSE OF OUR STUDENT SUSPECTS!
!
SO THEY'RE ON THE MOVE!
FIGURE OUT WHAT ROUTES THEY COULD BE TAKING FROM THERE, AND POSITION OUR TEAMS ALONG THE WAY. STOP ANY VAN THAT MATCHES THOSE PLATE NUMBERS!
BUT BE CAREFUL—THEY MIGHT BE CARRYING EXPLOSIVES!

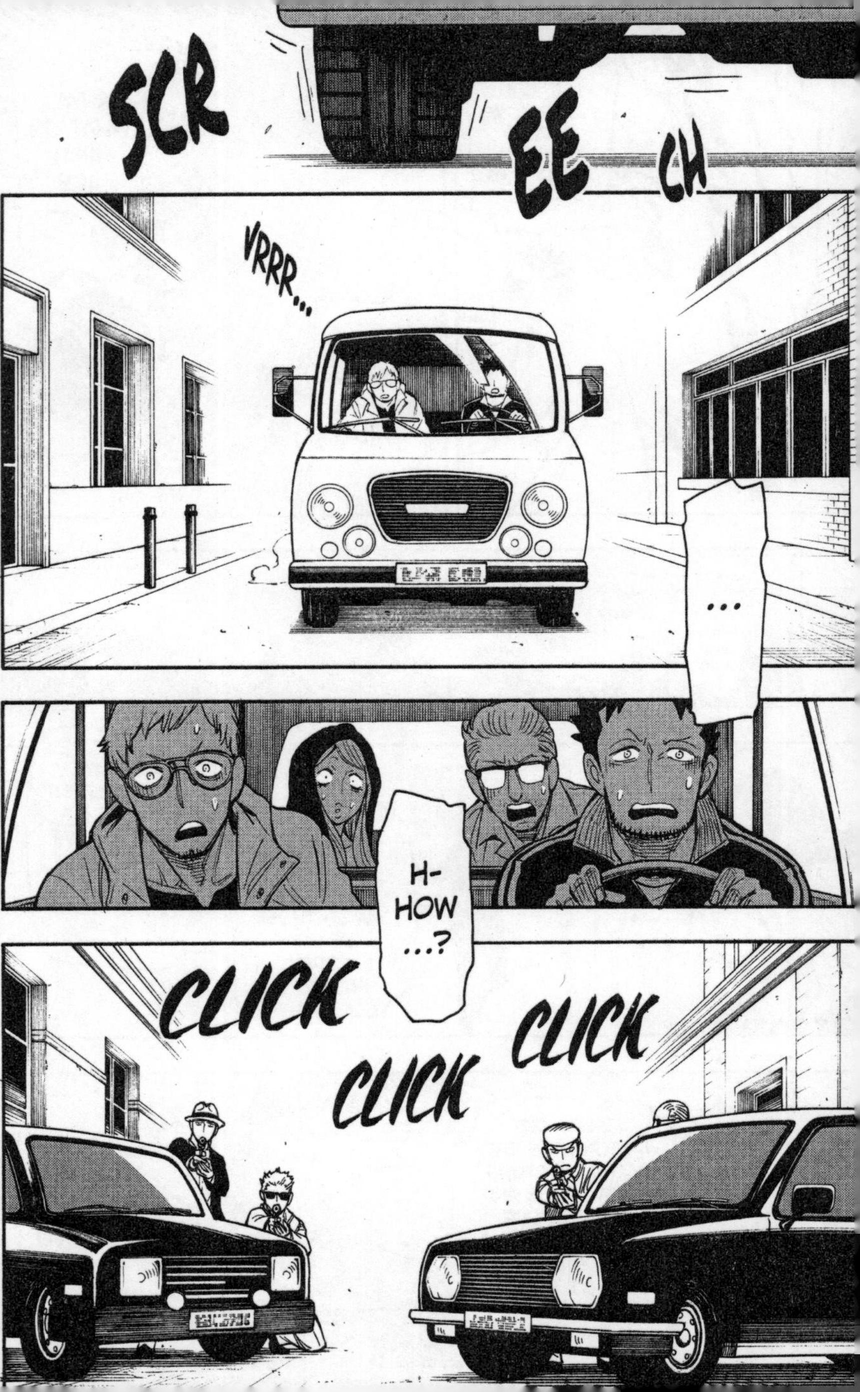
SCR
EE
CH
VRRR...
...
H-
HOW
...?
CLICK
CLICK
CLICK

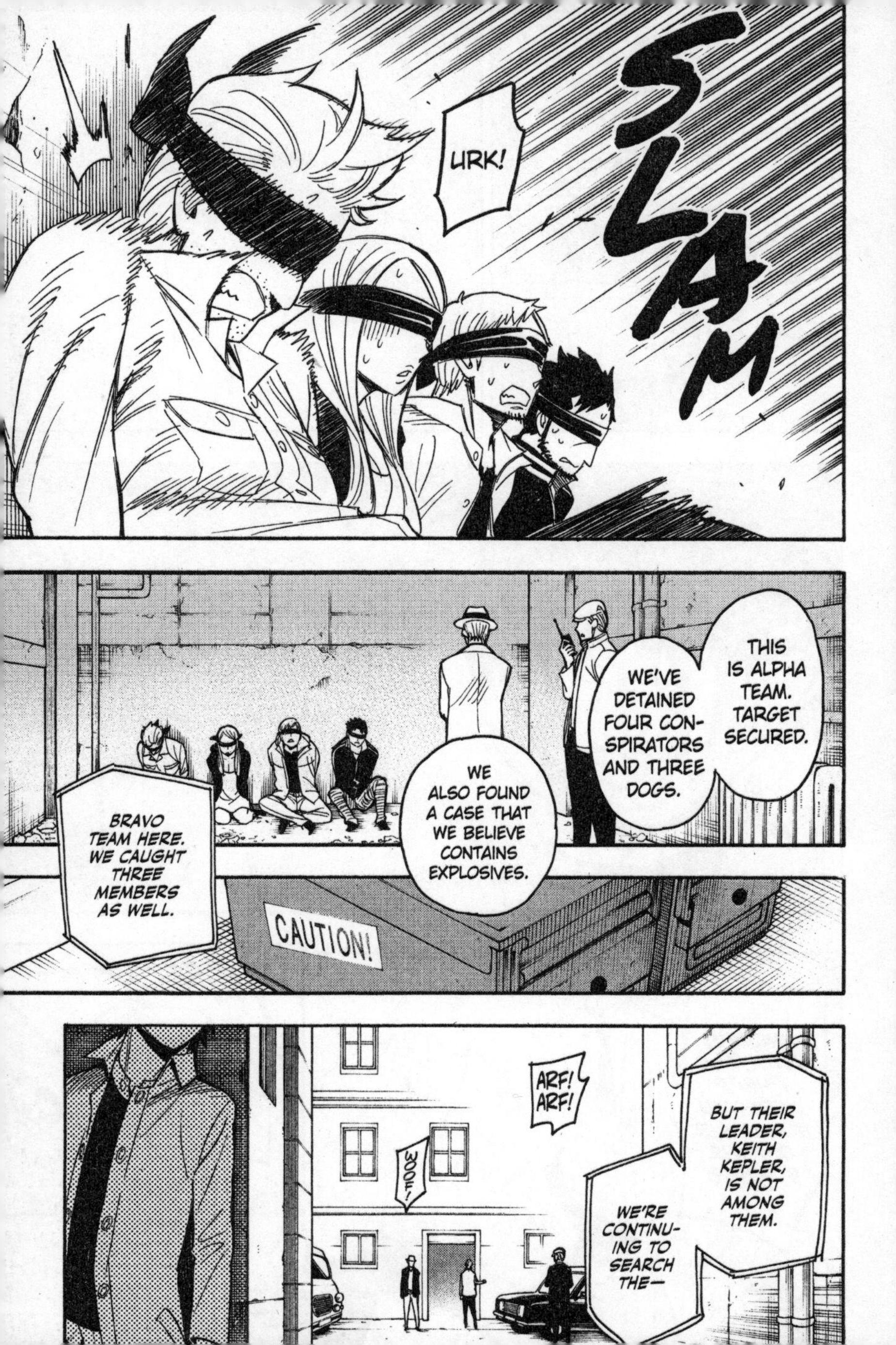
SLAM
URK!
THIS IS ALPHA TEAM. TARGET SECURED.
WE'VE DETAINED FOUR CON-SPIRATORS AND THREE DOGS.
WE ALSO FOUND A CASE THAT WE BELIEVE CONTAINS EXPLOSIVES.
BRAVO TEAM HERE. WE CAUGHT THREE MEMBERS AS WELL.
CAUTION!
BUT THEIR LEADER, KEITH KEPLER, IS NOT AMONG THEM.
WE'RE CONTINU-ING TO SEARCH THE—
ARF! ARF!
WOOF!

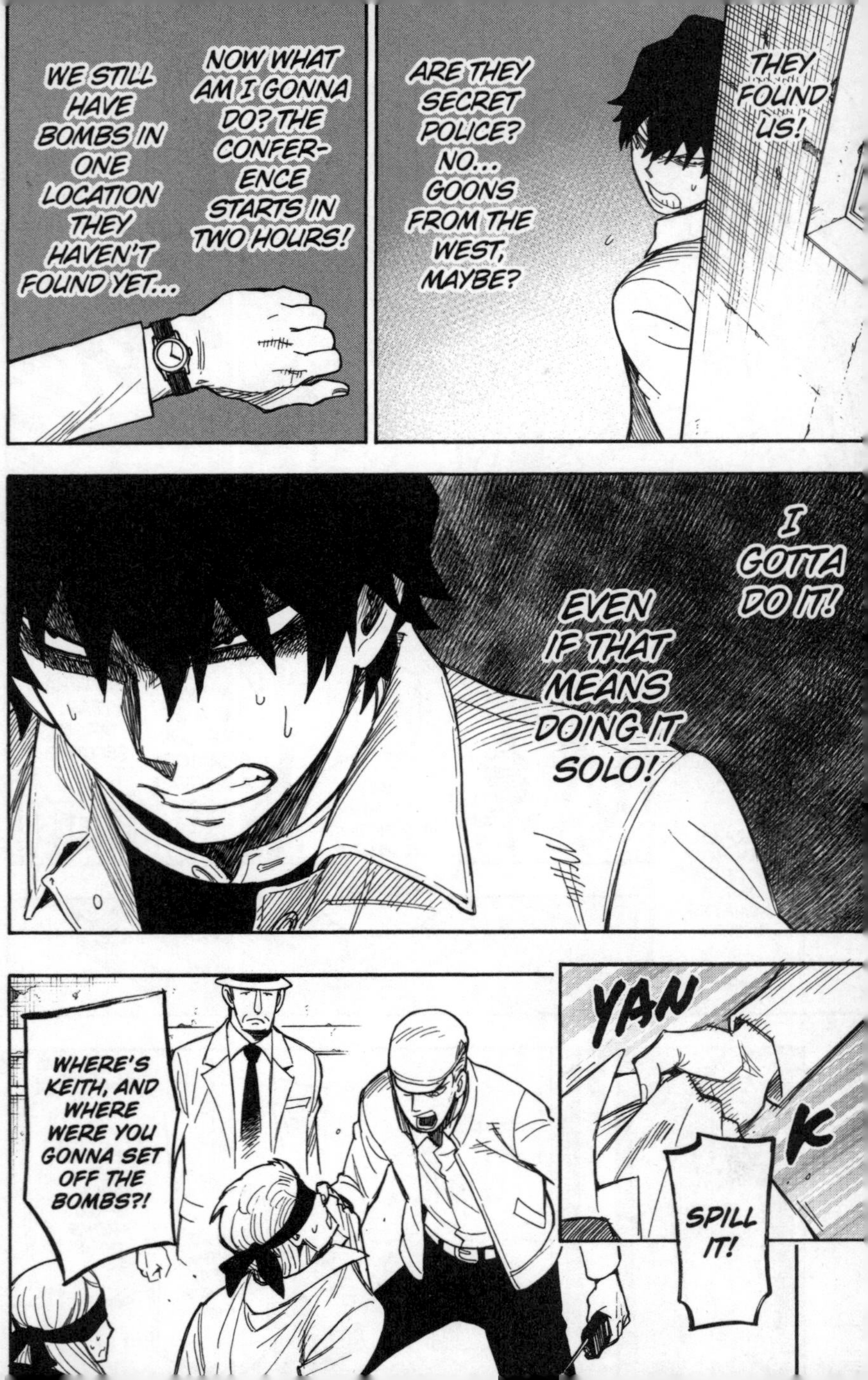
THEY FOUND US!
ARE THEY SECRET POLICE? NO... GOONS FROM THE WEST, MAYBE?
NOW WHAT AM I GONNA DO? THE CONFERENCE STARTS IN TWO HOURS!
WE STILL HAVE BOMBS IN ONE LOCATION THEY HAVEN'T FOUND YET...
I GOTTA DO IT!
EVEN IF THAT MEANS DOING IT SOLO!
YANK
SPILL IT!
WHERE'S KEITH, AND WHERE WERE YOU GONNA SET OFF THE BOMBS?!

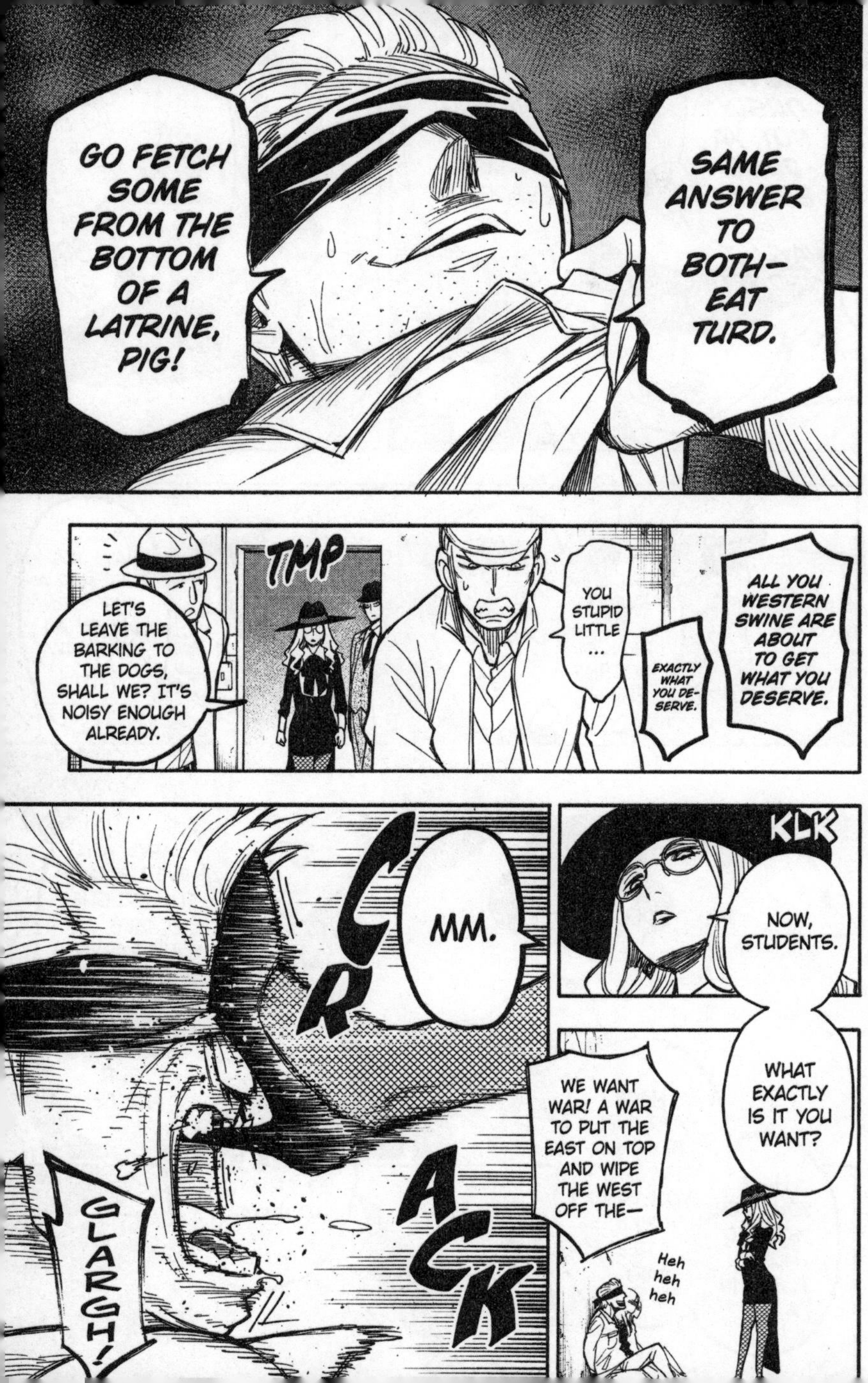
SAME ANSWER TO BOTH—EAT TURD.
GO FETCH SOME FROM THE BOTTOM OF A LATRINE, PIG!
ALL YOU WESTERN SWINE ARE ABOUT TO GET WHAT YOU DESERVE.
EXACTLY WHAT YOU DE-SERVE.
YOU STUPID LITTLE ...
TMP
LET'S LEAVE THE BARKING TO THE DOGS, SHALL WE? IT'S NOISY ENOUGH ALREADY.
KLK
NOW, STUDENTS.
WHAT EXACTLY IS IT YOU WANT?
WE WANT WAR! A WAR TO PUT THE EAST ON TOP AND WIPE THE WEST OFF THE—
Heh heh heh
CRACK
MM.
GLARGH!

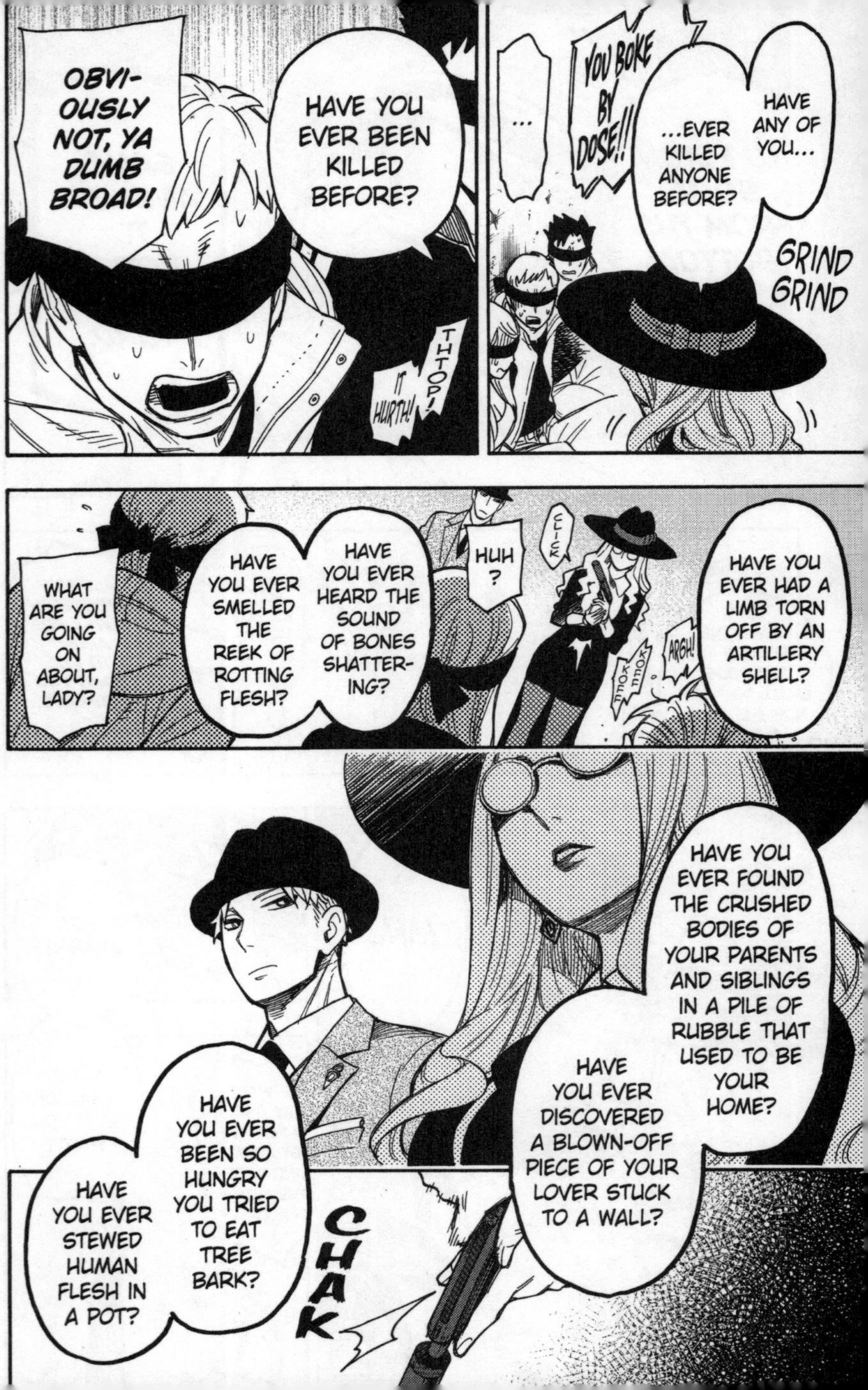
HAVE ANY OF YOU...
...EVER KILLED ANYONE BEFORE?
YOU BOKE BY DOSE!!
...
GRIND GRIND
HAVE YOU EVER BEEN KILLED BEFORE?
OBVI-OUSLY NOT, YA DUMB BROAD!
THTOP!
IT HURTH!
HAVE YOU EVER HAD A LIMB TORN OFF BY AN ARTILLERY SHELL?
ARGH!
KOFF KOFF
CLICK
HUH?
HAVE YOU EVER HEARD THE SOUND OF BONES SHATTER-ING?
HAVE YOU EVER SMELLED THE REEK OF ROTTING FLESH?
WHAT ARE YOU GOING ON ABOUT, LADY?
HAVE YOU EVER FOUND THE CRUSHED BODIES OF YOUR PARENTS AND SIBLINGS IN A PILE OF RUBBLE THAT USED TO BE YOUR HOME?
HAVE YOU EVER DISCOVERED A BLOWN-OFF PIECE OF YOUR LOVER STUCK TO A WALL?
CHAK
HAVE YOU EVER BEEN SO HUNGRY YOU TRIED TO EAT TREE BARK?
HAVE YOU EVER STEWED HUMAN FLESH IN A POT?

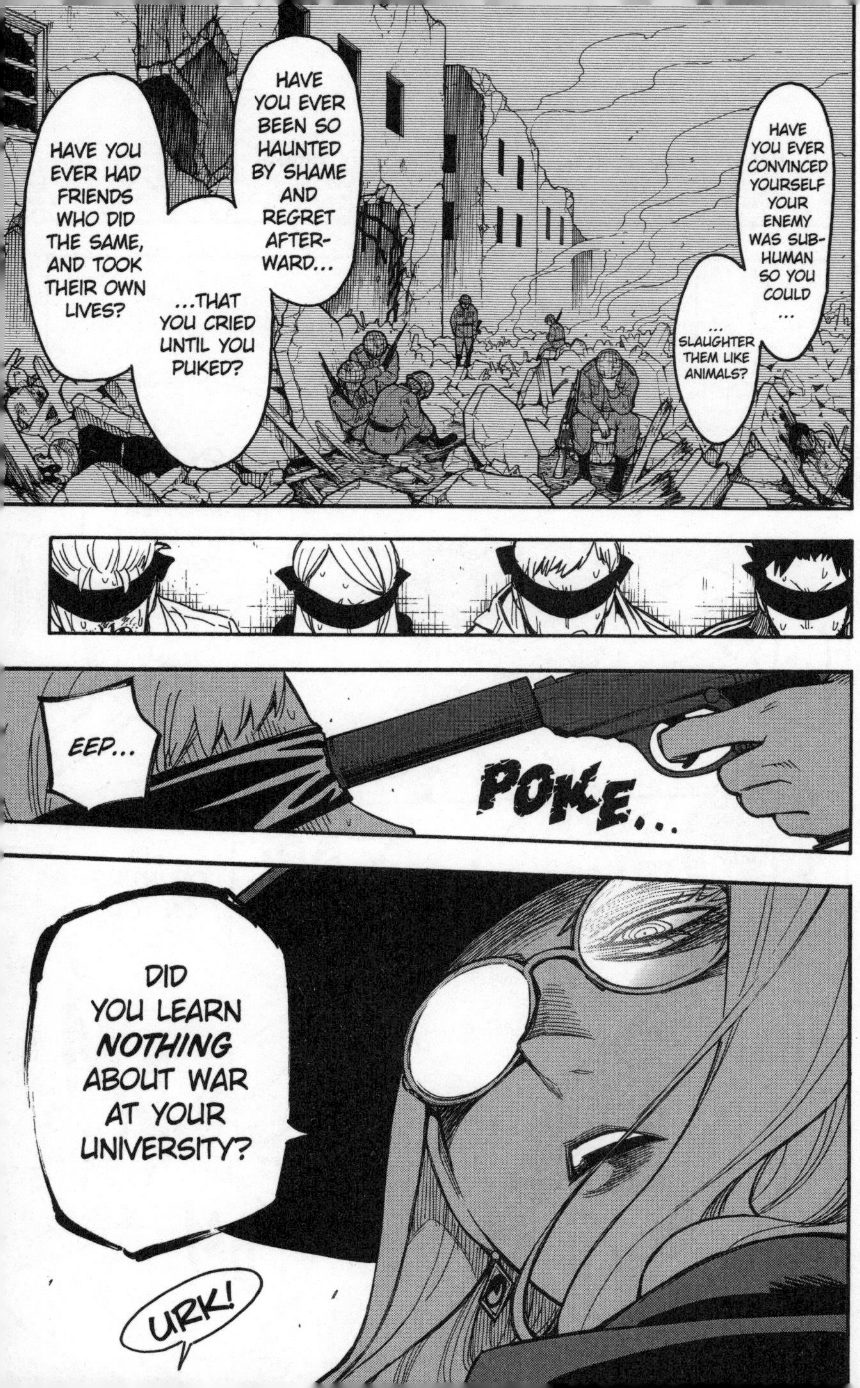
HAVE YOU EVER CONVINCED YOURSELF YOUR ENEMY WAS SUB-HUMAN SO YOU COULD ...
... SLAUGHTER THEM LIKE ANIMALS?
HAVE YOU EVER BEEN SO HAUNTED BY SHAME AND REGRET AFTER-WARD...
...THAT YOU CRIED UNTIL YOU PUKED?
HAVE YOU EVER HAD FRIENDS WHO DID THE SAME, AND TOOK THEIR OWN LIVES?
POKE...
EEP...
DID YOU LEARN ***NOTHING*** ABOUT WAR AT YOUR UNIVERSITY?
URK!

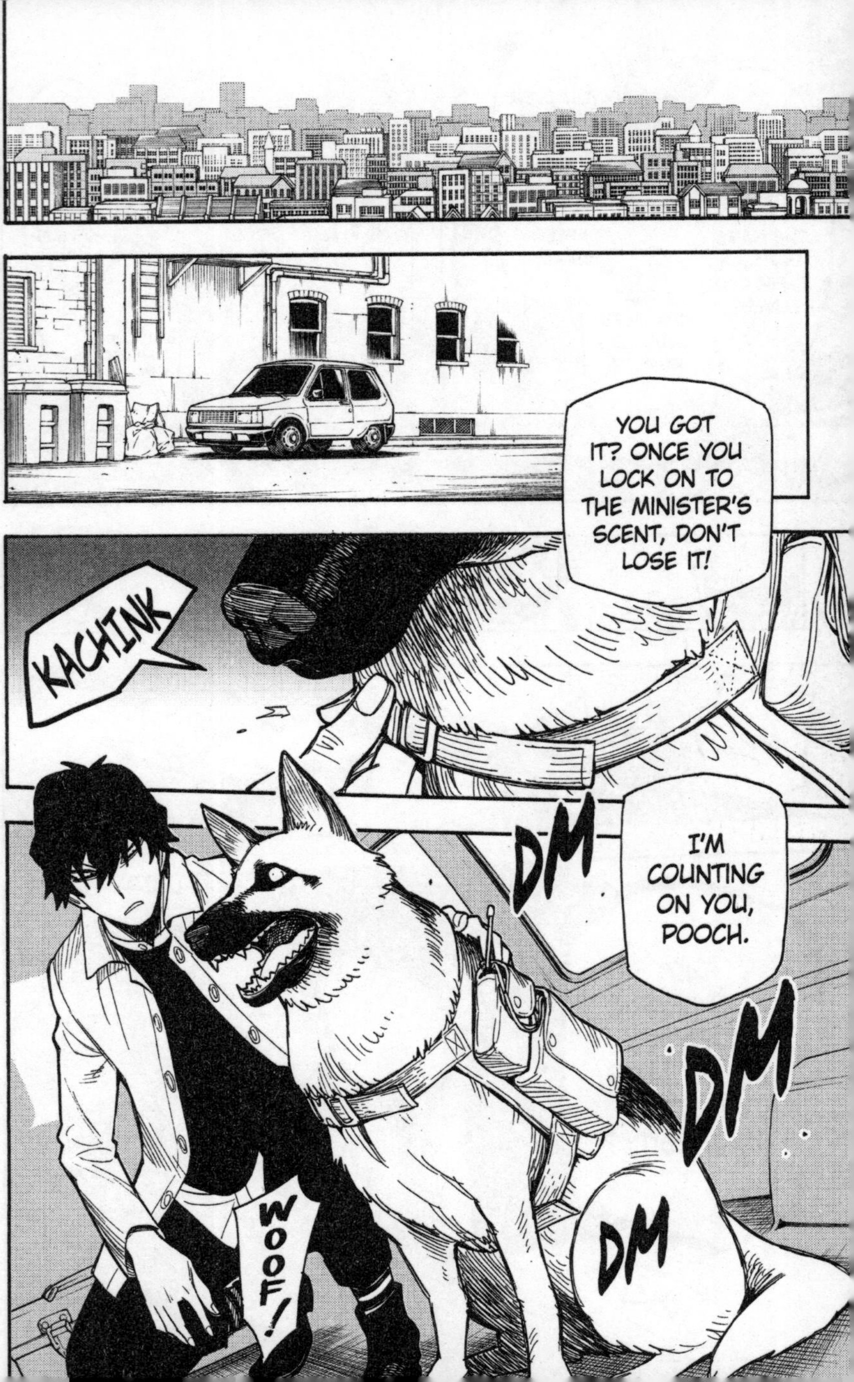
YOU GOT IT? ONCE YOU LOCK ON TO THE MINISTER'S SCENT, DON'T LOSE IT!
KACHINK
I'M COUNTING ON YOU, POOCH.
DM
DM
DM
WOOF!
DM

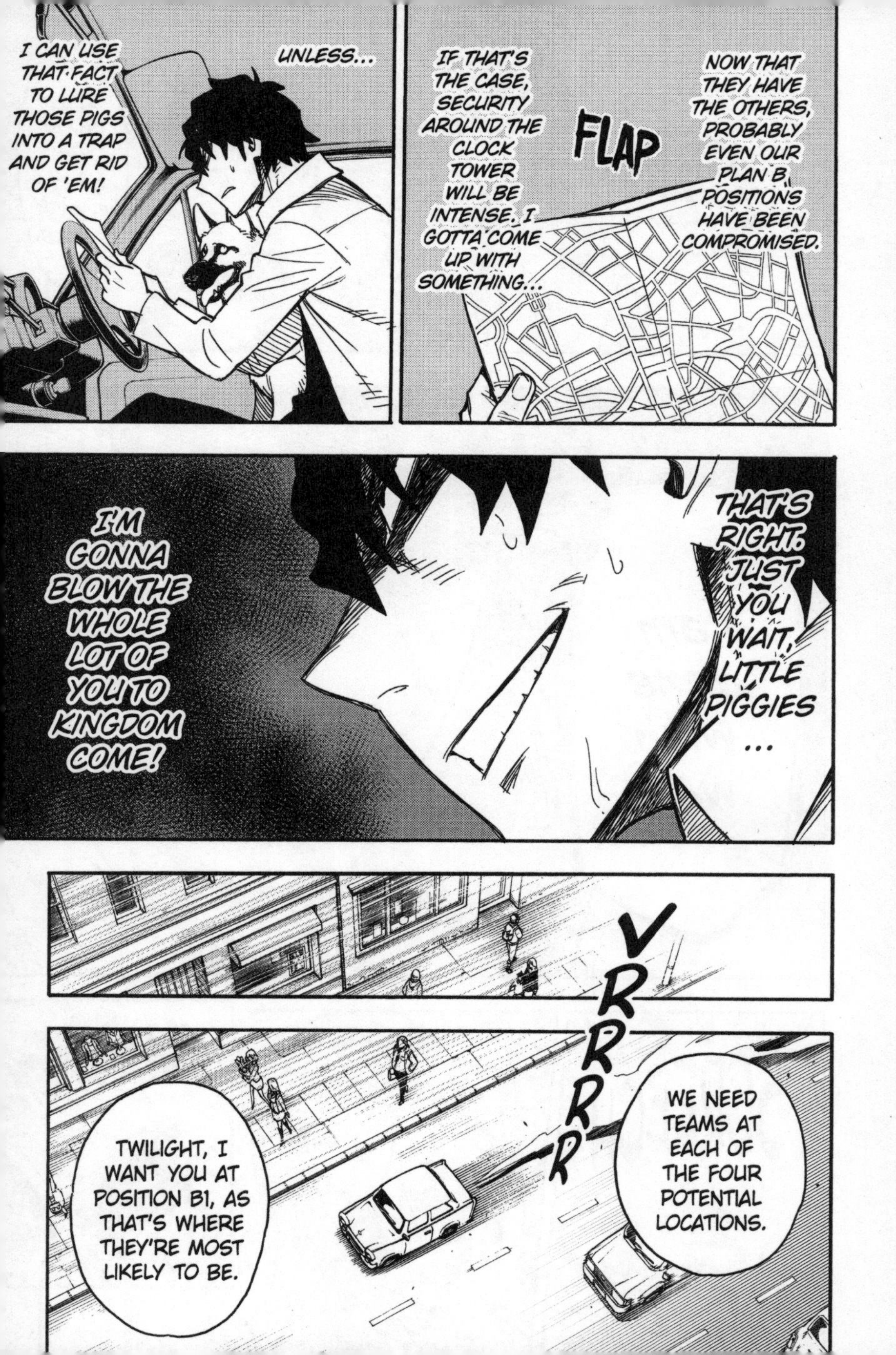
NOW THAT THEY HAVE THE OTHERS, PROBABLY EVEN OUR PLAN B POSITIONS HAVE BEEN COMPROMISED.
FLAP
IF THAT'S THE CASE, SECURITY AROUND THE CLOCK TOWER WILL BE INTENSE. I GOTTA COME UP WITH SOMETHING...
UNLESS...
I CAN USE THAT FACT TO LURE THOSE PIGS INTO A TRAP AND GET RID OF 'EM!
THAT'S RIGHT. JUST YOU WAIT, LITTLE PIGGIES ...
I'M GONNA BLOW THE WHOLE LOT OF YOU TO KINGDOM COME!
VRRRRR
WE NEED TEAMS AT EACH OF THE FOUR POTENTIAL LOCATIONS.
TWILIGHT, I WANT YOU AT POSITION B1, AS THAT'S WHERE THEY'RE MOST LIKELY TO BE.

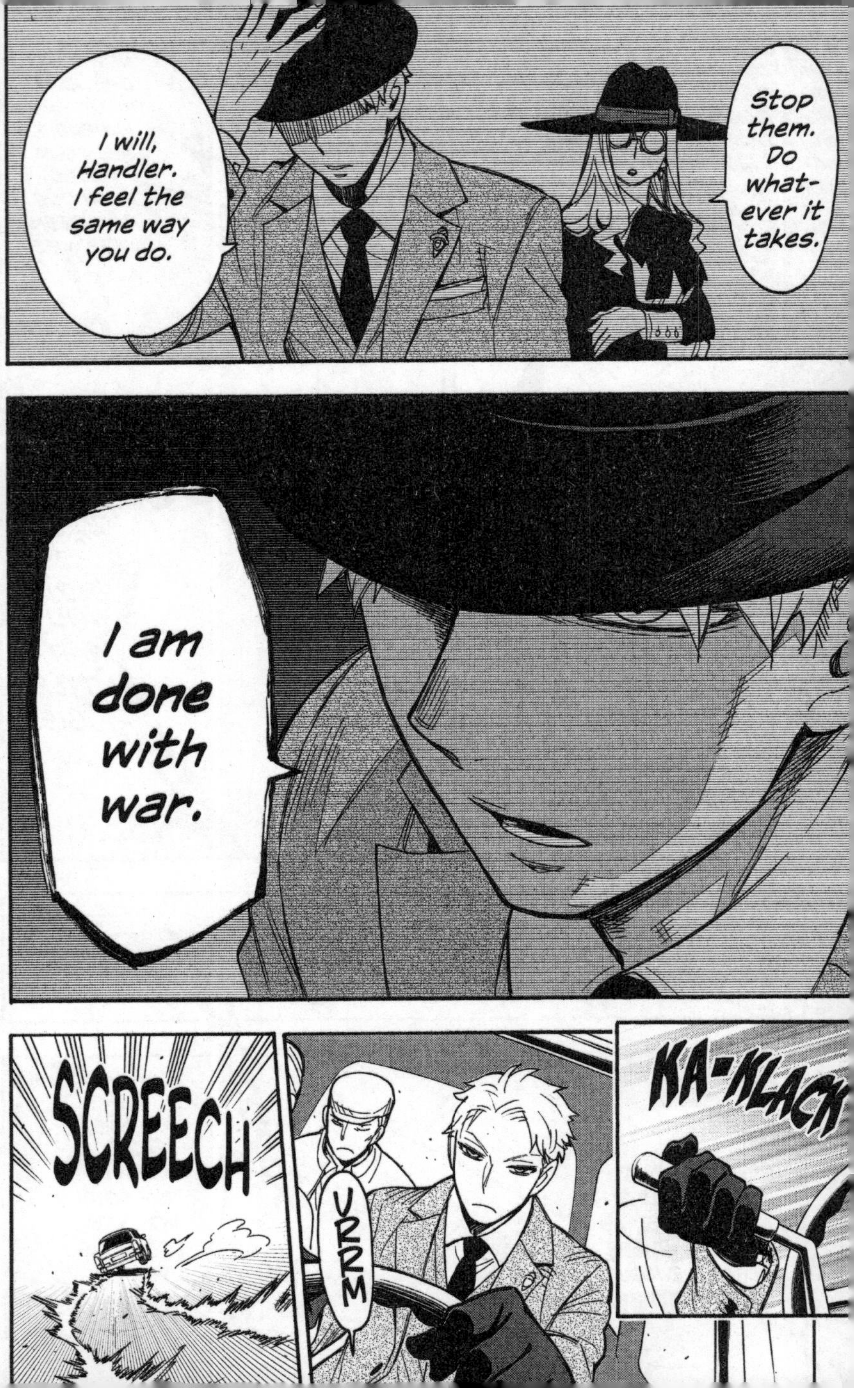
Stop them. Do whatever it takes.
I will, Handler. I feel the same way you do.
I am done with war.
KA-KLACK
VRRM
SCREECH

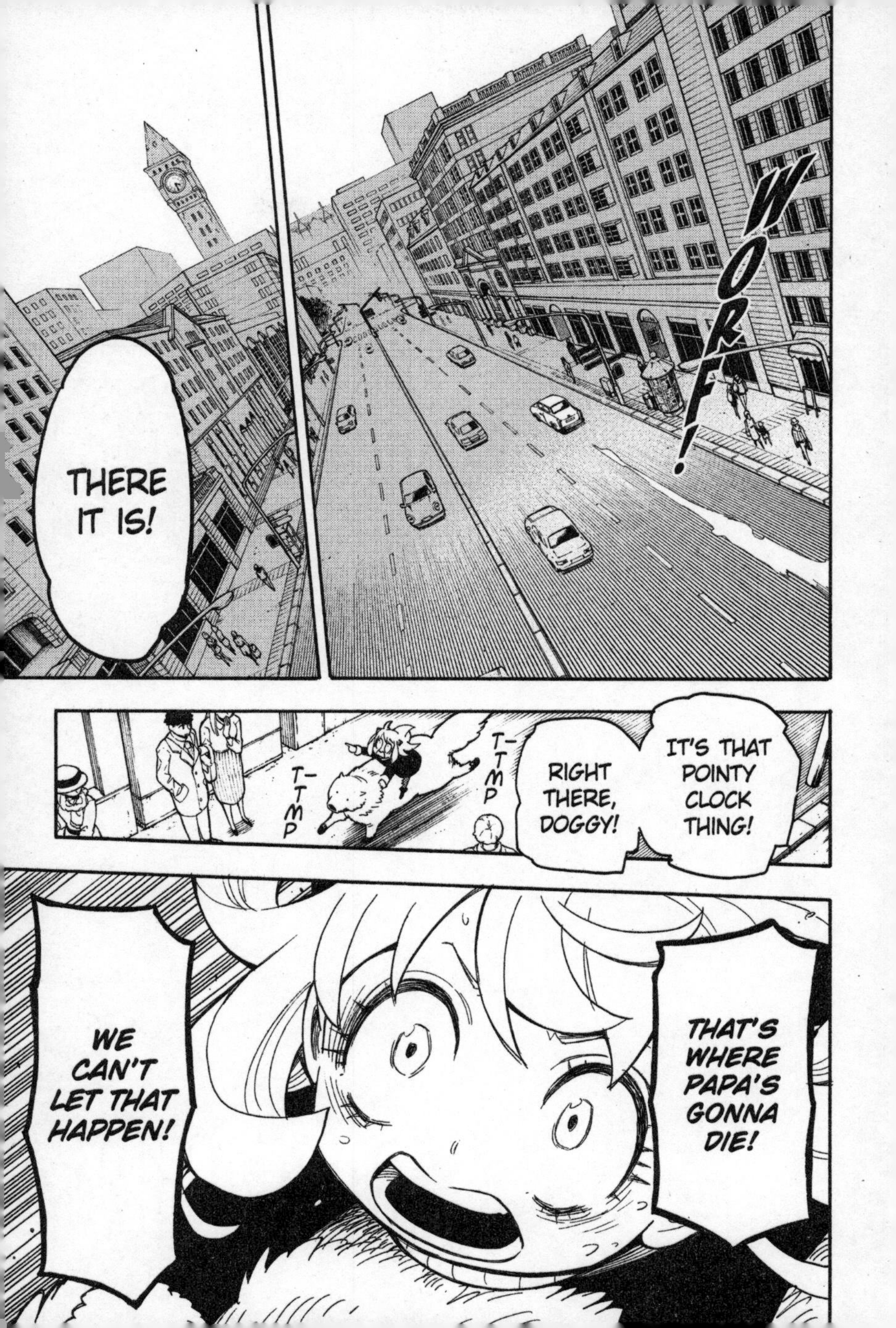
WORF!
THERE IT IS!
IT'S THAT POINTY CLOCK THING!
RIGHT THERE, DOGGY!
T-T-TMP
T-T-TMP
THAT'S WHERE PAPA'S GONNA DIE!
WE CAN'T LET THAT HAPPEN!

SPY×FAMILY

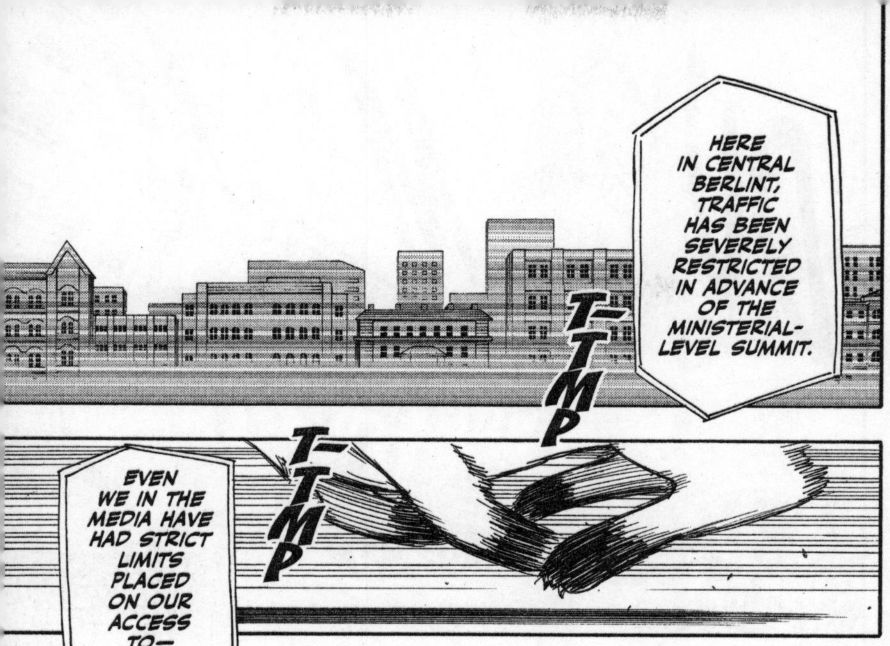
HERE IN CENTRAL BERLINT, TRAFFIC HAS BEEN SEVERELY RESTRICTED IN ADVANCE OF THE MINISTERIAL-LEVEL SUMMIT.
T-TMP
T-TMP
EVEN WE IN THE MEDIA HAVE HAD STRICT LIMITS PLACED ON OUR ACCESS TO—

SPY×FAMILY

MISSION 21

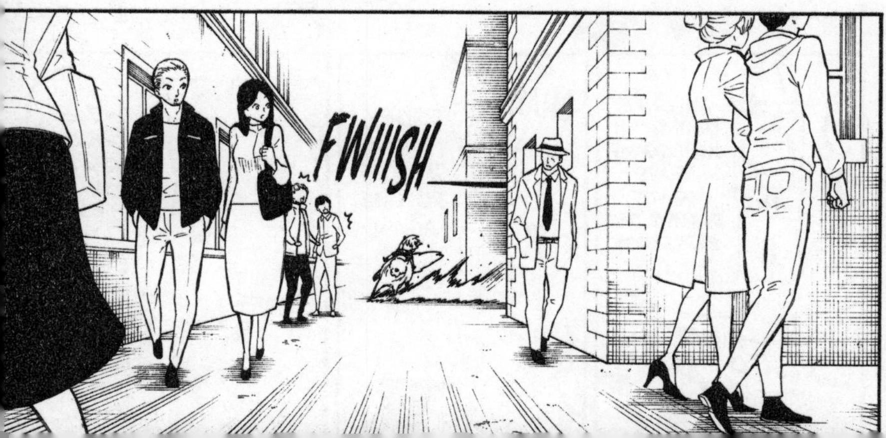
FWIIISH

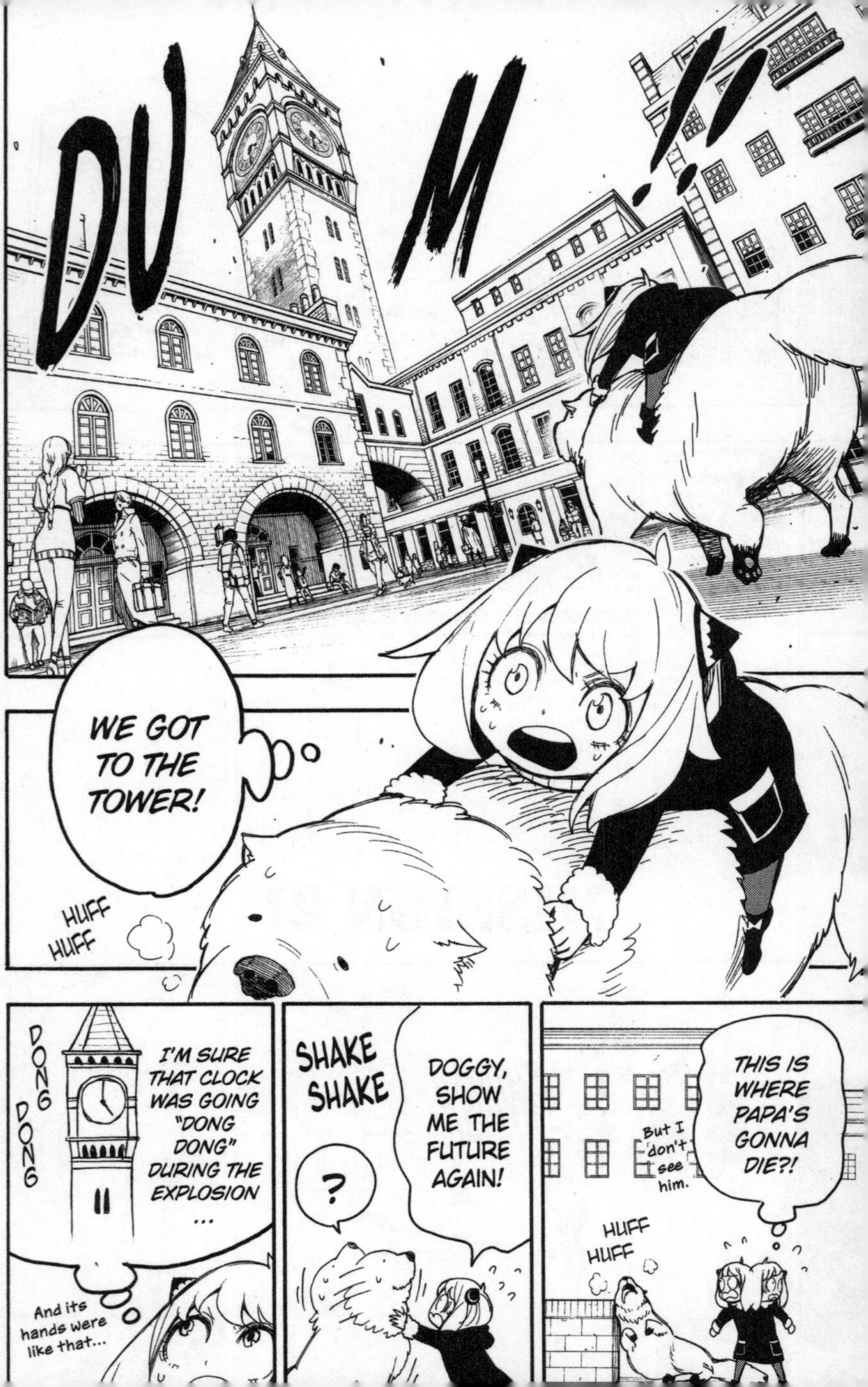
DU M!!
WE GOT TO THE TOWER!
HUFF HUFF
THIS IS WHERE PAPA'S GONNA DIE?!
But I don't see him.
HUFF HUFF
DOGGY, SHOW ME THE FUTURE AGAIN!
SHAKE SHAKE
?
I'M SURE THAT CLOCK WAS GOING "DONG DONG" DURING THE EXPLOSION...
DONG DONG
And its hands were like that...

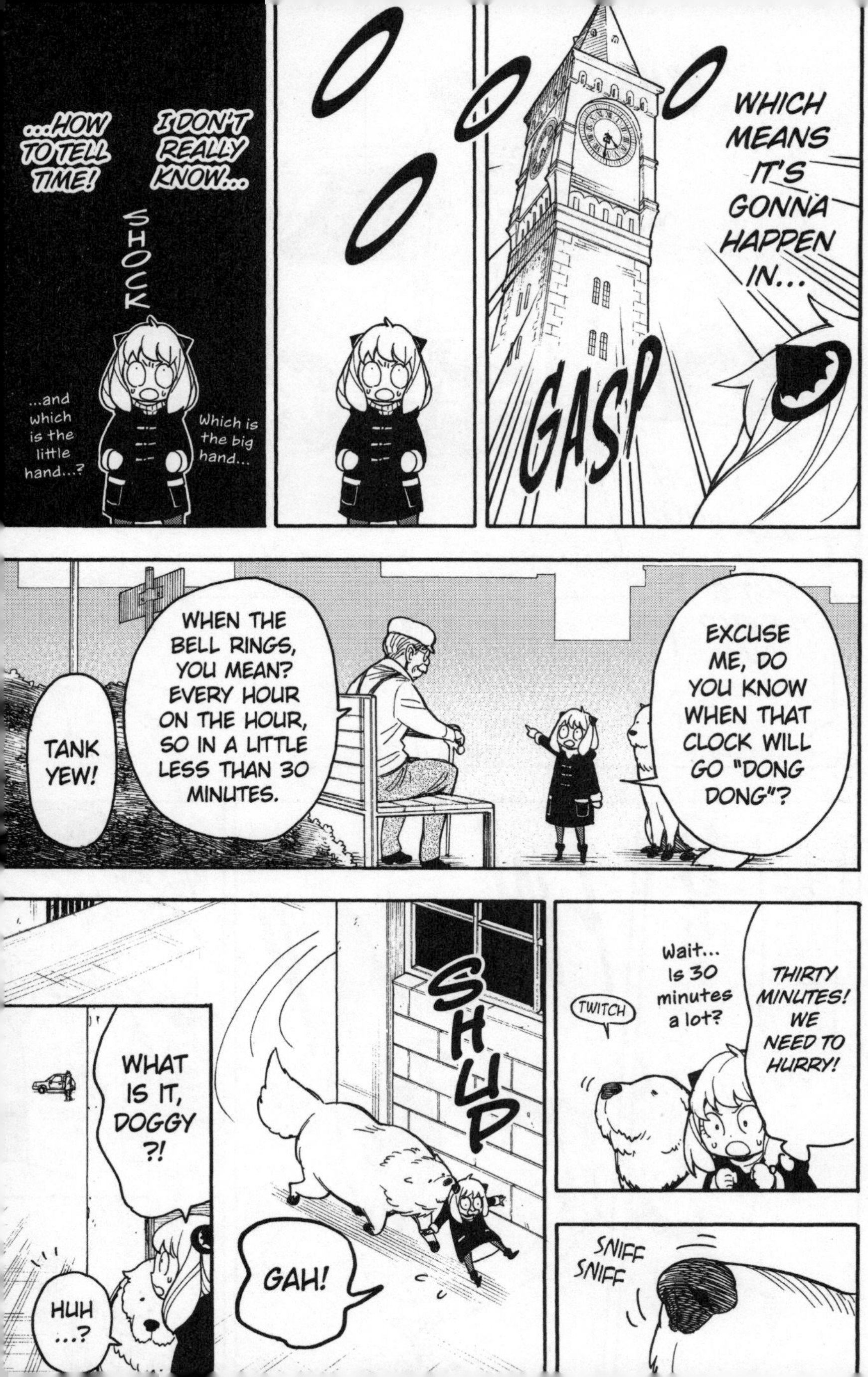
WHICH MEANS IT'S GONNA HAPPEN IN...
GASP
I DON'T REALLY KNOW...
...HOW TO TELL TIME!
SHOCK
Which is the big hand...
...and which is the little hand...?
EXCUSE ME, DO YOU KNOW WHEN THAT CLOCK WILL GO "DONG DONG"?
WHEN THE BELL RINGS, YOU MEAN? EVERY HOUR ON THE HOUR, SO IN A LITTLE LESS THAN 30 MINUTES.
TANK YEW!
THIRTY MINUTES! WE NEED TO HURRY!
Wait... Is 30 minutes a lot?
TWITCH
SNIFF SNIFF
SHUP
GAH!
WHAT IS IT, DOGGY?!
HUH...?

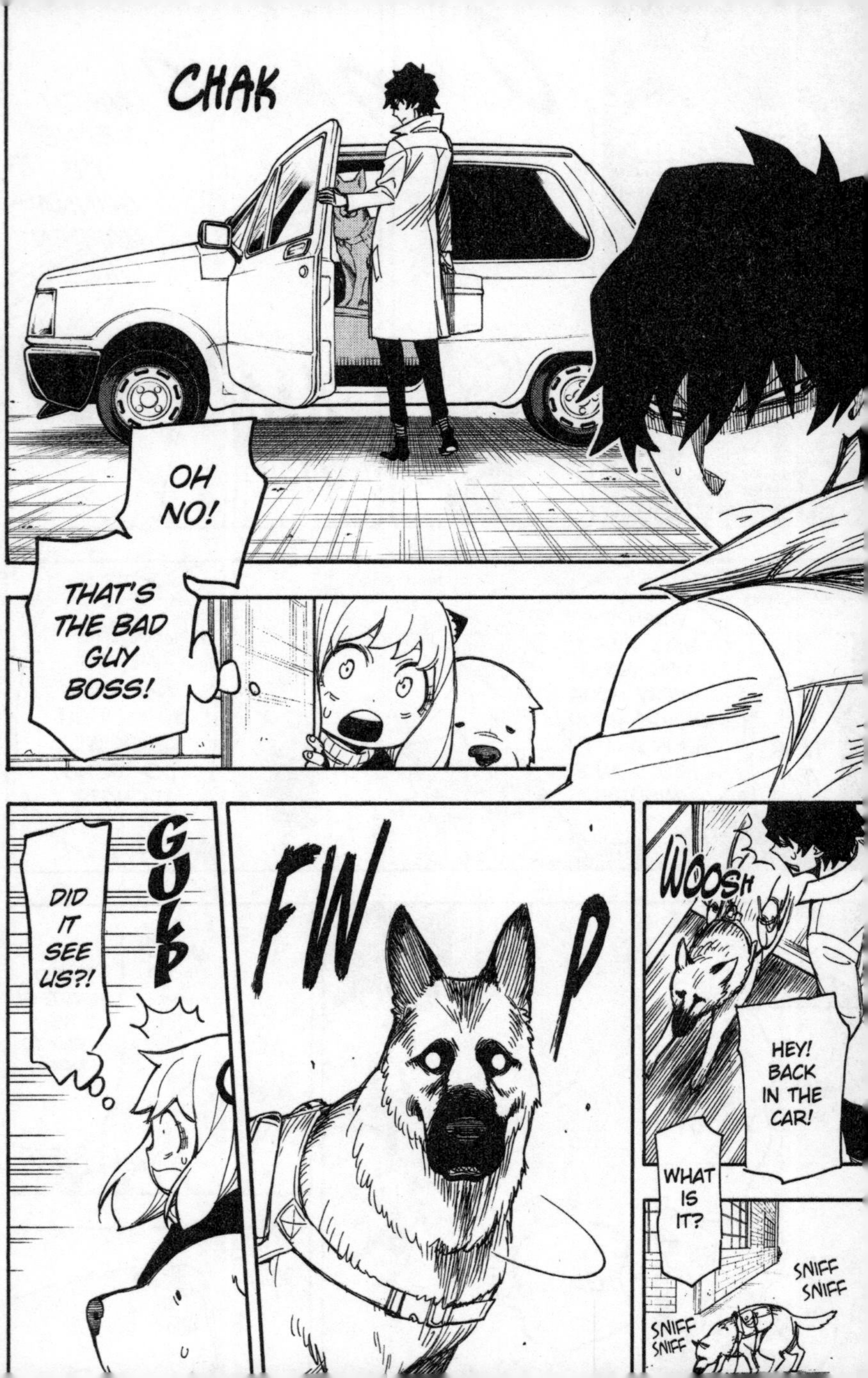
CHAK
OH NO!
THAT'S THE BAD GUY BOSS!
WOOSH
HEY! BACK IN THE CAR!
WHAT IS IT?
SNIFF SNIFF
SNIFF SNIFF
FW P
GULP
DID IT SEE US?!

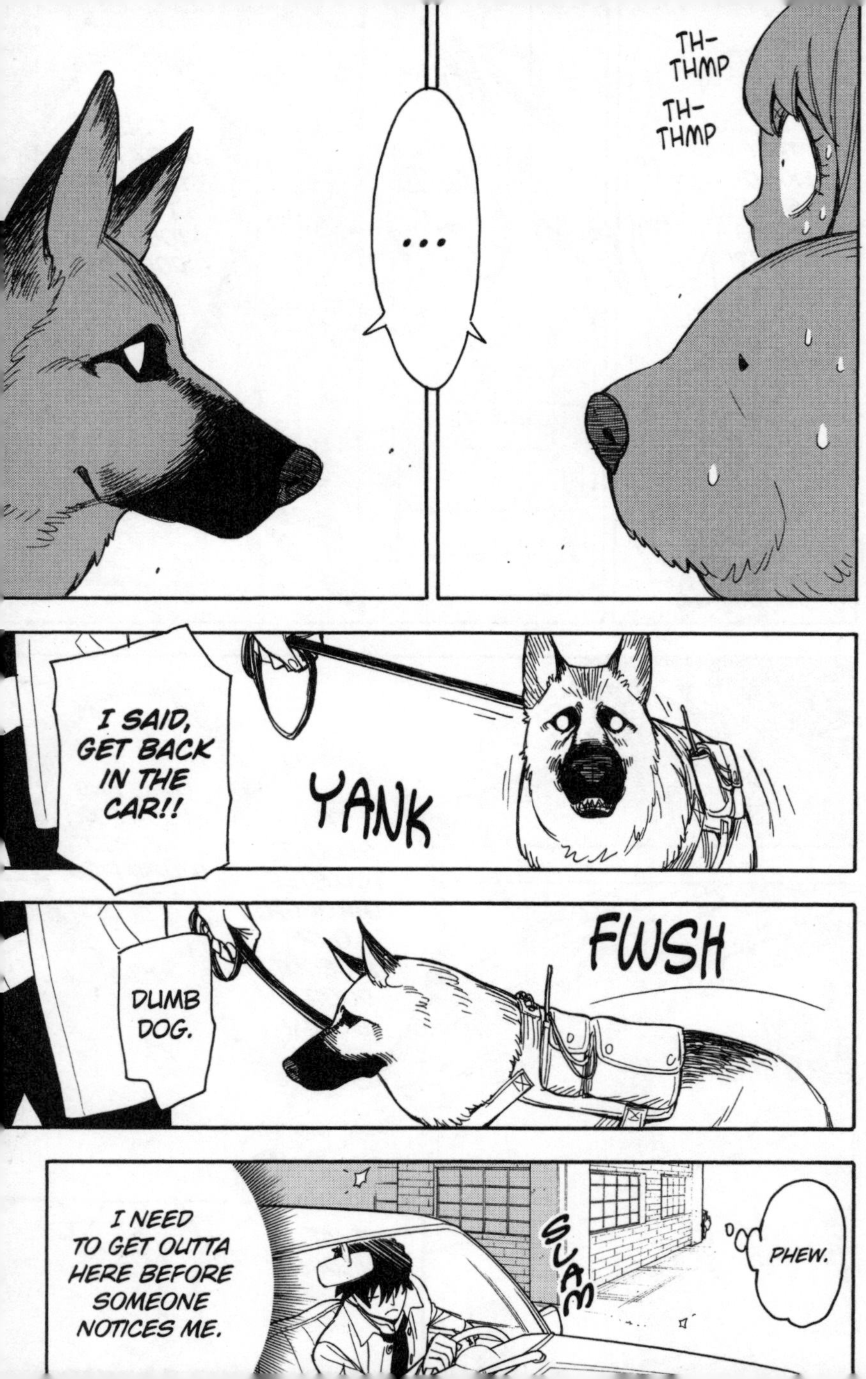
TH-THMP
TH-THMP
...
I SAID, GET BACK IN THE CAR!!
YANK
FWSH
DUMB DOG.
PHEW.
SLAM
I NEED TO GET OUTTA HERE BEFORE SOMEONE NOTICES ME.

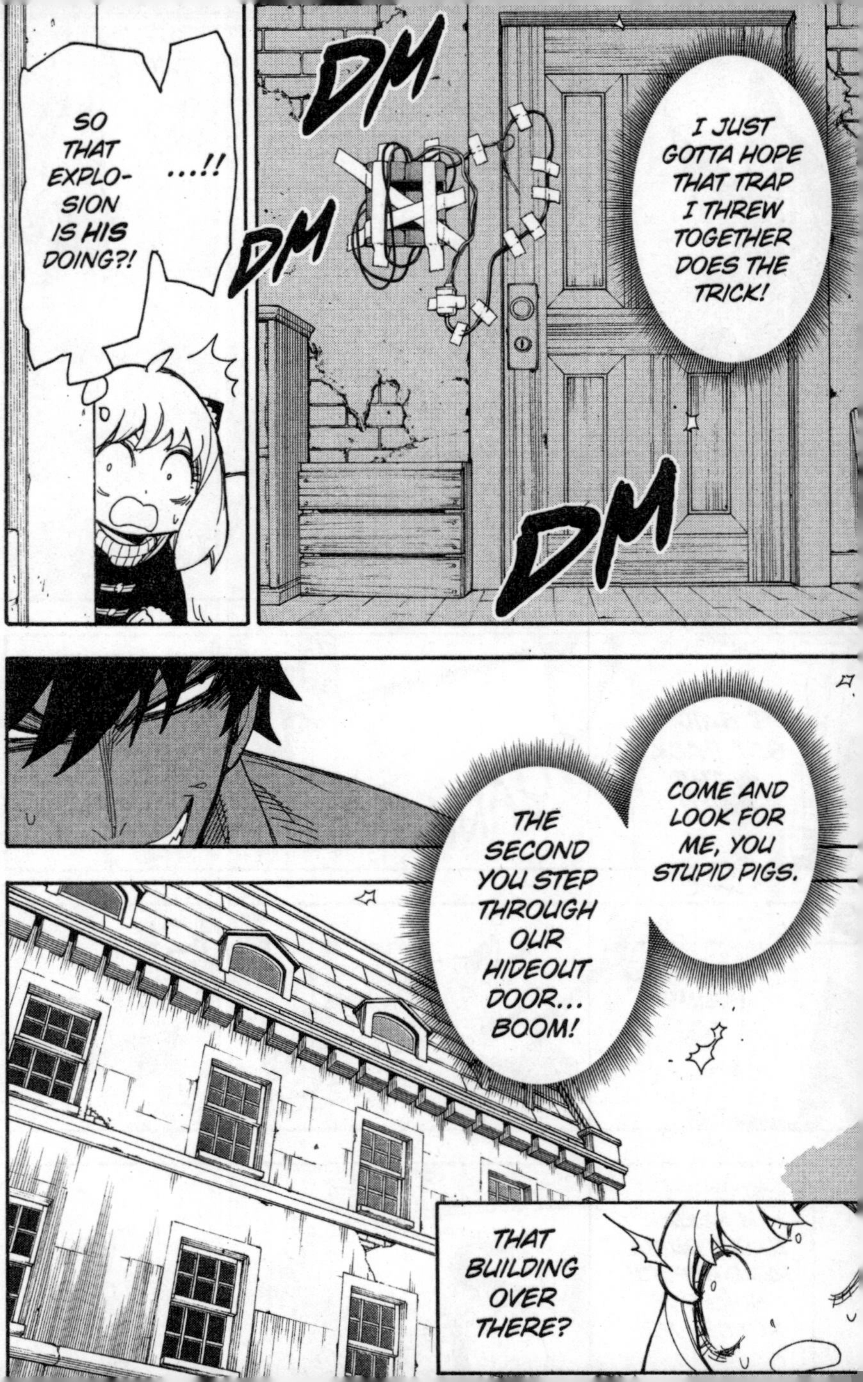
DM
DM
I JUST GOTTA HOPE THAT TRAP I THREW TOGETHER DOES THE TRICK!
DM
...!!
SO THAT EXPLOSION IS HIS DOING?!
COME AND LOOK FOR ME, YOU STUPID PIGS.
THE SECOND YOU STEP THROUGH OUR HIDEOUT DOOR... BOOM!
THAT BUILDING OVER THERE?

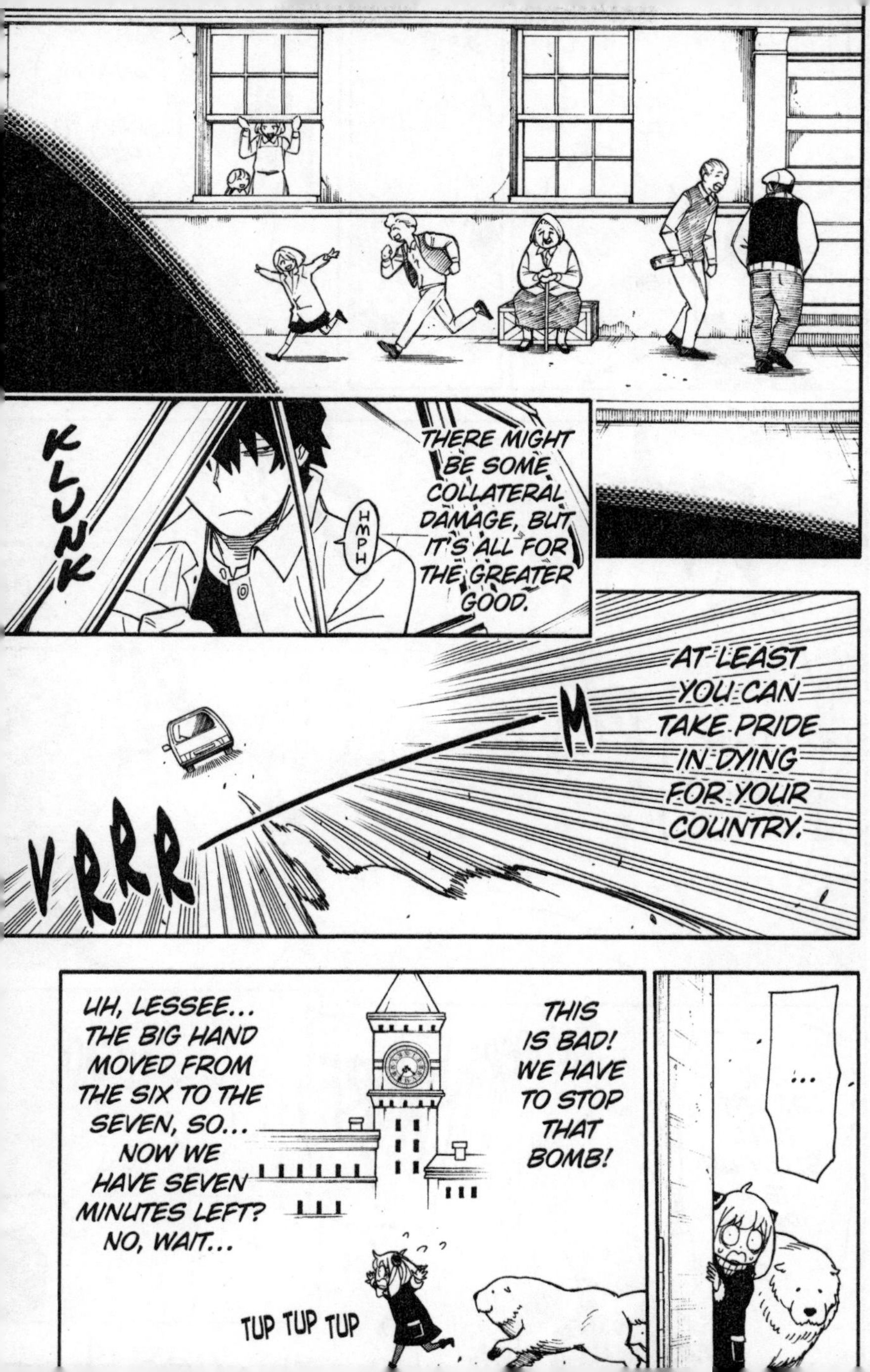
KLUNK
HMPH
THERE MIGHT BE SOME COLLATERAL DAMAGE, BUT IT'S ALL FOR THE GREATER GOOD.
AT LEAST YOU CAN TAKE PRIDE IN DYING FOR YOUR COUNTRY.
M
VRRR
...
THIS IS BAD! WE HAVE TO STOP THAT BOMB!
UH, LESSEE... THE BIG HAND MOVED FROM THE SIX TO THE SEVEN, SO... NOW WE HAVE SEVEN MINUTES LEFT? NO, WAIT...
TUP TUP TUP

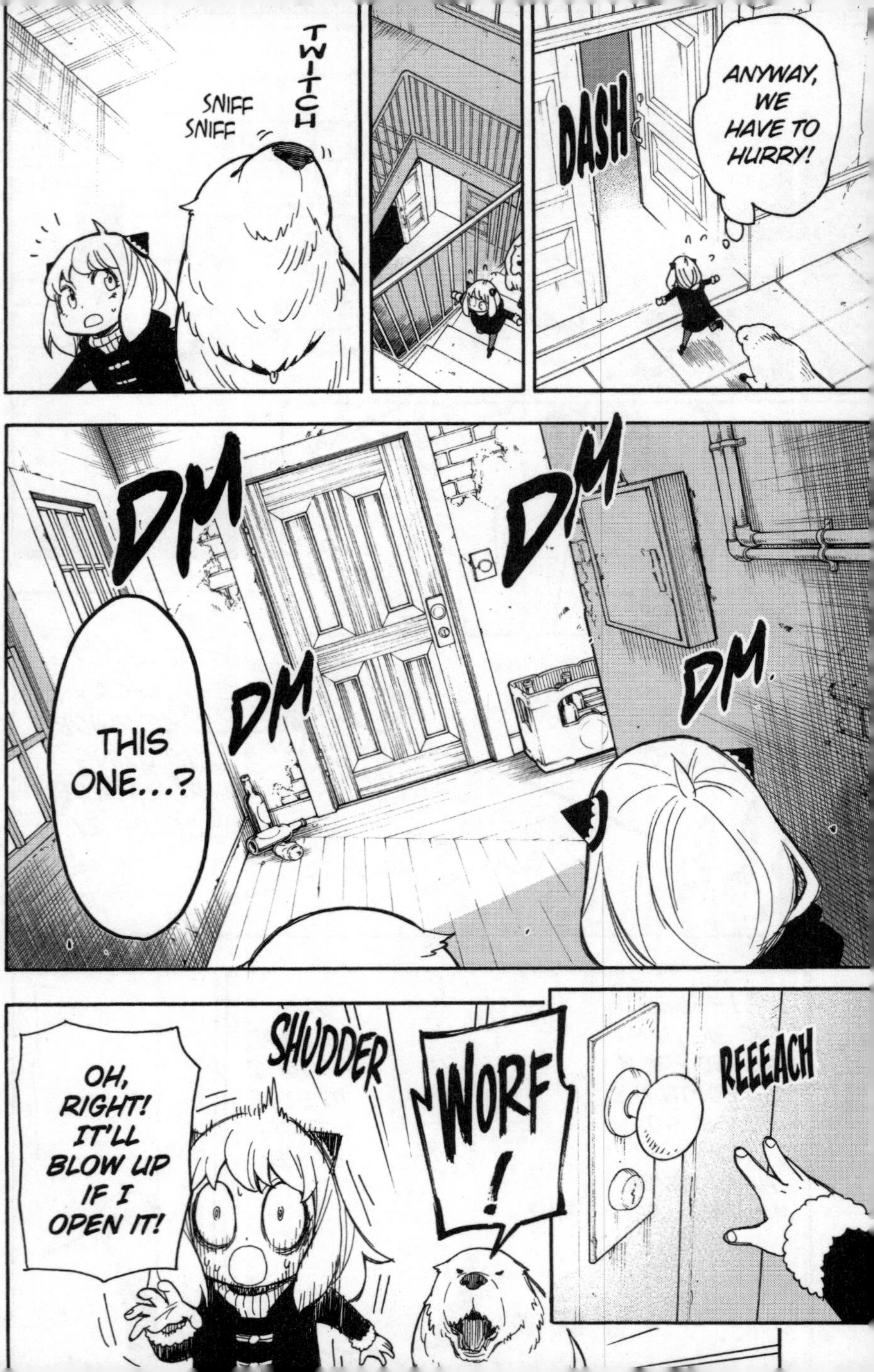
ANYWAY, WE HAVE TO HURRY!
DASH
TWITCH
SNIFF SNIFF
DM
DM
DM
DM.
THIS ONE...?
REEEACH
WORF !
SHUDDER
OH, RIGHT! IT'LL BLOW UP IF I OPEN IT!

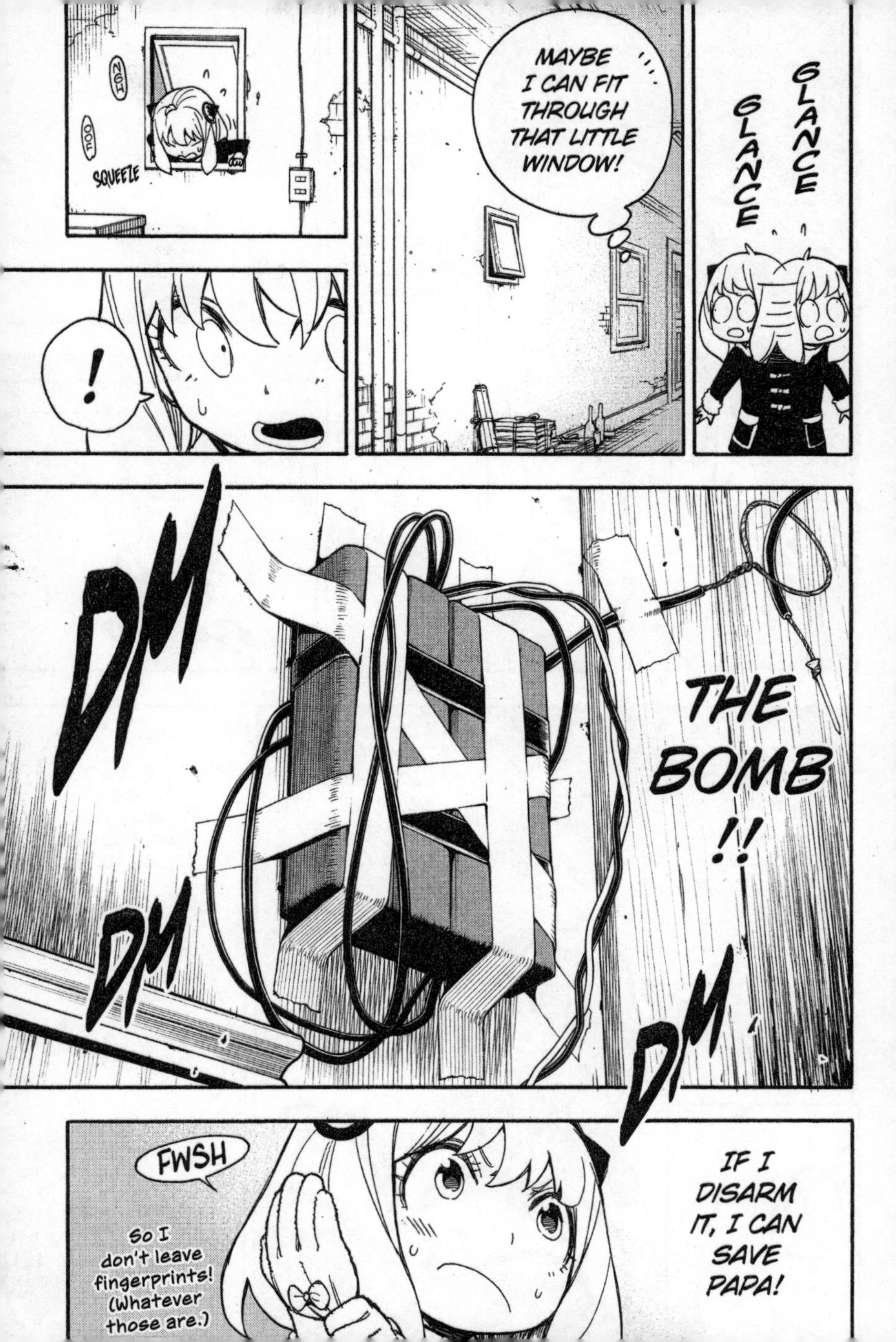
GLANCE
GLANCE
MAYBE I CAN FIT THROUGH THAT LITTLE WINDOW!
NGH
OOF
SQUEEZE
!
THE BOMB!!
DM
DM
DM
IF I DISARM IT, I CAN SAVE PAPA!
FWSH
So I don't leave fingerprints! (Whatever those are.)

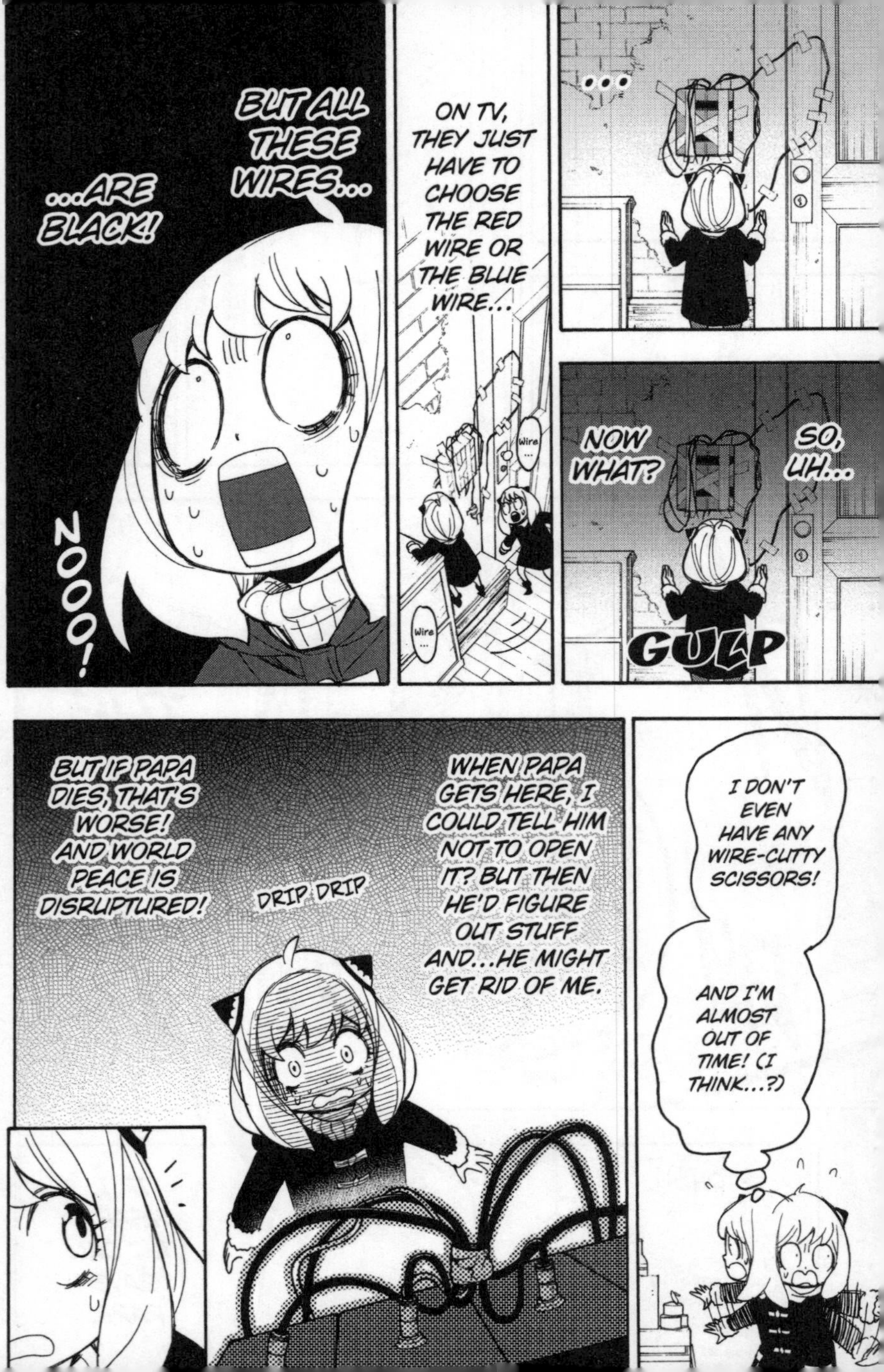
...
SO, UH...
NOW WHAT?
GULP
ON TV, THEY JUST HAVE TO CHOOSE THE RED WIRE OR THE BLUE WIRE...
Wire...
Wire...
BUT ALL THESE WIRES...
...ARE BLACK!
NOOOO!
I DON'T EVEN HAVE ANY WIRE-CUTTY SCISSORS!
AND I'M ALMOST OUT OF TIME! (I THINK...?)
WHEN PAPA GETS HERE, I COULD TELL HIM NOT TO OPEN IT? BUT THEN HE'D FIGURE OUT STUFF AND...HE MIGHT GET RID OF ME.
DRIP DRIP
BUT IF PAPA DIES, THAT'S WORSE! AND WORLD PEACE IS DISRUPTURED!

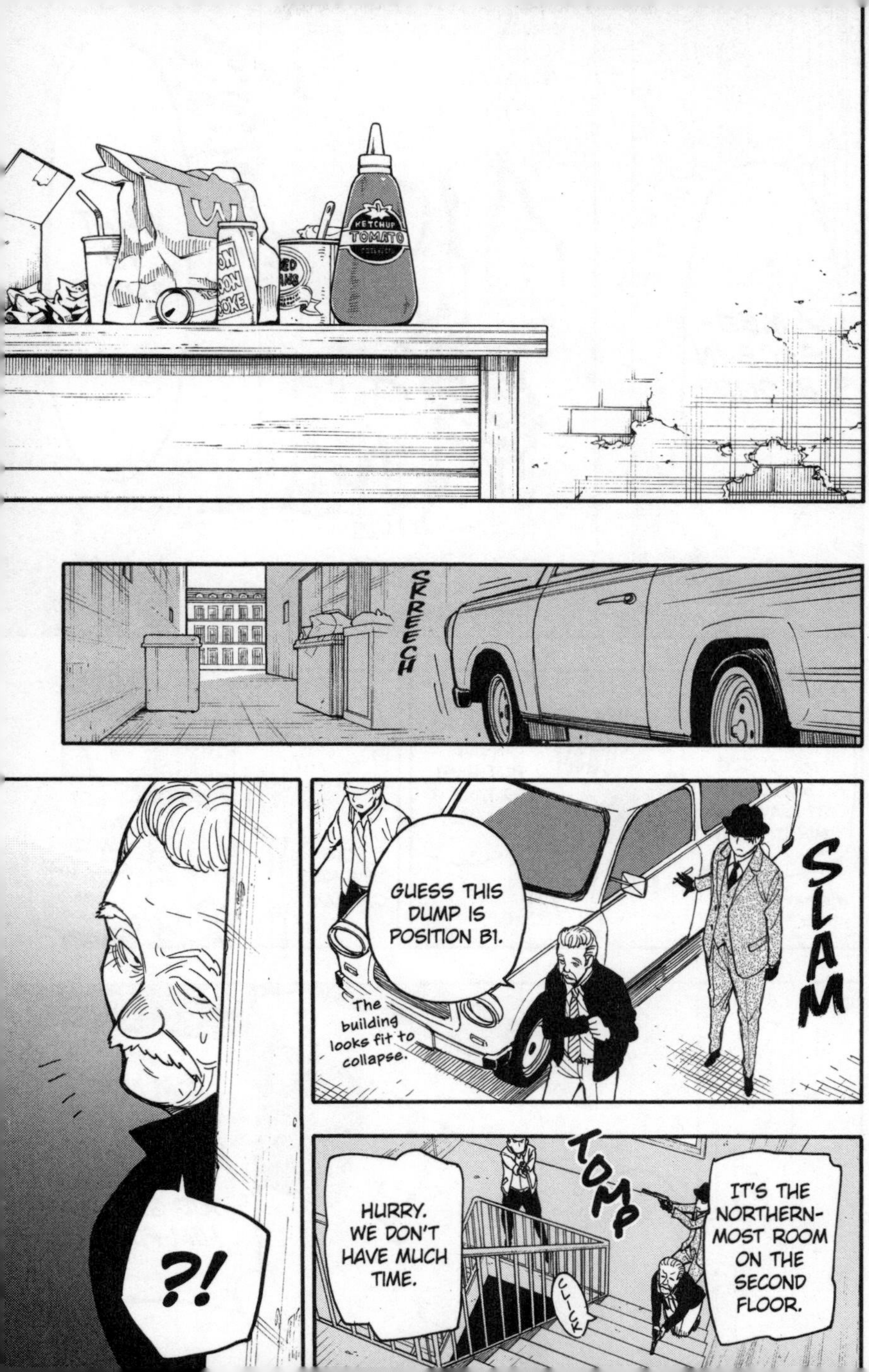
KETCHUP
TOMATO
SKREECH
SLAM
GUESS THIS DUMP IS POSITION B1.
The building looks fit to collapse.
TOMP
IT'S THE NORTHERN-MOST ROOM ON THE SECOND FLOOR.
HURRY. WE DON'T HAVE MUCH TIME.
CLICK
?!

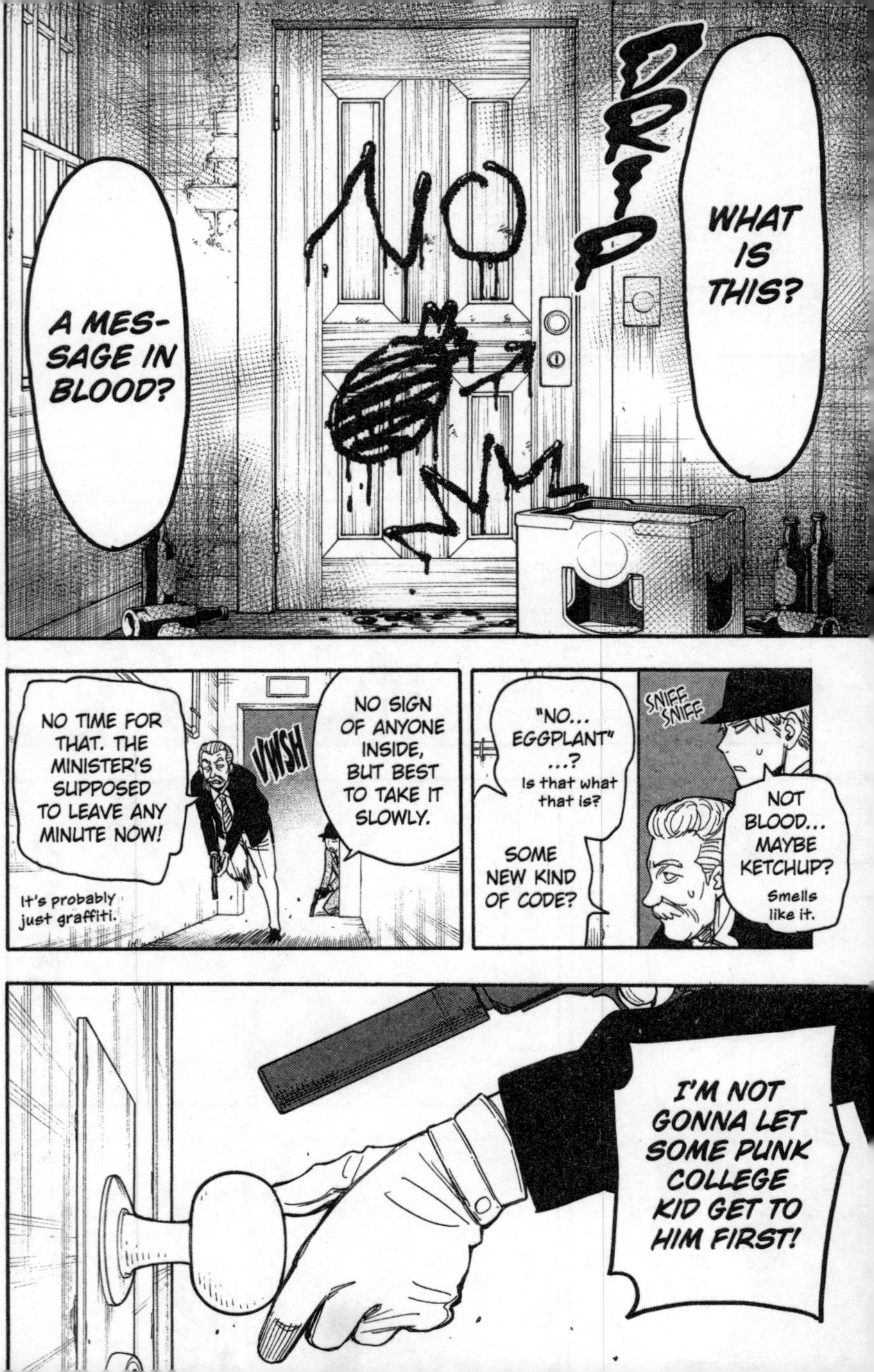
WHAT IS THIS?
DRIP
NO
A MES-SAGE IN BLOOD?
SNIFF SNIFF
NOT BLOOD... MAYBE KETCHUP?
Smells like it.
"NO... EGGPLANT" ...?
Is that what that is?
SOME NEW KIND OF CODE?
NO SIGN OF ANYONE INSIDE, BUT BEST TO TAKE IT SLOWLY.
VWSH
NO TIME FOR THAT. THE MINISTER'S SUPPOSED TO LEAVE ANY MINUTE NOW!
It's probably just graffiti.
I'M NOT GONNA LET SOME PUNK COLLEGE KID GET TO HIM FIRST!

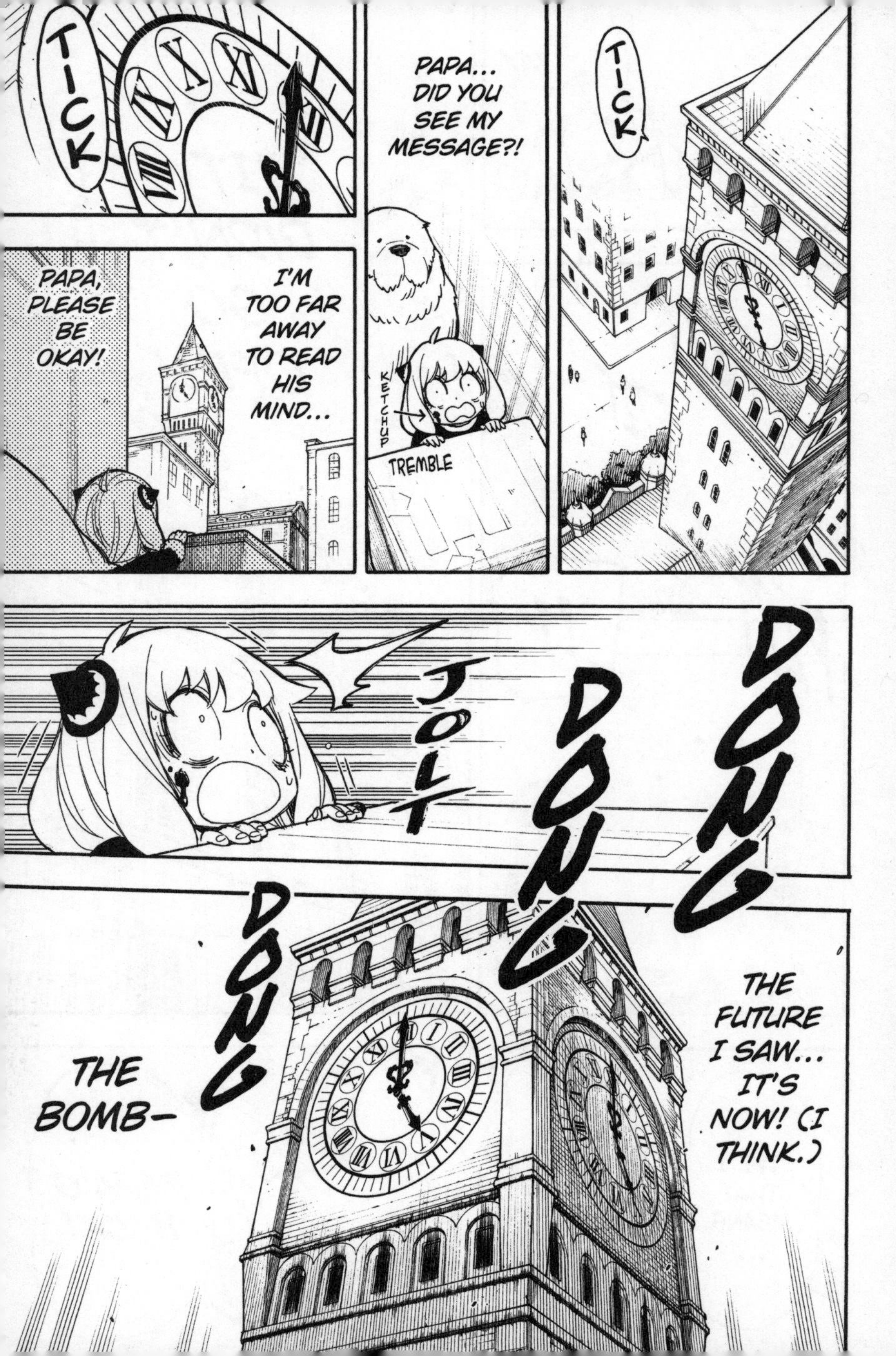
TICK
PAPA... DID YOU SEE MY MESSAGE?!
KETCHUP
TREMBLE
TICK
I'M TOO FAR AWAY TO READ HIS MIND...
PAPA, PLEASE BE OKAY!
JOLT
DONG
DONG
DONG
THE FUTURE I SAW... IT'S NOW! (I THINK.)
THE BOMB-

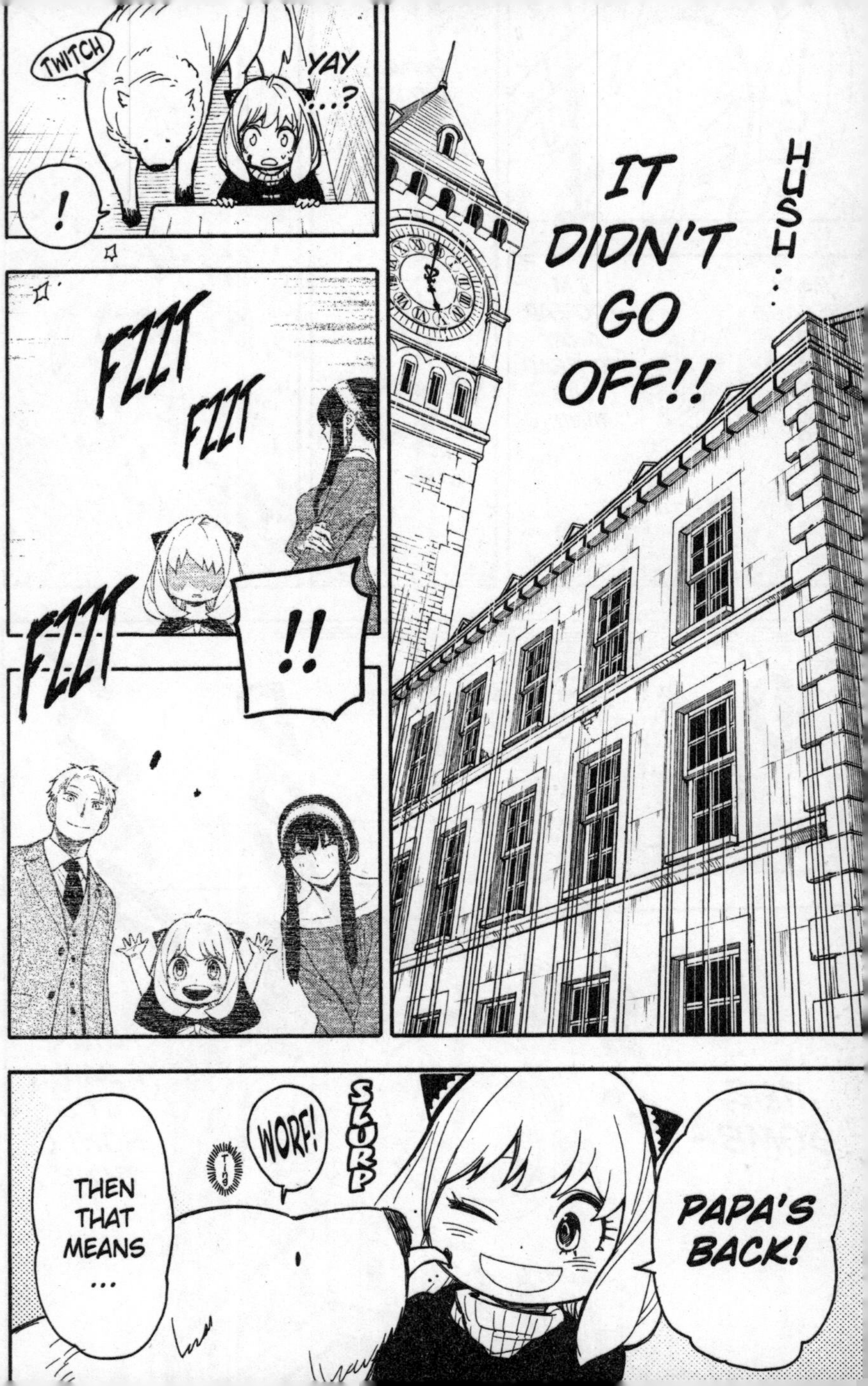
HUSH...
IT DIDN'T GO OFF!!
TWITCH
YAY...?
!
FZZT
FZZT
FZZT
!!
PAPA'S BACK!
SLURP
WORF!
Ting
THEN THAT MEANS ...

...WE SAVED THE FUTURE ...!

THIS FEELS WRONG.

THAT MESSAGE COULD BE A WARNING. I WANT TO BE SURE.

SHA

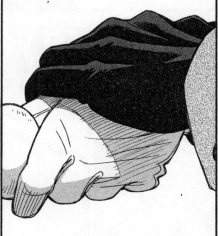

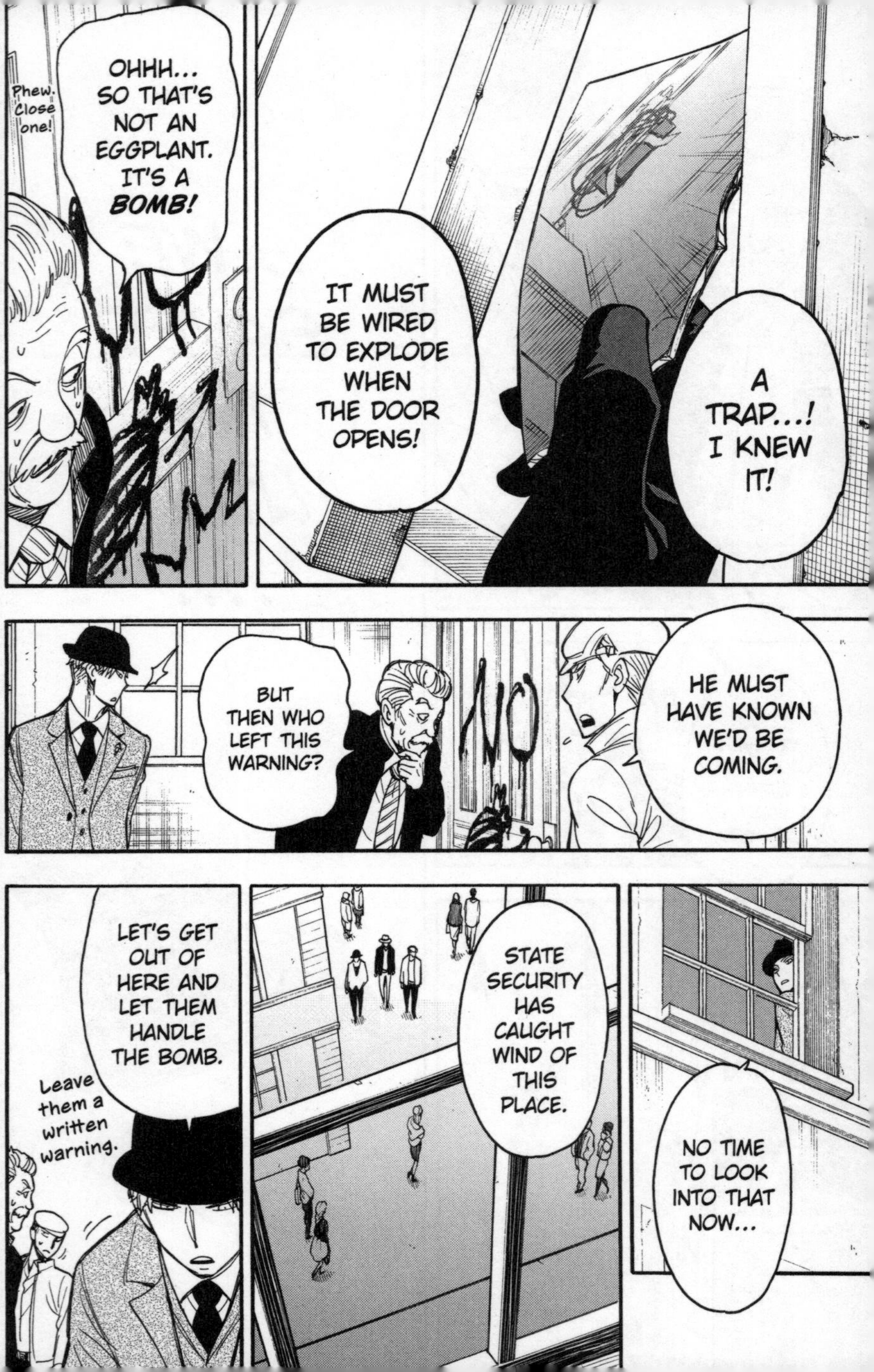
A TRAP...! I KNEW IT!
IT MUST BE WIRED TO EXPLODE WHEN THE DOOR OPENS!
OHHH... SO THAT'S NOT AN EGGPLANT. IT'S A BOMB!
Phew. Close one!
HE MUST HAVE KNOWN WE'D BE COMING.
BUT THEN WHO LEFT THIS WARNING?
NO
NO TIME TO LOOK INTO THAT NOW...
STATE SECURITY HAS CAUGHT WIND OF THIS PLACE.
LET'S GET OUT OF HERE AND LET THEM HANDLE THE BOMB.
Leave them a written warning.

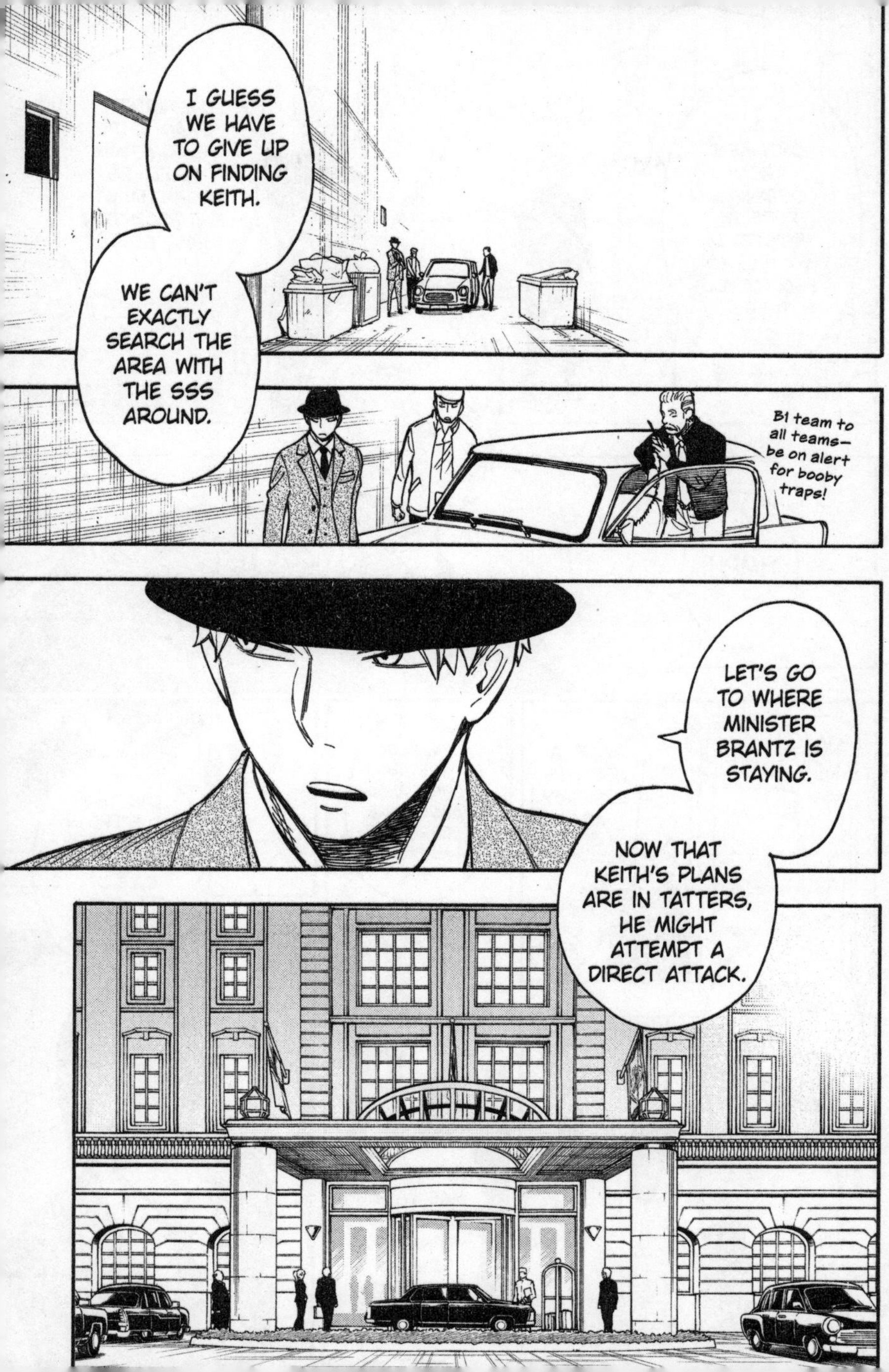
I GUESS WE HAVE TO GIVE UP ON FINDING KEITH.
WE CAN'T EXACTLY SEARCH THE AREA WITH THE SSS AROUND.
B1 team to all teams—be on alert for booby traps!
LET'S GO TO WHERE MINISTER BRANTZ IS STAYING.
NOW THAT KEITH'S PLANS ARE IN TATTERS, HE MIGHT ATTEMPT A DIRECT ATTACK.

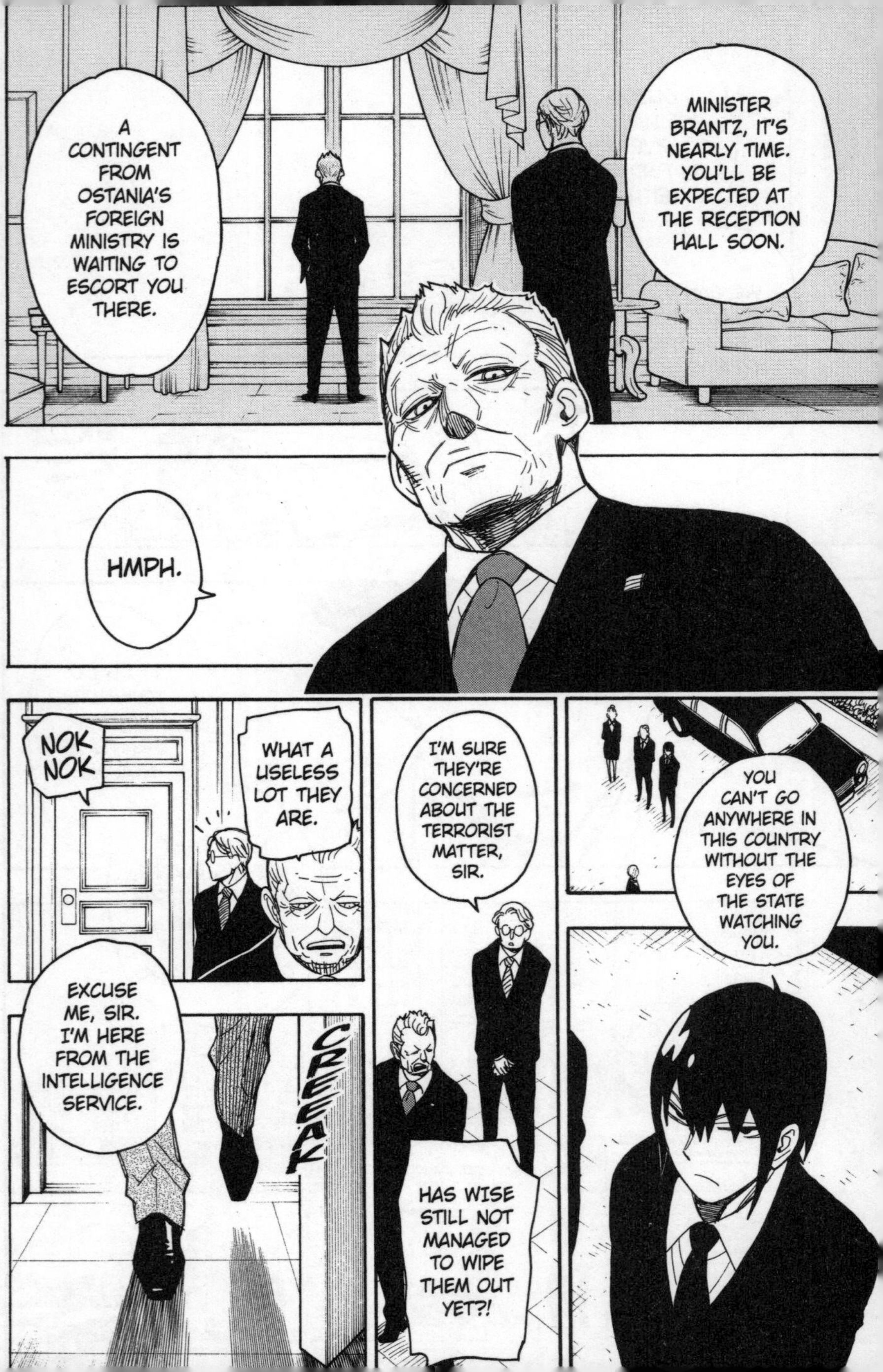
MINISTER BRANTZ, IT'S NEARLY TIME. YOU'LL BE EXPECTED AT THE RECEPTION HALL SOON.
A CONTINGENT FROM OSTANIA'S FOREIGN MINISTRY IS WAITING TO ESCORT YOU THERE.
HMPH.
YOU CAN'T GO ANYWHERE IN THIS COUNTRY WITHOUT THE EYES OF THE STATE WATCHING YOU.
I'M SURE THEY'RE CONCERNED ABOUT THE TERRORIST MATTER, SIR.
HAS WISE STILL NOT MANAGED TO WIPE THEM OUT YET?!
WHAT A USELESS LOT THEY ARE.
NOK NOK
EXCUSE ME, SIR. I'M HERE FROM THE INTELLIGENCE SERVICE.
CREEEAK

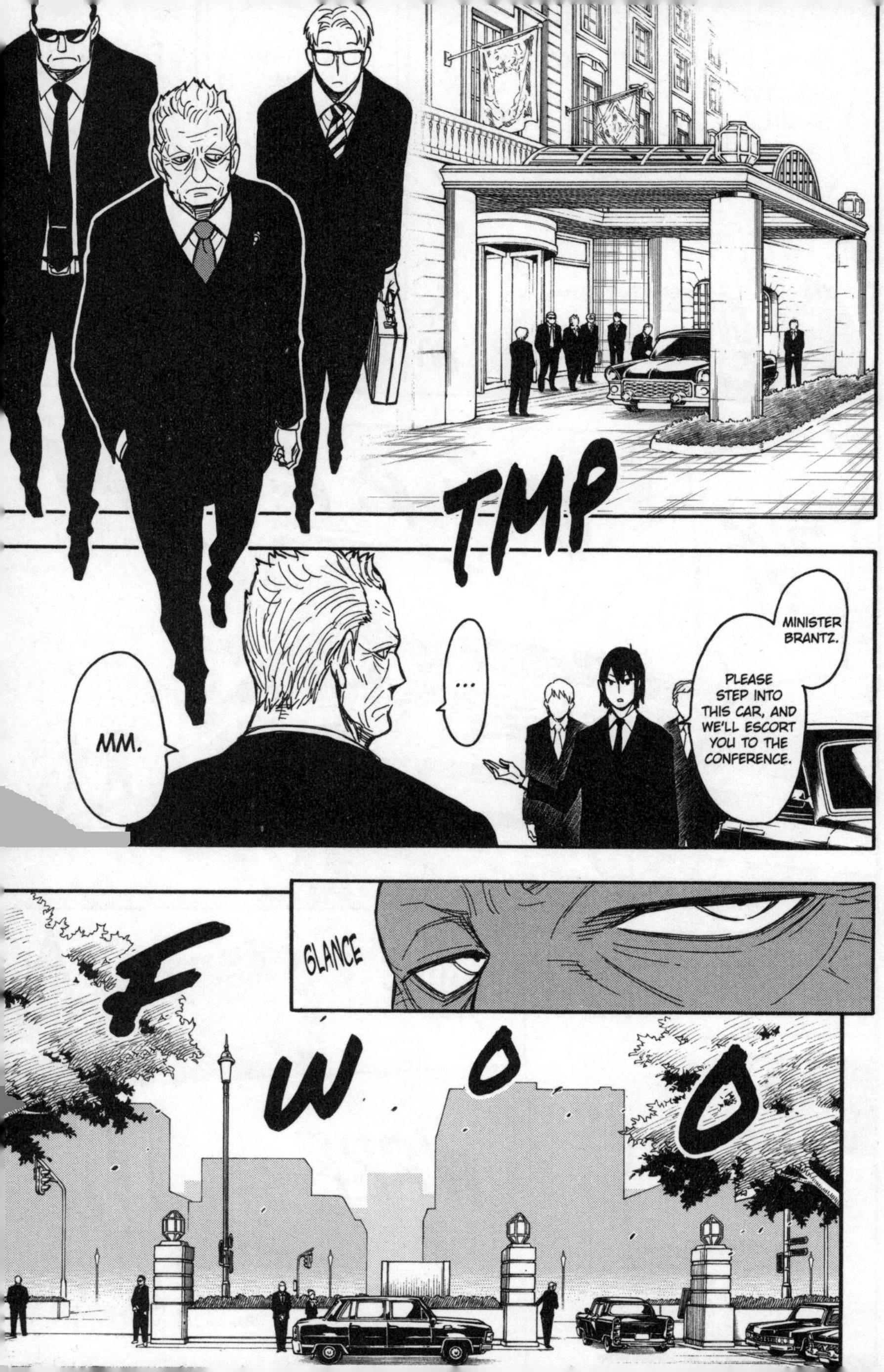
TMP
MINISTER BRANTZ.
PLEASE STEP INTO THIS CAR, AND WE'LL ESCORT YOU TO THE CONFERENCE.
...
MM.
GLANCE
FWOO

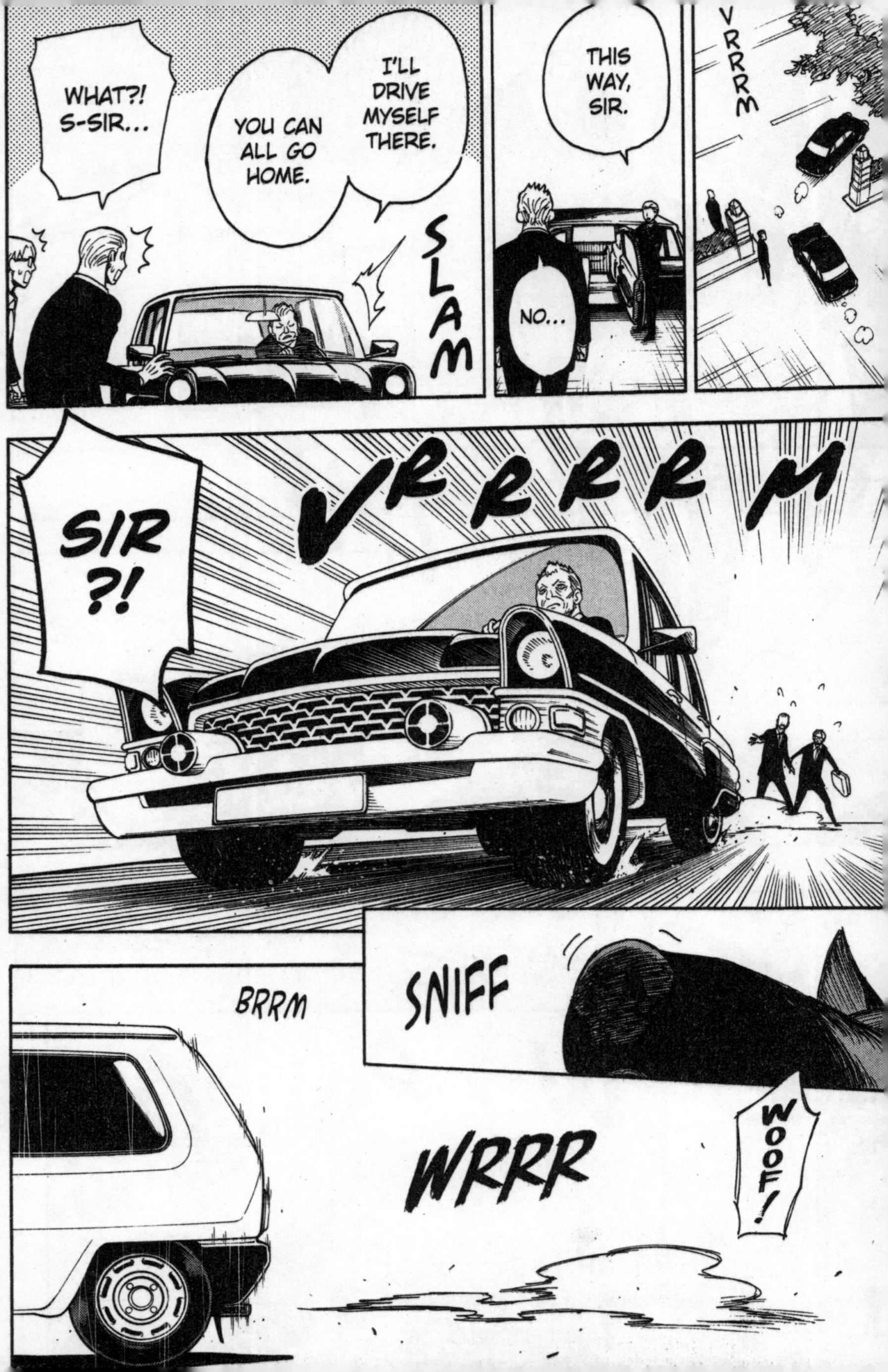
VRRRM
THIS WAY, SIR.
NO...
I'LL DRIVE MYSELF THERE.
YOU CAN ALL GO HOME.
WHAT?! S-SIR...
SLAM
VRRRRM
SIR?!
SNIFF
BRRM
WOOF!
WRRR

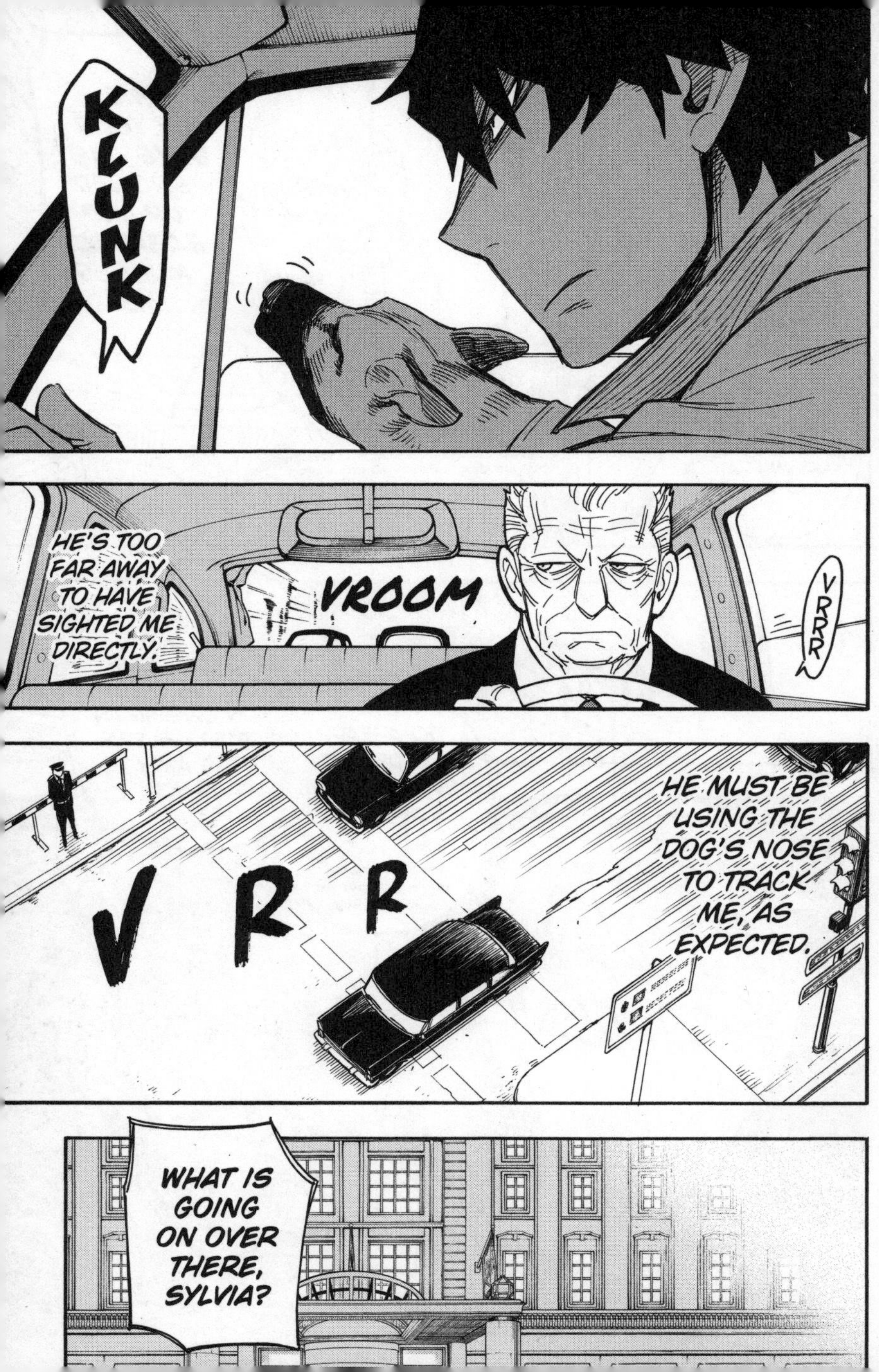
KLUNK
HE'S TOO FAR AWAY TO HAVE SIGHTED ME DIRECTLY.
VROOM
VRRR
HE MUST BE USING THE DOG'S NOSE TO TRACK ME, AS EXPECTED.
VRR
WHAT IS GOING ON OVER THERE, SYLVIA?

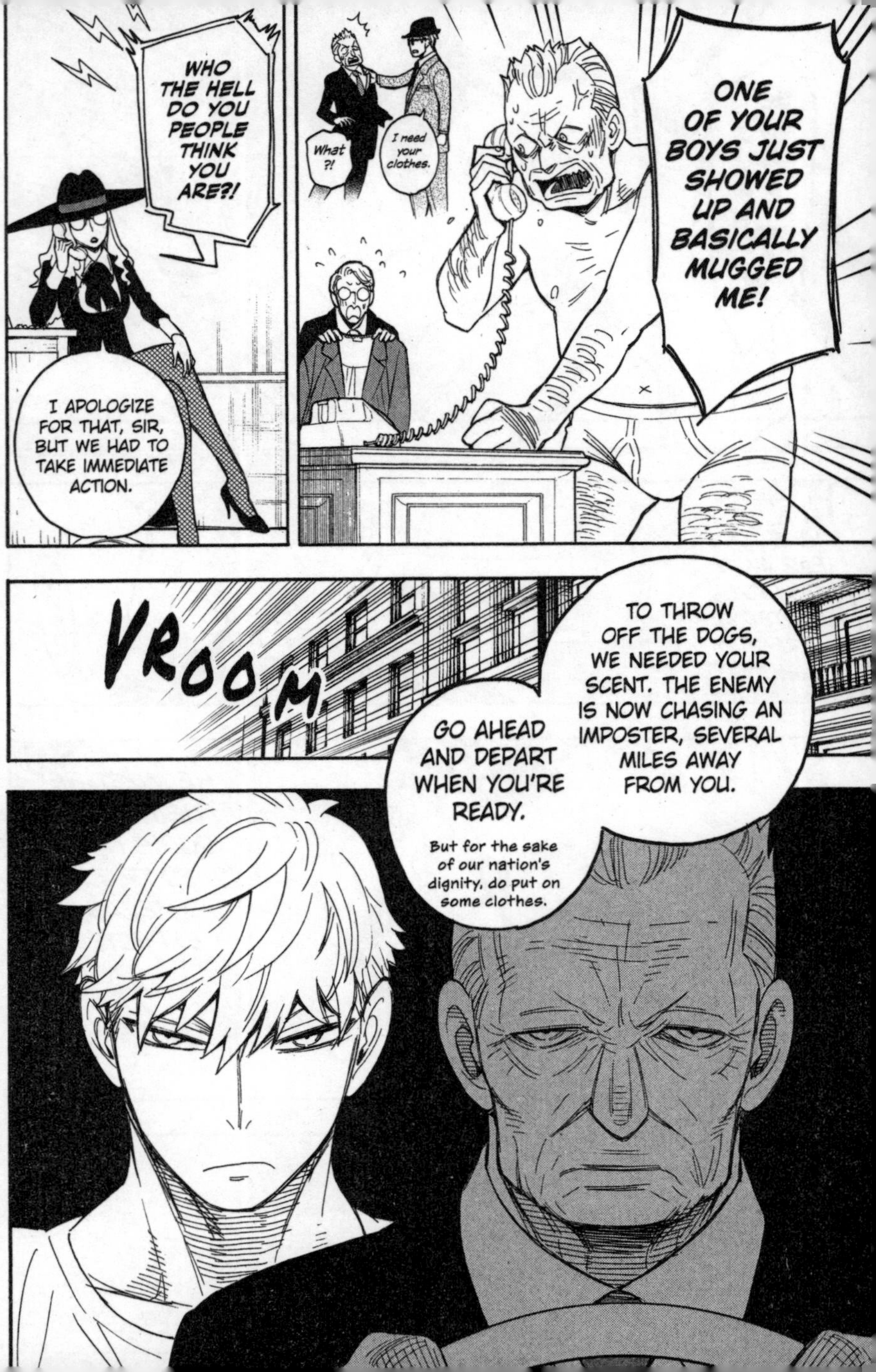
ONE OF YOUR BOYS JUST SHOWED UP AND BASICALLY MUGGED ME!
I need your clothes.
What?!
WHO THE HELL DO YOU PEOPLE THINK YOU ARE?!
I APOLOGIZE FOR THAT, SIR, BUT WE HAD TO TAKE IMMEDIATE ACTION.
VROOM
TO THROW OFF THE DOGS, WE NEEDED YOUR SCENT. THE ENEMY IS NOW CHASING AN IMPOSTER, SEVERAL MILES AWAY FROM YOU.
GO AHEAD AND DEPART WHEN YOU'RE READY.
But for the sake of our nation's dignity, do put on some clothes.

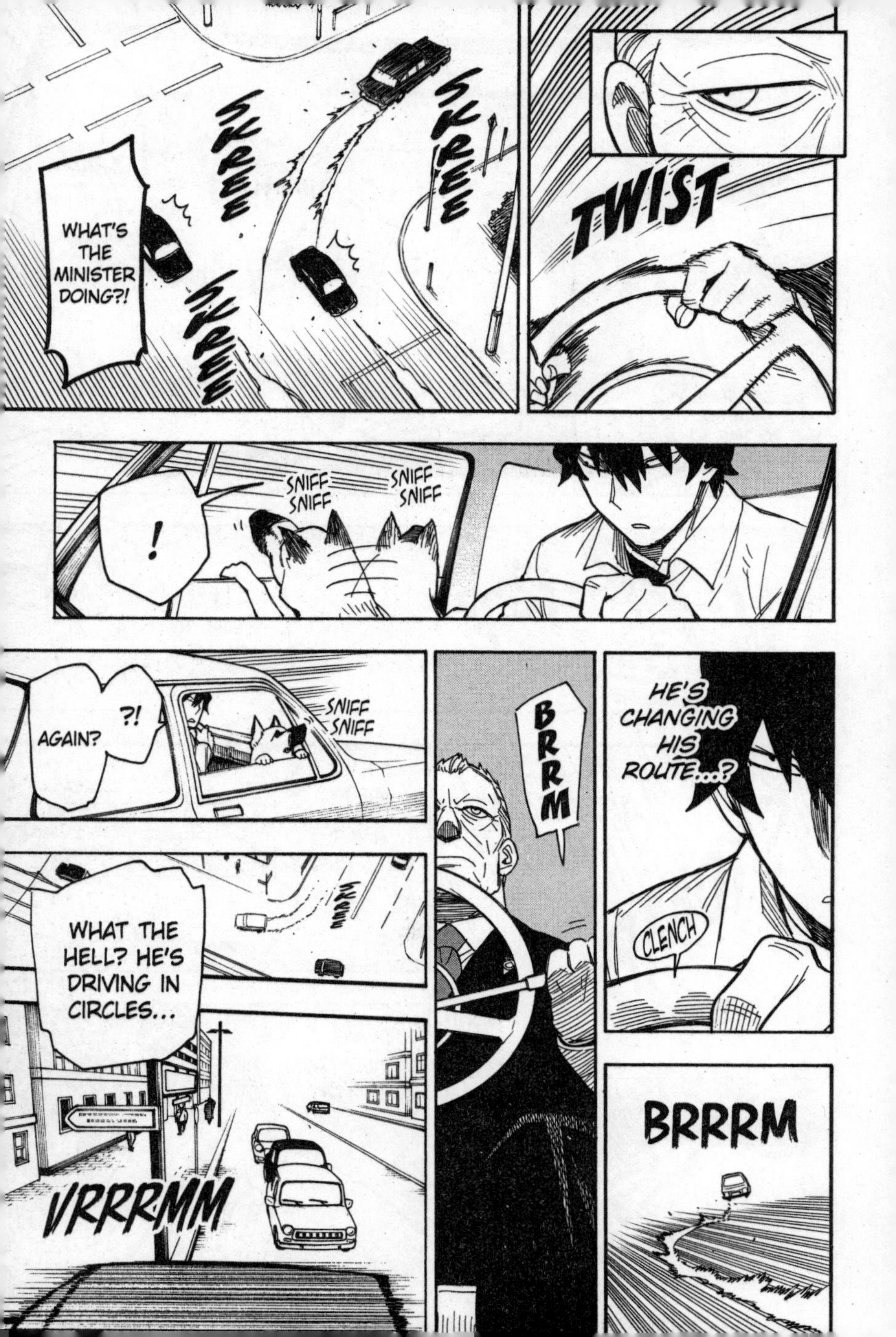
TWIST
SKREE
SKREE
WHAT'S THE MINISTER DOING?!
SNIFF SNIFF
SNIFF SNIFF
!
HE'S CHANGING HIS ROUTE...?
CLENCH
BRRM
SNIFF SNIFF
?!
AGAIN?
BRRRM
WHAT THE HELL? HE'S DRIVING IN CIRCLES...
VRRRMM

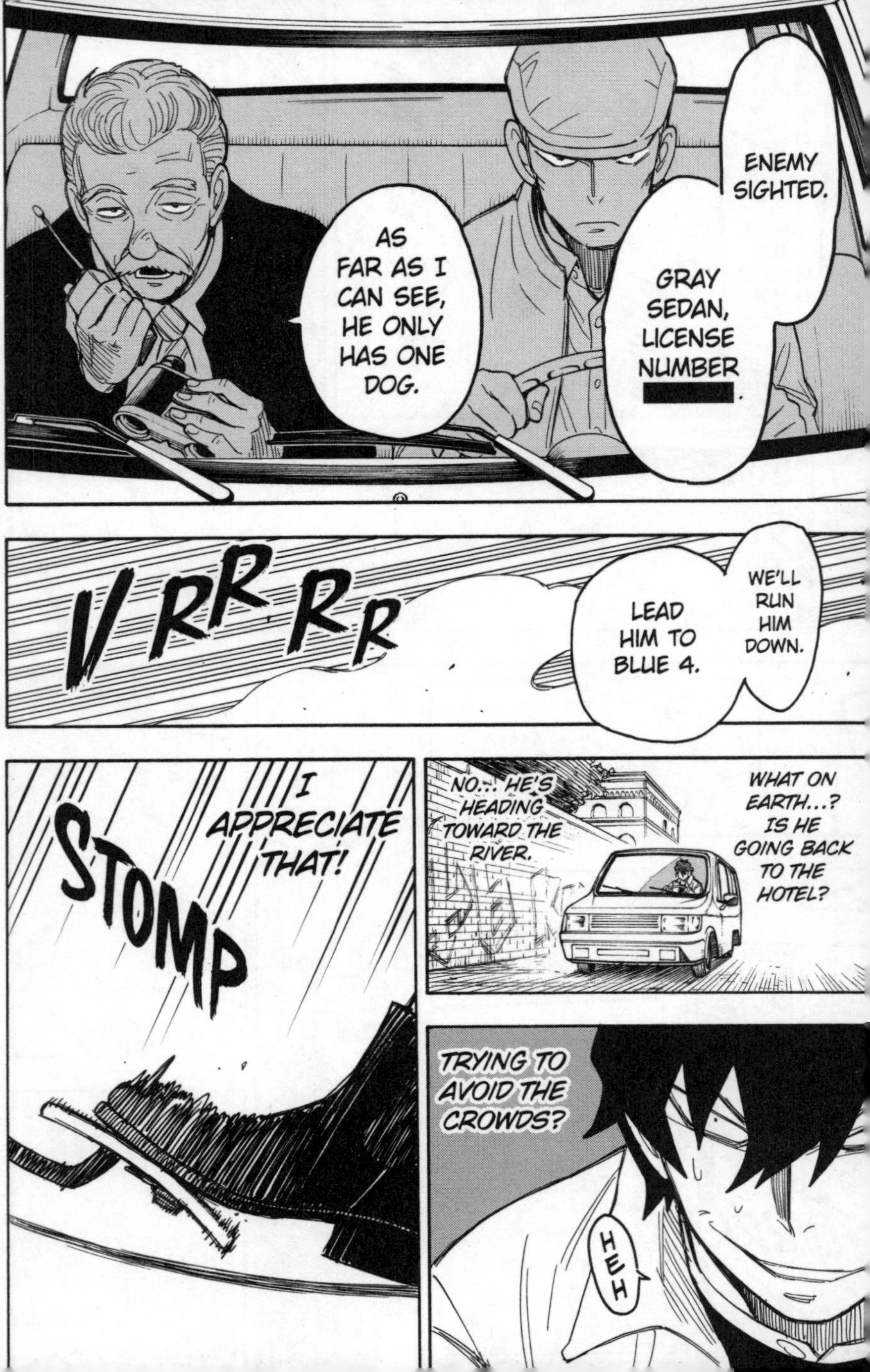
ENEMY SIGHTED.
GRAY SEDAN, LICENSE NUMBER [redacted].
AS FAR AS I CAN SEE, HE ONLY HAS ONE DOG.
WE'LL RUN HIM DOWN.
LEAD HIM TO BLUE 4.
VRRRRR
WHAT ON EARTH...? IS HE GOING BACK TO THE HOTEL?
NO... HE'S HEADING TOWARD THE RIVER.
TRYING TO AVOID THE CROWDS?
HEH
I APPRECIATE THAT!
STOMP

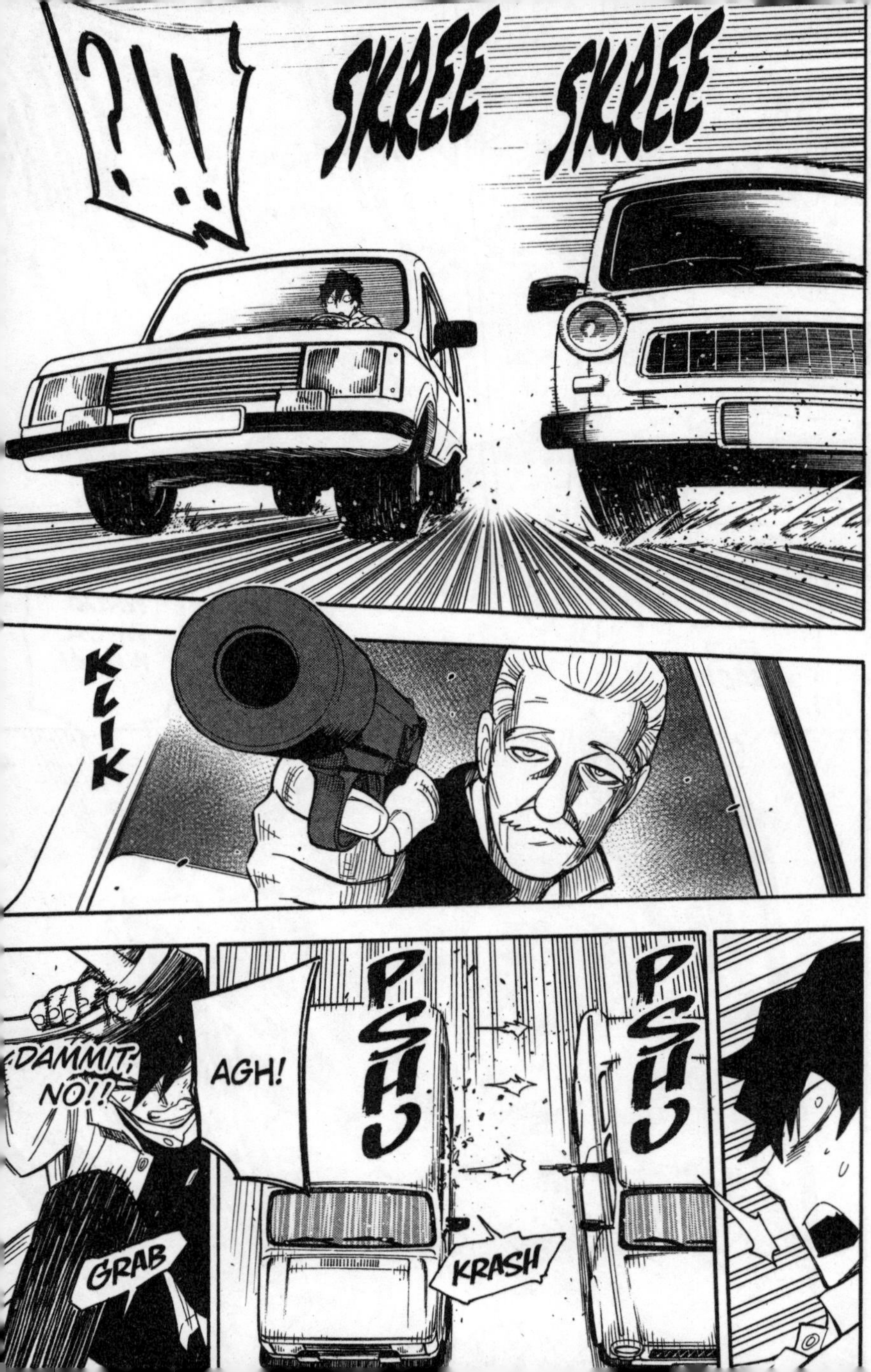
?!!
SKREE
SKREE
KLIK
PSHU
PSHU
AGH!
KRASH
DAMMIT, NO!!
GRAB

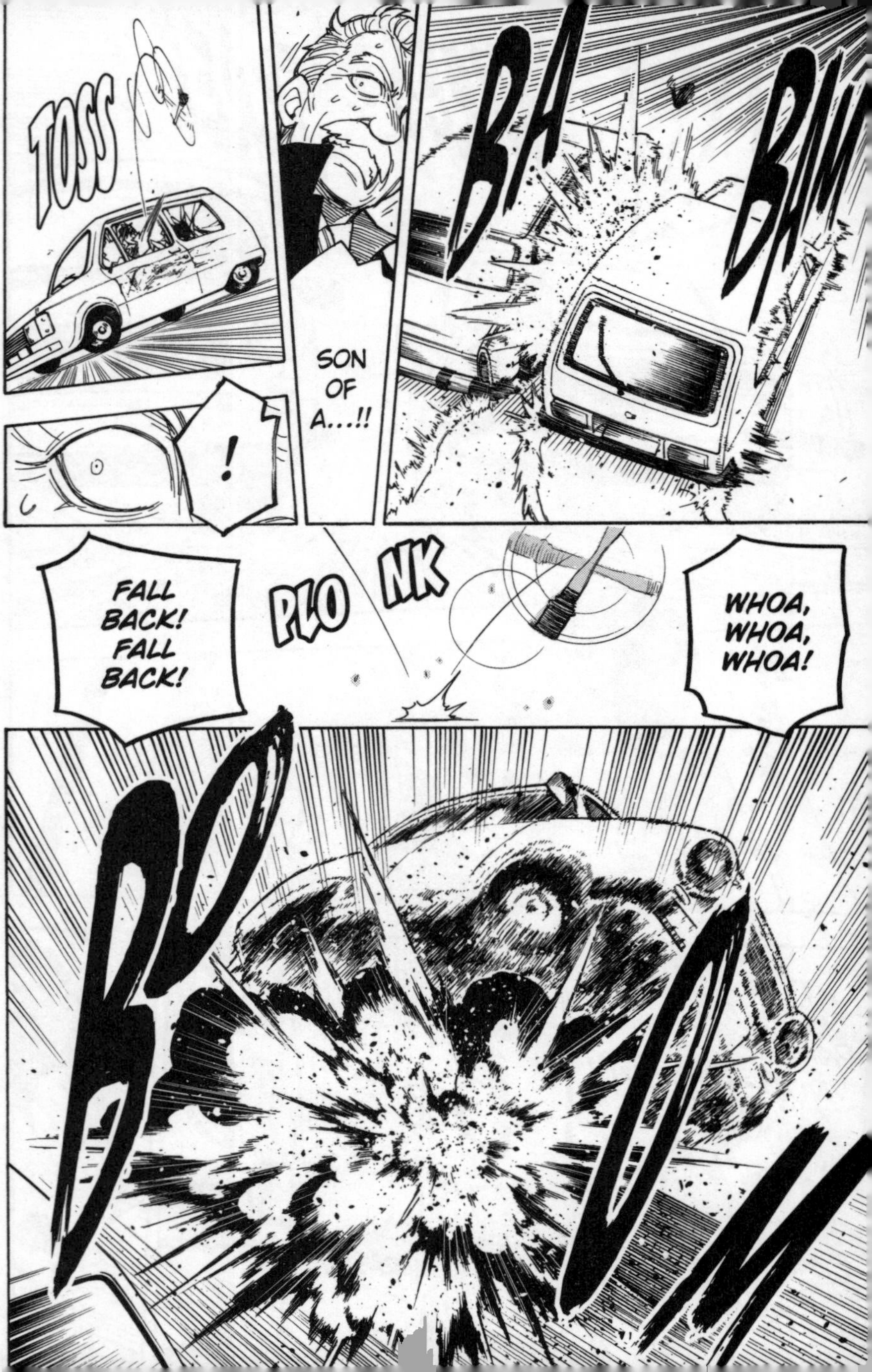
BA
BAM
SON OF A...!!
TOSS
!
WHOA, WHOA, WHOA!
PLONK
FALL BACK! FALL BACK!
BOOM

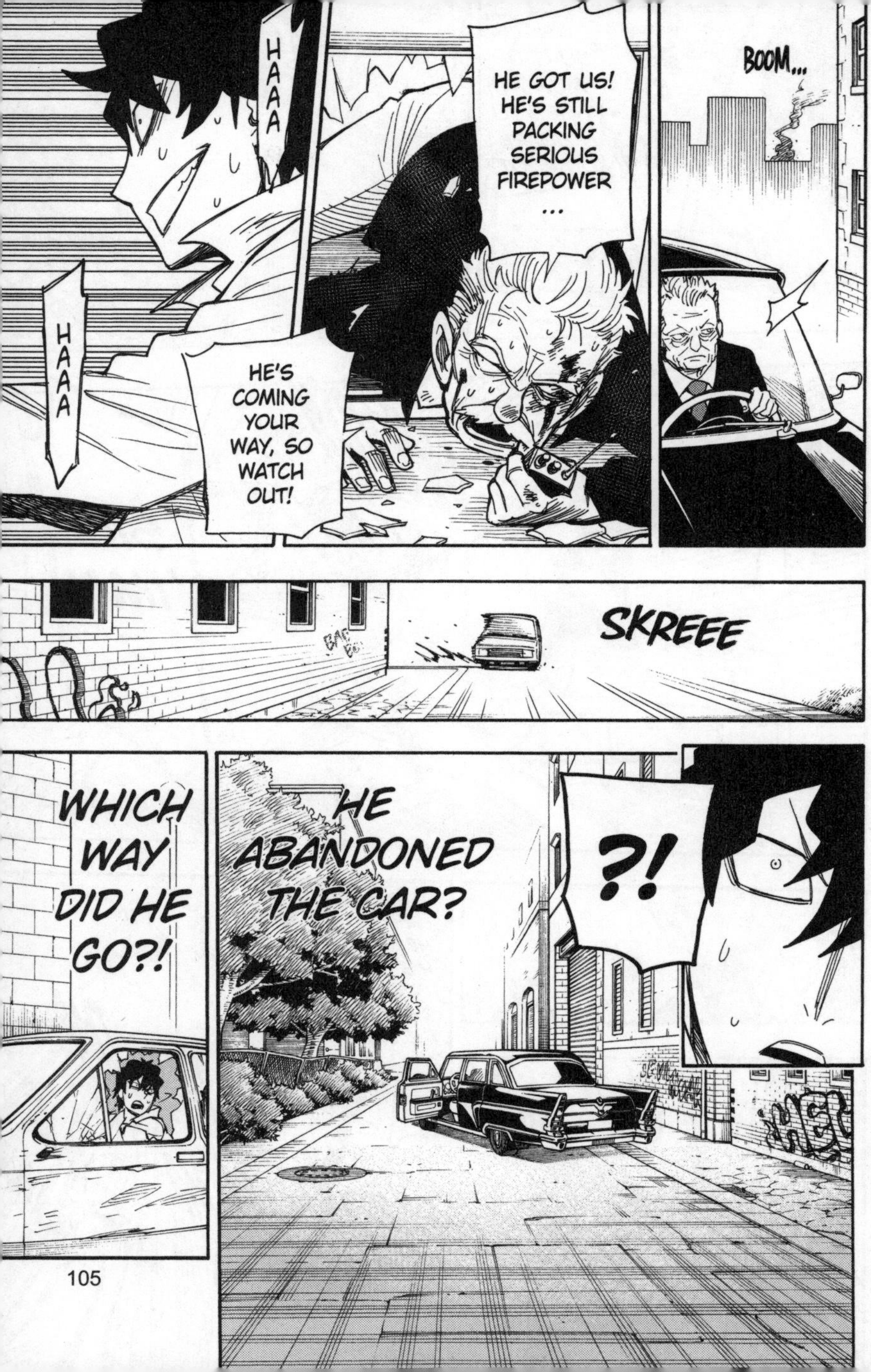
BOOM...
HE GOT US! HE'S STILL PACKING SERIOUS FIREPOWER ...
HE'S COMING YOUR WAY, SO WATCH OUT!
HAAA
HAAA
SKREEE
?!
HE ABANDONED THE CAR?
WHICH WAY DID HE GO?!

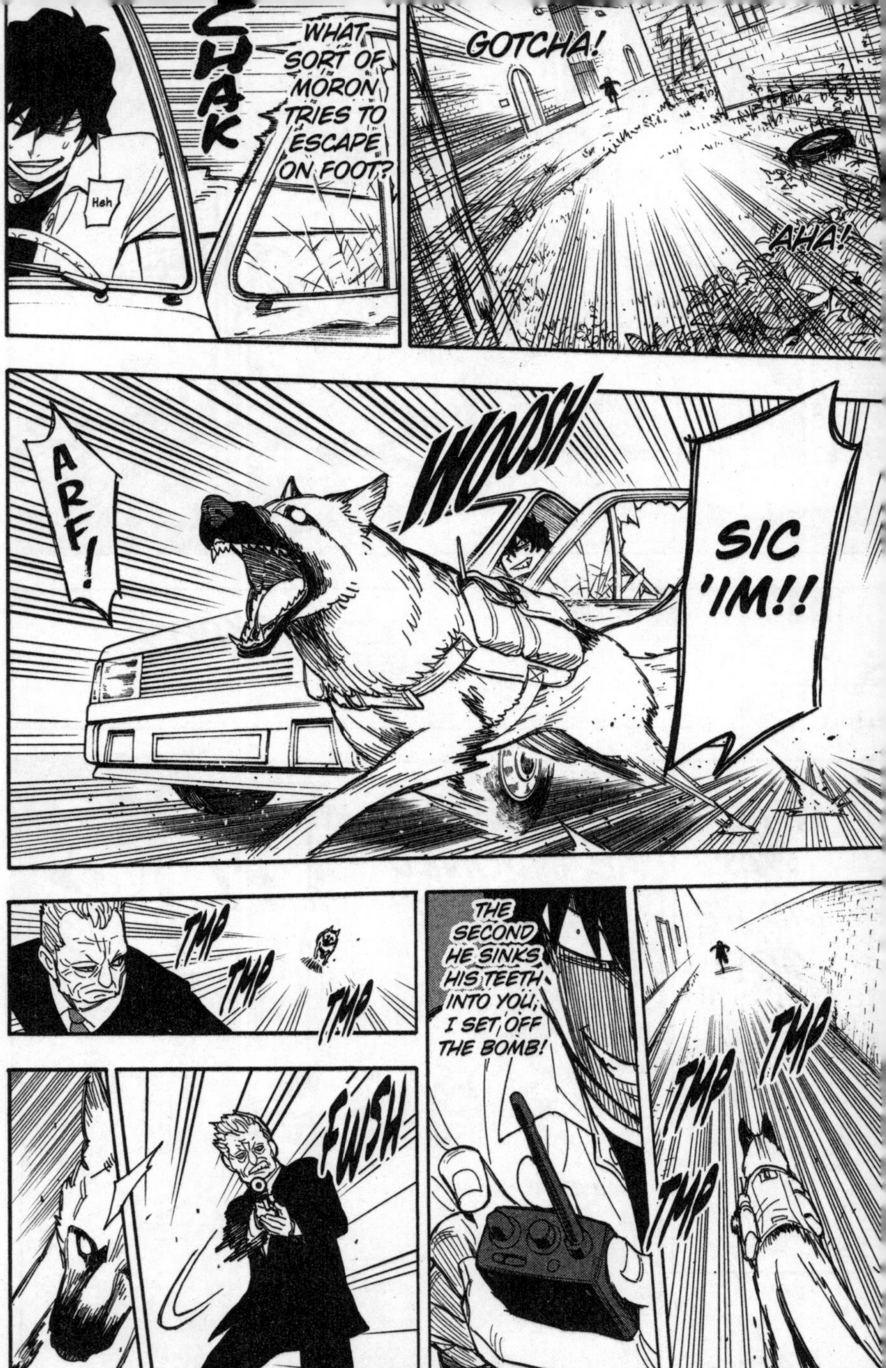
GOTCHA!
AHA!
SHAK
WHAT SORT OF MORON TRIES TO ESCAPE ON FOOT?
Heh
SIC 'IM!!
WOOSH
ARF!
TMP TMP TMP TMP
THE SECOND HE SINKS HIS TEETH INTO YOU, I SET OFF THE BOMB!
TMP TMP TMP
FWSH

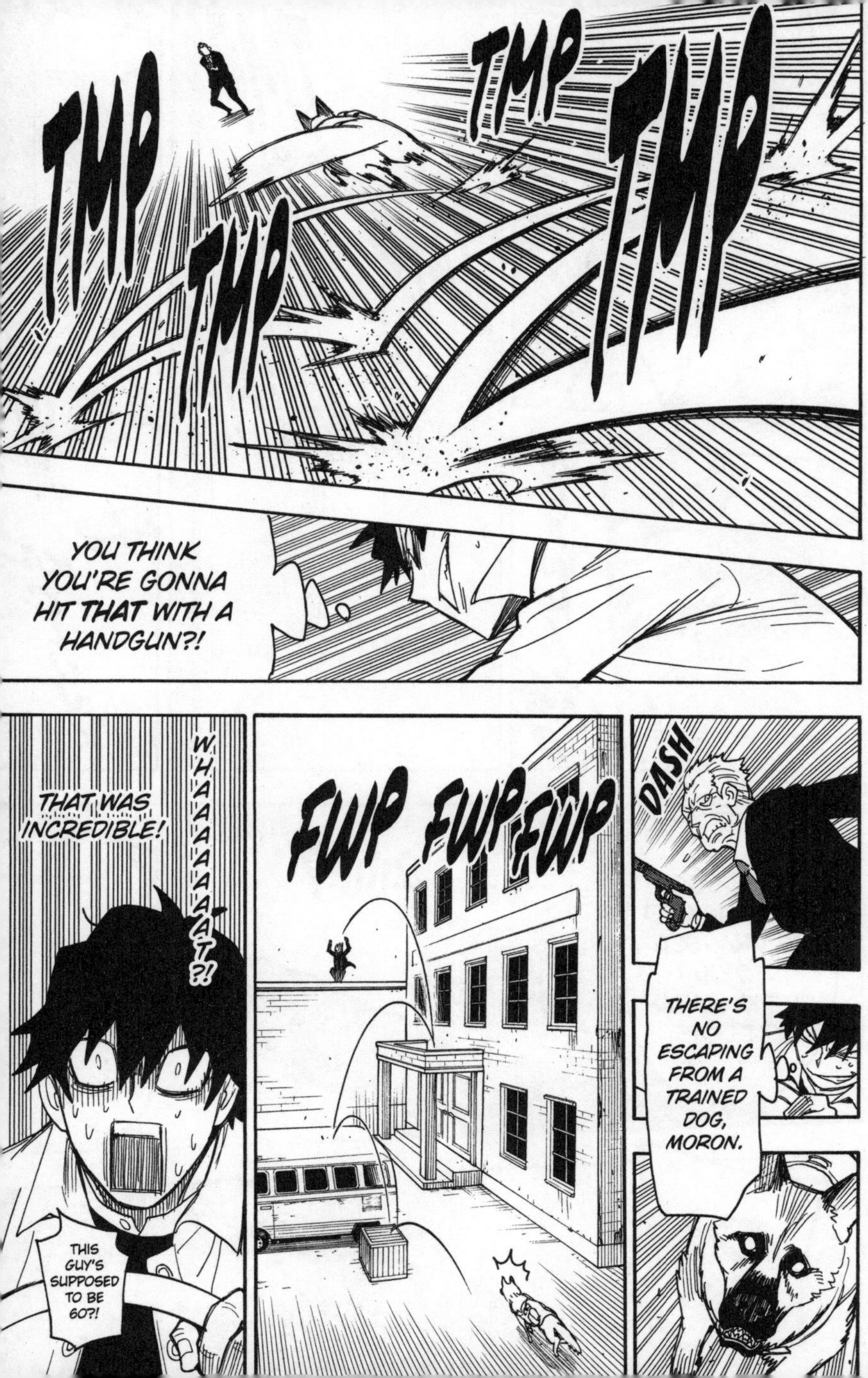
TMP
TMP
TMP
TMP
YOU THINK YOU'RE GONNA HIT THAT WITH A HANDGUN?!
DASH
THERE'S NO ESCAPING FROM A TRAINED DOG, MORON.
FWP FWP FWP
WHAAAAAAAAAT?!
THAT WAS INCREDIBLE!
THIS GUY'S SUPPOSED TO BE 60?!

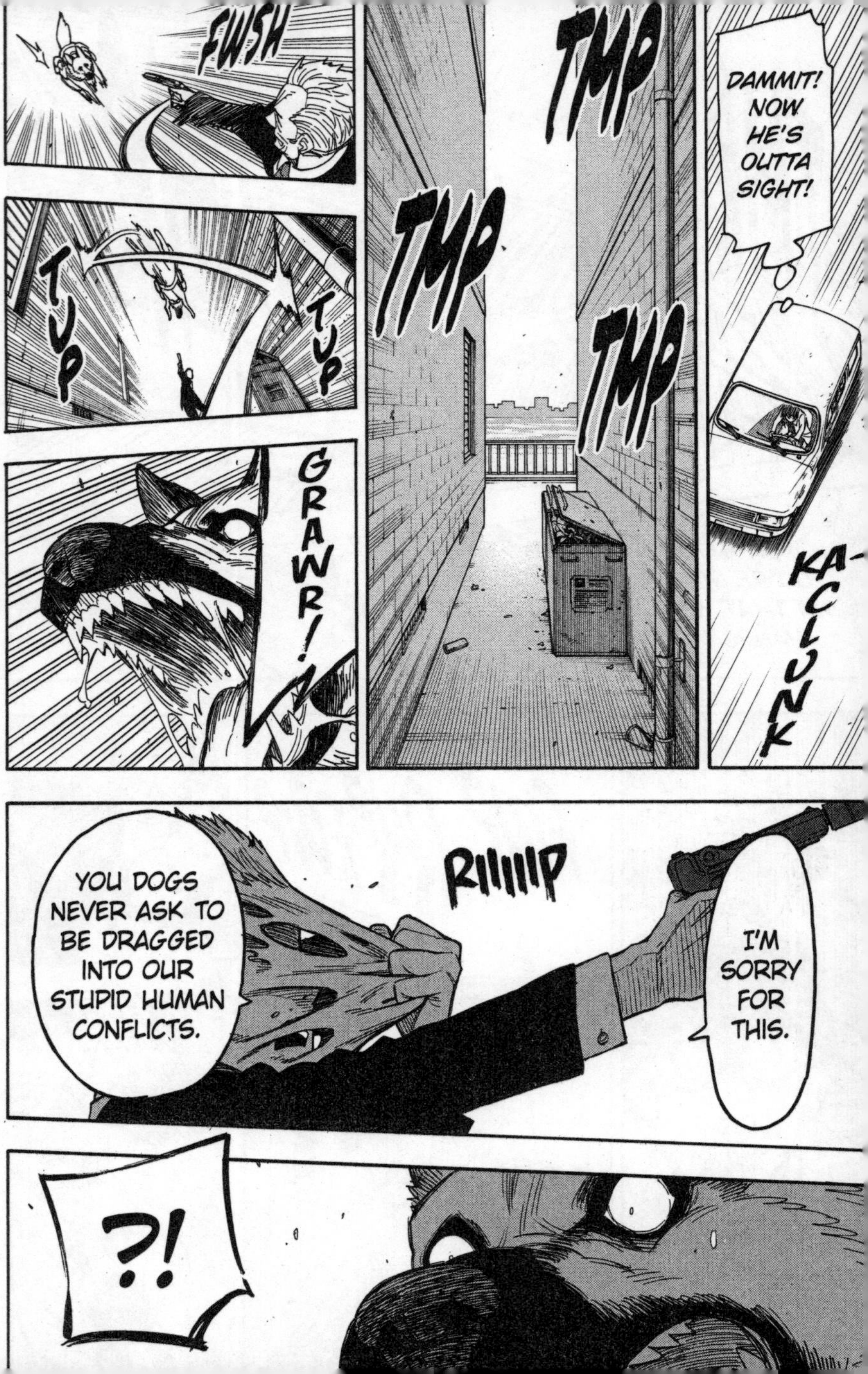
DAMMIT! NOW HE'S OUTTA SIGHT!
KA-CLUNK
TMP
TMP
TMP
FWSH
TUP
TUP
GRAWR!
RIIIIP
YOU DOGS NEVER ASK TO BE DRAGGED INTO OUR STUPID HUMAN CONFLICTS.
I'M SORRY FOR THIS.
?!

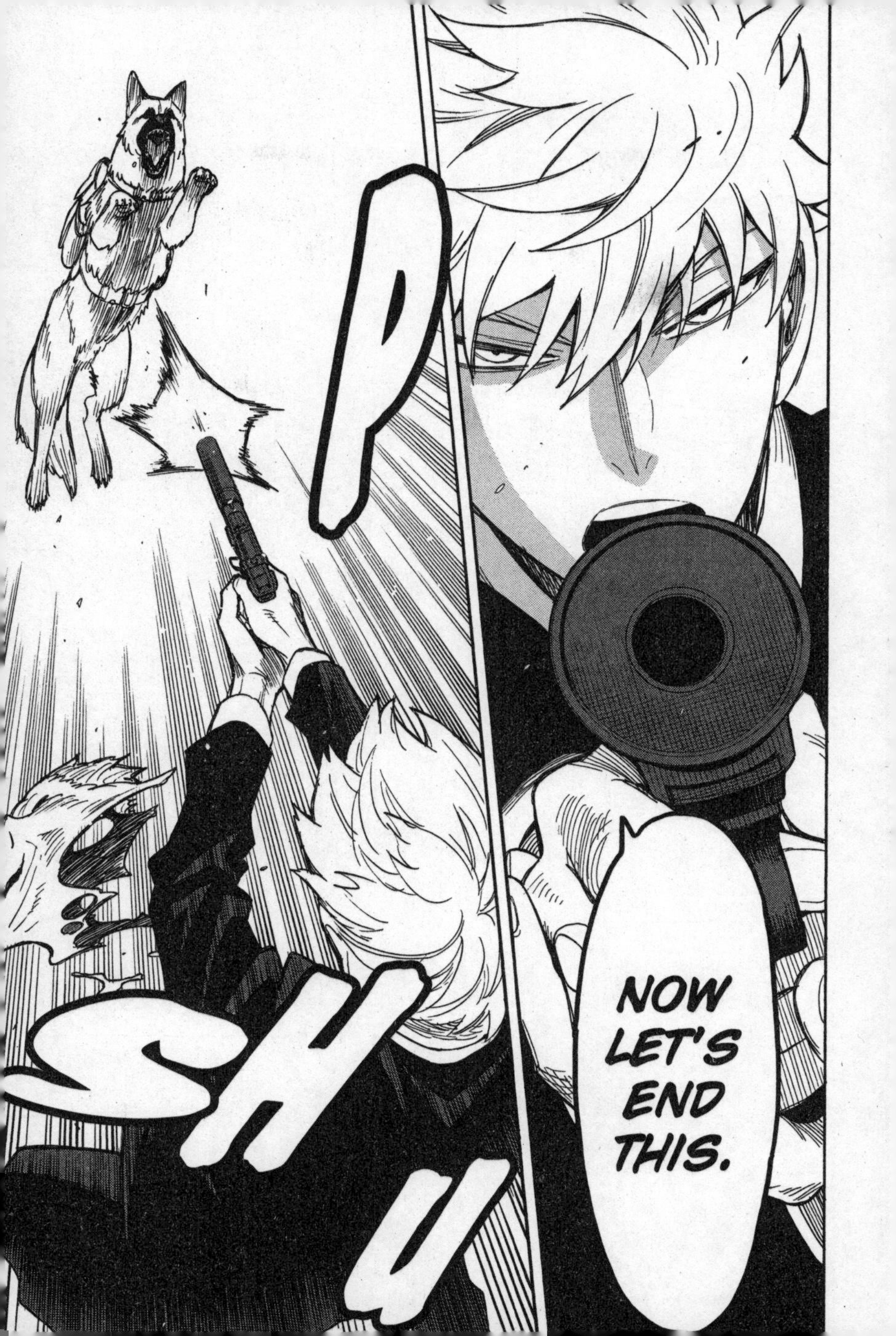
NOW LET'S END THIS.
P
SHH

SPY×FAMILY

MISSION 22

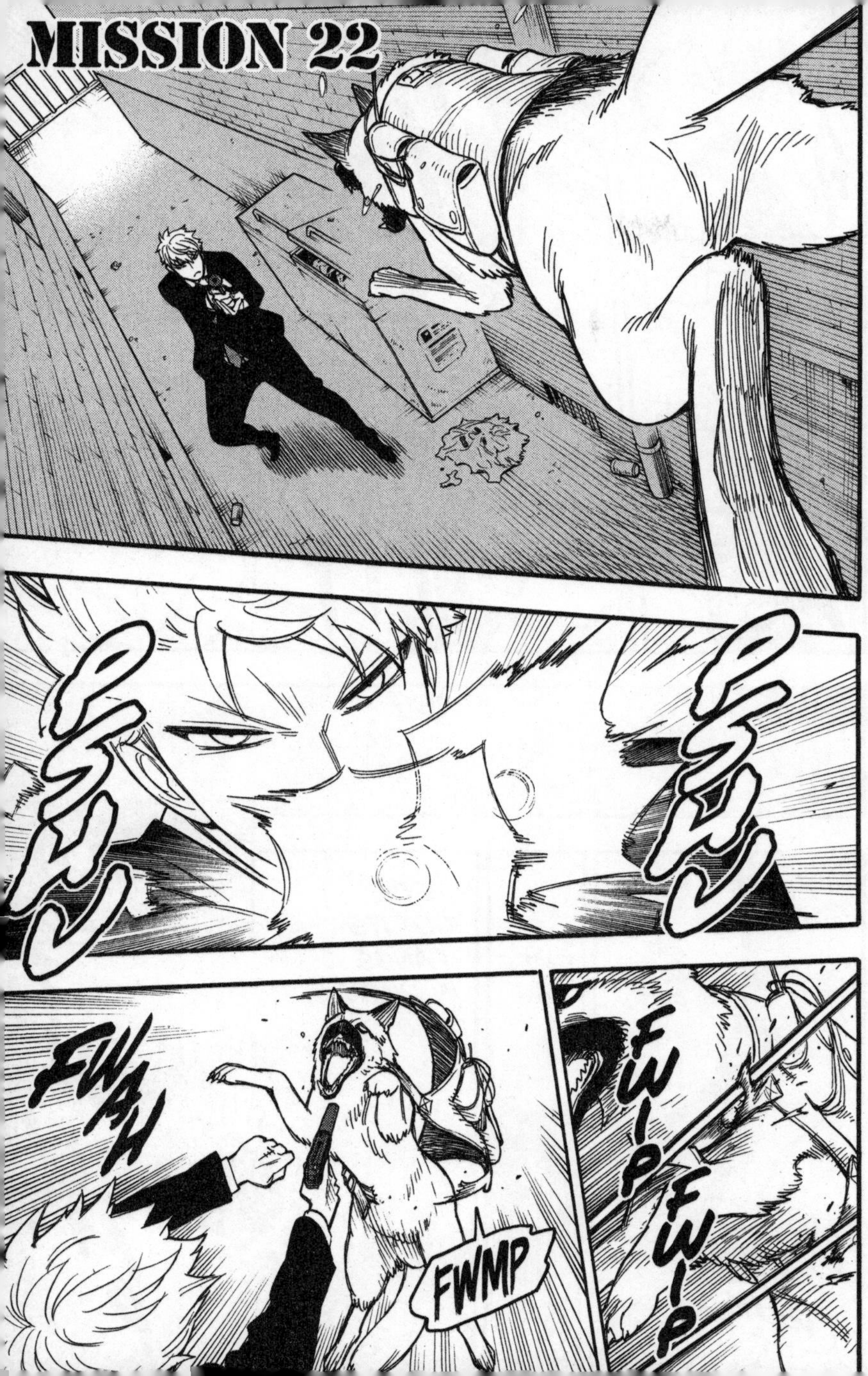
FWIP
FWIP
FWAH
FWMP

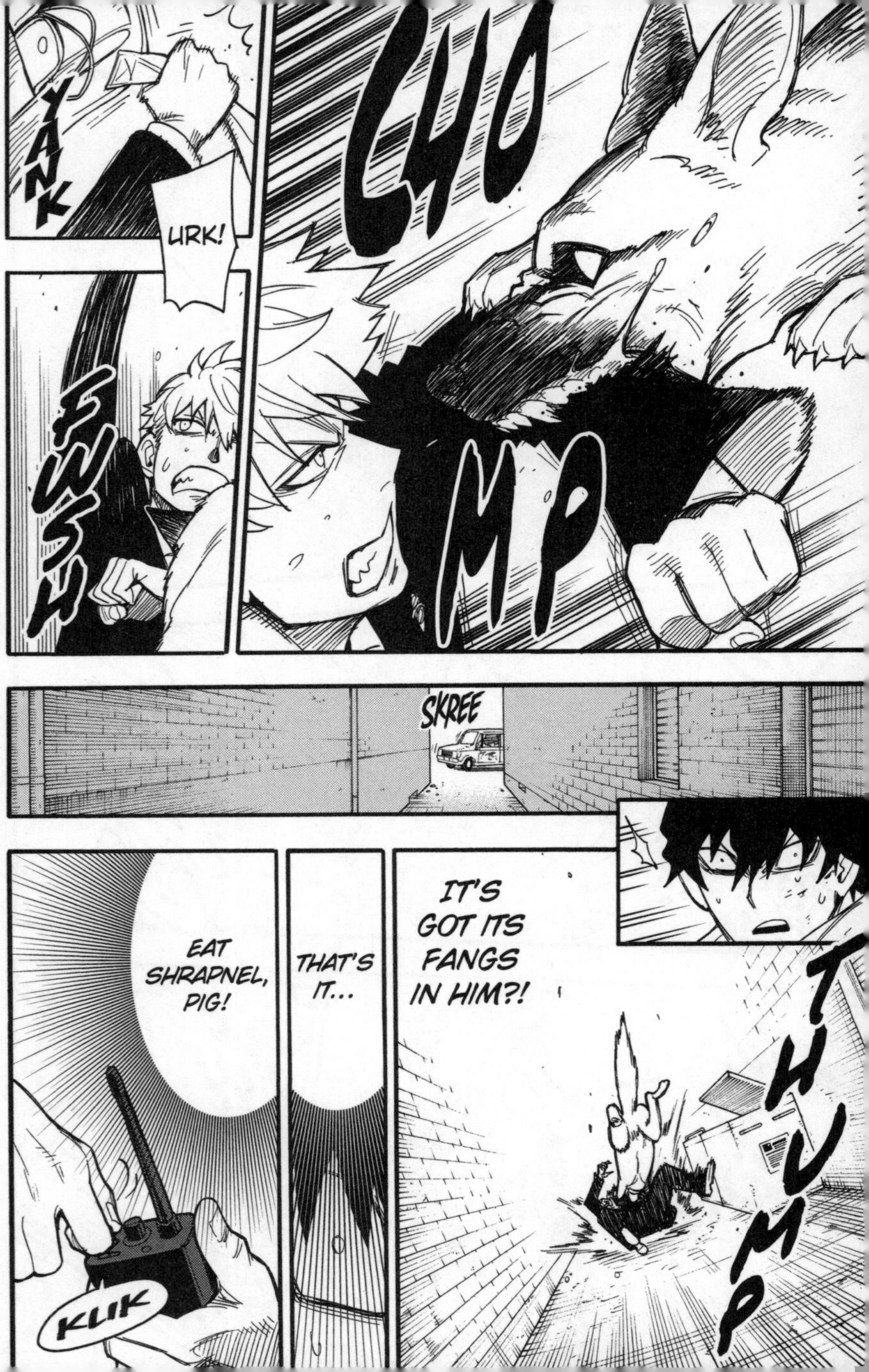
CHOMP
YANK
URK!
FWUSH
SKREE
IT'S GOT ITS FANGS IN HIM?!
THUMP
THAT'S IT...
EAT SHRAPNEL, PIG!
KLIK

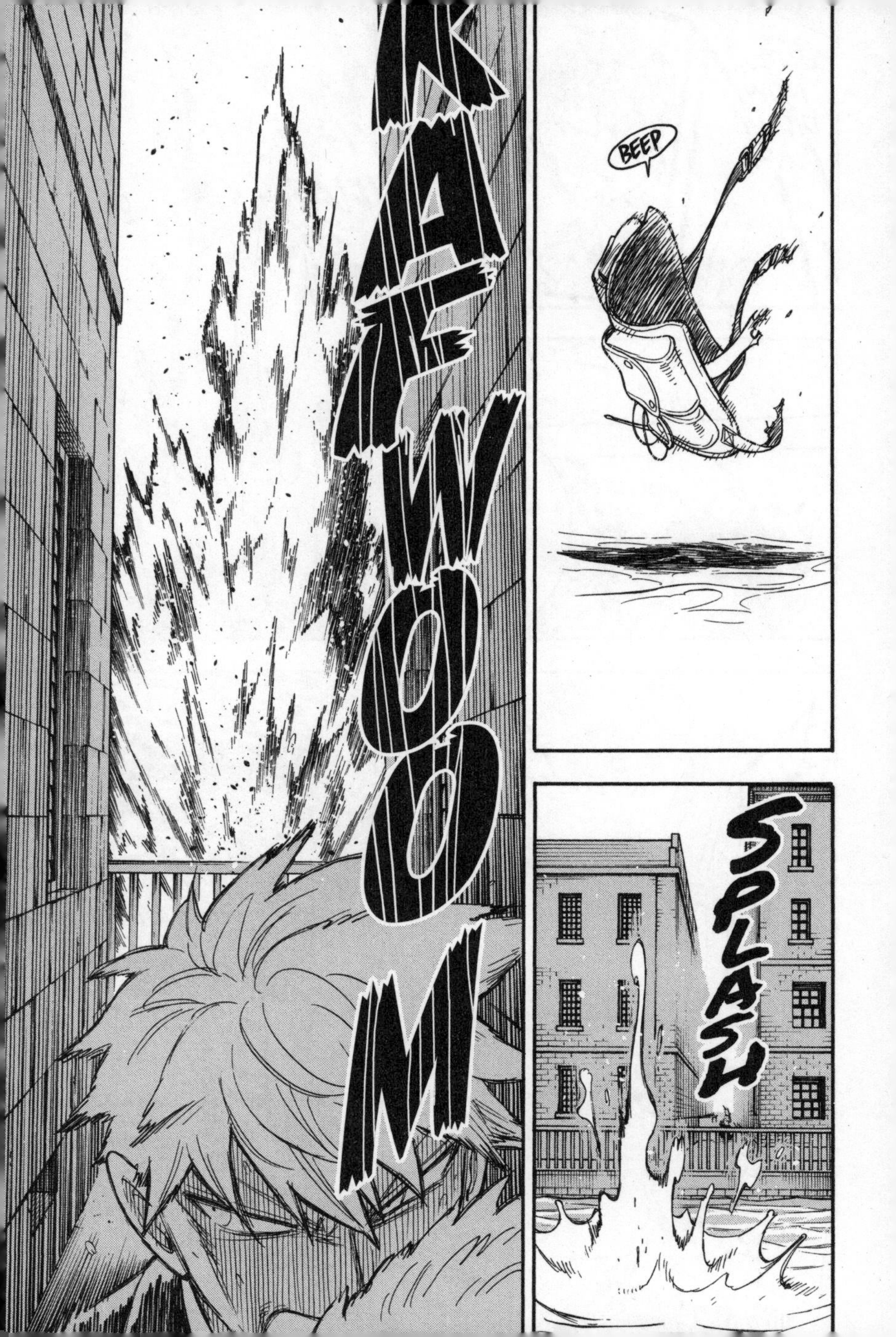
BEEP
SPLASH
KABWOOM

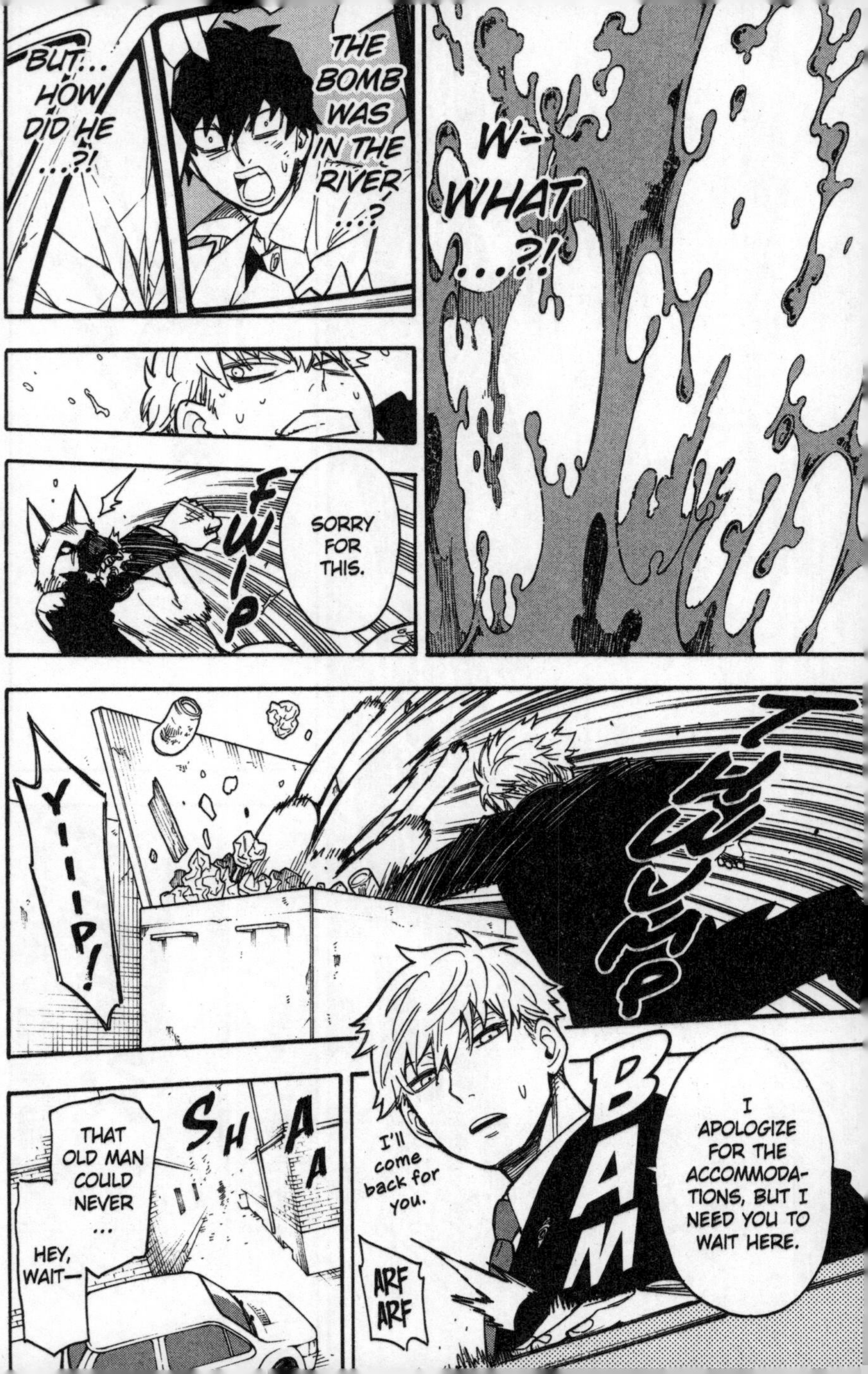
W-WHAT...?!
THE BOMB WAS IN THE RIVER...?
BUT... HOW DID HE ...?!
FWIP
SORRY FOR THIS.
THUMP
YIIIP!
BAM
I APOLOGIZE FOR THE ACCOMMODATIONS, BUT I NEED YOU TO WAIT HERE.
I'll come back for you.
ARF ARF
SHAA
THAT OLD MAN COULD NEVER ...
HEY, WAIT—

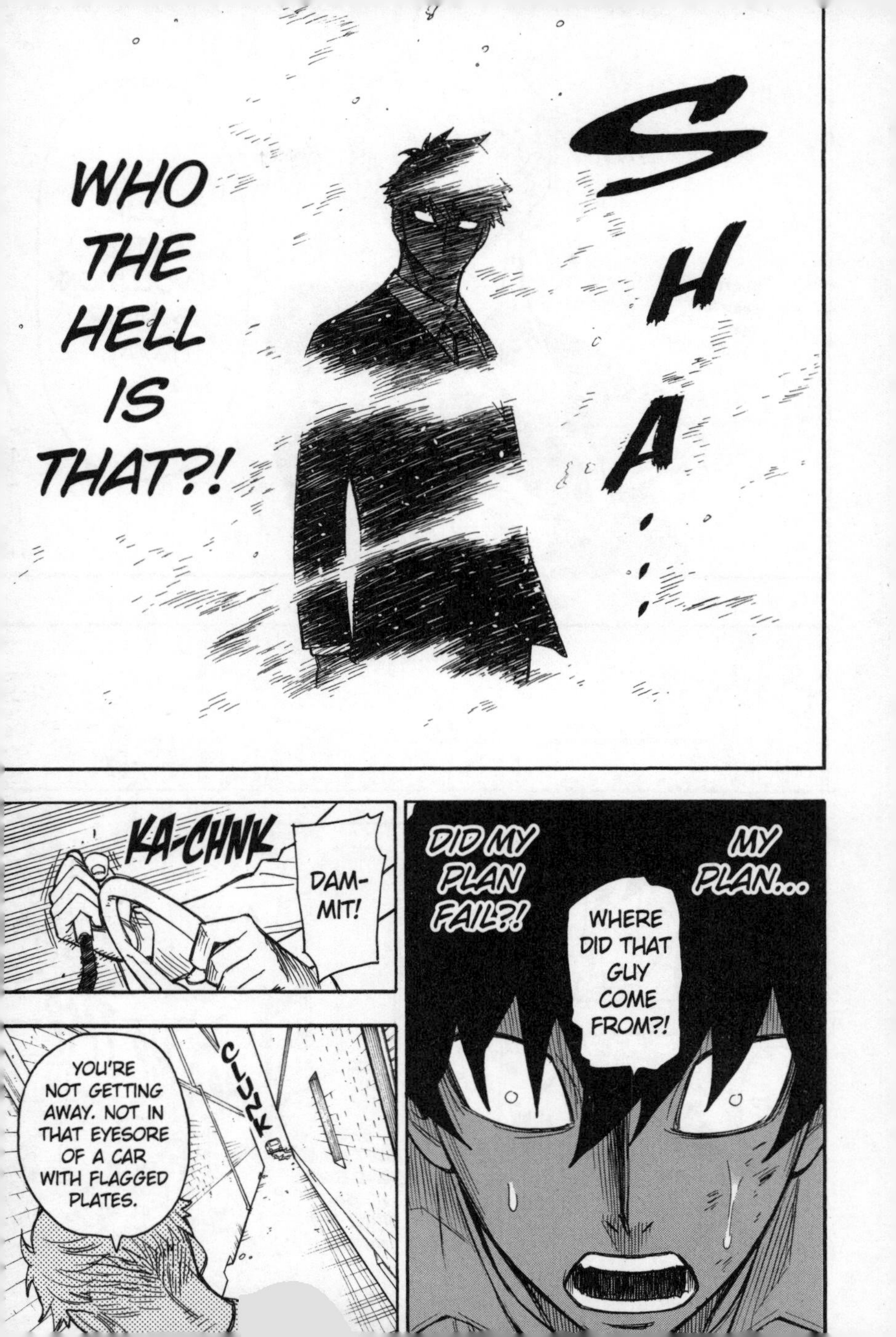
SHA...
WHO THE HELL IS THAT?!
MY PLAN...
DID MY PLAN FAIL?!
WHERE DID THAT GUY COME FROM?!
KA-CHNK
DAM-MIT!
CLUNK
YOU'RE NOT GETTING AWAY. NOT IN THAT EYESORE OF A CAR WITH FLAGGED PLATES.

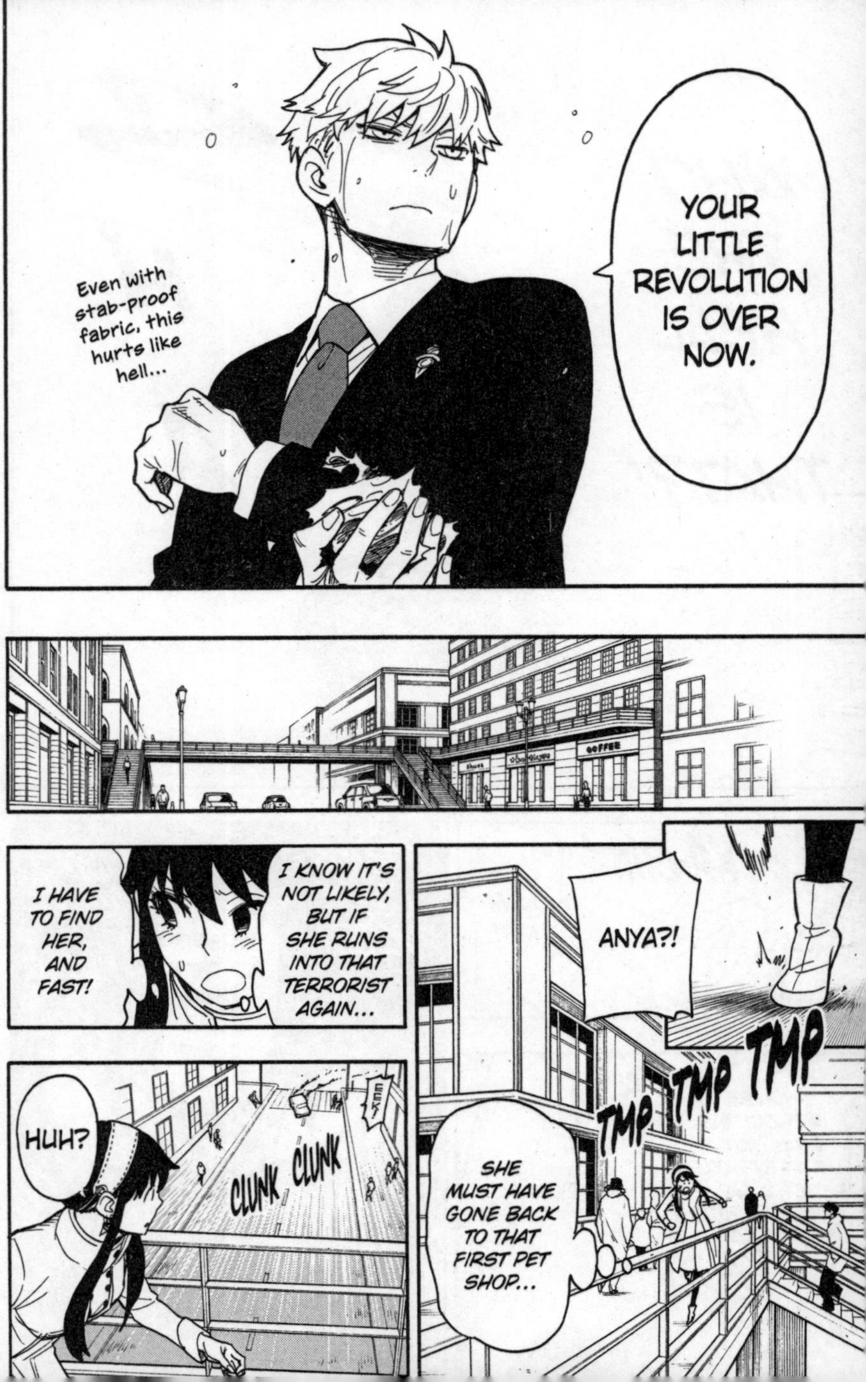
YOUR LITTLE REVOLUTION IS OVER NOW.
Even with stab-proof fabric, this hurts like hell...
COFFEE
ANYA?!
TMP TMP TMP TMP
SHE MUST HAVE GONE BACK TO THAT FIRST PET SHOP...
I KNOW IT'S NOT LIKELY, BUT IF SHE RUNS INTO THAT TERRORIST AGAIN...
I HAVE TO FIND HER, AND FAST!
EEK!
CLUNK CLUNK
HUH?

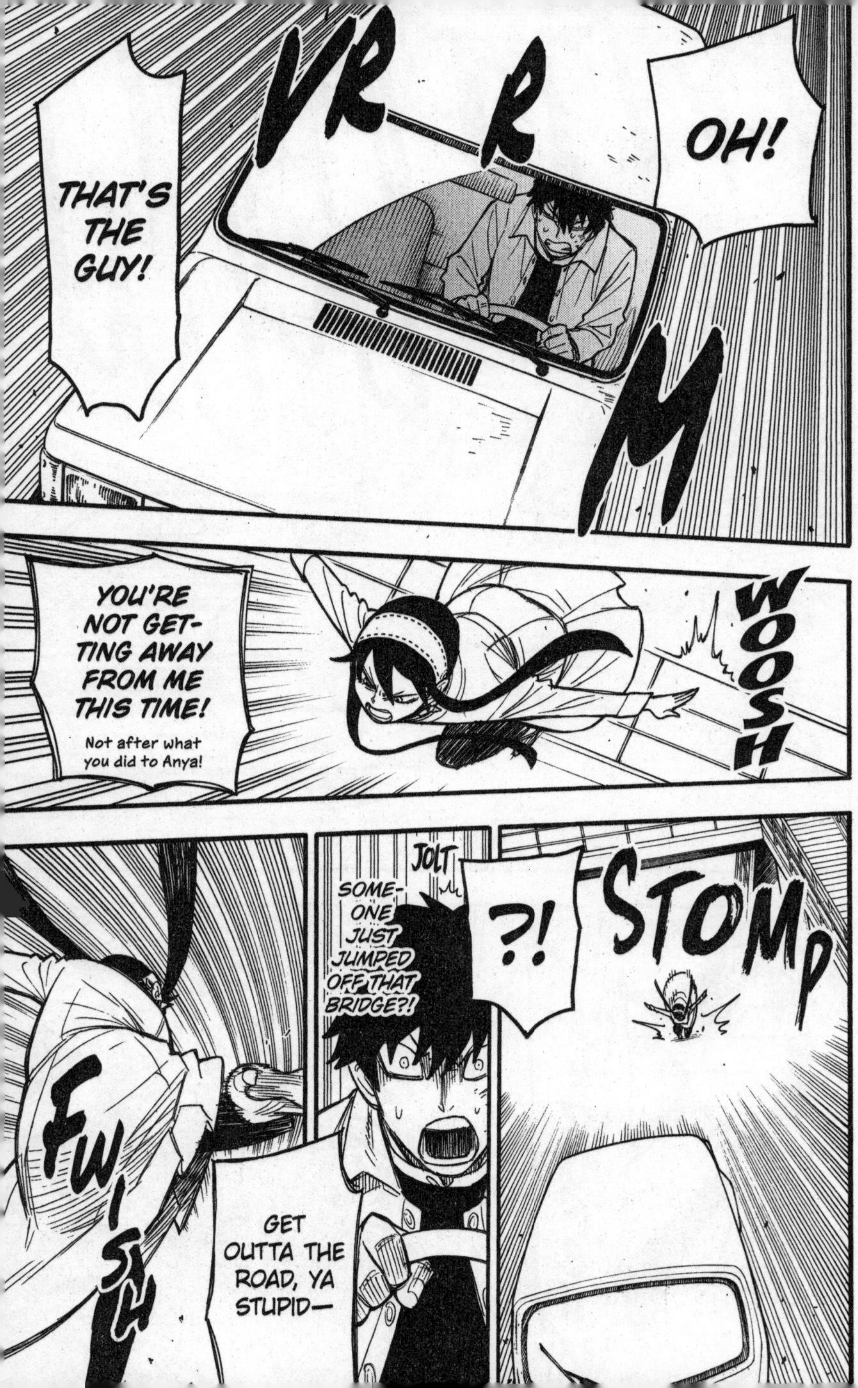
OH!
VRRM
THAT'S THE GUY!
WOOSH
YOU'RE NOT GET-TING AWAY FROM ME THIS TIME!
Not after what you did to Anya!
STOMP
?!
JOLT
SOME-ONE JUST JUMPED OFF THAT BRIDGE?!
GET OUTTA THE ROAD, YA STUPID—
FWISH

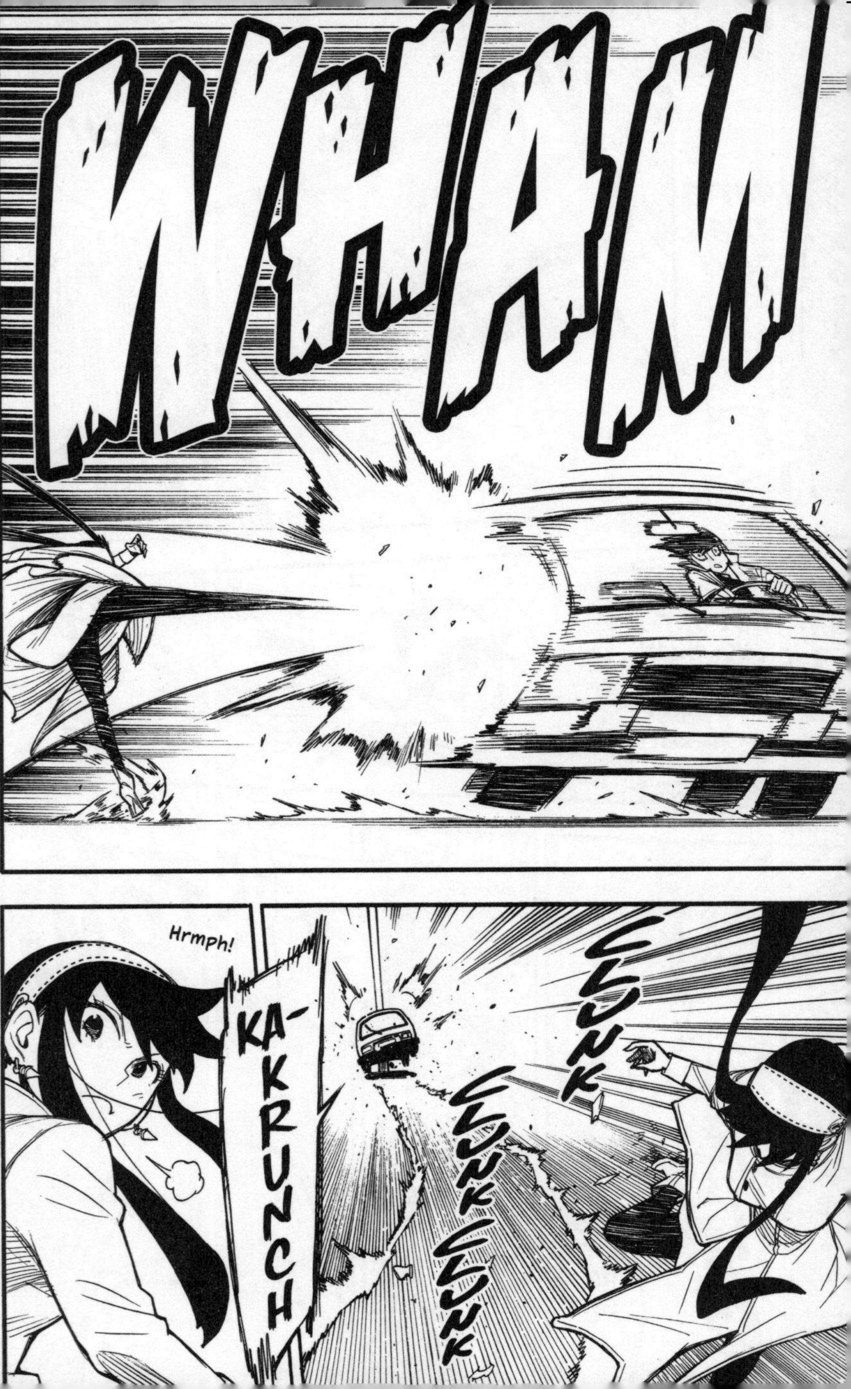
WHAM
CLUNK
CLUNK
CLUNK
KA-KRUNCH
Hrmph!

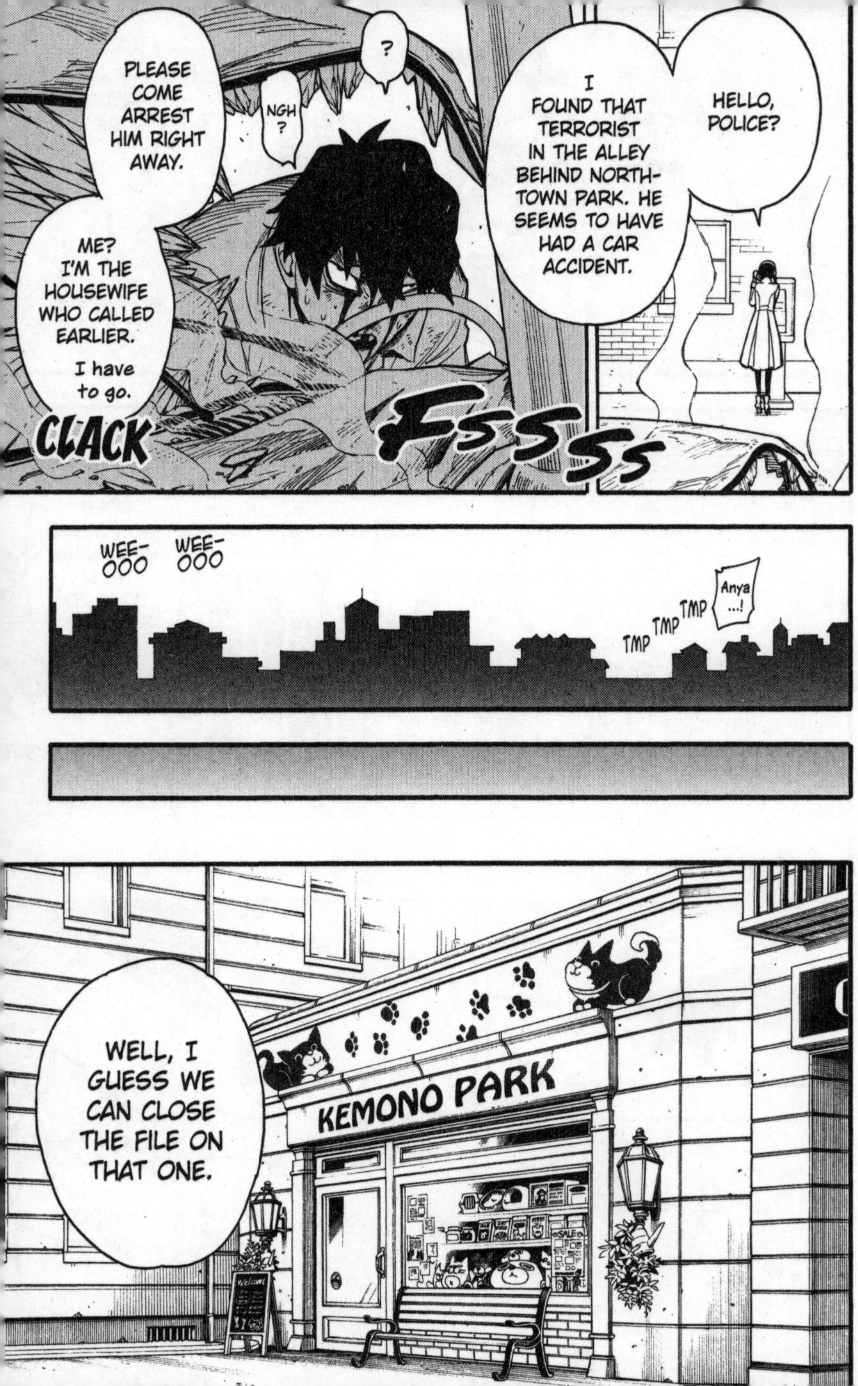
HELLO, POLICE?
I FOUND THAT TERRORIST IN THE ALLEY BEHIND NORTH-TOWN PARK. HE SEEMS TO HAVE HAD A CAR ACCIDENT.
?
NGH?
PLEASE COME ARREST HIM RIGHT AWAY.
ME? I'M THE HOUSEWIFE WHO CALLED EARLIER.
I have to go.
FSSSSS
CLACK
Anya ...!
TMP TMP TMP
WEE-OOO WEE-OOO
KEMONO PARK
WELL, I GUESS WE CAN CLOSE THE FILE ON THAT ONE.

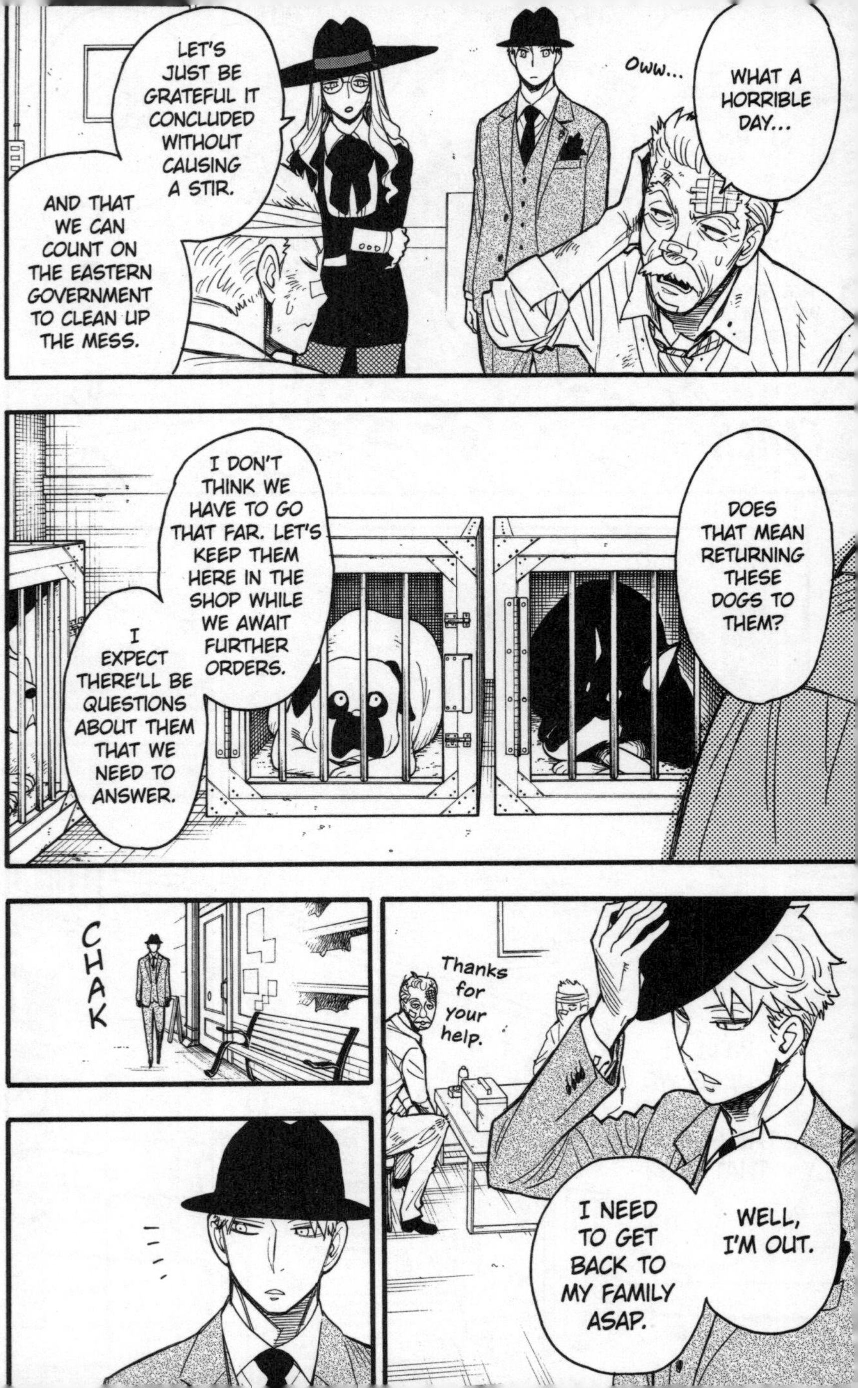
Oww...
WHAT A HORRIBLE DAY...
LET'S JUST BE GRATEFUL IT CONCLUDED WITHOUT CAUSING A STIR.
AND THAT WE CAN COUNT ON THE EASTERN GOVERNMENT TO CLEAN UP THE MESS.
DOES THAT MEAN RETURNING THESE DOGS TO THEM?
I DON'T THINK WE HAVE TO GO THAT FAR. LET'S KEEP THEM HERE IN THE SHOP WHILE WE AWAIT FURTHER ORDERS.
I EXPECT THERE'LL BE QUESTIONS ABOUT THEM THAT WE NEED TO ANSWER.
WELL, I'M OUT.
I NEED TO GET BACK TO MY FAMILY ASAP.
Thanks for your help.
CHAK

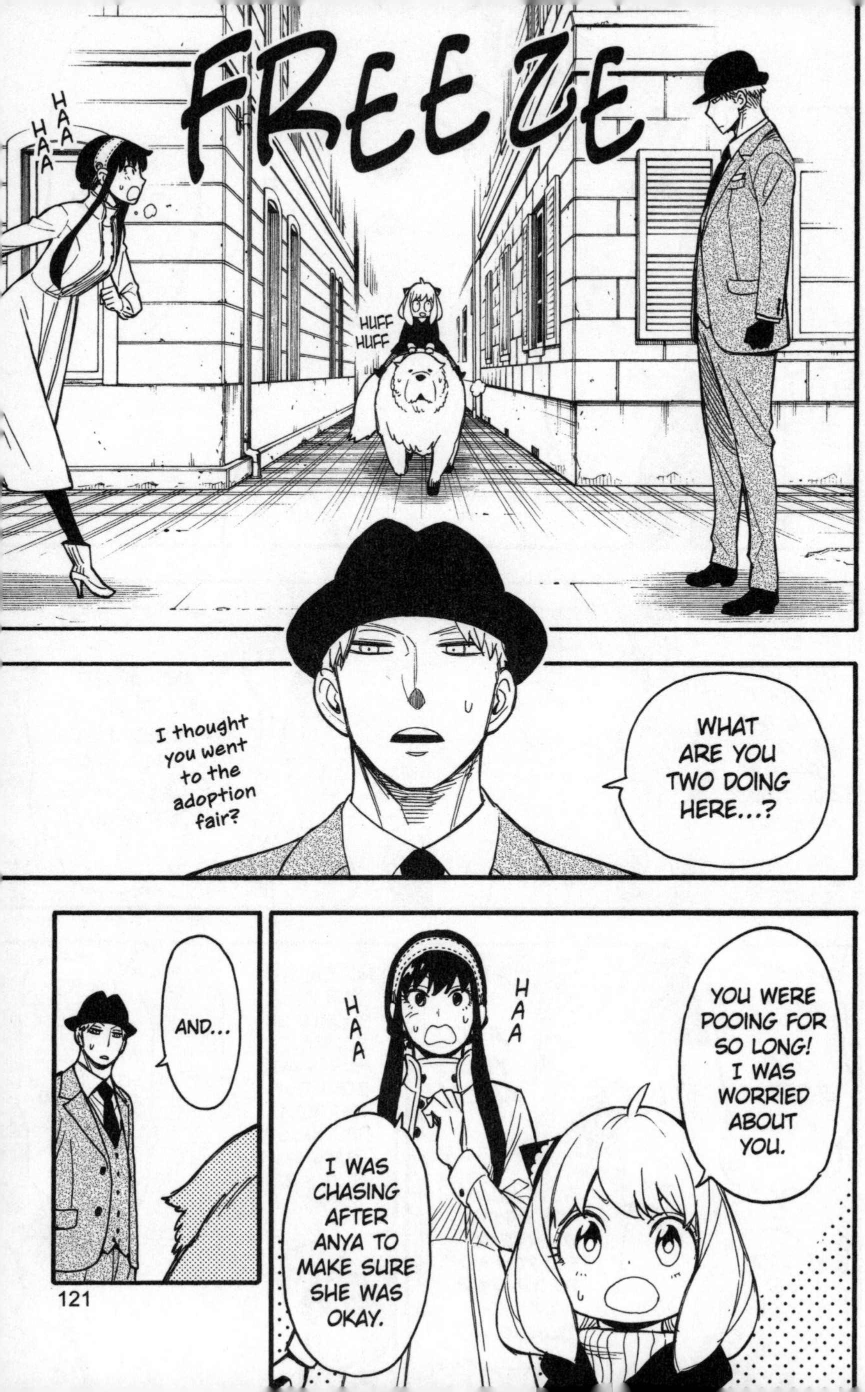
FREEZE
HUFF HUFF
HAA HA-A HAA
WHAT ARE YOU TWO DOING HERE...?
I thought you went to the adoption fair?
YOU WERE POOING FOR SO LONG! I WAS WORRIED ABOUT YOU.
HAA HAA
I WAS CHASING AFTER ANYA TO MAKE SURE SHE WAS OKAY.
AND...

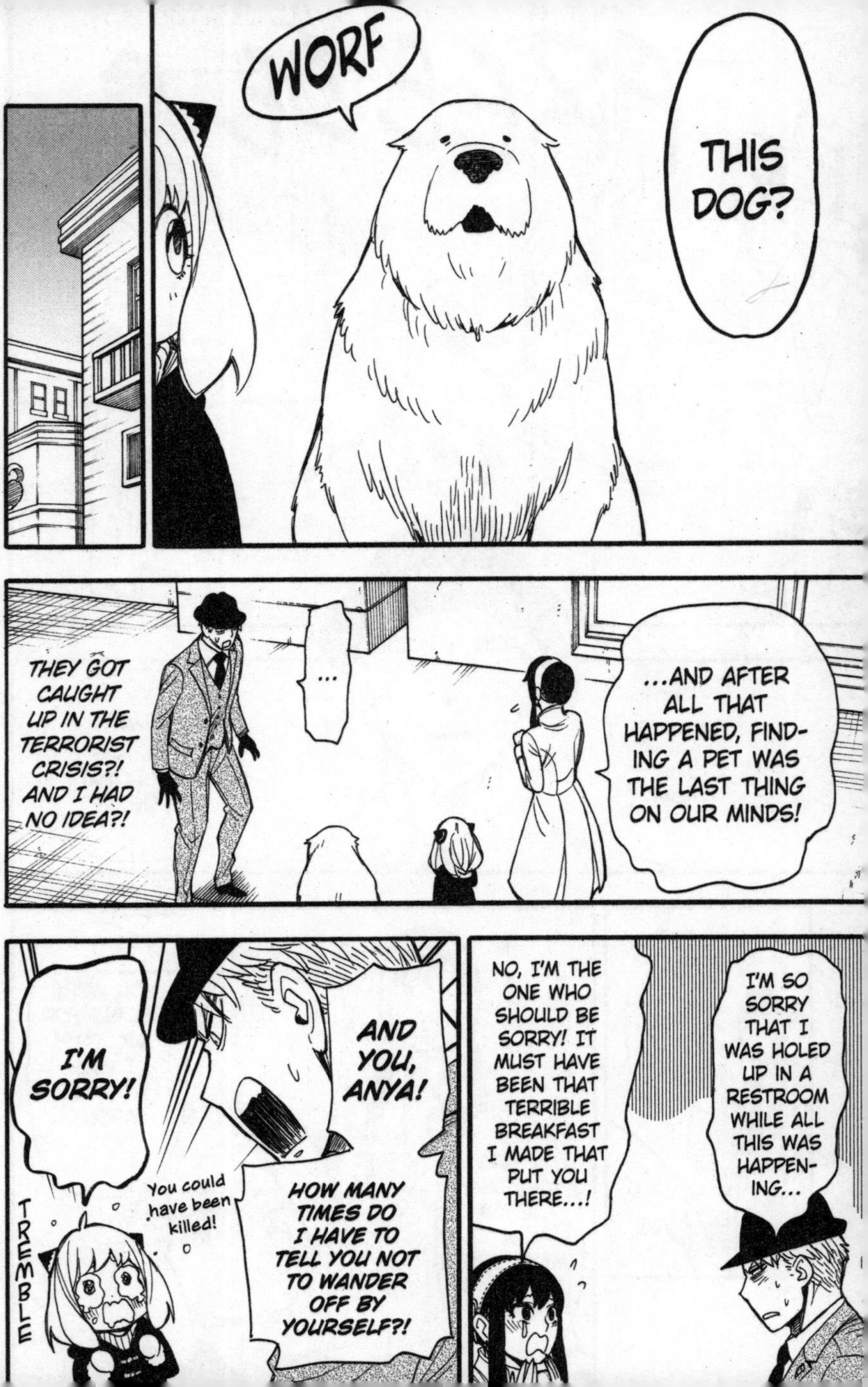

THIS DOG?
WORF
...AND AFTER ALL THAT HAPPENED, FINDING A PET WAS THE LAST THING ON OUR MINDS!
...
THEY GOT CAUGHT UP IN THE TERRORIST CRISIS?! AND I HAD NO IDEA?!
I'M SO SORRY THAT I WAS HOLED UP IN A RESTROOM WHILE ALL THIS WAS HAPPENING...
NO, I'M THE ONE WHO SHOULD BE SORRY! IT MUST HAVE BEEN THAT TERRIBLE BREAKFAST I MADE THAT PUT YOU THERE...!
AND YOU, ANYA!
HOW MANY TIMES DO I HAVE TO TELL YOU NOT TO WANDER OFF BY YOURSELF?!
You could have been killed!
I'M SORRY!
TREMBLE

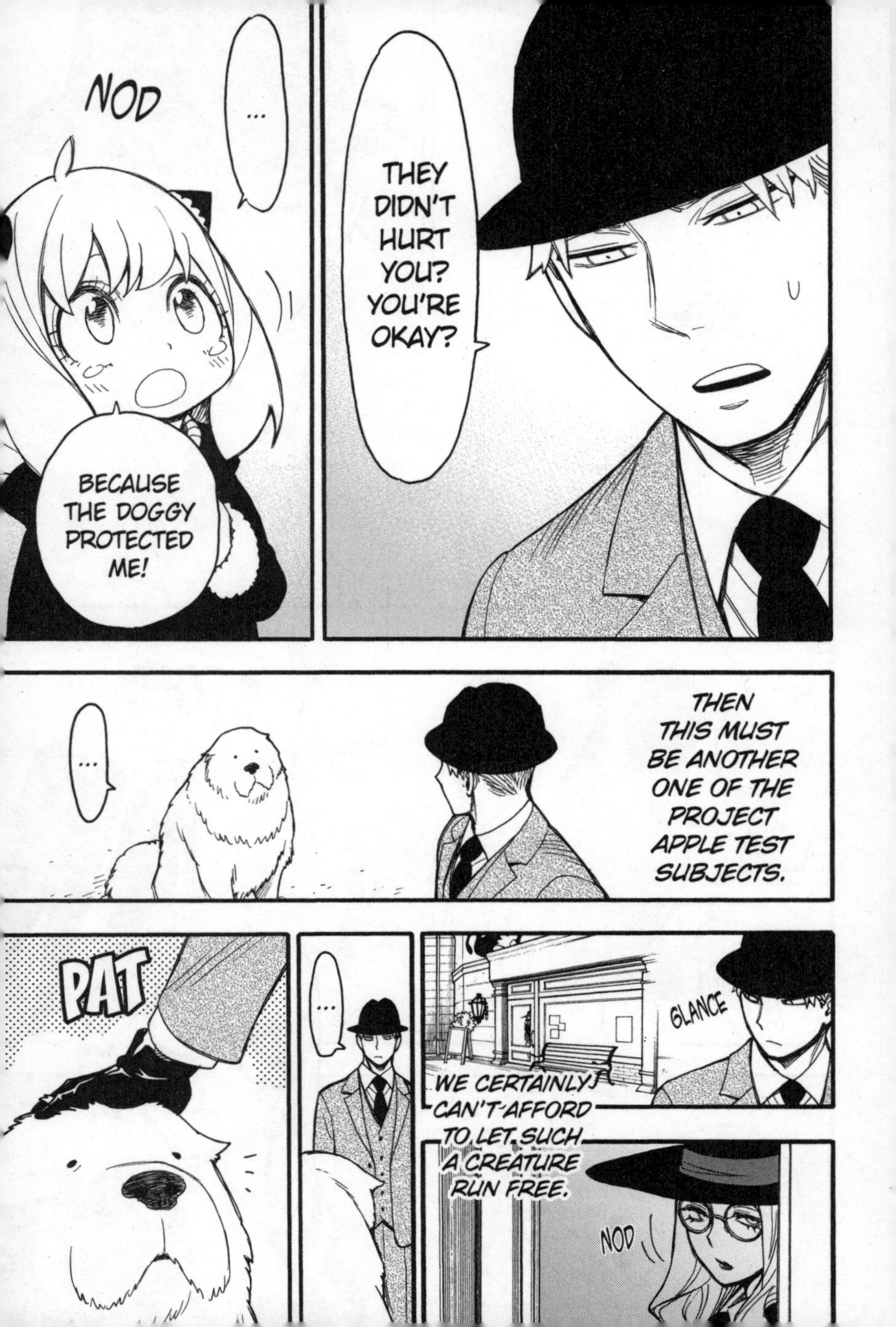
THEY DIDN'T HURT YOU? YOU'RE OKAY?
...
NOD
BECAUSE THE DOGGY PROTECTED ME!
THEN THIS MUST BE ANOTHER ONE OF THE PROJECT APPLE TEST SUBJECTS.
...
GLANCE
WE CERTAINLY CAN'T AFFORD TO LET SUCH A CREATURE RUN FREE.
NOD
...
PAT

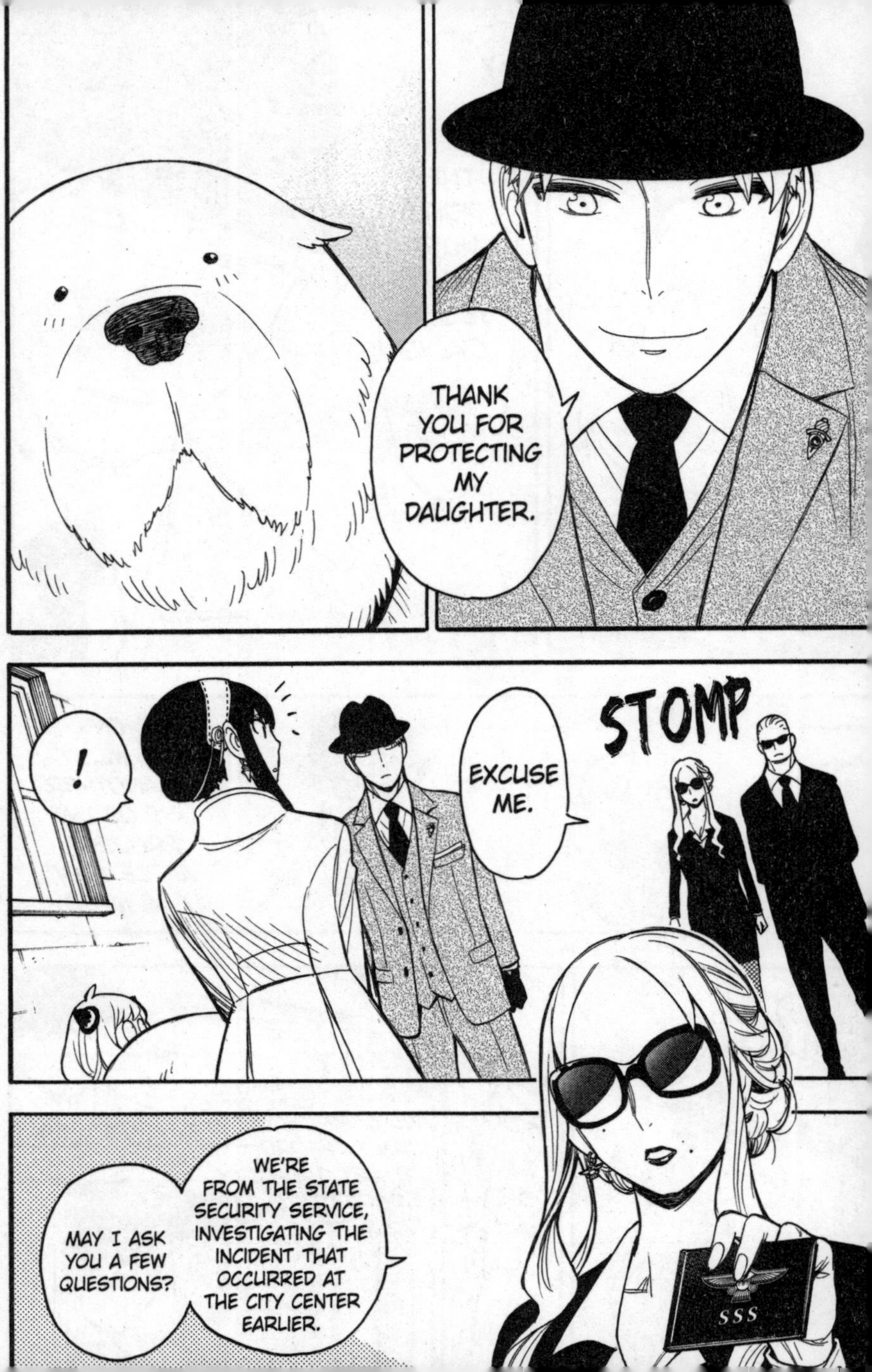
THANK YOU FOR PROTECTING MY DAUGHTER.
STOMP
EXCUSE ME.
!
WE'RE FROM THE STATE SECURITY SERVICE, INVESTIGATING THE INCIDENT THAT OCCURRED AT THE CITY CENTER EARLIER.
MAY I ASK YOU A FEW QUESTIONS?
SSS

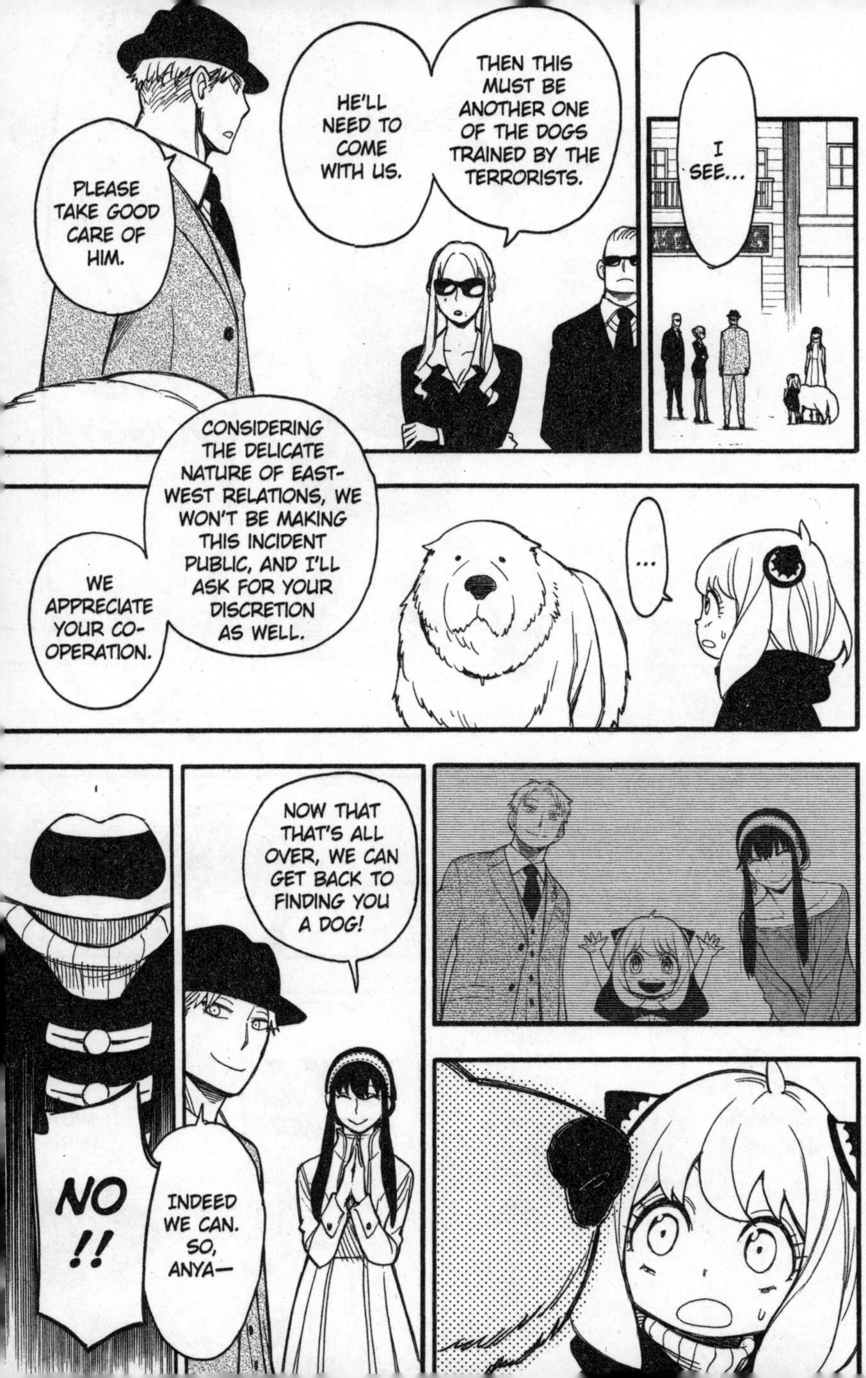
I SEE...
THEN THIS MUST BE ANOTHER ONE OF THE DOGS TRAINED BY THE TERRORISTS.
HE'LL NEED TO COME WITH US.
PLEASE TAKE GOOD CARE OF HIM.
...
CONSIDERING THE DELICATE NATURE OF EAST-WEST RELATIONS, WE WON'T BE MAKING THIS INCIDENT PUBLIC, AND I'LL ASK FOR YOUR DISCRETION AS WELL.
WE APPRECIATE YOUR CO-OPERATION.
NOW THAT THAT'S ALL OVER, WE CAN GET BACK TO FINDING YOU A DOG!
INDEED WE CAN. SO, ANYA—
NO !!

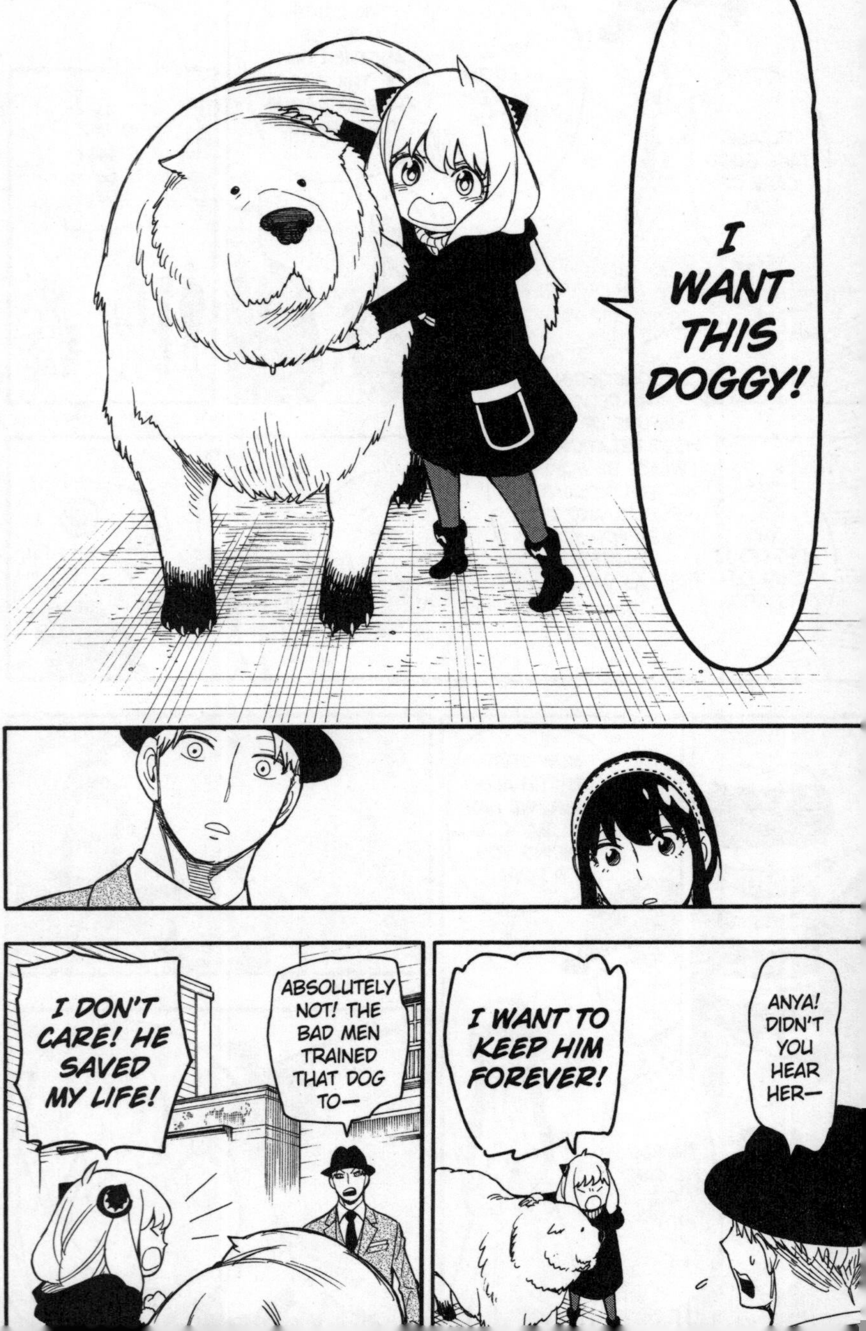
I WANT THIS DOGGY!
ANYA! DIDN'T YOU HEAR HER—
I WANT TO KEEP HIM FOREVER!
ABSOLULTELY NOT! THE BAD MEN TRAINED THAT DOG TO—
I DON'T CARE! HE SAVED MY LIFE!

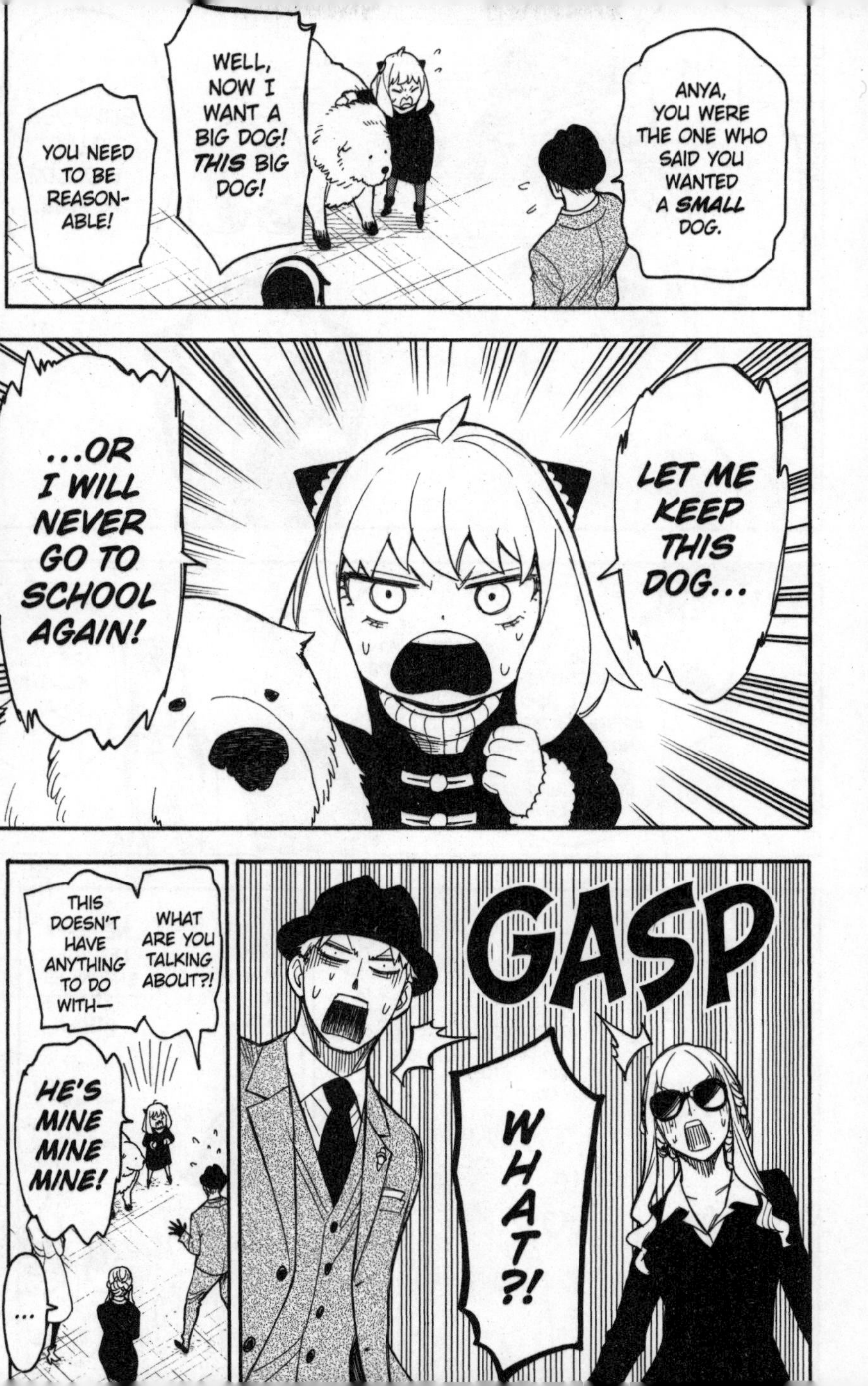
ANYA, YOU WERE THE ONE WHO SAID YOU WANTED A SMALL DOG.
WELL, NOW I WANT A BIG DOG! THIS BIG DOG!
YOU NEED TO BE REASON-ABLE!
LET ME KEEP THIS DOG...
...OR I WILL NEVER GO TO SCHOOL AGAIN!
GASP
WHAT?!
WHAT ARE YOU TALKING ABOUT?!
THIS DOESN'T HAVE ANYTHING TO DO WITH—
HE'S MINE MINE MINE!
...

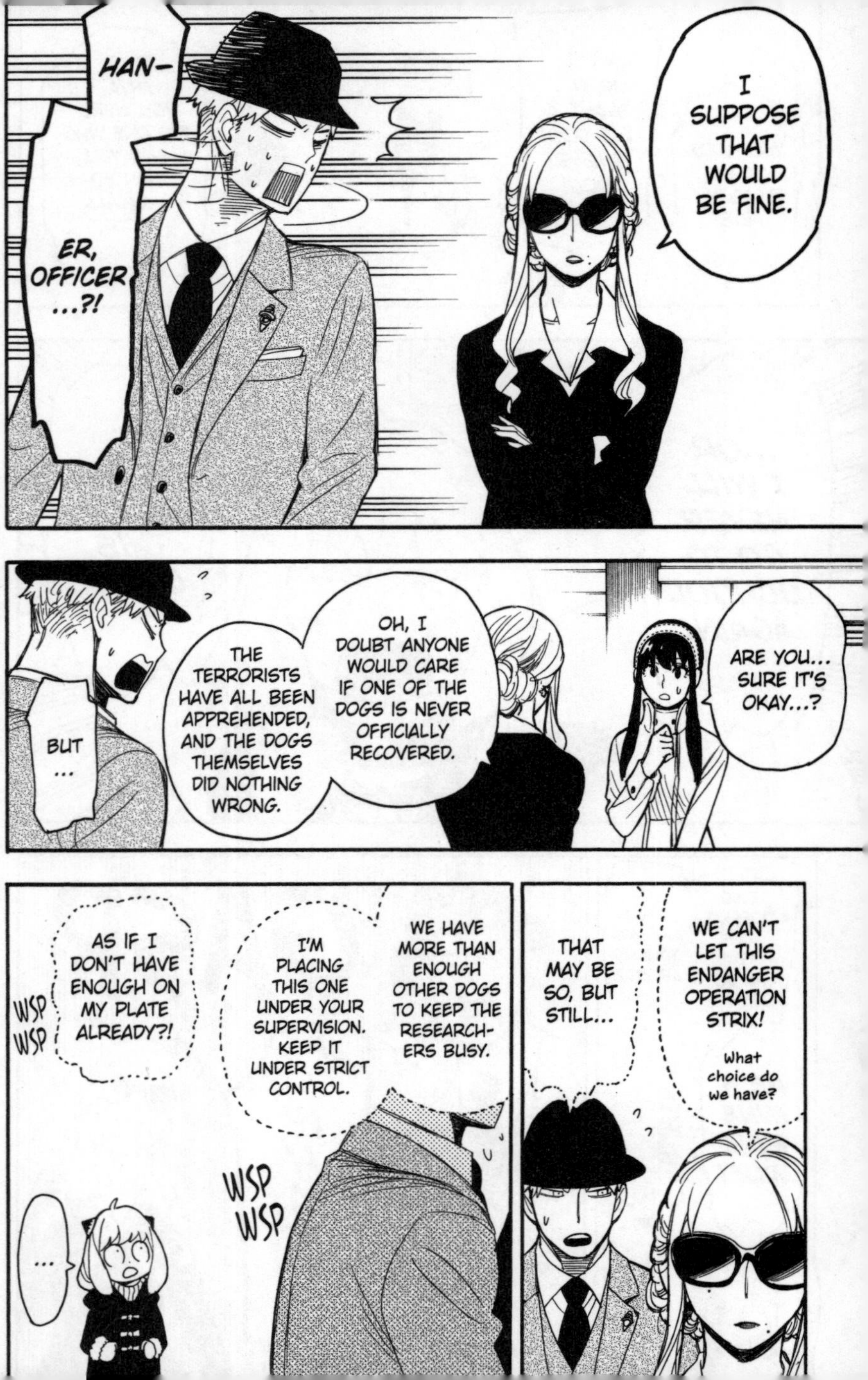
I SUPPOSE THAT WOULD BE FINE.
HAN–
ER, OFFICER ...?!
ARE YOU... SURE IT'S OKAY...?
OH, I DOUBT ANYONE WOULD CARE IF ONE OF THE DOGS IS NEVER OFFICIALLY RECOVERED.
THE TERRORISTS HAVE ALL BEEN APPREHENDED, AND THE DOGS THEMSELVES DID NOTHING WRONG.
BUT ...
WE CAN'T LET THIS ENDANGER OPERATION STRIX!
What choice do we have?
THAT MAY BE SO, BUT STILL...
WE HAVE MORE THAN ENOUGH OTHER DOGS TO KEEP THE RESEARCH-ERS BUSY.
I'M PLACING THIS ONE UNDER YOUR SUPERVISION. KEEP IT UNDER STRICT CONTROL.
AS IF I DON'T HAVE ENOUGH ON MY PLATE ALREADY?!
WSP WSP
WSP WSP
...

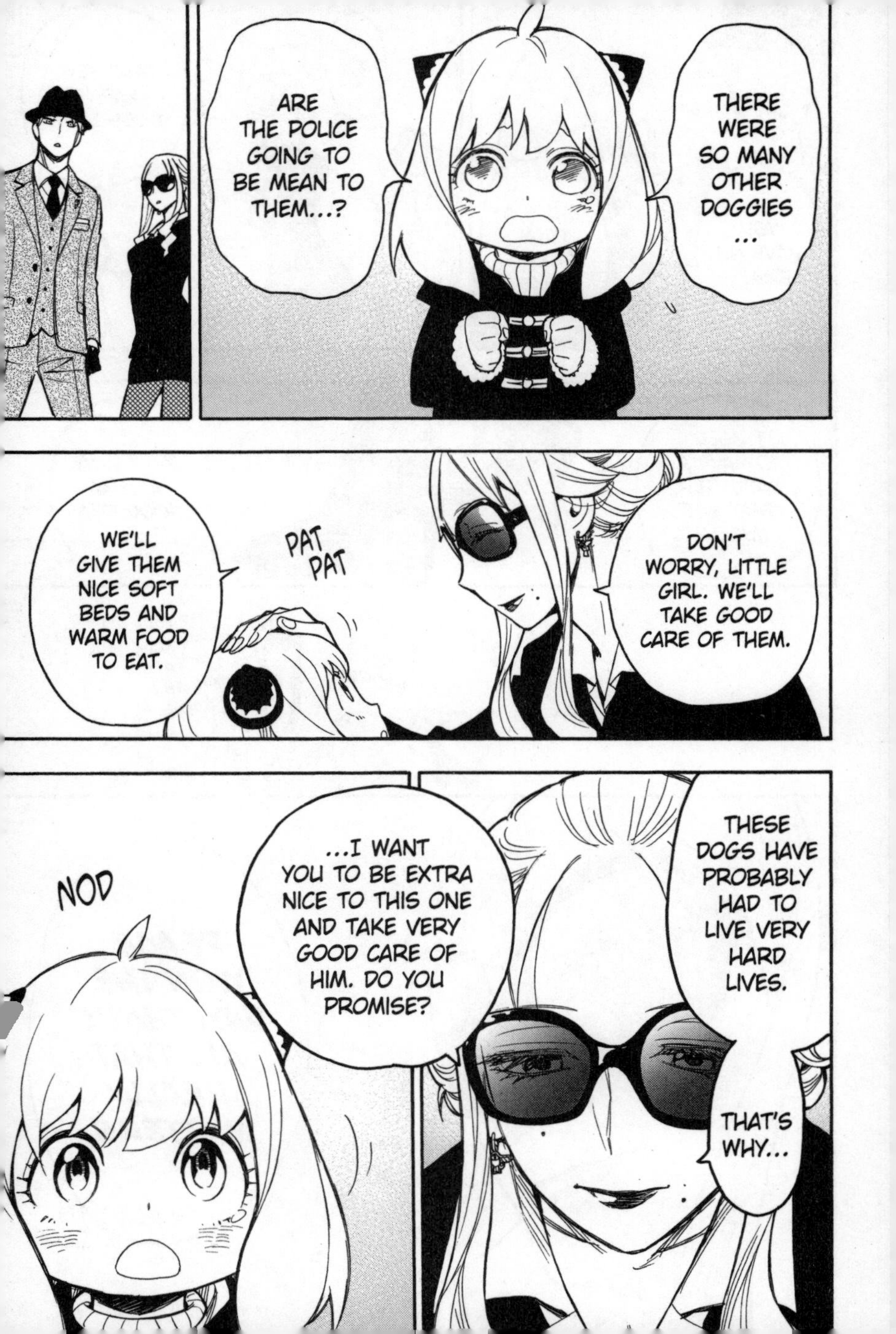
THERE WERE SO MANY OTHER DOGGIES ...
ARE THE POLICE GOING TO BE MEAN TO THEM...?
DON'T WORRY, LITTLE GIRL. WE'LL TAKE GOOD CARE OF THEM.
PAT PAT
WE'LL GIVE THEM NICE SOFT BEDS AND WARM FOOD TO EAT.
THESE DOGS HAVE PROBABLY HAD TO LIVE VERY HARD LIVES.
THAT'S WHY...
...I WANT YOU TO BE EXTRA NICE TO THIS ONE AND TAKE VERY GOOD CARE OF HIM. DO YOU PROMISE?
NOD

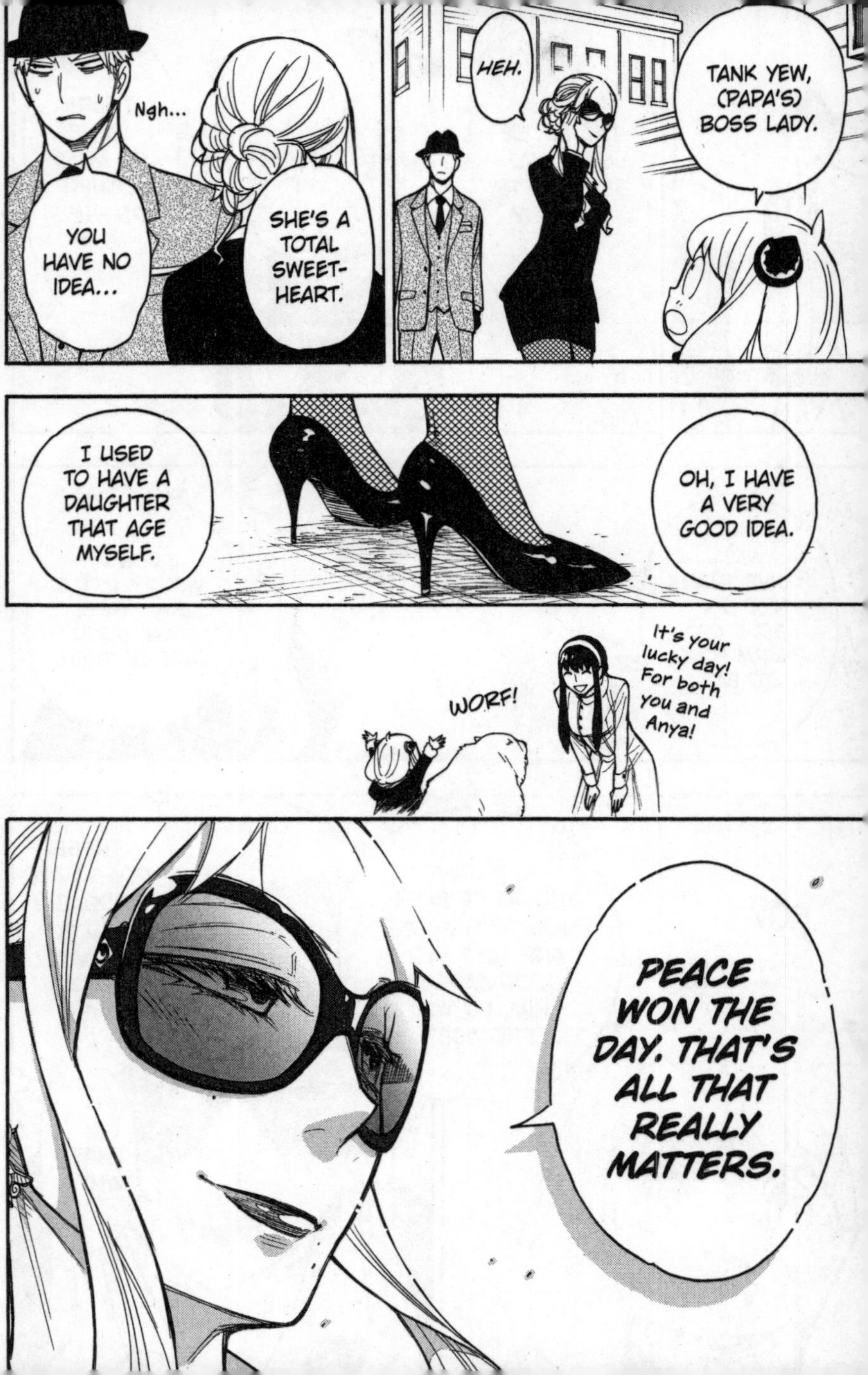
TANK YEW, (PAPA'S) BOSS LADY.
HEH.
SHE'S A TOTAL SWEET-HEART.
Ngh...
YOU HAVE NO IDEA...
OH, I HAVE A VERY GOOD IDEA.
I USED TO HAVE A DAUGHTER THAT AGE MYSELF.
It's your lucky day! For both you and Anya!
WORF!
PEACE WON THE DAY. THAT'S ALL THAT REALLY MATTERS.

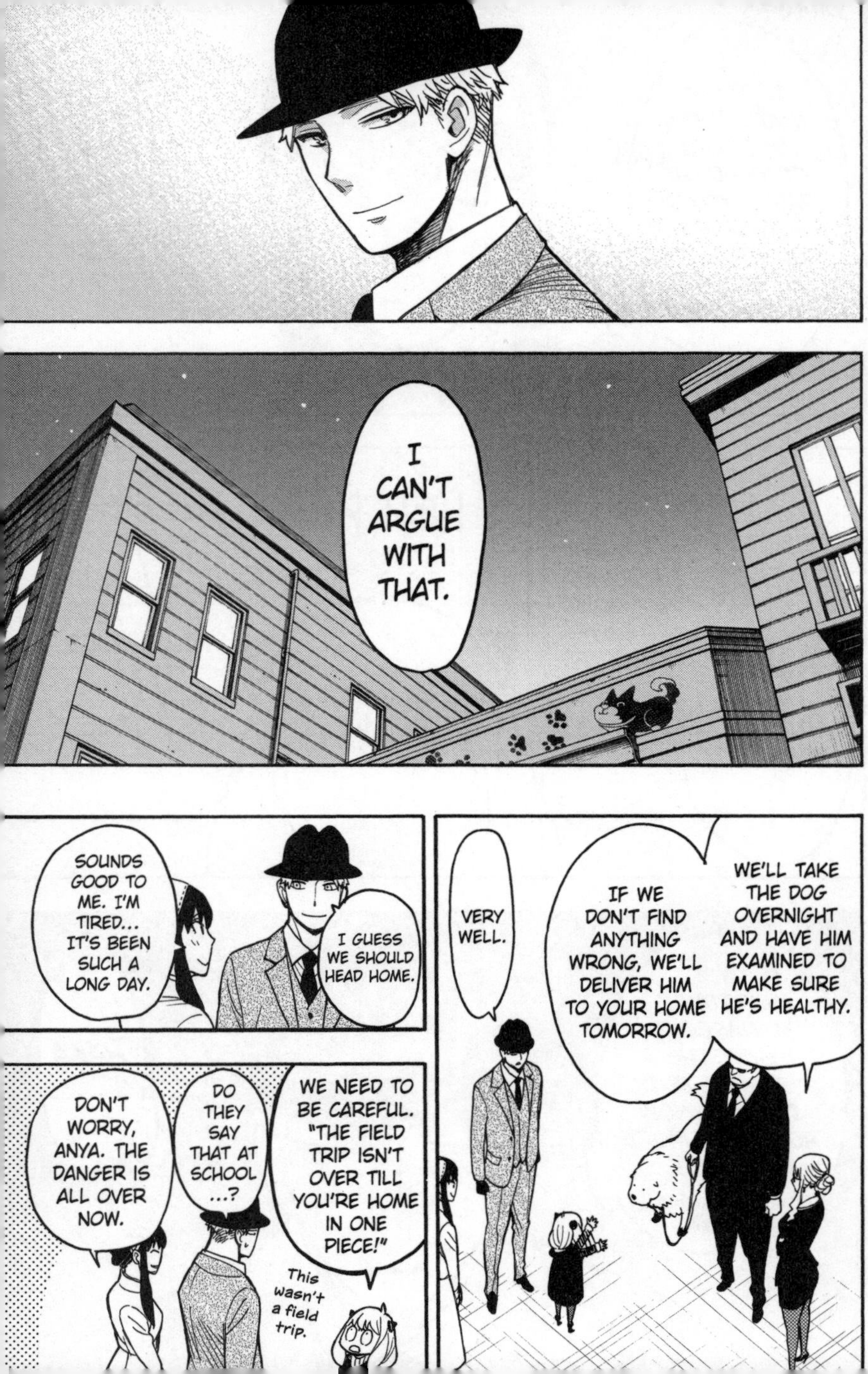
I CAN'T ARGUE WITH THAT.
WE'LL TAKE THE DOG OVERNIGHT AND HAVE HIM EXAMINED TO MAKE SURE HE'S HEALTHY.
IF WE DON'T FIND ANYTHING WRONG, WE'LL DELIVER HIM TO YOUR HOME TOMORROW.
VERY WELL.
I GUESS WE SHOULD HEAD HOME.
SOUNDS GOOD TO ME. I'M TIRED... IT'S BEEN SUCH A LONG DAY.
WE NEED TO BE CAREFUL. "THE FIELD TRIP ISN'T OVER TILL YOU'RE HOME IN ONE PIECE!"
DO THEY SAY THAT AT SCHOOL ...?
DON'T WORRY, ANYA. THE DANGER IS ALL OVER NOW.
This wasn't a field trip.

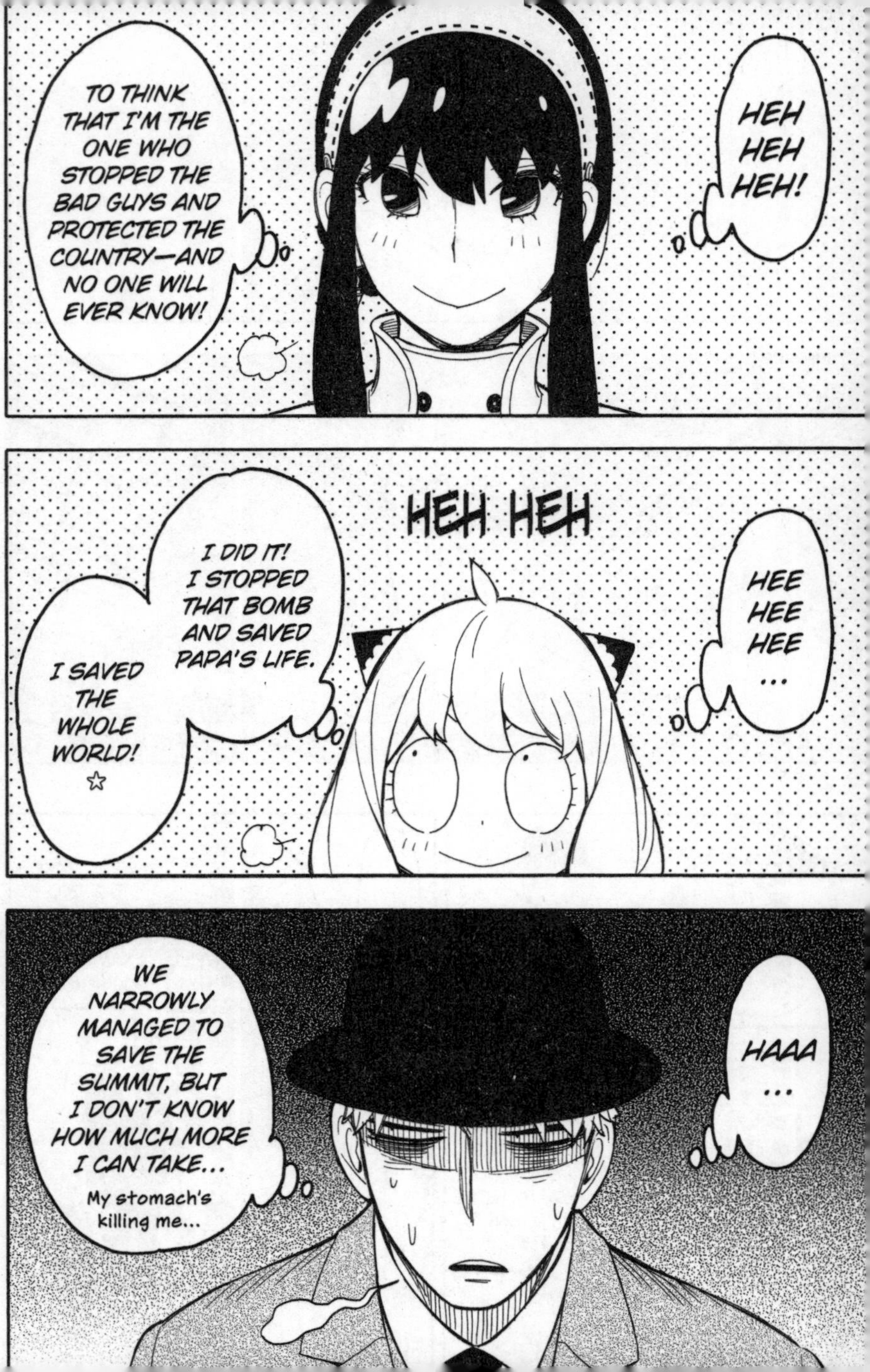
HEH HEH HEH!
TO THINK THAT I'M THE ONE WHO STOPPED THE BAD GUYS AND PROTECTED THE COUNTRY—AND NO ONE WILL EVER KNOW!
HEE HEE HEE ...
HEH HEH
I DID IT! I STOPPED THAT BOMB AND SAVED PAPA'S LIFE.
I SAVED THE WHOLE WORLD! ☆
HAAA ...
WE NARROWLY MANAGED TO SAVE THE SUMMIT, BUT I DON'T KNOW HOW MUCH MORE I CAN TAKE...
My stomach's killing me...

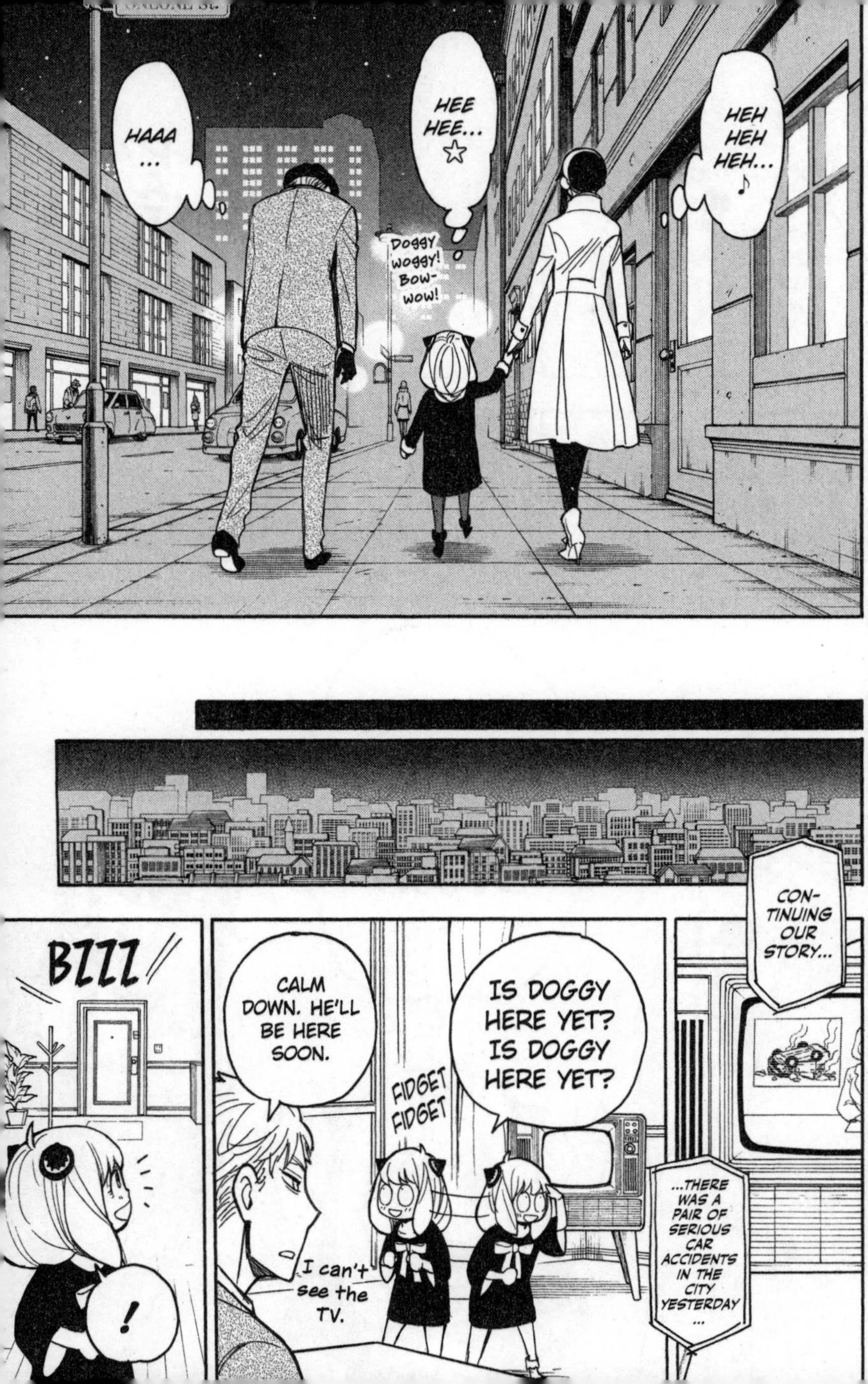
HEH HEH HEH... ♪
HEE HEE... ☆
Doggy woggy! Bow-wow!
HAAA...
CON-TINUING OUR STORY...
...THERE WAS A PAIR OF SERIOUS CAR ACCIDENTS IN THE CITY YESTERDAY...
IS DOGGY HERE YET? IS DOGGY HERE YET?
FIDGET FIDGET
CALM DOWN. HE'LL BE HERE SOON.
I can't see the TV.
BZZZ
!

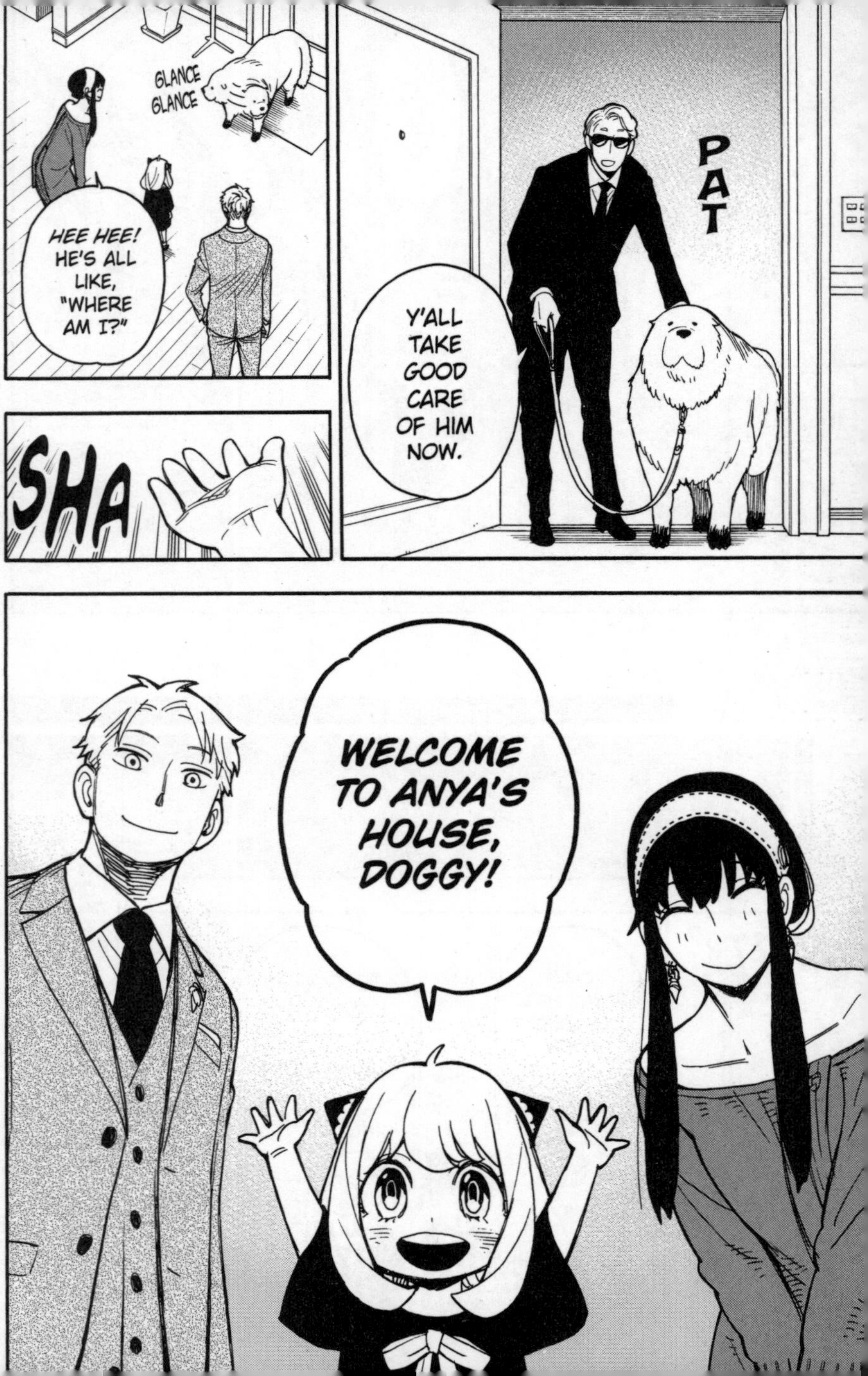
PAT
Y'ALL TAKE GOOD CARE OF HIM NOW.
GLANCE GLANCE
HEE HEE! HE'S ALL LIKE, "WHERE AM I?"
SHA
WELCOME TO ANYA'S HOUSE, DOGGY!

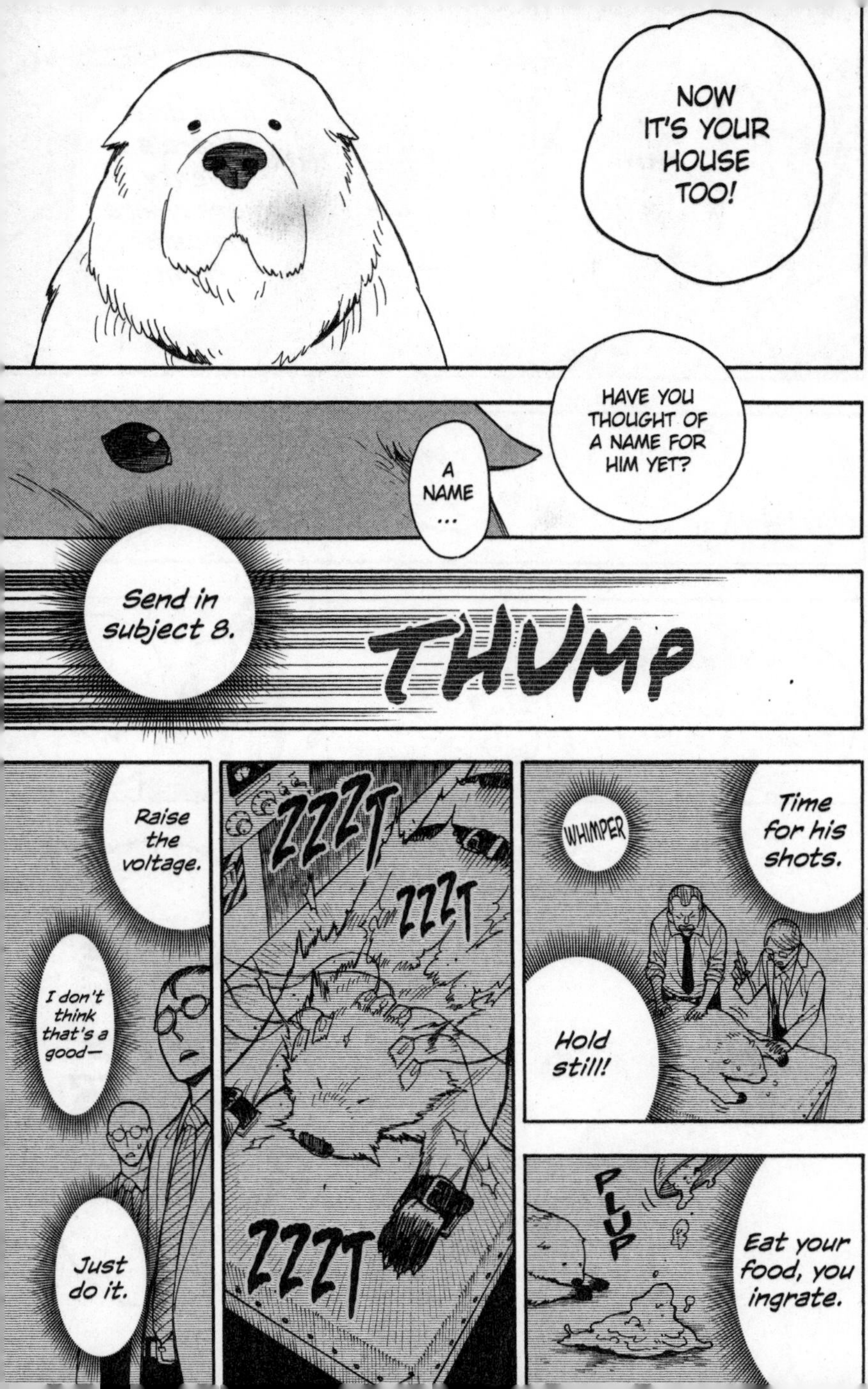
NOW IT'S YOUR HOUSE TOO!
HAVE YOU THOUGHT OF A NAME FOR HIM YET?
A NAME ...
THUMP
Send in subject 8.
Time for his shots.
WHIMPER
Hold still!
Eat your food, you ingrate.
PLUP
ZZZT
ZZZT
ZZZT
Raise the voltage.
I don't think that's a good—
Just do it.

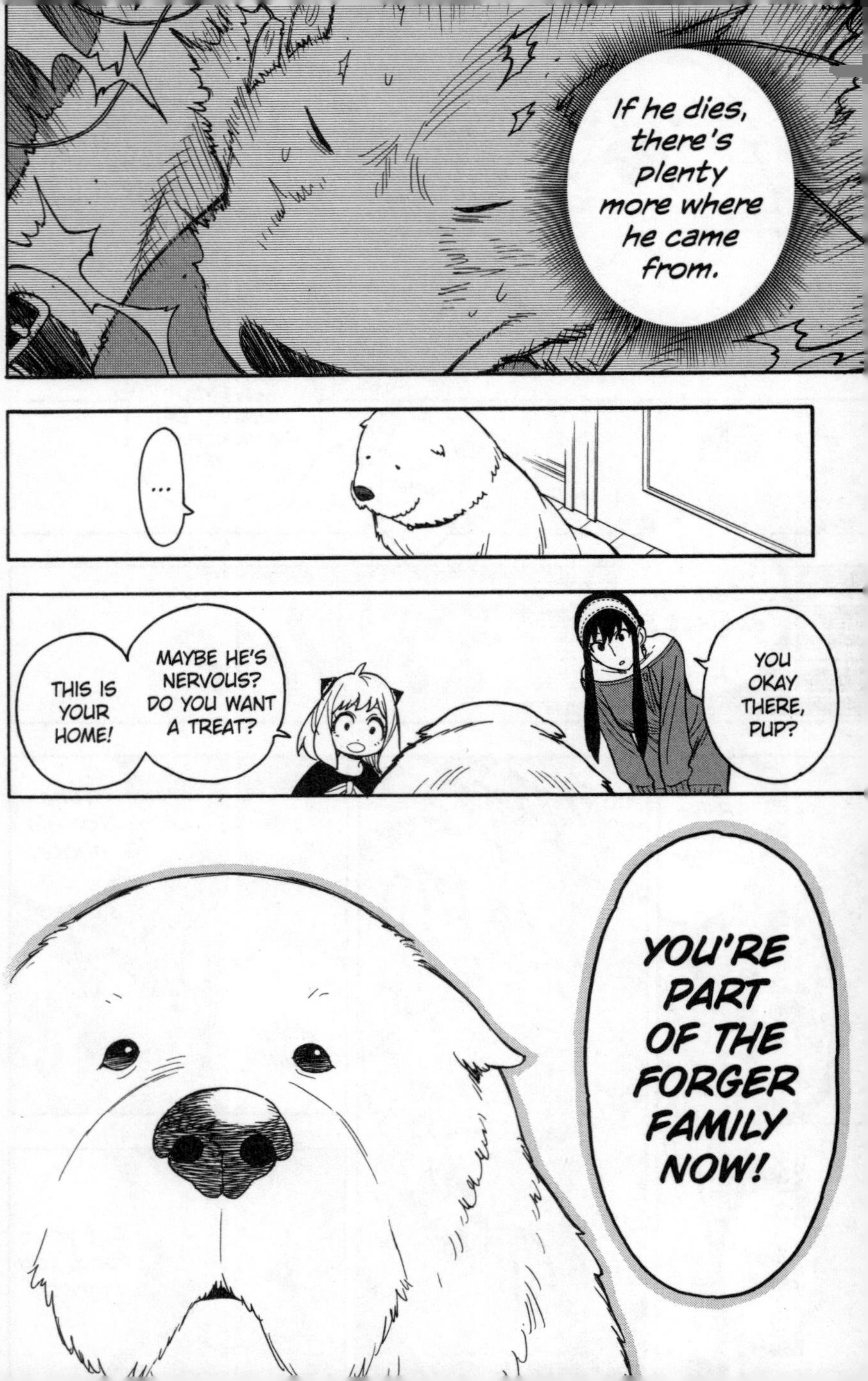
If he dies, there's plenty more where he came from.
...
YOU OKAY THERE, PUP?
MAYBE HE'S NERVOUS? DO YOU WANT A TREAT?
THIS IS YOUR HOME!
YOU'RE PART OF THE FORGER FAMILY NOW!

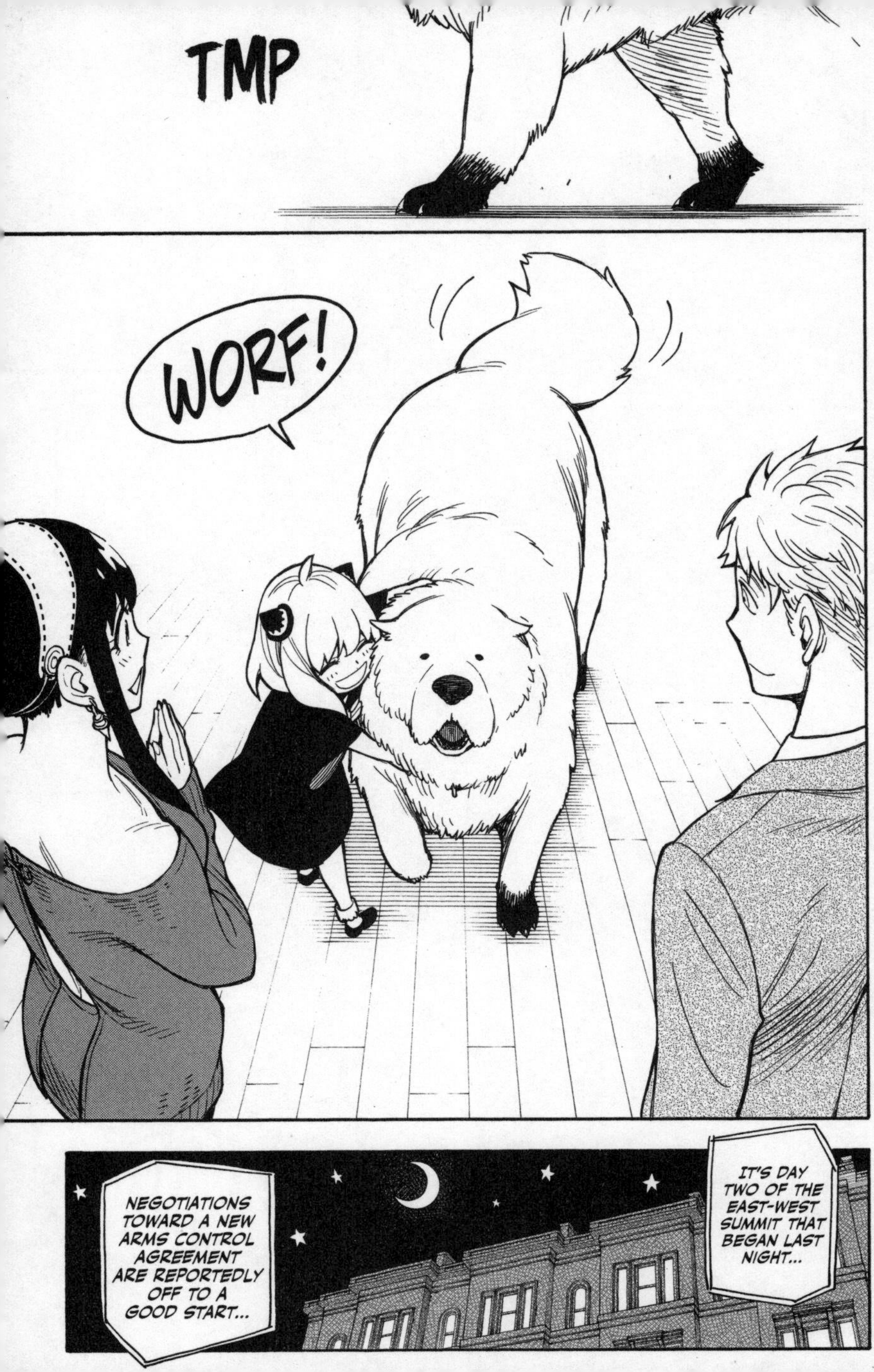
TMP
WORF!
IT'S DAY TWO OF THE EAST-WEST SUMMIT THAT BEGAN LAST NIGHT...
NEGOTIATIONS TOWARD A NEW ARMS CONTROL AGREEMENT ARE REPORTEDLY OFF TO A GOOD START...

SPY×FAMILY

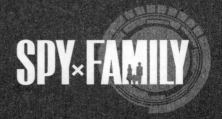

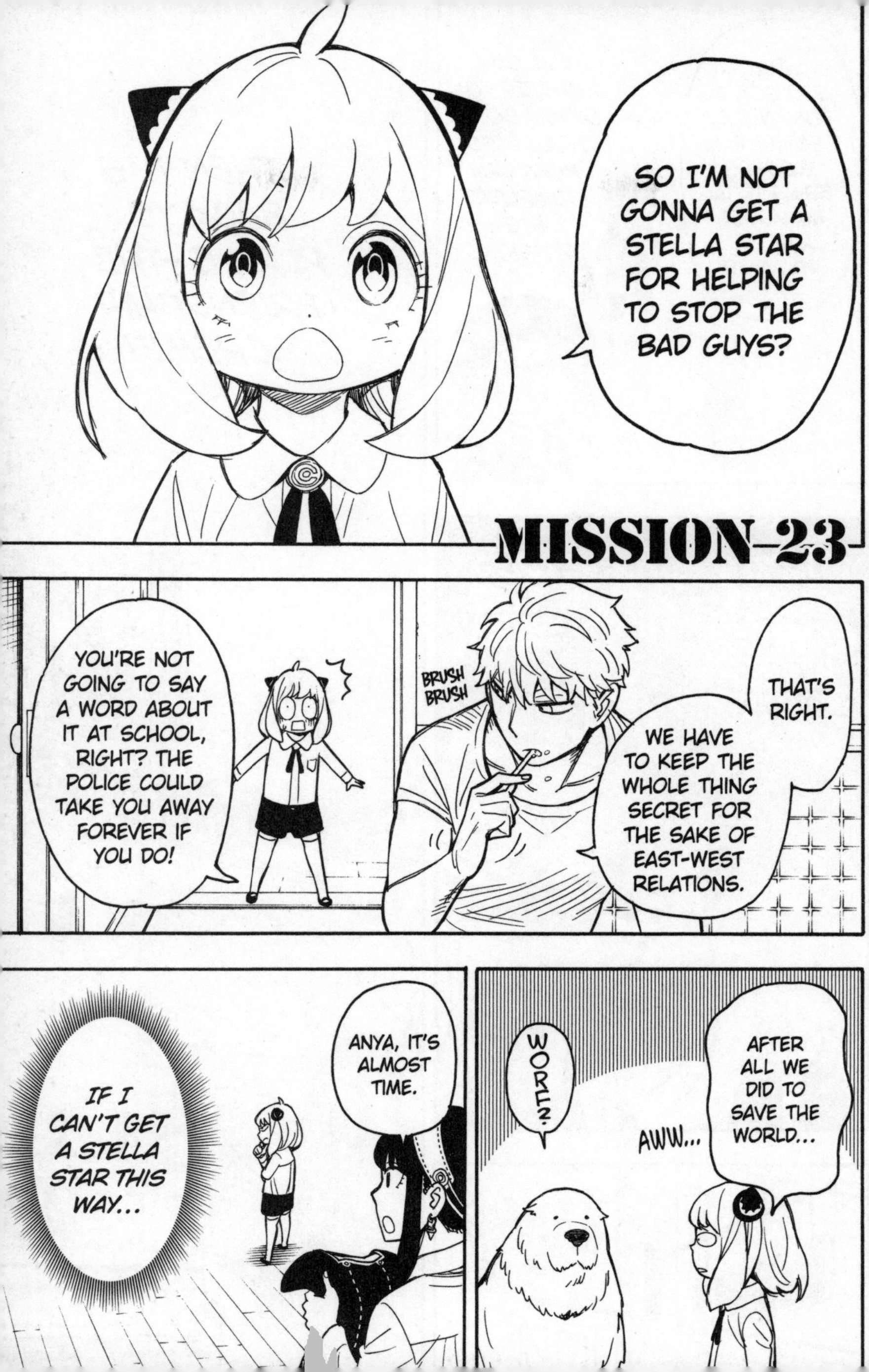
SO I'M NOT GONNA GET A STELLA STAR FOR HELPING TO STOP THE BAD GUYS?
MISSION 23
THAT'S RIGHT.
WE HAVE TO KEEP THE WHOLE THING SECRET FOR THE SAKE OF EAST-WEST RELATIONS.
BRUSH BRUSH
YOU'RE NOT GOING TO SAY A WORD ABOUT IT AT SCHOOL, RIGHT? THE POLICE COULD TAKE YOU AWAY FOREVER IF YOU DO!
AFTER ALL WE DID TO SAVE THE WORLD...
AWW...
WORF?
ANYA, IT'S ALMOST TIME.
IF I CAN'T GET A STELLA STAR THIS WAY...

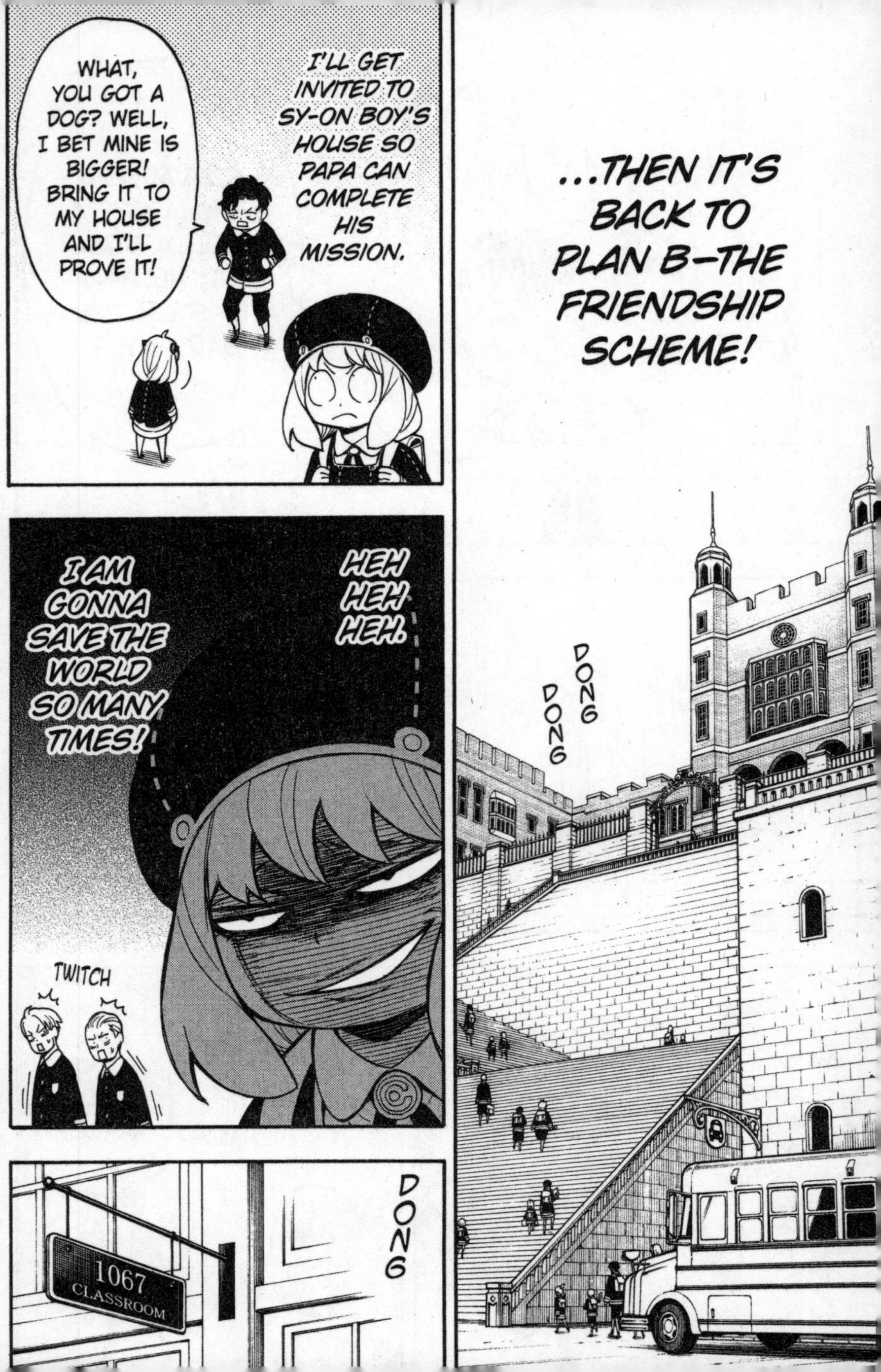
...THEN IT'S BACK TO PLAN B—THE FRIENDSHIP SCHEME!
DONG
DONG
I'LL GET INVITED TO SY-ON BOY'S HOUSE SO PAPA CAN COMPLETE HIS MISSION.
WHAT, YOU GOT A DOG? WELL, I BET MINE IS BIGGER! BRING IT TO MY HOUSE AND I'LL PROVE IT!
HEH HEH HEH.
I AM GONNA SAVE THE WORLD SO MANY TIMES!
TWITCH
DONG
1067 CLASSROOM

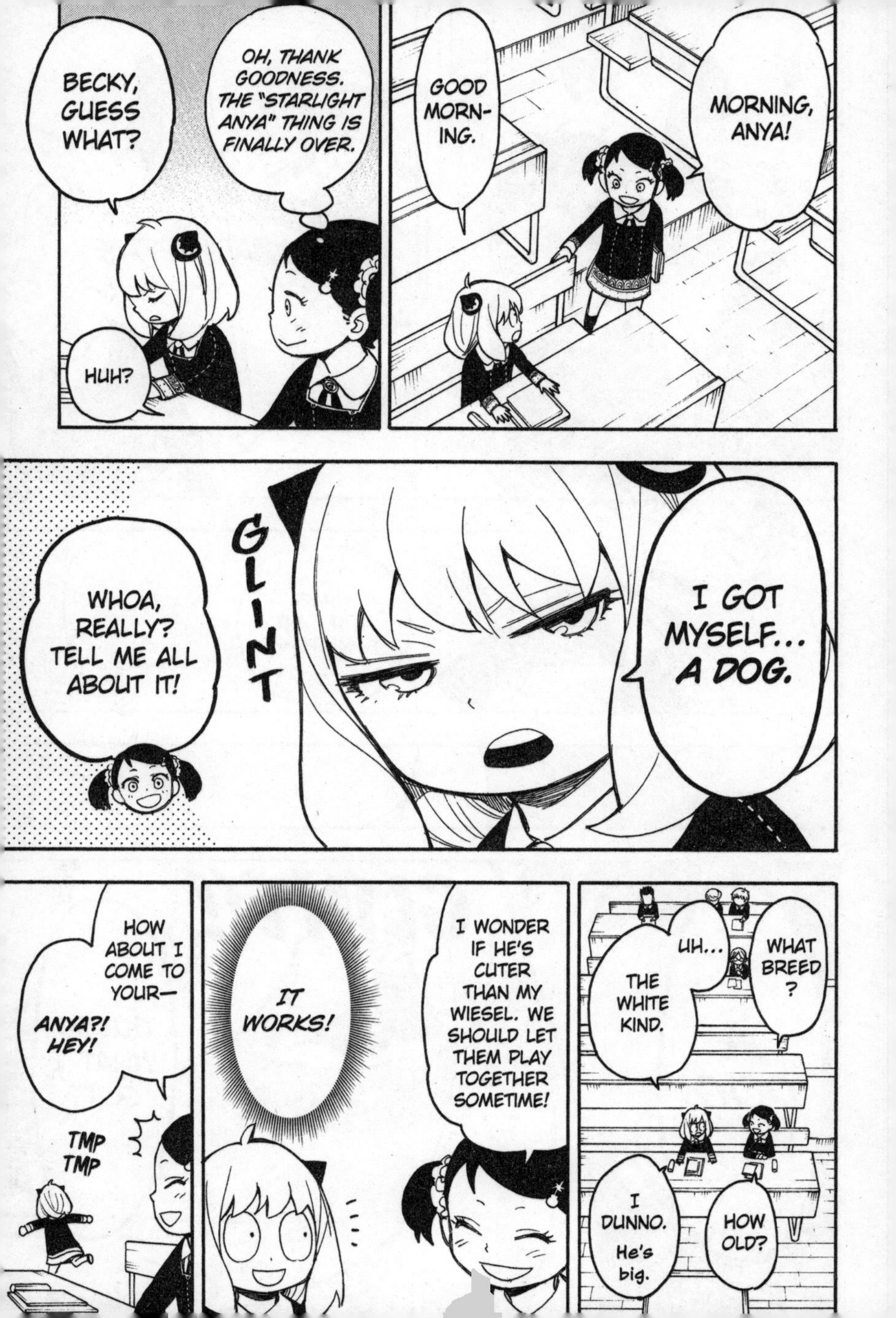
MORNING, ANYA!
GOOD MORN-ING.
OH, THANK GOODNESS. THE "STARLIGHT ANYA" THING IS FINALLY OVER.
BECKY, GUESS WHAT?
HUH?
I GOT MYSELF... A DOG.
GLINT
WHOA, REALLY? TELL ME ALL ABOUT IT!
WHAT BREED?
UH... THE WHITE KIND.
HOW OLD?
I DUNNO. He's big.
I WONDER IF HE'S CUTER THAN MY WIESEL. WE SHOULD LET THEM PLAY TOGETHER SOMETIME!
IT WORKS!
HOW ABOUT I COME TO YOUR—
ANYA?! HEY!
TMP TMP

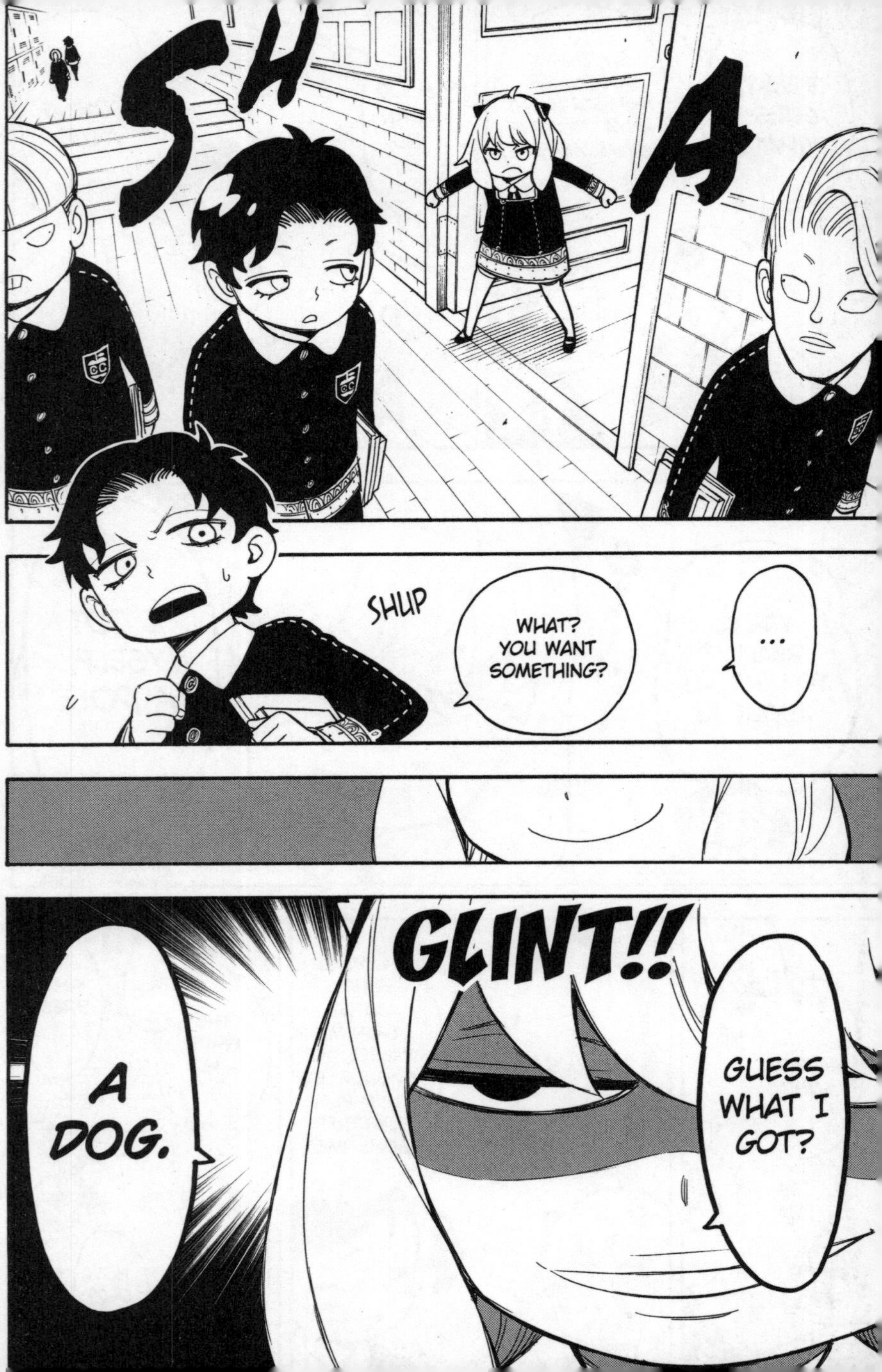
SHA
...
WHAT? YOU WANT SOMETHING?
SHUP
GLINT!!
GUESS WHAT I GOT?
A DOG.

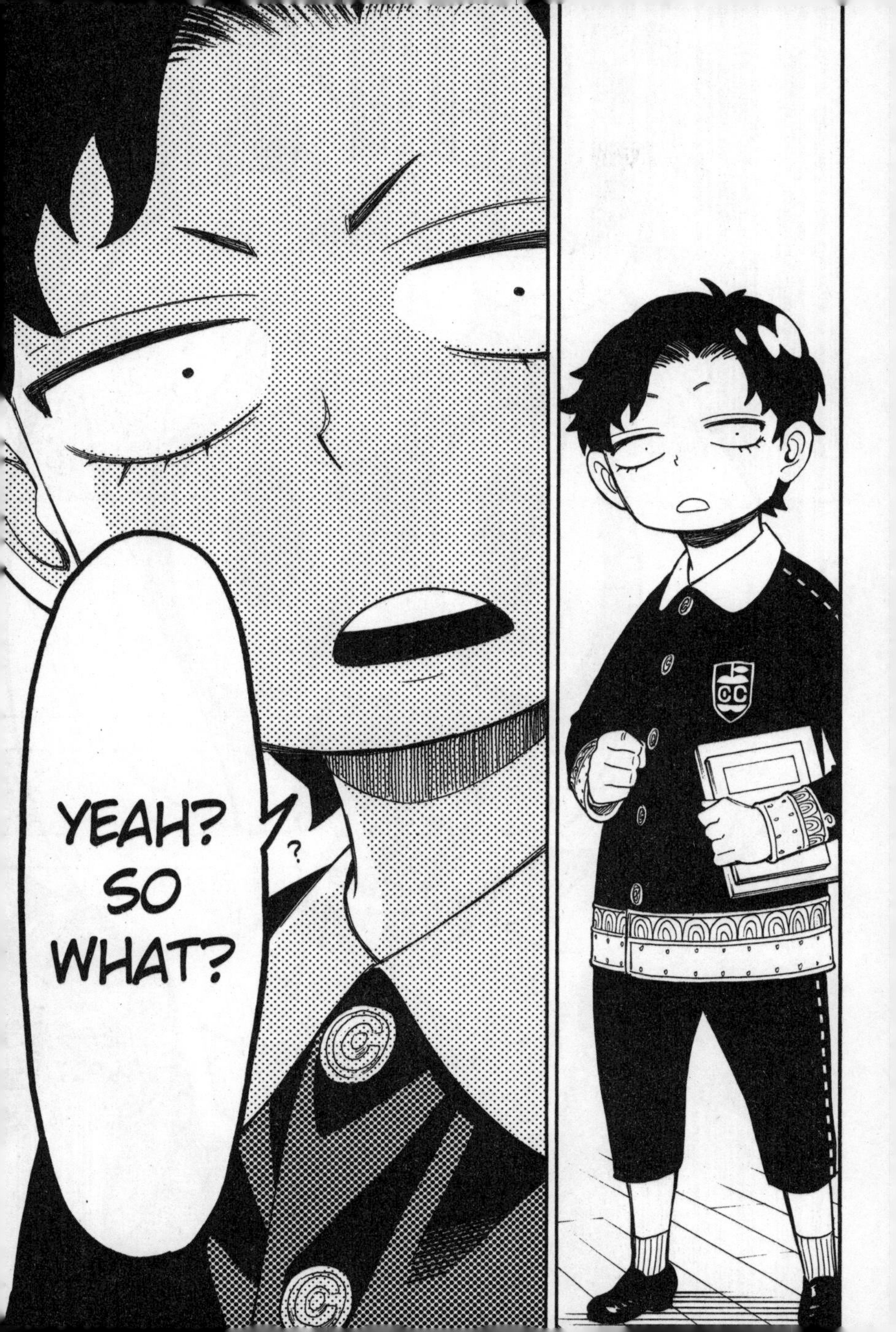
YEAH? SO WHAT?

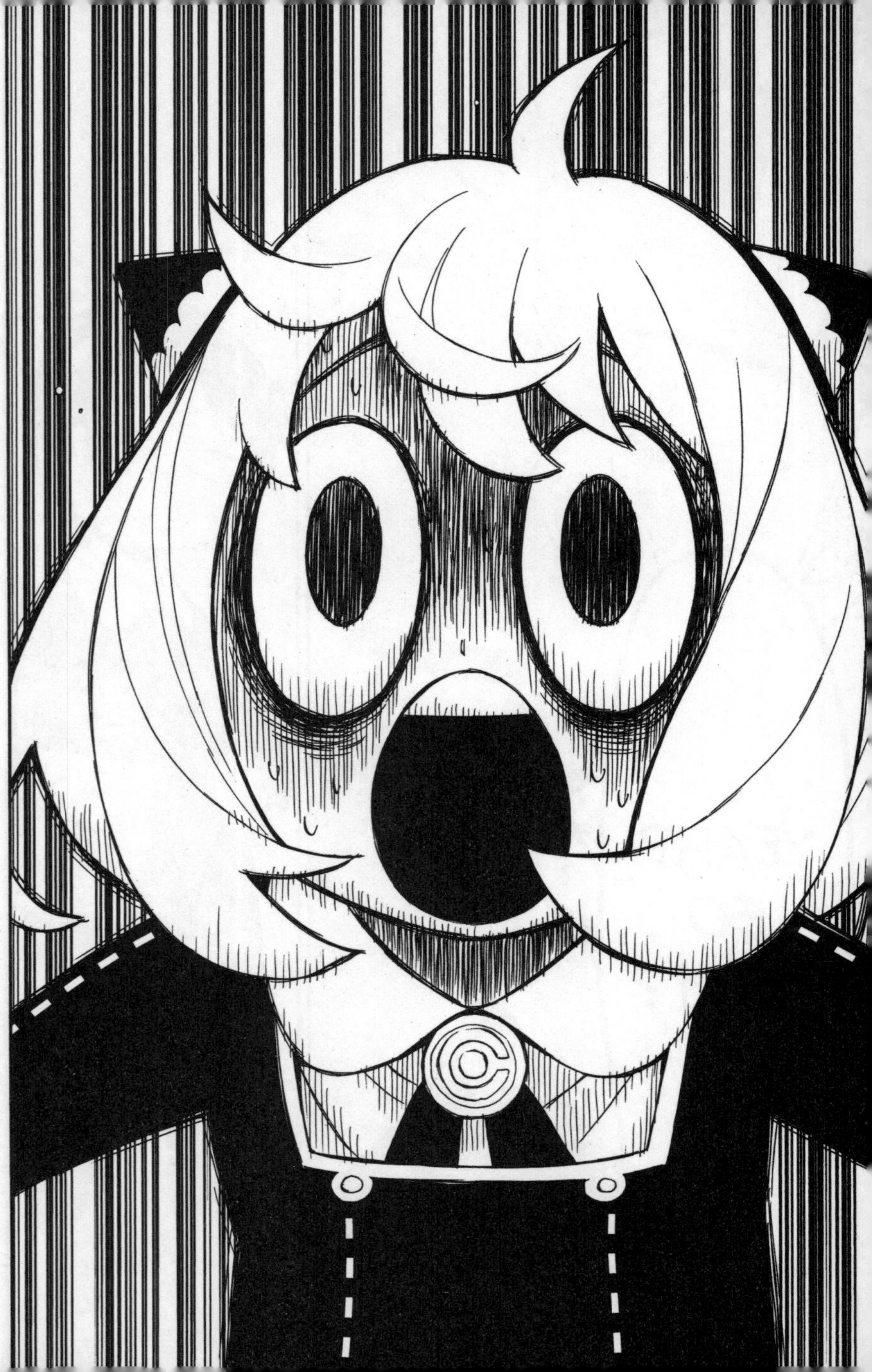

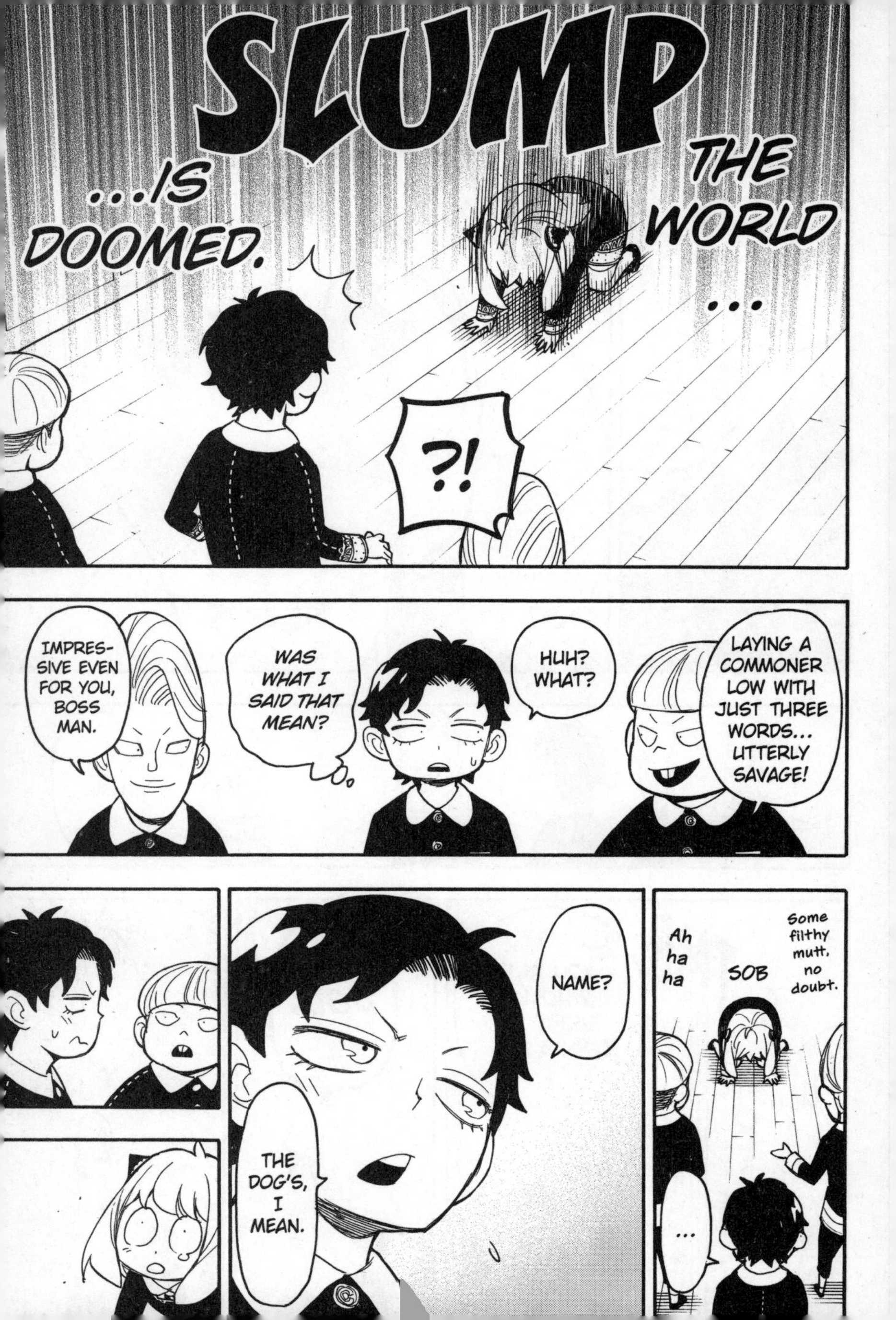
SLUMP
THE WORLD ...
...IS DOOMED.
?!
LAYING A COMMONER LOW WITH JUST THREE WORDS... UTTERLY SAVAGE!
HUH? WHAT?
WAS WHAT I SAID THAT MEAN?
IMPRES-SIVE EVEN FOR YOU, BOSS MAN.
Some filthy mutt, no doubt.
SOB
Ah ha ha
...
NAME?
THE DOG'S, I MEAN.

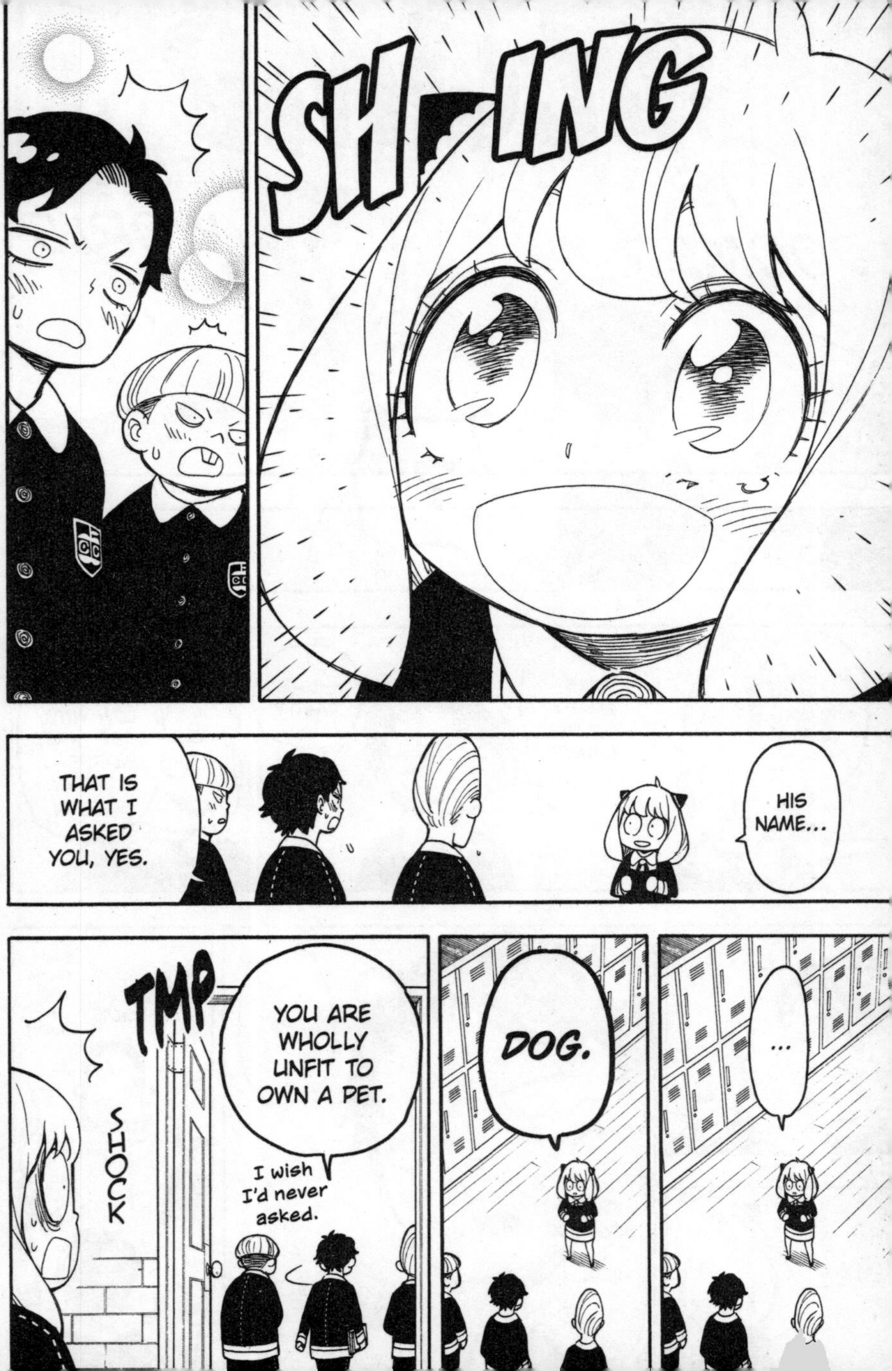
SH ING
HIS NAME...
THAT IS WHAT I ASKED YOU, YES.
...
DOG.
YOU ARE WHOLLY UNFIT TO OWN A PET.
TMP
I wish I'd never asked.
SHOCK

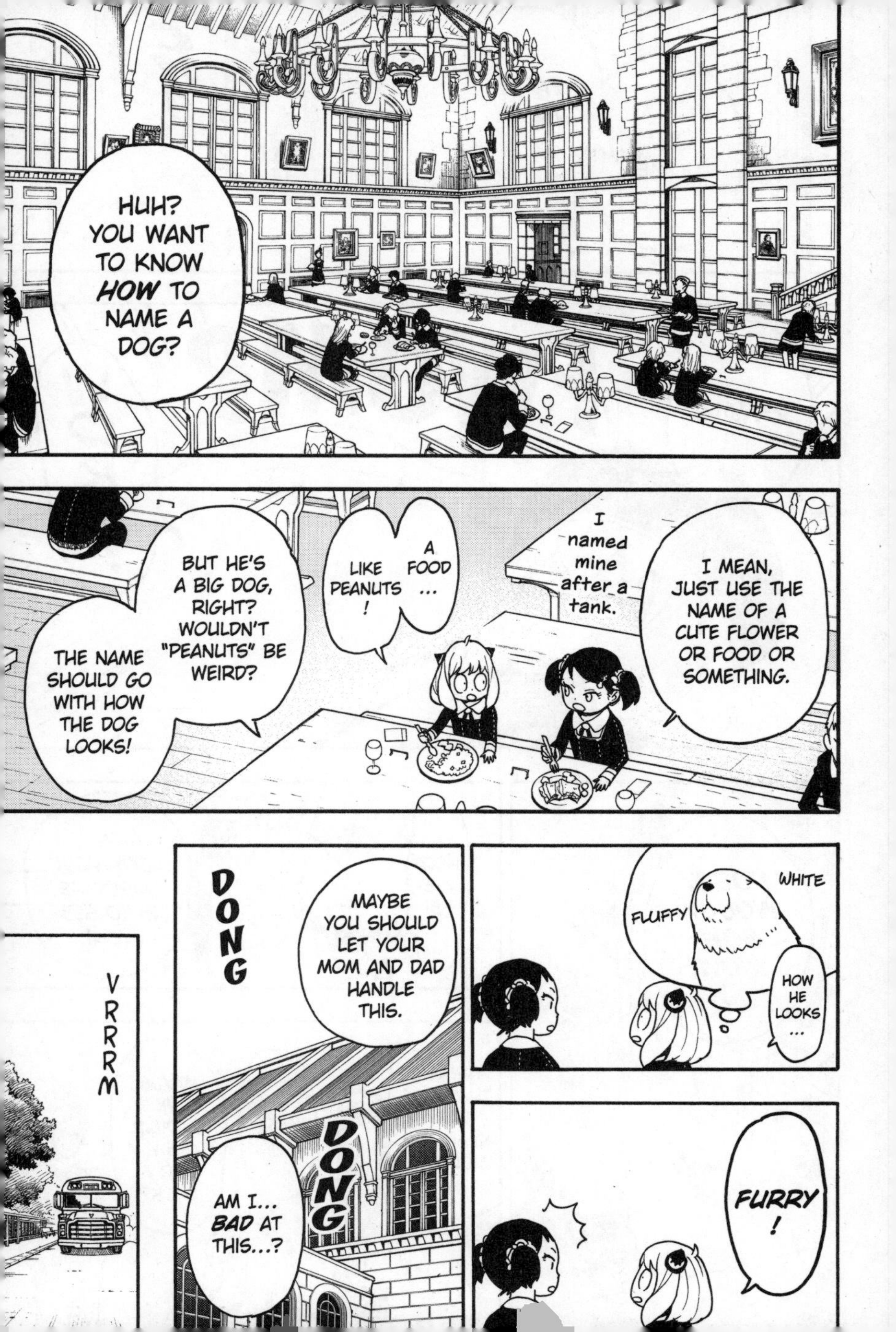
HUH? YOU WANT TO KNOW HOW TO NAME A DOG?
I MEAN, JUST USE THE NAME OF A CUTE FLOWER OR FOOD OR SOMETHING.
I named mine after a tank.
A FOOD ...
LIKE PEANUTS !
BUT HE'S A BIG DOG, RIGHT? WOULDN'T "PEANUTS" BE WEIRD?
THE NAME SHOULD GO WITH HOW THE DOG LOOKS!
WHITE
FLUFFY
HOW HE LOOKS ...
FURRY !
DONG
MAYBE YOU SHOULD LET YOUR MOM AND DAD HANDLE THIS.
DONG
AM I... BAD AT THIS...?
VRRRM

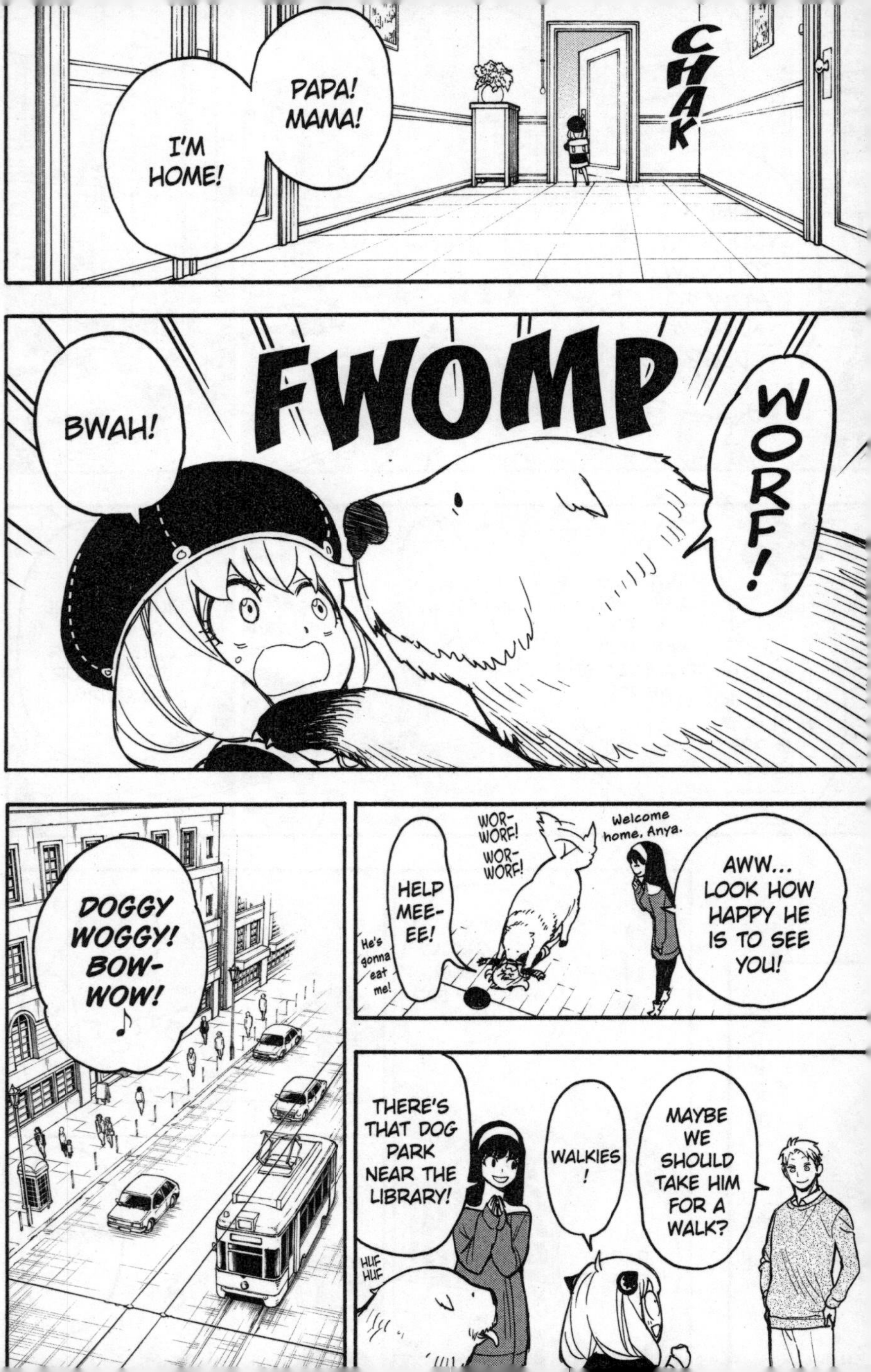
CHAK
PAPA! MAMA!
I'M HOME!
WORF!
FWOMP
BWAH!
AWW... LOOK HOW HAPPY HE IS TO SEE YOU!
Welcome home, Anya.
WOR-WORF! WOR-WORF!
HELP MEEE-EE!
He's gonna eat me!
MAYBE WE SHOULD TAKE HIM FOR A WALK?
WALKIES!
THERE'S THAT DOG PARK NEAR THE LIBRARY!
HUF HUF
DOGGY WOGGY! BOW-WOW! ♪

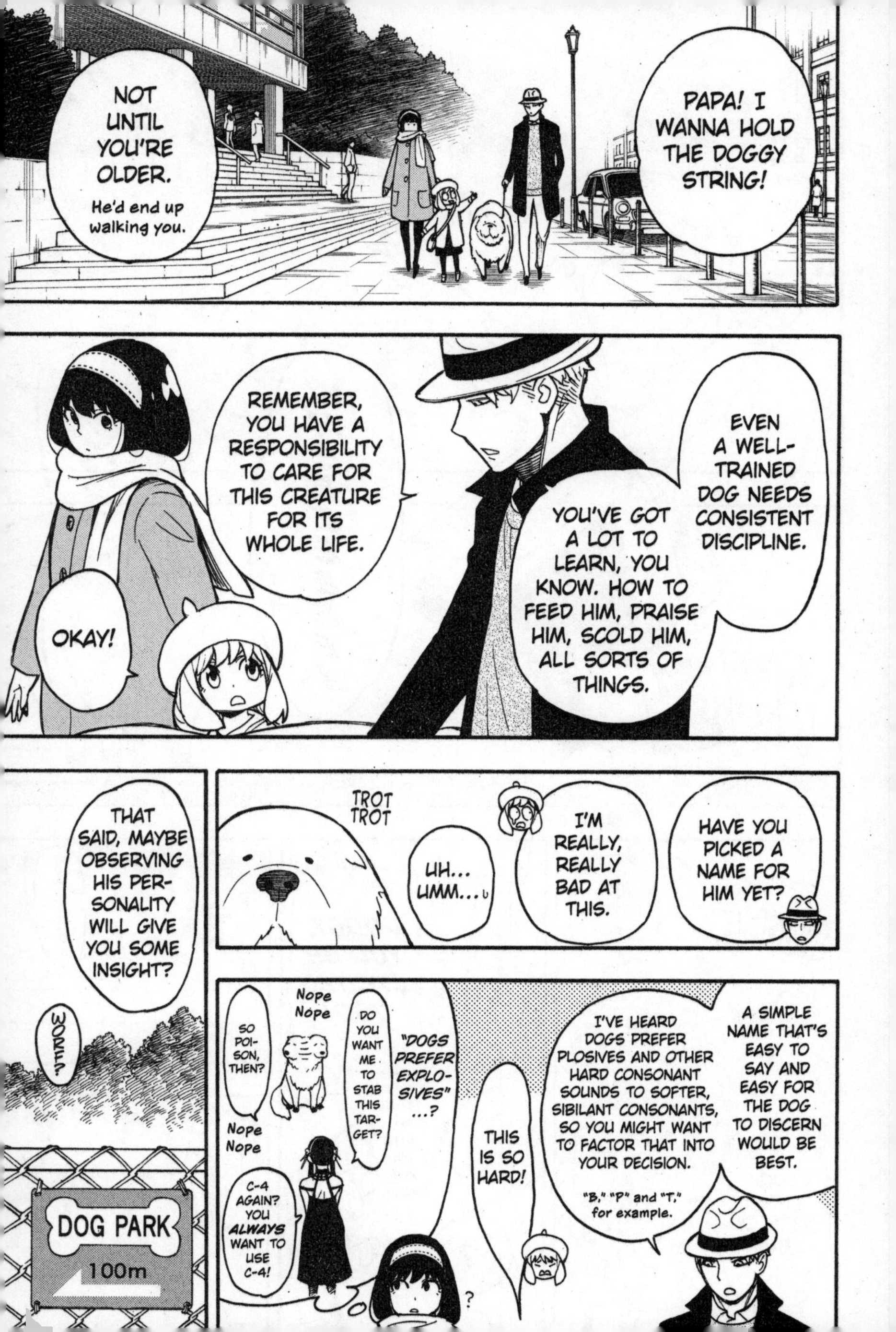
PAPA! I WANNA HOLD THE DOGGY STRING!
NOT UNTIL YOU'RE OLDER.
He'd end up walking you.
EVEN A WELL-TRAINED DOG NEEDS CONSISTENT DISCIPLINE.
YOU'VE GOT A LOT TO LEARN, YOU KNOW. HOW TO FEED HIM, PRAISE HIM, SCOLD HIM, ALL SORTS OF THINGS.
REMEMBER, YOU HAVE A RESPONSIBILITY TO CARE FOR THIS CREATURE FOR ITS WHOLE LIFE.
OKAY!
HAVE YOU PICKED A NAME FOR HIM YET?
I'M REALLY, REALLY BAD AT THIS.
UH... UMM...
TROT TROT
A SIMPLE NAME THAT'S EASY TO SAY AND EASY FOR THE DOG TO DISCERN WOULD BE BEST.
I'VE HEARD DOGS PREFER PLOSIVES AND OTHER HARD CONSONANT SOUNDS TO SOFTER, SIBILANT CONSONANTS, SO YOU MIGHT WANT TO FACTOR THAT INTO YOUR DECISION.
"B," "P" and "T," for example.
THIS IS SO HARD!
"DOGS PREFER EXPLOSIVES" ...?
DO YOU WANT ME TO STAB THIS TARGET?
Nope Nope
SO POISON, THEN?
Nope Nope
C-4 AGAIN? YOU *ALWAYS* WANT TO USE C-4!
THAT SAID, MAYBE OBSERVING HIS PER-SONALITY WILL GIVE YOU SOME INSIGHT?
WORF?
DOG PARK
100m

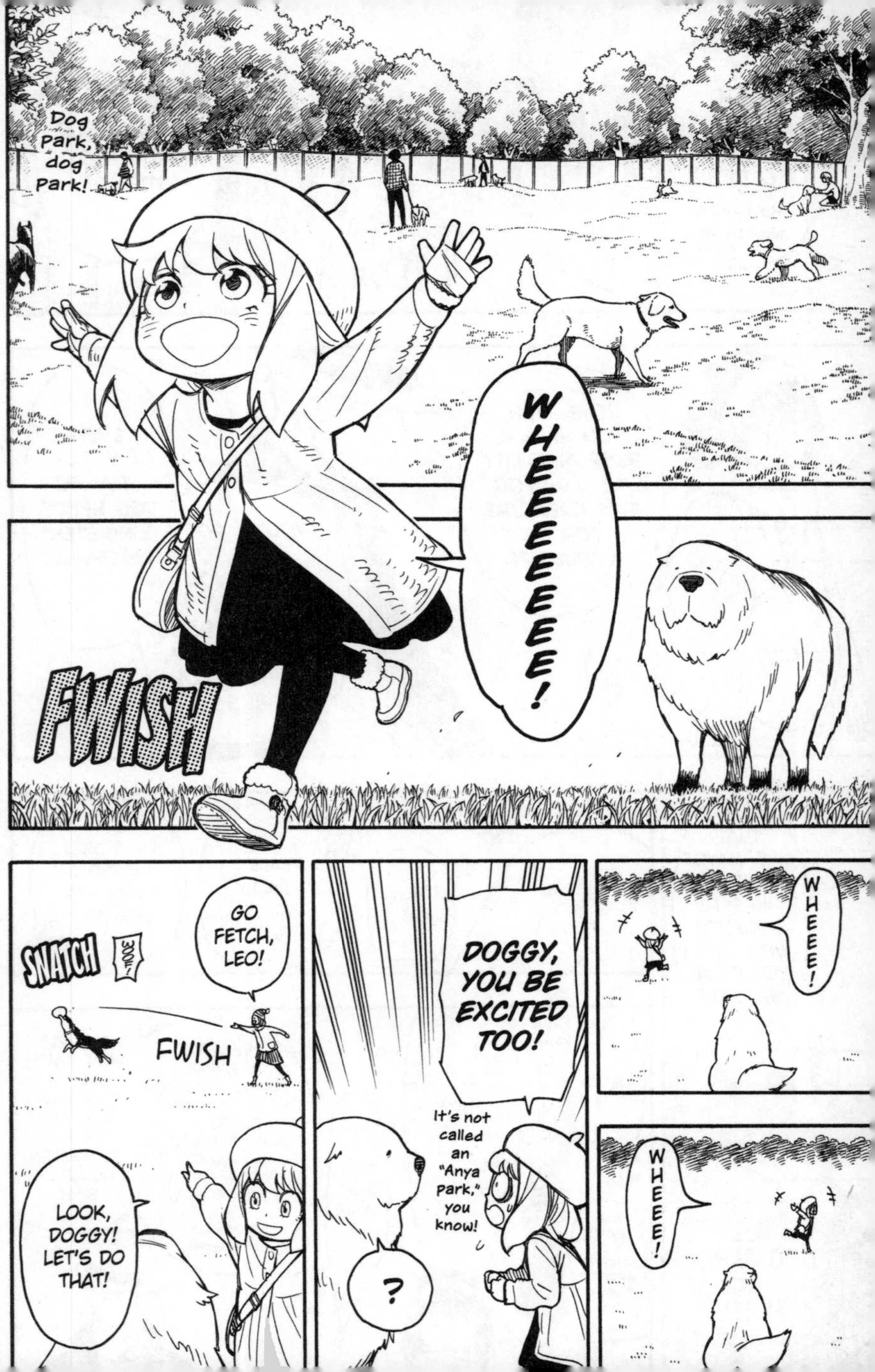
Dog Park, dog Park!
WHEEEEEEEE!
FWISH
WHEEE!
WHEEE!
DOGGY, YOU BE EXCITED TOO!
?
It's not called an "Anya park," you know!
GO FETCH, LEO!
SNATCH
WOOF!
FWISH
LOOK, DOGGY! LET'S DO THAT!

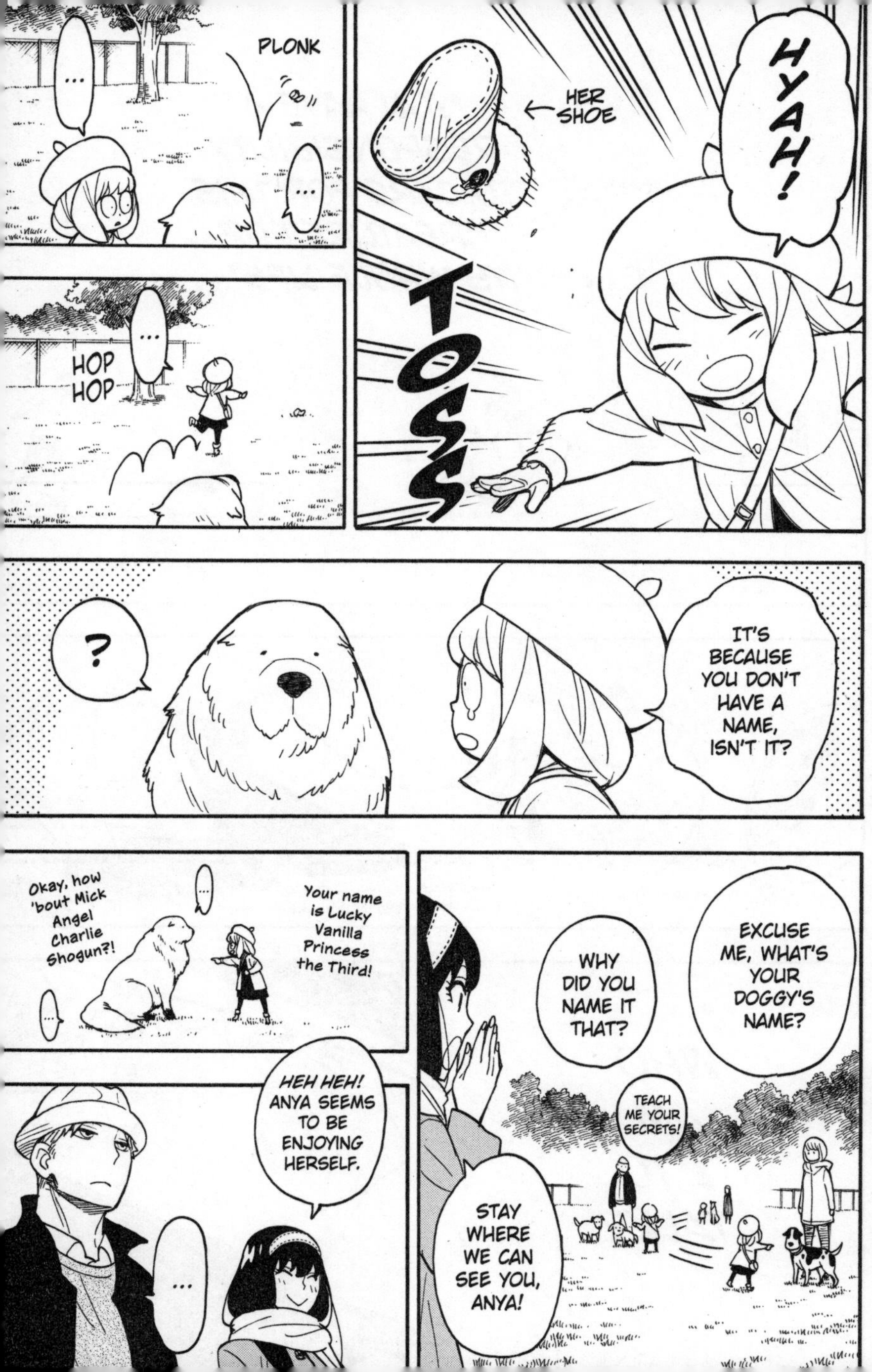
HYAH!
HER SHOE
TOSS
PLONK
...
...
...
HOP HOP
IT'S BECAUSE YOU DON'T HAVE A NAME, ISN'T IT?
?
EXCUSE ME, WHAT'S YOUR DOGGY'S NAME?
WHY DID YOU NAME IT THAT?
TEACH ME YOUR SECRETS!
STAY WHERE WE CAN SEE YOU, ANYA!
Your name is Lucky Vanilla Princess the Third!
...
Okay, how 'bout Mick Angel Charlie Shogun?!
...
HEH HEH! ANYA SEEMS TO BE ENJOYING HERSELF.
...

"YOU HAVE A RESPONSIBILITY TO CARE FOR THIS CREATURE FOR ITS WHOLE LIFE"...

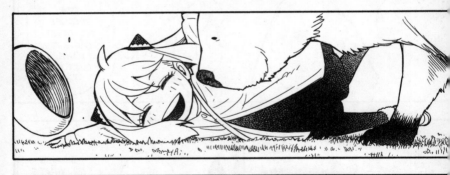

WHO AM I TO TALK?

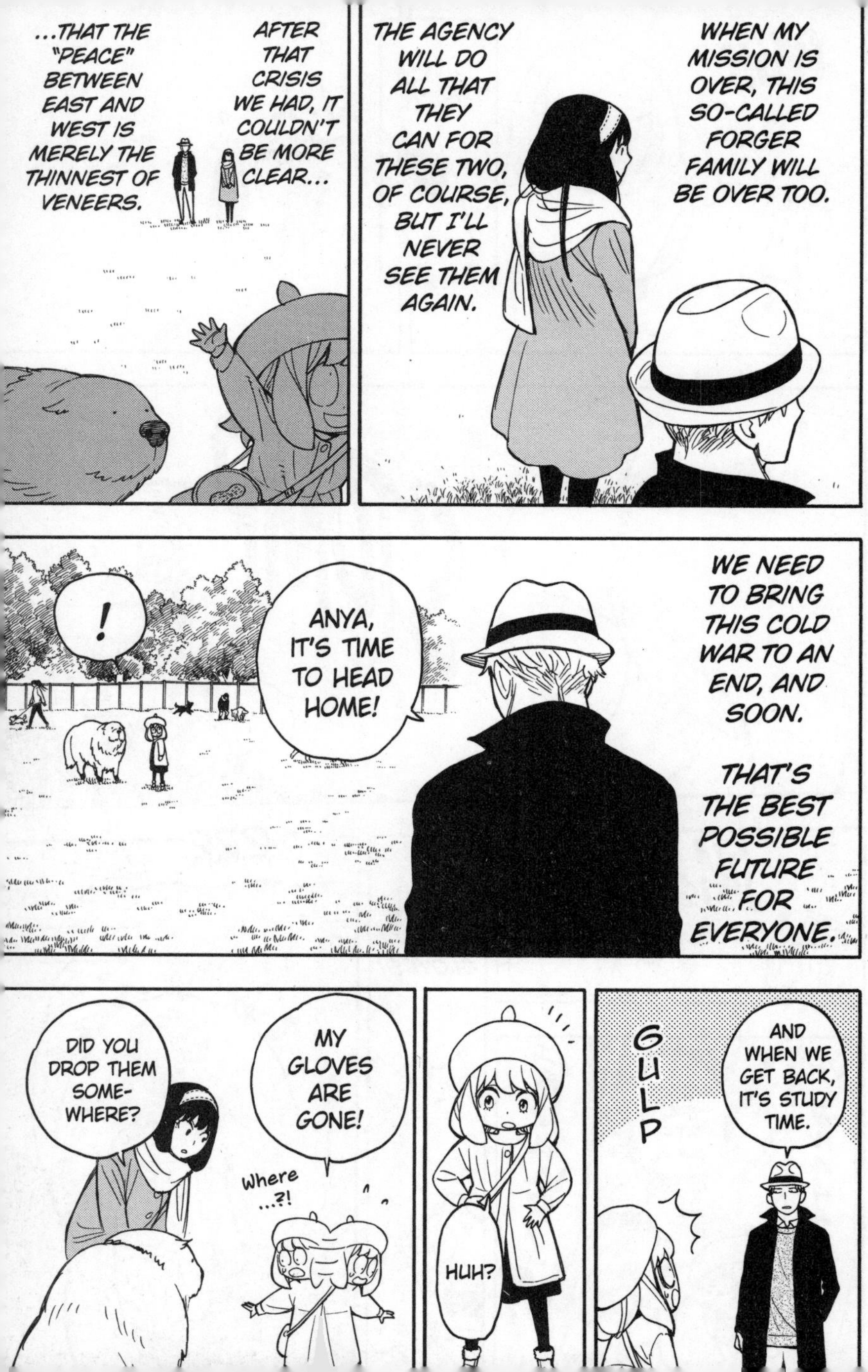
WHEN MY MISSION IS OVER, THIS SO-CALLED FORGER FAMILY WILL BE OVER TOO.
THE AGENCY WILL DO ALL THAT THEY CAN FOR THESE TWO, OF COURSE, BUT I'LL NEVER SEE THEM AGAIN.
AFTER THAT CRISIS WE HAD, IT COULDN'T BE MORE CLEAR...
...THAT THE "PEACE" BETWEEN EAST AND WEST IS MERELY THE THINNEST OF VENEERS.
WE NEED TO BRING THIS COLD WAR TO AN END, AND SOON.
THAT'S THE BEST POSSIBLE FUTURE FOR EVERYONE.
ANYA, IT'S TIME TO HEAD HOME!
!
AND WHEN WE GET BACK, IT'S STUDY TIME.
GULP
HUH?
MY GLOVES ARE GONE!
Where ...?!
DID YOU DROP THEM SOME-WHERE?

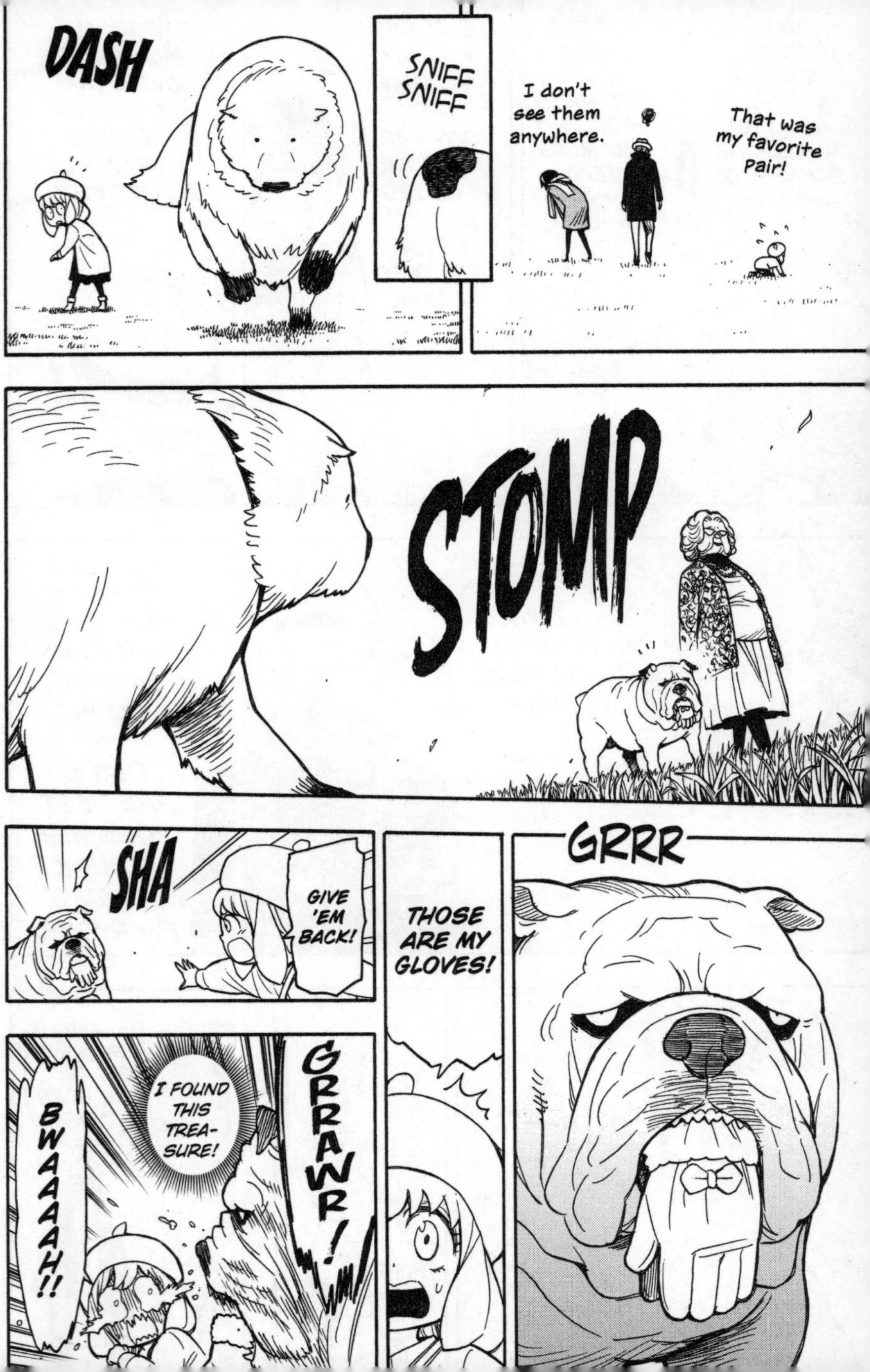

That was my favorite Pair!
I don't see them anywhere.
SNIFF SNIFF
DASH
STOMP
GRRR
THOSE ARE MY GLOVES!
GIVE 'EM BACK!
SHA
GRRAWR!
I FOUND THIS TREA-SURE!
BWAAAAAH!!

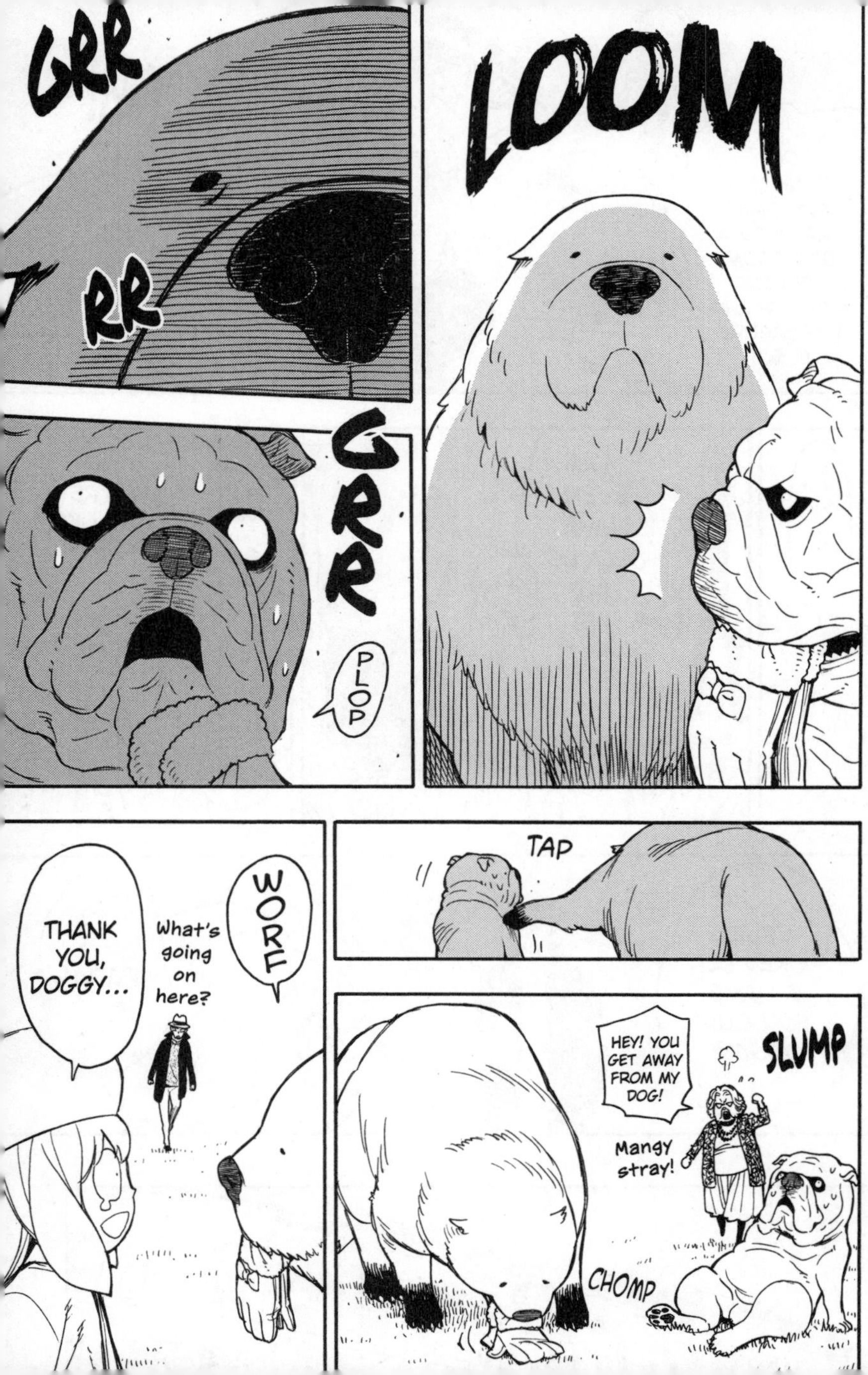
LOOM
GRR
RR
GRR
PLOP
TAP
HEY! YOU GET AWAY FROM MY DOG!
SLUMP
Mangy stray!
CHOMP
WORF
What's going on here?
THANK YOU, DOGGY...

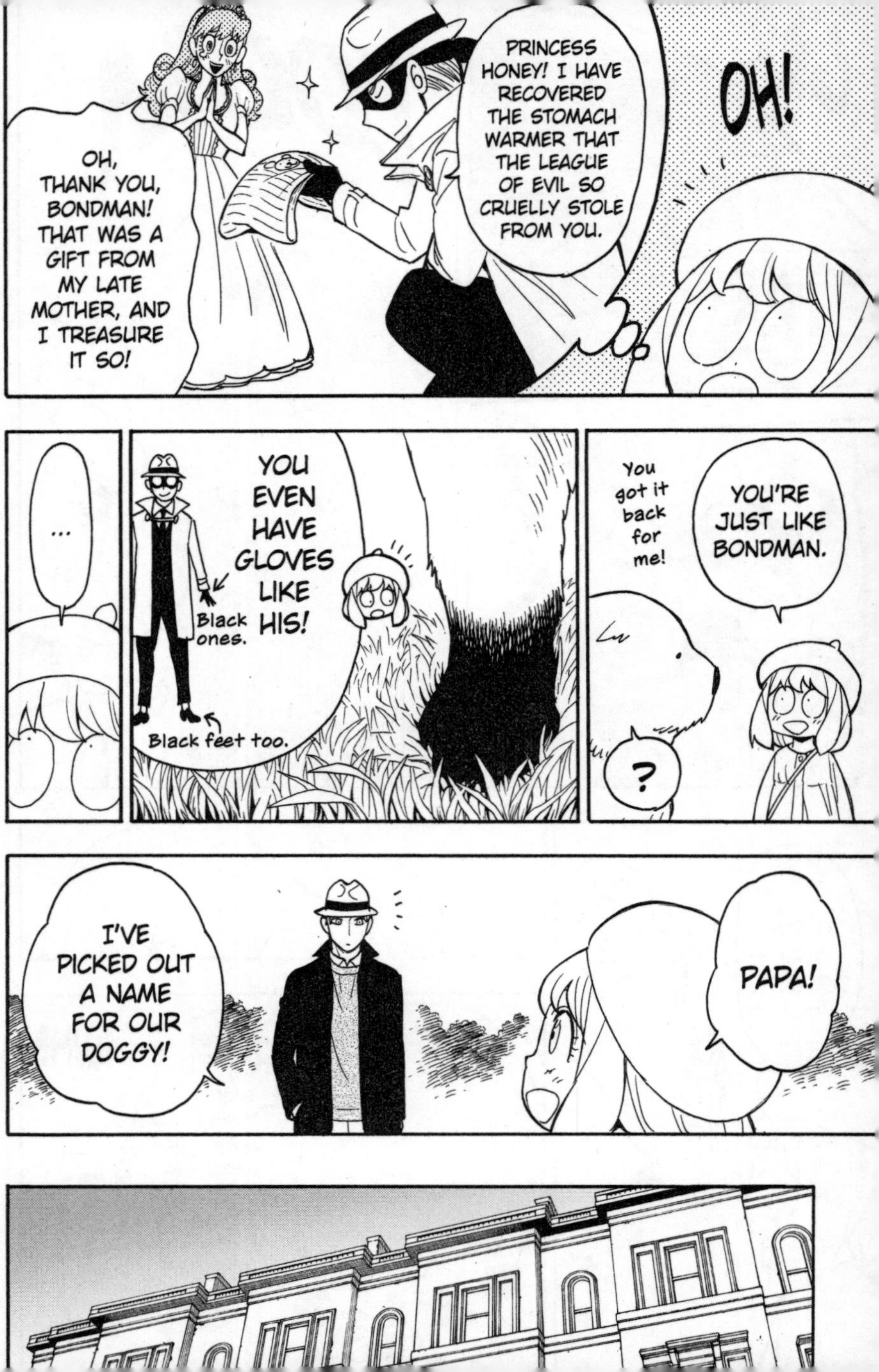
OH!
PRINCESS HONEY! I HAVE RECOVERED THE STOMACH WARMER THAT THE LEAGUE OF EVIL SO CRUELLY STOLE FROM YOU.
OH, THANK YOU, BONDMAN! THAT WAS A GIFT FROM MY LATE MOTHER, AND I TREASURE IT SO!
YOU'RE JUST LIKE BONDMAN.
You got it back for me!
?
YOU EVEN HAVE GLOVES LIKE HIS!
Black ones.
Black feet too.
...
PAPA!
I'VE PICKED OUT A NAME FOR OUR DOGGY!

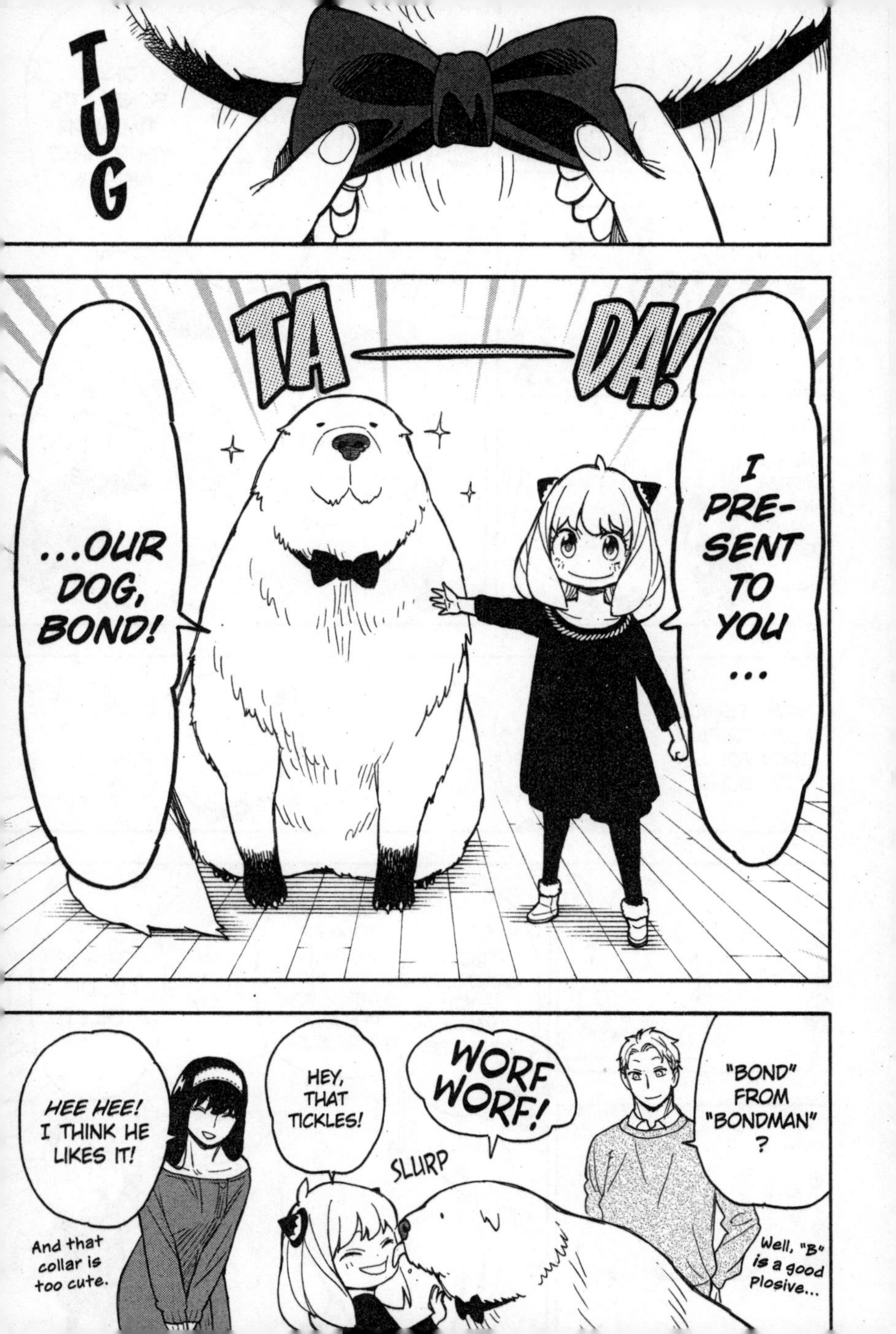
TUG
I PRESENT TO YOU...
TA—DA!
...OUR DOG, BOND!
"BOND" FROM "BONDMAN"?
Well, "B" is a good plosive...
WORF WORF!
SLURP
HEY, THAT TICKLES!
HEE HEE! I THINK HE LIKES IT!
And that collar is too cute.

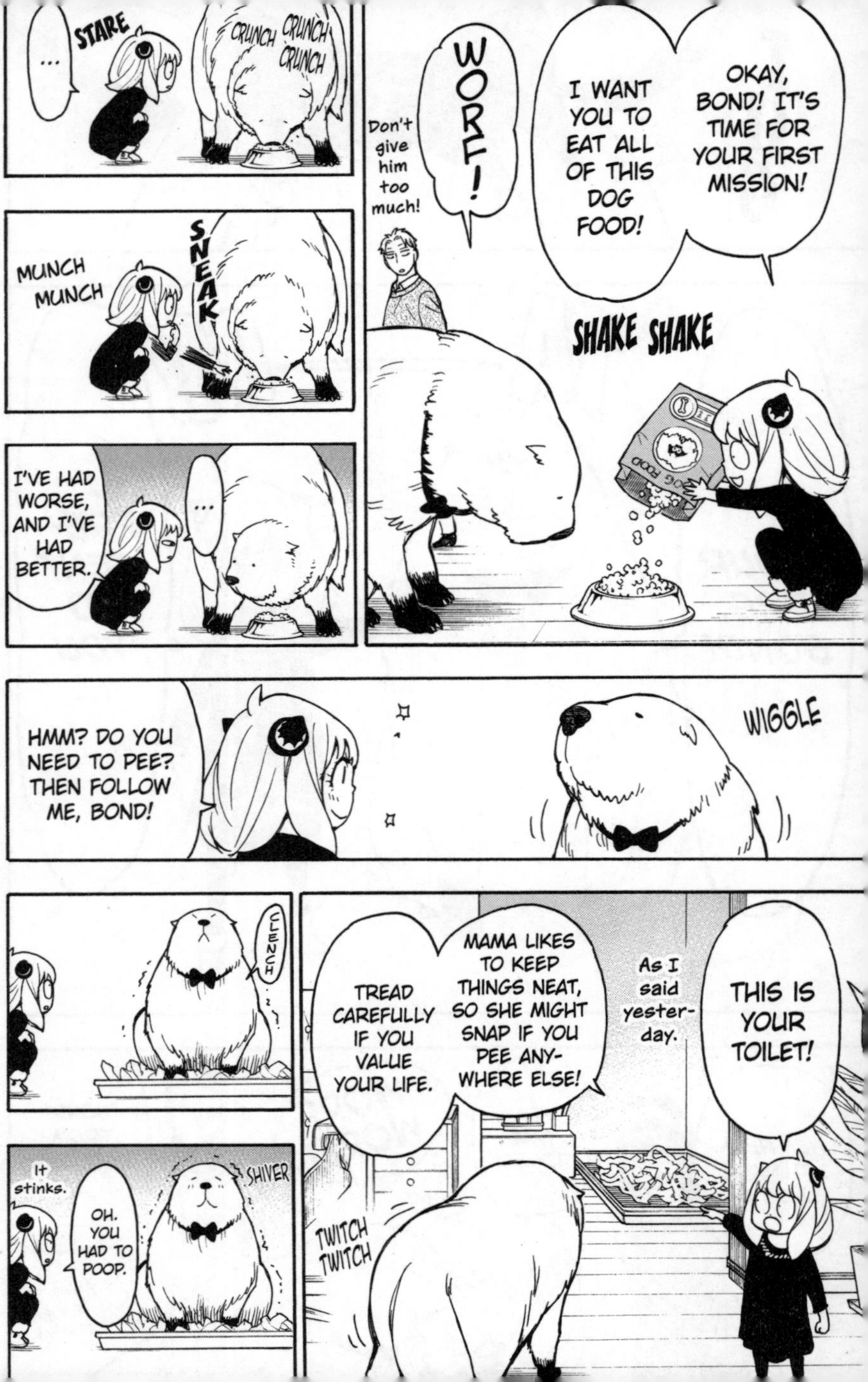
OKAY, BOND! IT'S TIME FOR YOUR FIRST MISSION!
I WANT YOU TO EAT ALL OF THIS DOG FOOD!
WORF!
Don't give him too much!
SHAKE SHAKE
STARE
...
CRUNCH CRUNCH CRUNCH
SNEAK
MUNCH MUNCH
...
I'VE HAD WORSE, AND I'VE HAD BETTER.
WIGGLE
HMM? DO YOU NEED TO PEE? THEN FOLLOW ME, BOND!
THIS IS YOUR TOILET!
As I said yester-day.
MAMA LIKES TO KEEP THINGS NEAT, SO SHE MIGHT SNAP IF YOU PEE ANY-WHERE ELSE!
TREAD CAREFULLY IF YOU VALUE YOUR LIFE.
TWITCH TWITCH
CLENCH
SHIVER
OH. YOU HAD TO POOP.
It stinks.

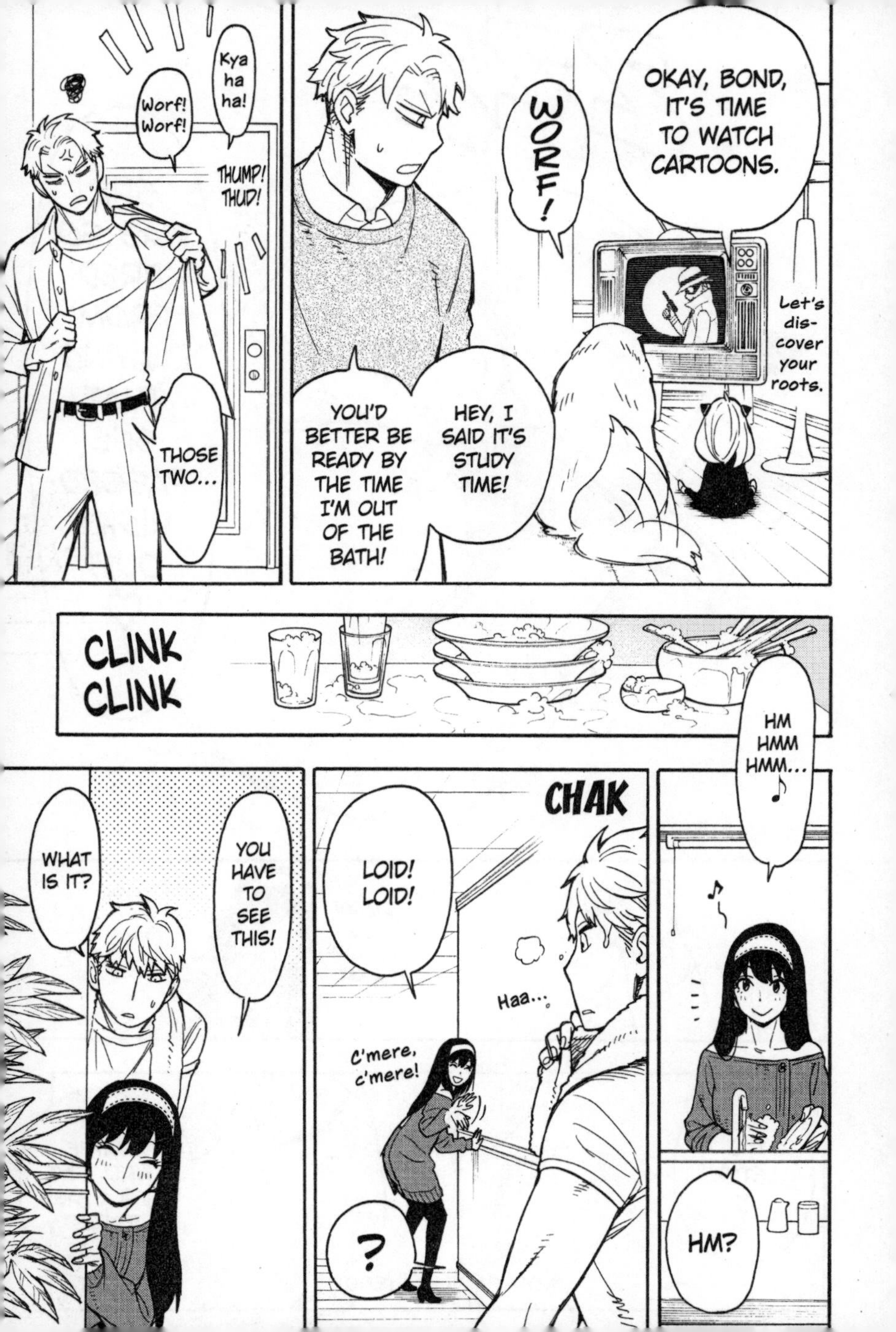
OKAY, BOND, IT'S TIME TO WATCH CARTOONS.
WORF!
Let's dis-cover your roots.
HEY, I SAID IT'S STUDY TIME!
YOU'D BETTER BE READY BY THE TIME I'M OUT OF THE BATH!
Kya ha ha!
Worf! Worf!
THUMP! THUD!
THOSE TWO...
CLINK CLINK
HM HMM HMM... ♪
HM?
CHAK
LOID! LOID!
Haa...
C'mere, c'mere!
?
YOU HAVE TO SEE THIS!
WHAT IS IT?

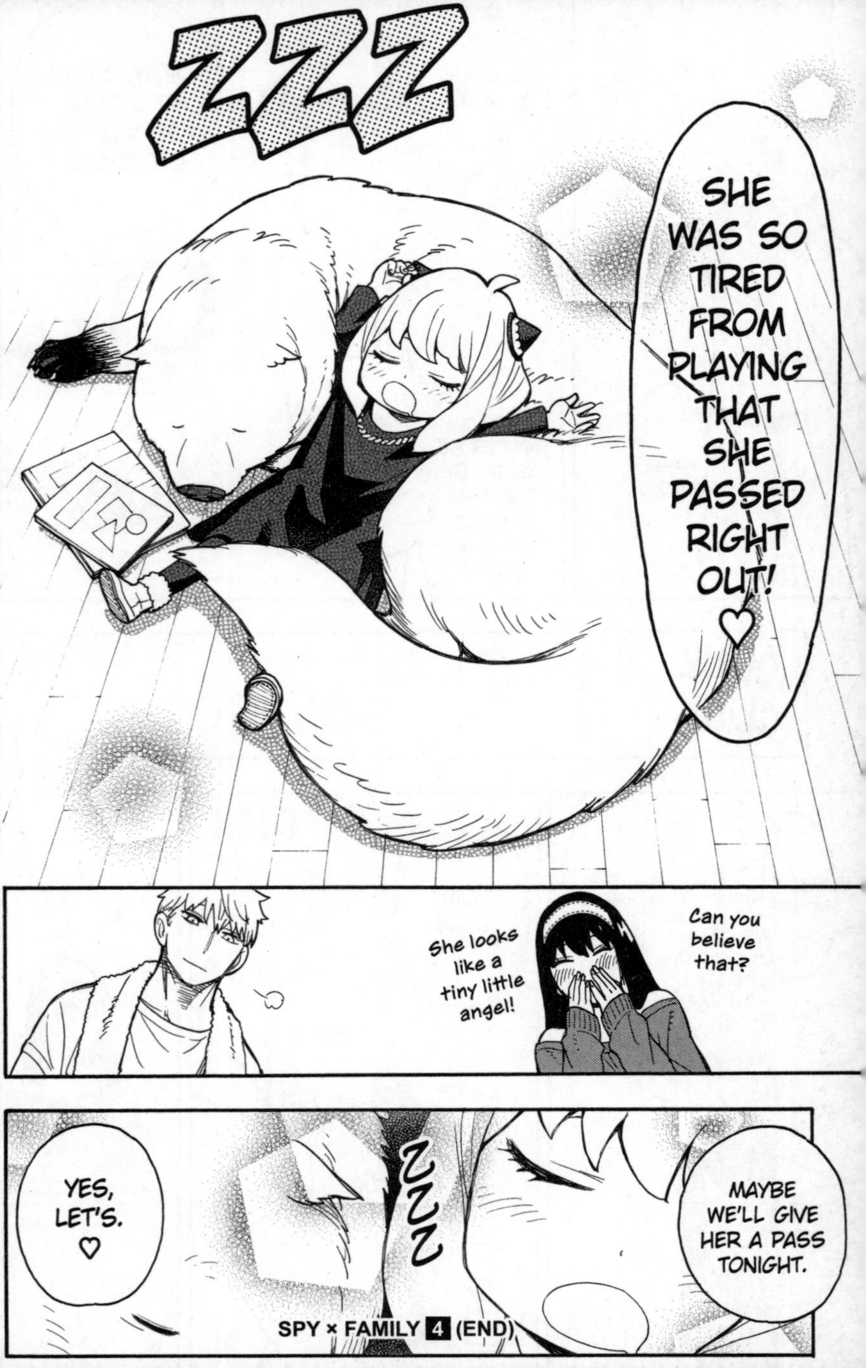
ZZZ
SHE WAS SO TIRED FROM PLAYING THAT SHE PASSED RIGHT OUT! ♡
Can you believe that?
She looks like a tiny little angel!
MAYBE WE'LL GIVE HER A PASS TONIGHT.
ZZZ
YES, LET'S. ♡
SPY × FAMILY 4 (END)

SPY×FAMILY

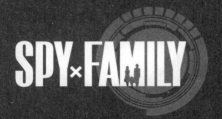

AFTERWARD, THE DOG WAS ADOPTED BY A KINDLY AGENT.

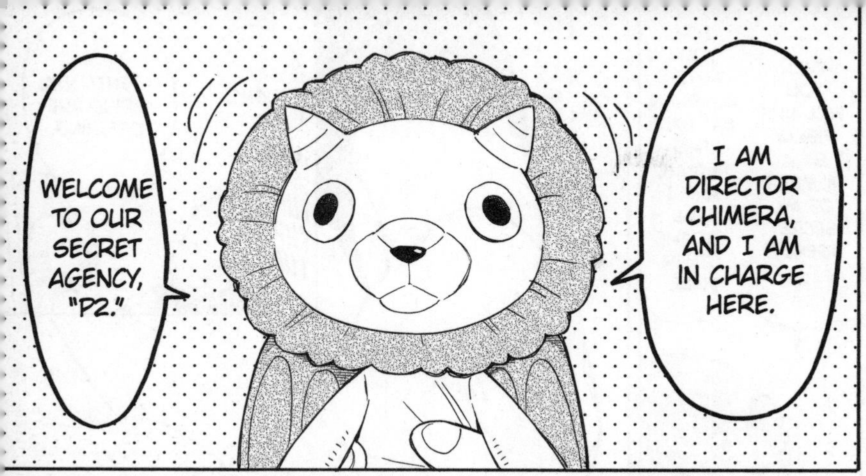
I AM DIRECTOR CHIMERA, AND I AM IN CHARGE HERE.
WELCOME TO OUR SECRET AGENCY, "P2."

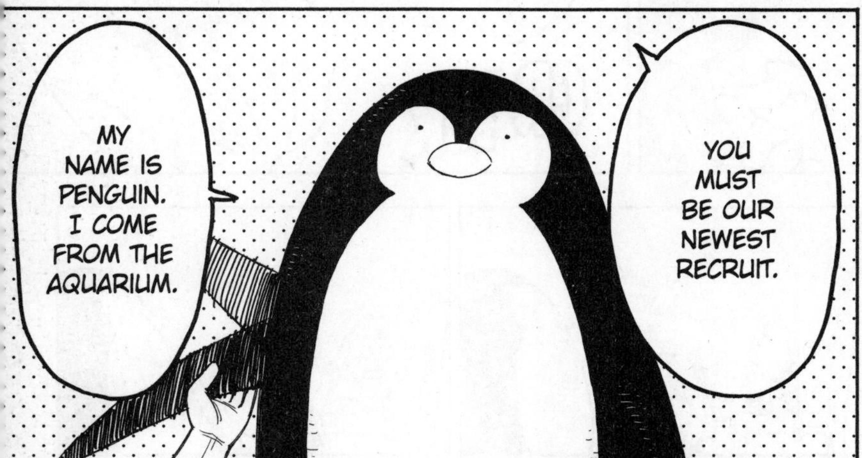
YOU MUST BE OUR NEWEST RECRUIT.
MY NAME IS PENGUIN. I COME FROM THE AQUARIUM.

SHORT MISSION 1

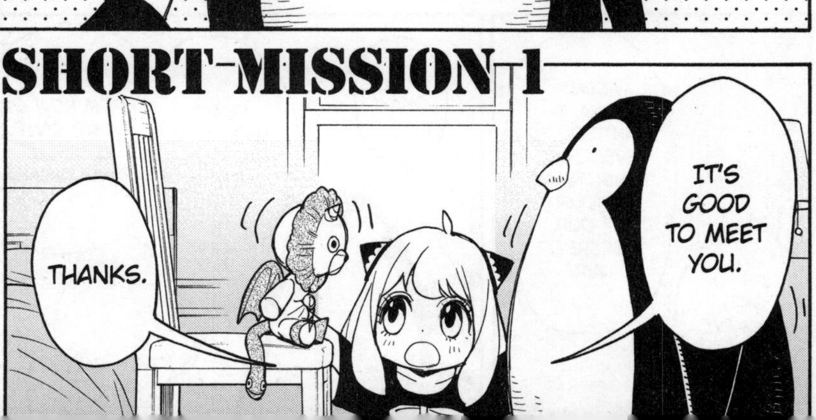
IT'S GOOD TO MEET YOU.
THANKS.

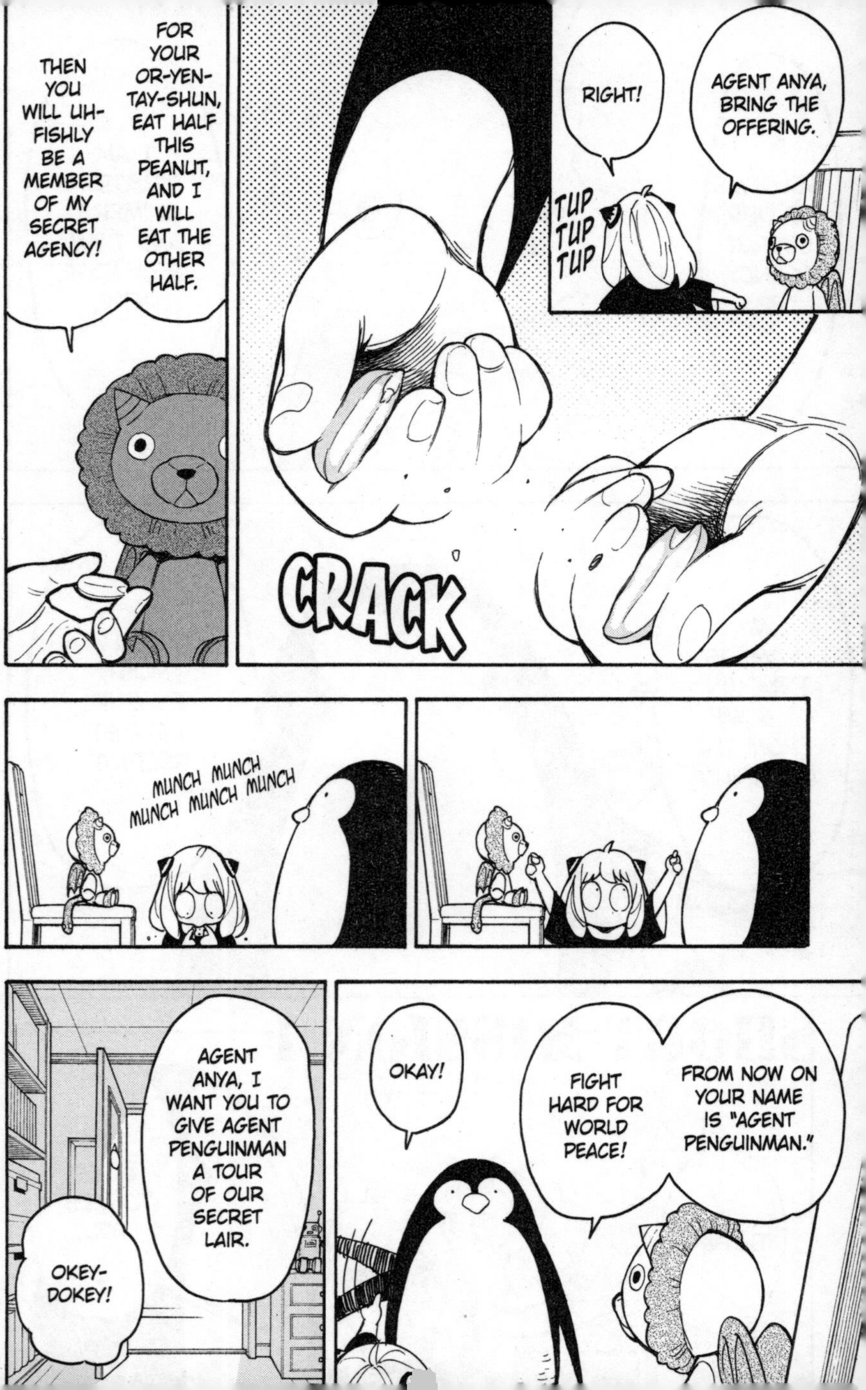
AGENT ANYA, BRING THE OFFERING.
RIGHT!
TUP TUP TUP
CRACK
FOR YOUR OR-YEN-TAY-SHUN, EAT HALF THIS PEANUT, AND I WILL EAT THE OTHER HALF.
THEN YOU WILL UH-FISHLY BE A MEMBER OF MY SECRET AGENCY!
MUNCH MUNCH MUNCH MUNCH MUNCH
FROM NOW ON YOUR NAME IS "AGENT PENGUINMAN."
FIGHT HARD FOR WORLD PEACE!
OKAY!
AGENT ANYA, I WANT YOU TO GIVE AGENT PENGUINMAN A TOUR OF OUR SECRET LAIR.
OKEY-DOKEY!

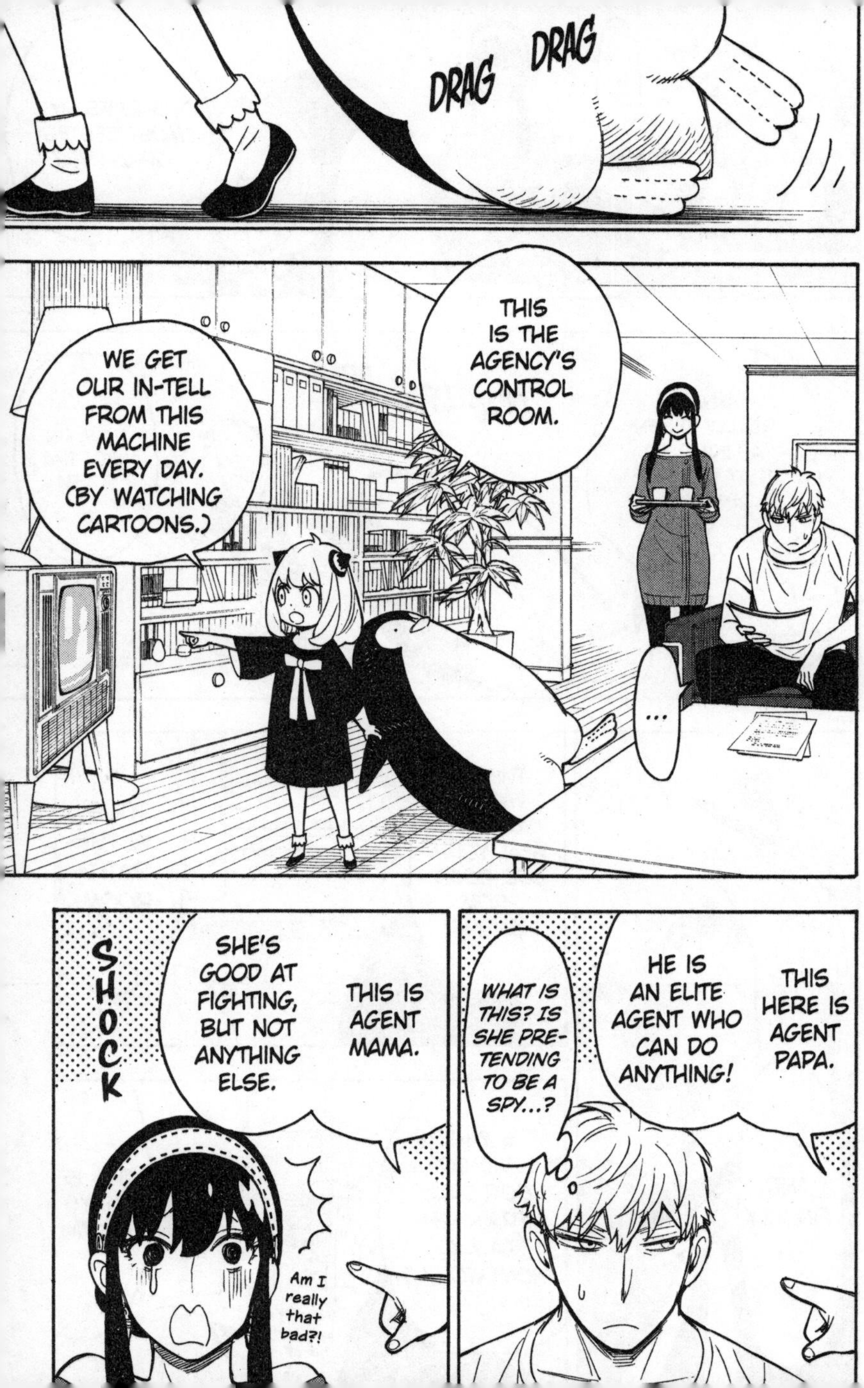
DRAG DRAG
THIS IS THE AGENCY'S CONTROL ROOM.
WE GET OUR IN-TELL FROM THIS MACHINE EVERY DAY. (BY WATCHING CARTOONS.)
...
THIS HERE IS AGENT PAPA.
HE IS AN ELITE AGENT WHO CAN DO ANYTHING!
WHAT IS THIS? IS SHE PRETENDING TO BE A SPY...?
THIS IS AGENT MAMA.
SHE'S GOOD AT FIGHTING, BUT NOT ANYTHING ELSE.
SHOCK
Am I really that bad?!

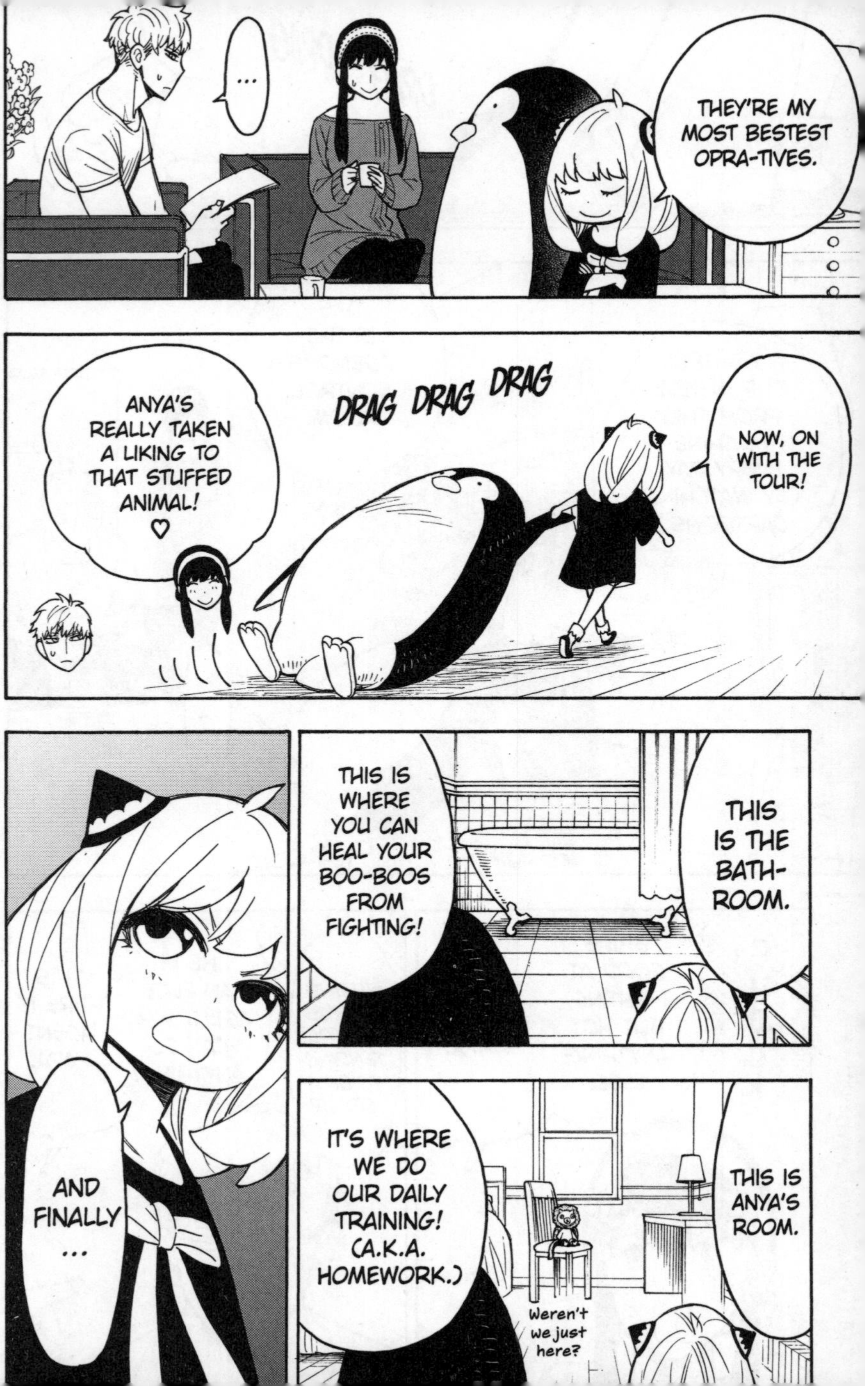
THEY'RE MY MOST BESTEST OPRA-TIVES.
...
NOW, ON WITH THE TOUR!
DRAG DRAG DRAG
ANYA'S REALLY TAKEN A LIKING TO THAT STUFFED ANIMAL! ♡
THIS IS THE BATH-ROOM.
THIS IS WHERE YOU CAN HEAL YOUR BOO-BOOS FROM FIGHTING!
THIS IS ANYA'S ROOM.
IT'S WHERE WE DO OUR DAILY TRAINING! (A.K.A. HOMEWORK.)
Weren't we just here?
AND FINALLY ...

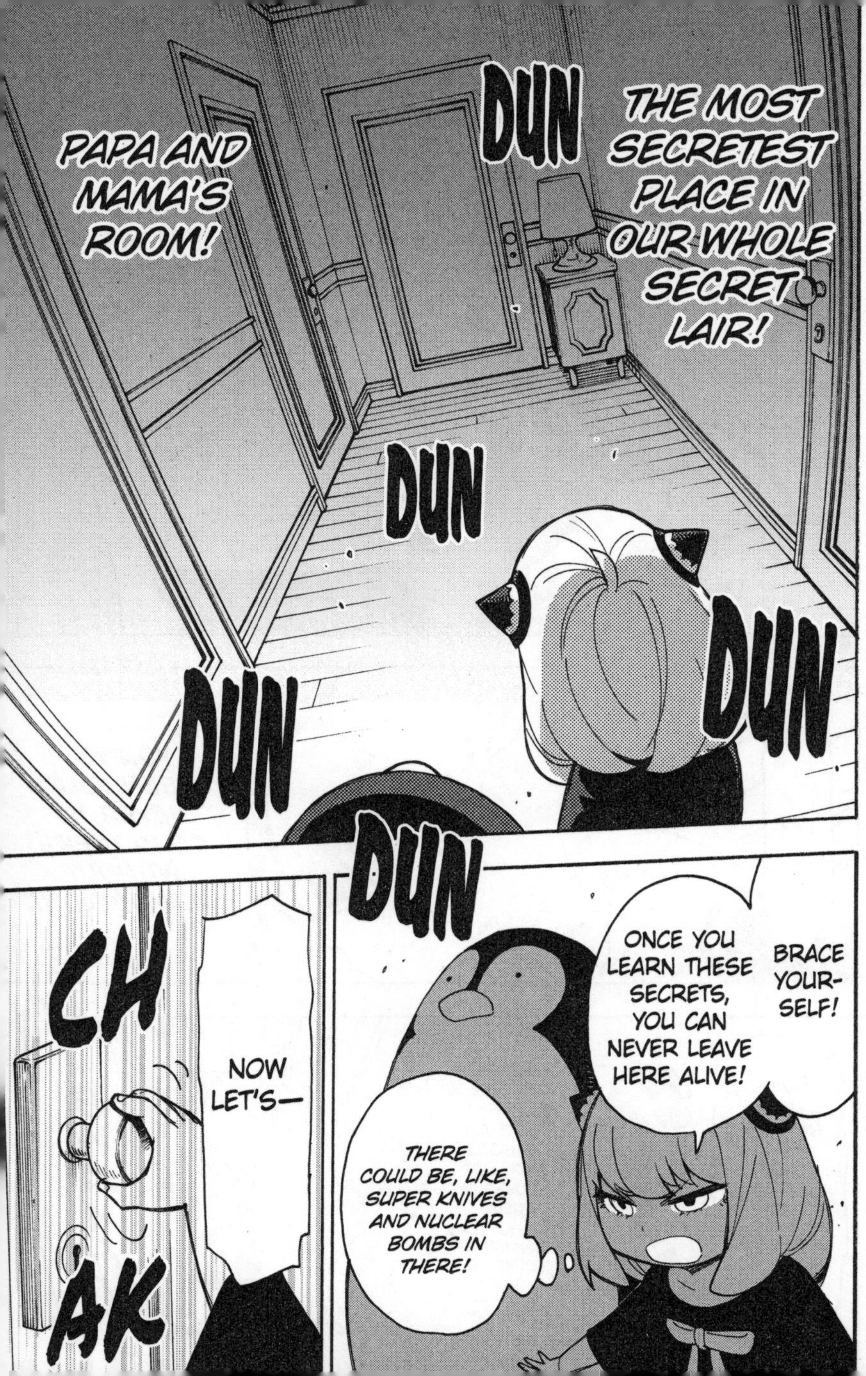
THE MOST SECRETEST PLACE IN OUR WHOLE SECRET LAIR!
DUN
PAPA AND MAMA'S ROOM!
DUN
DUN
DUN
DUN
BRACE YOURSELF!
ONCE YOU LEARN THESE SECRETS, YOU CAN NEVER LEAVE HERE ALIVE!
THERE COULD BE, LIKE, SUPER KNIVES AND NUCLEAR BOMBS IN THERE!
NOW LET'S—
CHAK

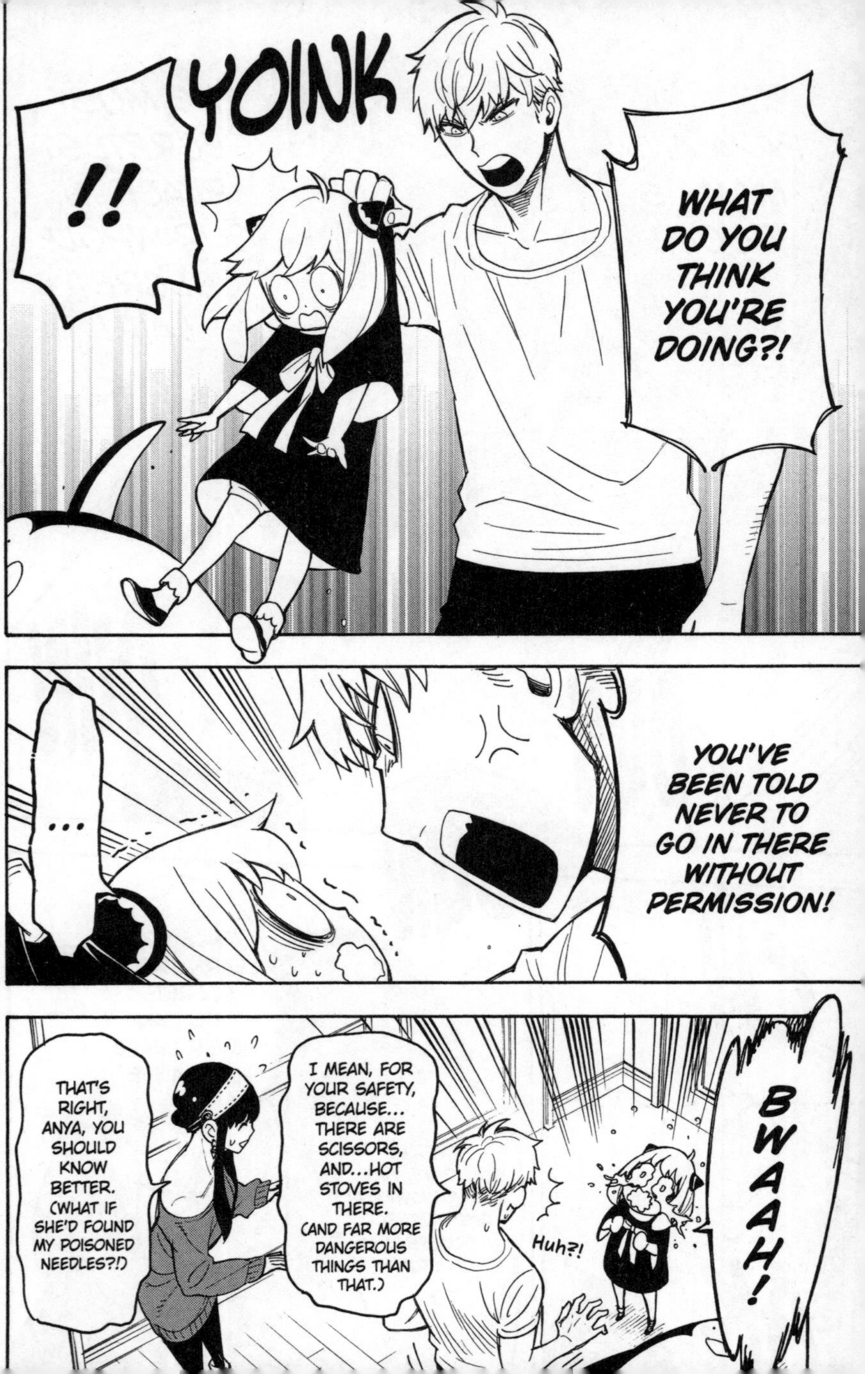
WHAT DO YOU THINK YOU'RE DOING?!
YOINK
!!
YOU'VE BEEN TOLD NEVER TO GO IN THERE WITHOUT PERMISSION!
...
BWAAAH!
Huh?!
I MEAN, FOR YOUR SAFETY, BECAUSE... THERE ARE SCISSORS, AND...HOT STOVES IN THERE. (AND FAR MORE DANGEROUS THINGS THAN THAT.)
THAT'S RIGHT, ANYA, YOU SHOULD KNOW BETTER. (WHAT IF SHE'D FOUND MY POISONED NEEDLES?!)

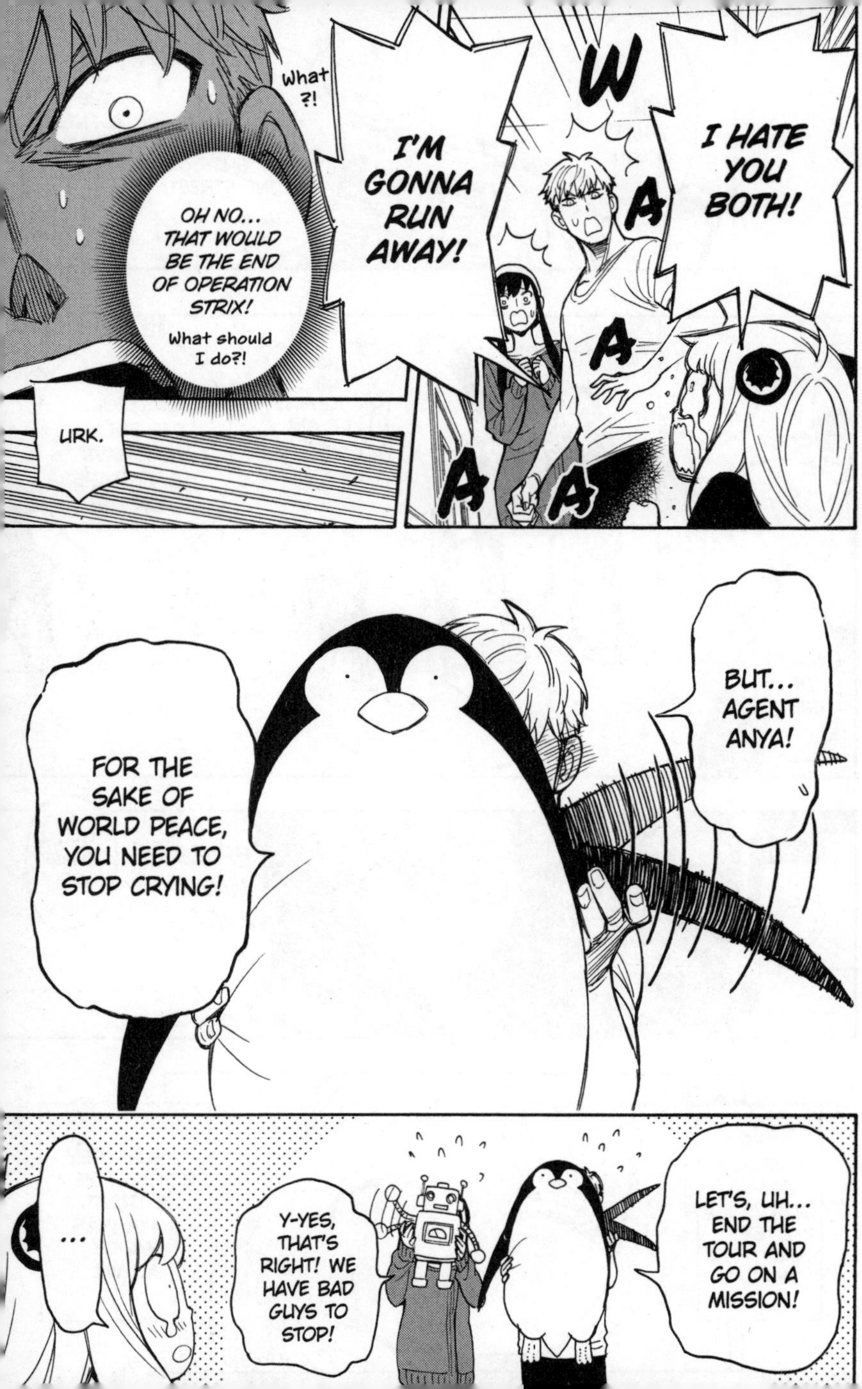
I HATE YOU BOTH!
I'M GONNA RUN AWAY!
WAAAAA
What?!
OH NO... THAT WOULD BE THE END OF OPERATION STRIX!
What should I do?!
URK.
BUT... AGENT ANYA!
FOR THE SAKE OF WORLD PEACE, YOU NEED TO STOP CRYING!
LET'S, UH... END THE TOUR AND GO ON A MISSION!
Y-YES, THAT'S RIGHT! WE HAVE BAD GUYS TO STOP!
...

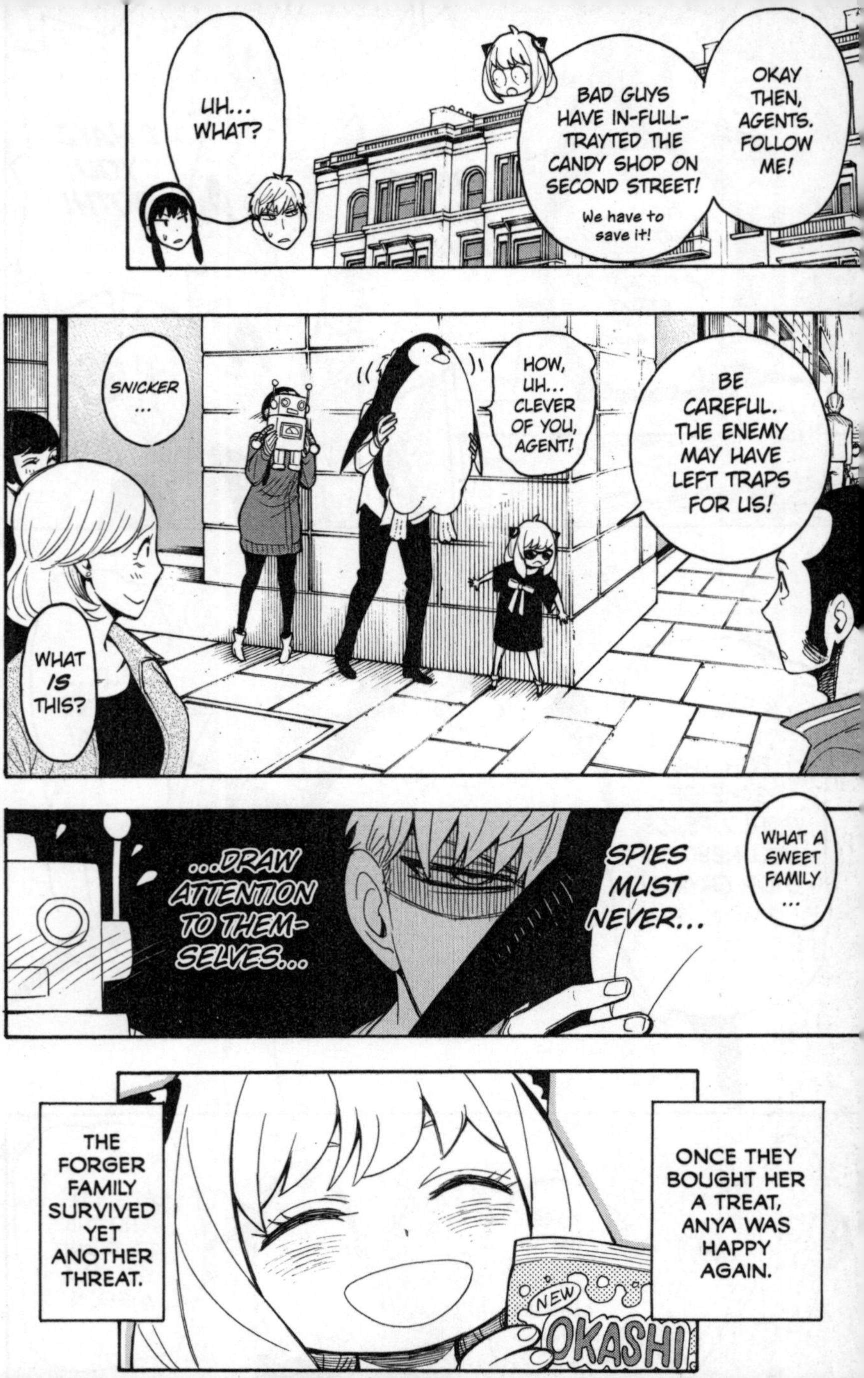
OKAY THEN, AGENTS. FOLLOW ME!
BAD GUYS HAVE IN-FULL-TRAYTED THE CANDY SHOP ON SECOND STREET!
We have to save it!
UH... WHAT?
BE CAREFUL. THE ENEMY MAY HAVE LEFT TRAPS FOR US!
HOW, UH... CLEVER OF YOU, AGENT!
SNICKER ...
WHAT IS THIS?
WHAT A SWEET FAMILY ...
SPIES MUST NEVER...
...DRAW ATTENTION TO THEM-SELVES...
ONCE THEY BOUGHT HER A TREAT, ANYA WAS HAPPY AGAIN.
THE FORGER FAMILY SURVIVED YET ANOTHER THREAT.
NEW
OKASHI

SECRET AGENCY "P2"

DIRECTOR CHIMERA

LEVEL: 100 BAJILLION
LEADERSHIP: 100 / KARIZMA: 100
EASYNESS TO CARRY: 80 / DURTYNESS: 20

AGENT ANYA

LEVEL: 100,000
POWER: 10 / SMARTS: 10
CUTENESS: 1,000,000 / TALLNESS: 99.5

AGENT PENGUINMAN

LEVEL: 1
POWER: 2 / SMARTS: 3
EAGERNESS: 80 / SOFTNESS: 50

AGENT PAPA

LEVEL: 100
POWER: 100 / SMARTS: 500
COOLNESS: 80 / STOMACHACHEYNESS: 90

AGENT MAMA

LEVEL: 100
POWER: 10,000 / SMARTS: 2
KINDNESS: 100 / LIFE SKILLS: 5

INFORMANT SCRUFFY

LEVEL: 30
POWER: 20 / SMARTS: 50
LIKABULLITY: 2 / USEFULNESS: 100

SPY×FAMILY

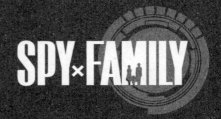

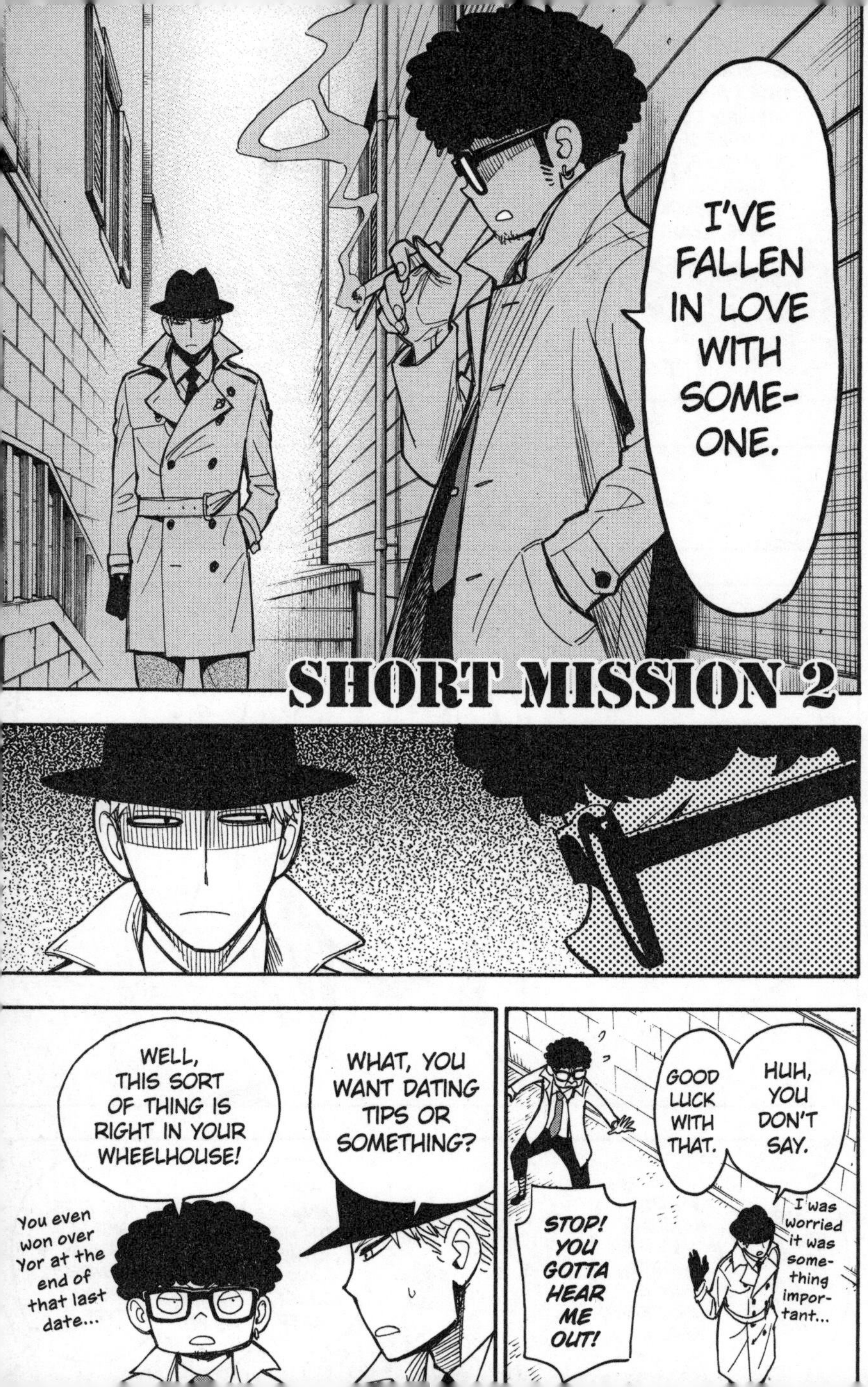
I'VE FALLEN IN LOVE WITH SOME-ONE.
SHORT MISSION 2
HUH, YOU DON'T SAY.
GOOD LUCK WITH THAT.
I was worried it was some-thing impor-tant...
STOP! YOU GOTTA HEAR ME OUT!
WHAT, YOU WANT DATING TIPS OR SOMETHING?
WELL, THIS SORT OF THING IS RIGHT IN YOUR WHEELHOUSE!
You even won over Yor at the end of that last date...

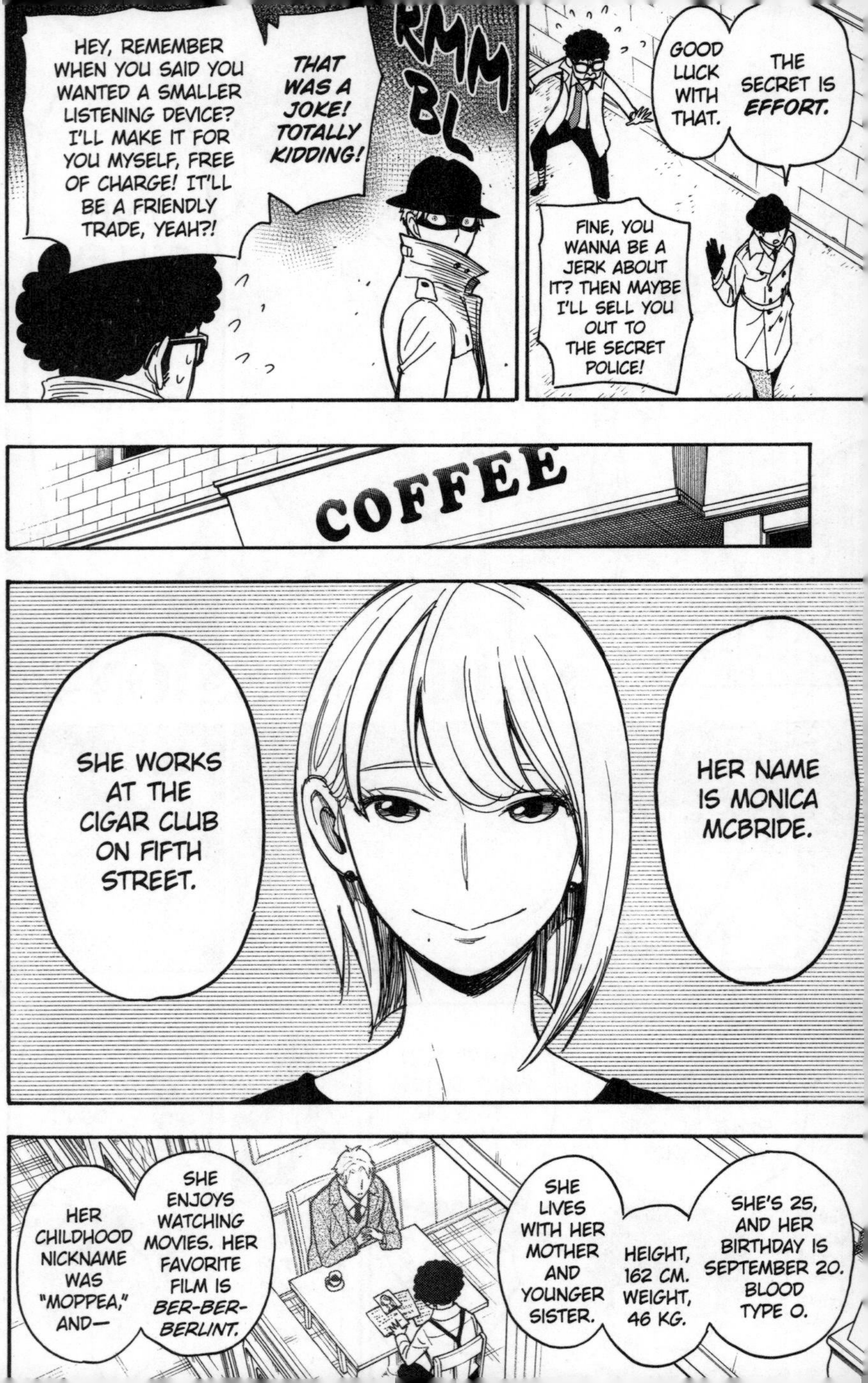
THE SECRET IS *EFFORT.*
GOOD LUCK WITH THAT.
FINE, YOU WANNA BE A JERK ABOUT IT? THEN MAYBE I'LL SELL YOU OUT TO THE SECRET POLICE!
RMMMBL
THAT WAS A JOKE! TOTALLY KIDDING!
HEY, REMEMBER WHEN YOU SAID YOU WANTED A SMALLER LISTENING DEVICE? I'LL MAKE IT FOR YOU MYSELF, FREE OF CHARGE! IT'LL BE A FRIENDLY TRADE, YEAH?!
COFFEE
HER NAME IS MONICA MCBRIDE.
SHE WORKS AT THE CIGAR CLUB ON FIFTH STREET.
SHE'S 25, AND HER BIRTHDAY IS SEPTEMBER 20. BLOOD TYPE O.
HEIGHT, 162 CM. WEIGHT, 46 KG.
SHE LIVES WITH HER MOTHER AND YOUNGER SISTER.
SHE ENJOYS WATCHING MOVIES. HER FAVORITE FILM IS *BER-BER-BERLINT.*
HER CHILDHOOD NICKNAME WAS "MOPPEA," AND—

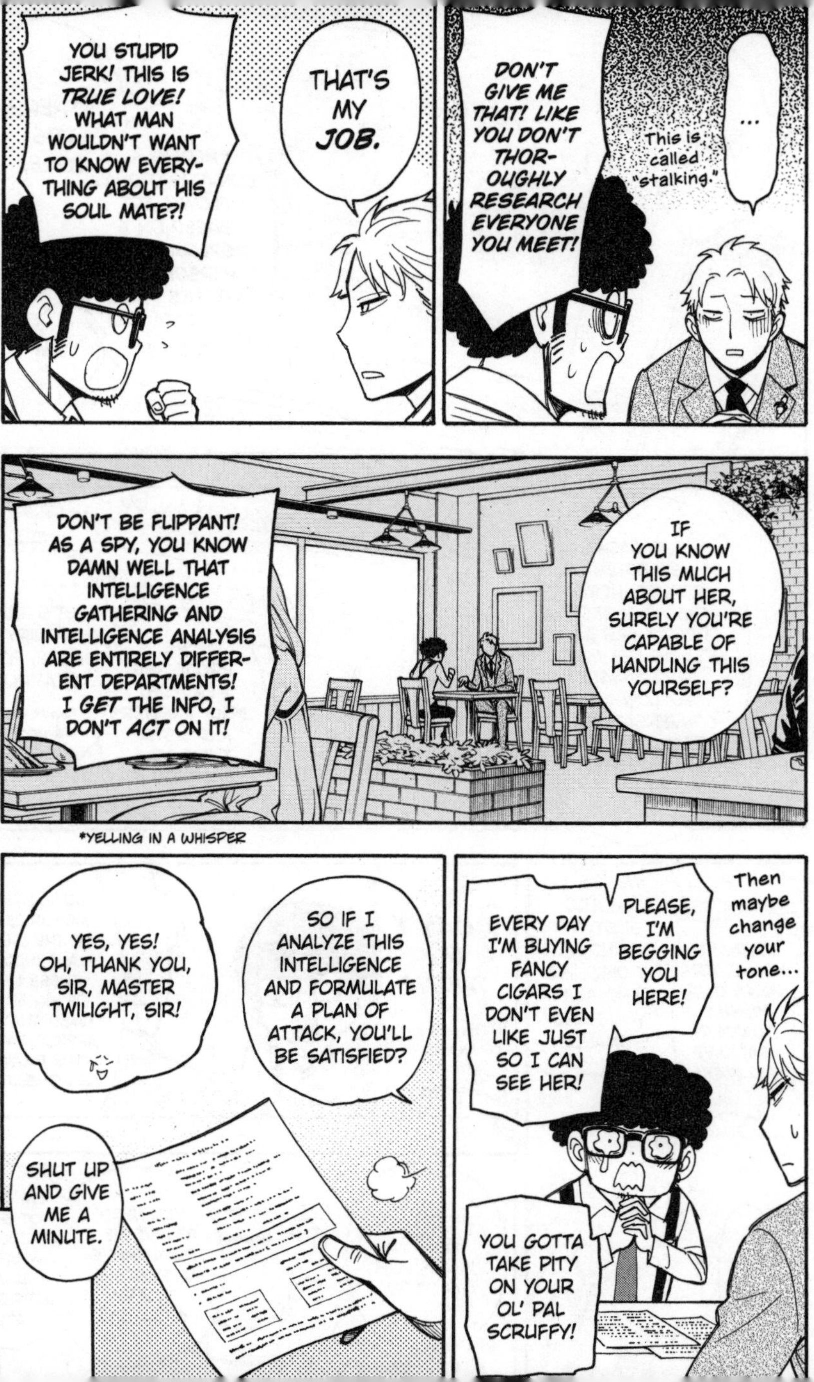
...
This is called "stalking."
DON'T GIVE ME THAT! LIKE YOU DON'T THOROUGHLY RESEARCH EVERYONE YOU MEET!
THAT'S MY JOB.
YOU STUPID JERK! THIS IS TRUE LOVE! WHAT MAN WOULDN'T WANT TO KNOW EVERYTHING ABOUT HIS SOUL MATE?!
IF YOU KNOW THIS MUCH ABOUT HER, SURELY YOU'RE CAPABLE OF HANDLING THIS YOURSELF?
DON'T BE FLIPPANT! AS A SPY, YOU KNOW DAMN WELL THAT INTELLIGENCE GATHERING AND INTELLIGENCE ANALYSIS ARE ENTIRELY DIFFERENT DEPARTMENTS! I GET THE INFO, I DON'T ACT ON IT!
*YELLING IN A WHISPER
Then maybe change your tone...
PLEASE, I'M BEGGING YOU HERE!
EVERY DAY I'M BUYING FANCY CIGARS I DON'T EVEN LIKE JUST SO I CAN SEE HER!
YOU GOTTA TAKE PITY ON YOUR OL' PAL SCRUFFY!
SO IF I ANALYZE THIS INTELLIGENCE AND FORMULATE A PLAN OF ATTACK, YOU'LL BE SATISFIED?
YES, YES! OH, THANK YOU, SIR, MASTER TWILIGHT, SIR!
SHUT UP AND GIVE ME A MINUTE.

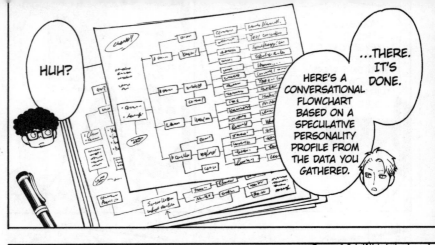

...THERE. IT'S DONE.
HERE'S A CONVERSATIONAL FLOWCHART BASED ON A SPECULATIVE PERSONALITY PROFILE FROM THE DATA YOU GATHERED.
HUH?
LET'S TAKE INQUIRY 1 HERE, FOR EXAMPLE.
About her favorite foods...
I'VE PROJECTED HER MOST LIKELY ANSWERS AND LISTED THEM AS *A* THROUGH *D*.
UH, OKAY...
A. STRAWBERRIES
B. PICKLES
FOOD?
FOR EACH OF HER POTENTIAL REPLIES, HERE ARE YOUR BEST RESPONSES AS WELL AS THE MOST APPROPRIATE FOLLOW-UP CONVERSATIONAL BRANCHES FOR THE POSSIBLE PATHS.
UH-HUH...
YOU'LL NEED TO MEMORIZE ALL OF THE CHARTS AND INITIATE THESE LINES OF INQUIRY AT TIMES THAT ARE APPROPRIATE TO THE FLOW OF CONVERSATION...
I CAN'T DO THIS!!
There are thousands of them!
I'M JUST NOT GOOD AT JUDGING WHAT IS AND ISN'T APPROPRIATE.
YOU NEED TO GIVE ME A PLAN THAT'S APPLICABLE IN *ANY* SITUATION!
IT'D BE LESS WORK FOR YOU TOO!
MAYBE I SHOULD JUST SIT BEHIND HER IN DISGUISE AND GIVE YOU HAND SIGNALS...
AND LET YOU OVERHEAR OUR WHOLE CONVERSATION? NO WAY!
...

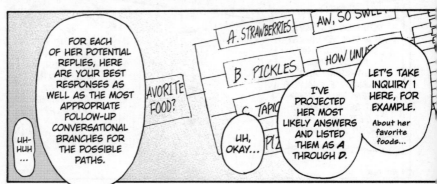

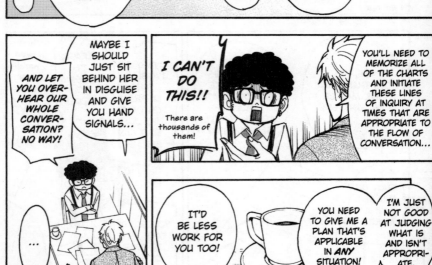

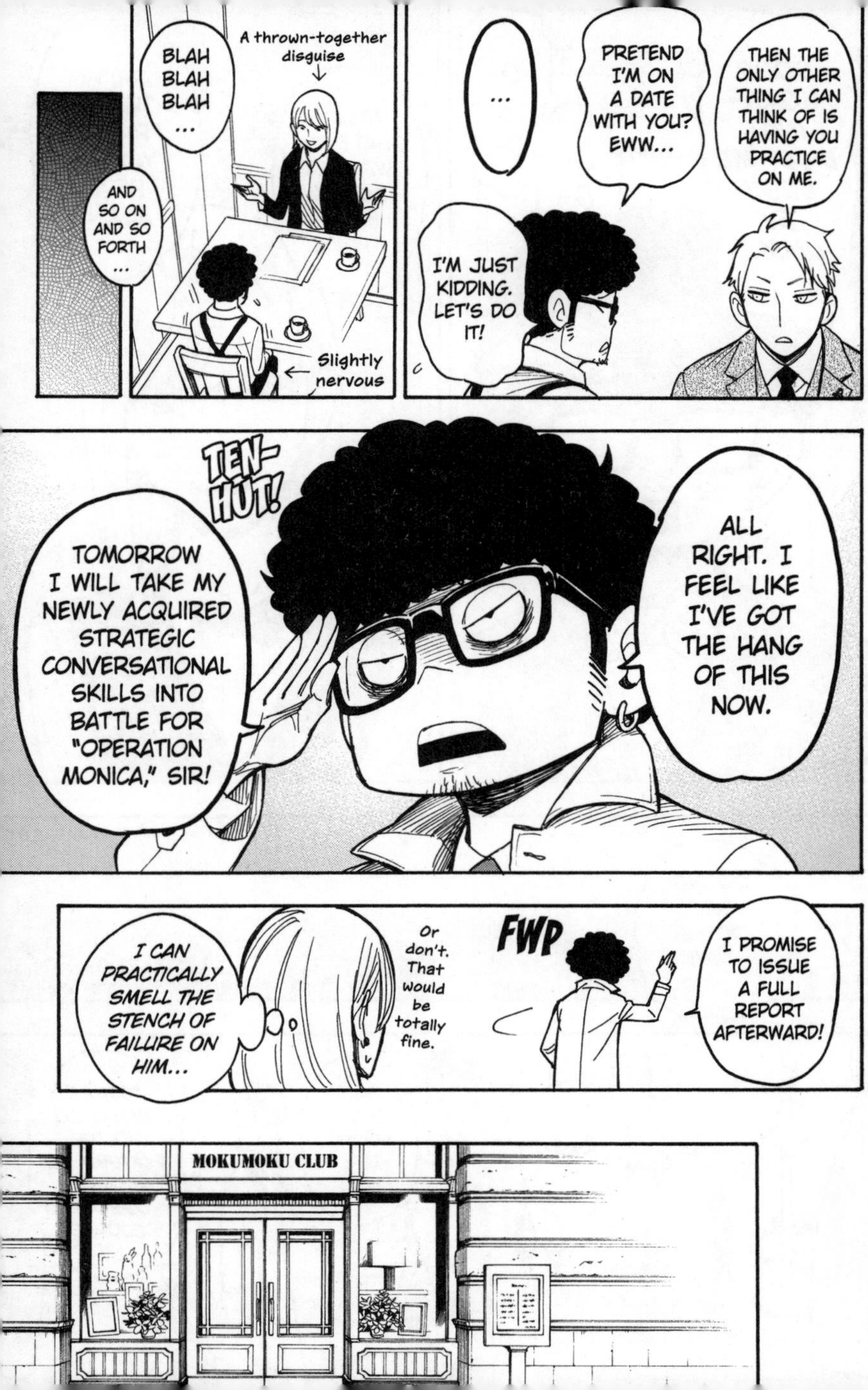
THEN THE ONLY OTHER THING I CAN THINK OF IS HAVING YOU PRACTICE ON ME.
PRETEND I'M ON A DATE WITH YOU? EWW...
...
I'M JUST KIDDING. LET'S DO IT!
A thrown-together disguise
BLAH BLAH BLAH ...
AND SO ON AND SO FORTH ...
Slightly nervous
ALL RIGHT. I FEEL LIKE I'VE GOT THE HANG OF THIS NOW.
TEN-HUT!
TOMORROW I WILL TAKE MY NEWLY ACQUIRED STRATEGIC CONVERSATIONAL SKILLS INTO BATTLE FOR "OPERATION MONICA," SIR!
I PROMISE TO ISSUE A FULL REPORT AFTERWARD!
FWP
Or don't. That would be totally fine.
I CAN PRACTICALLY SMELL THE STENCH OF FAILURE ON HIM...
MOKUMOKU CLUB

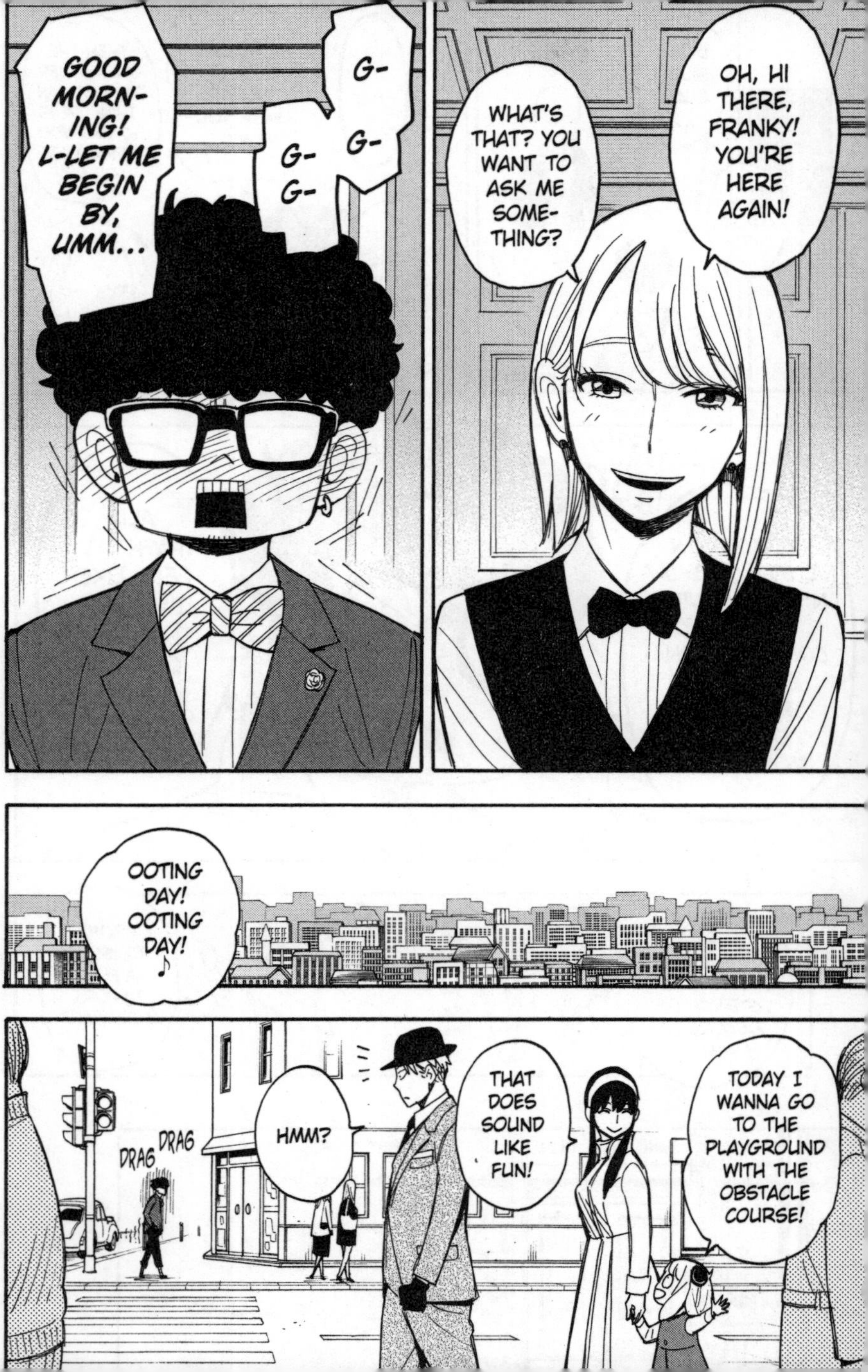
OH, HI THERE, FRANKY! YOU'RE HERE AGAIN!
WHAT'S THAT? YOU WANT TO ASK ME SOMETHING?
G- G-
G- G-
GOOD MORNING! L-LET ME BEGIN BY, UMM...
OOTING DAY! OOTING DAY! ♪
TODAY I WANNA GO TO THE PLAYGROUND WITH THE OBSTACLE COURSE!
THAT DOES SOUND LIKE FUN!
HMM?
DRAG DRAG

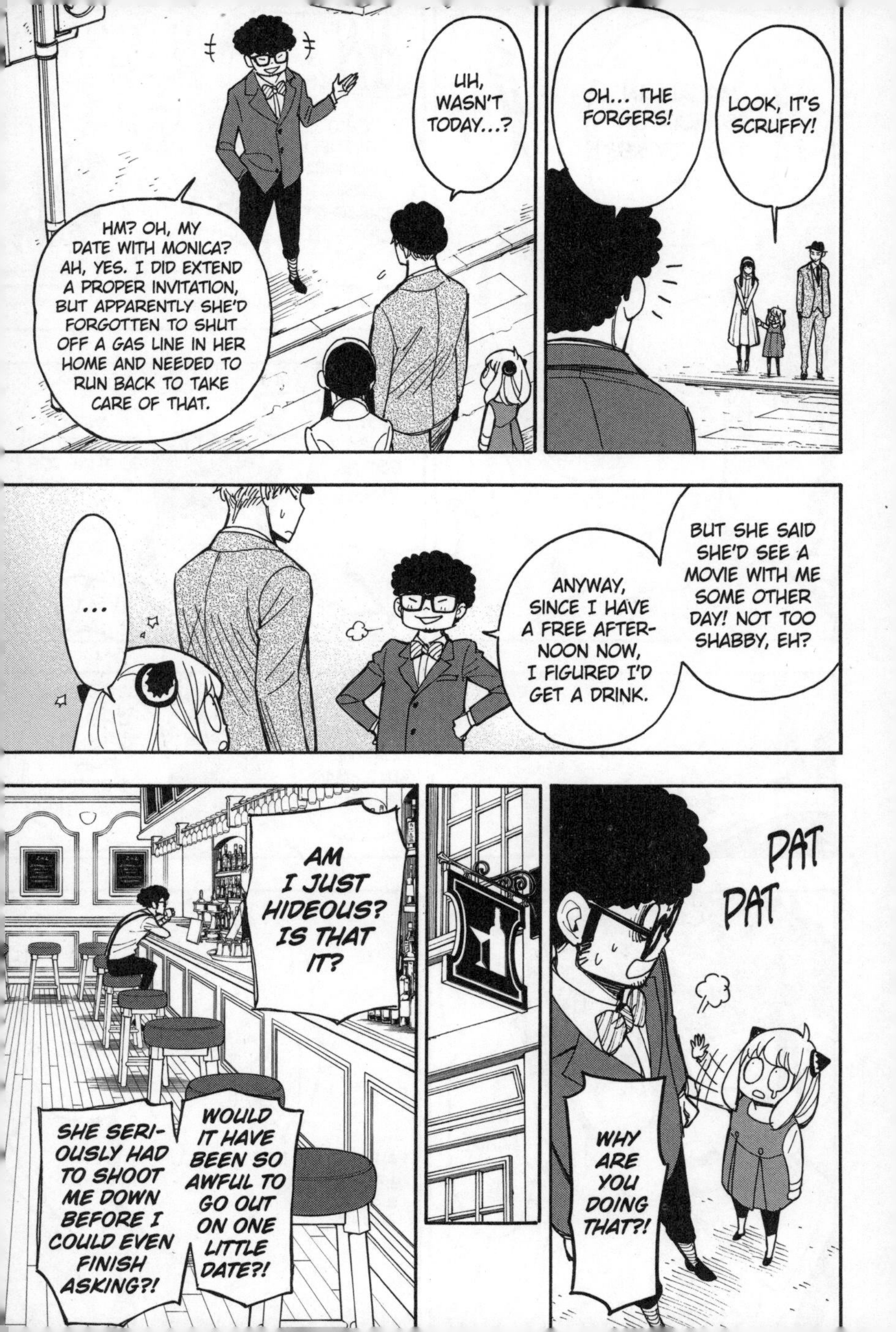
LOOK, IT'S SCRUFFY!
OH... THE FORGERS!
UH, WASN'T TODAY...?
HM? OH, MY DATE WITH MONICA? AH, YES. I DID EXTEND A PROPER INVITATION, BUT APPARENTLY SHE'D FORGOTTEN TO SHUT OFF A GAS LINE IN HER HOME AND NEEDED TO RUN BACK TO TAKE CARE OF THAT.
BUT SHE SAID SHE'D SEE A MOVIE WITH ME SOME OTHER DAY! NOT TOO SHABBY, EH?
ANYWAY, SINCE I HAVE A FREE AFTER-NOON NOW, I FIGURED I'D GET A DRINK.
...
PAT
PAT
WHY ARE YOU DOING THAT?!
AM I JUST HIDEOUS? IS THAT IT?
WOULD IT HAVE BEEN SO AWFUL TO GO OUT ON ONE LITTLE DATE?!
SHE SERI-OUSLY HAD TO SHOOT ME DOWN BEFORE I COULD EVEN FINISH ASKING?!

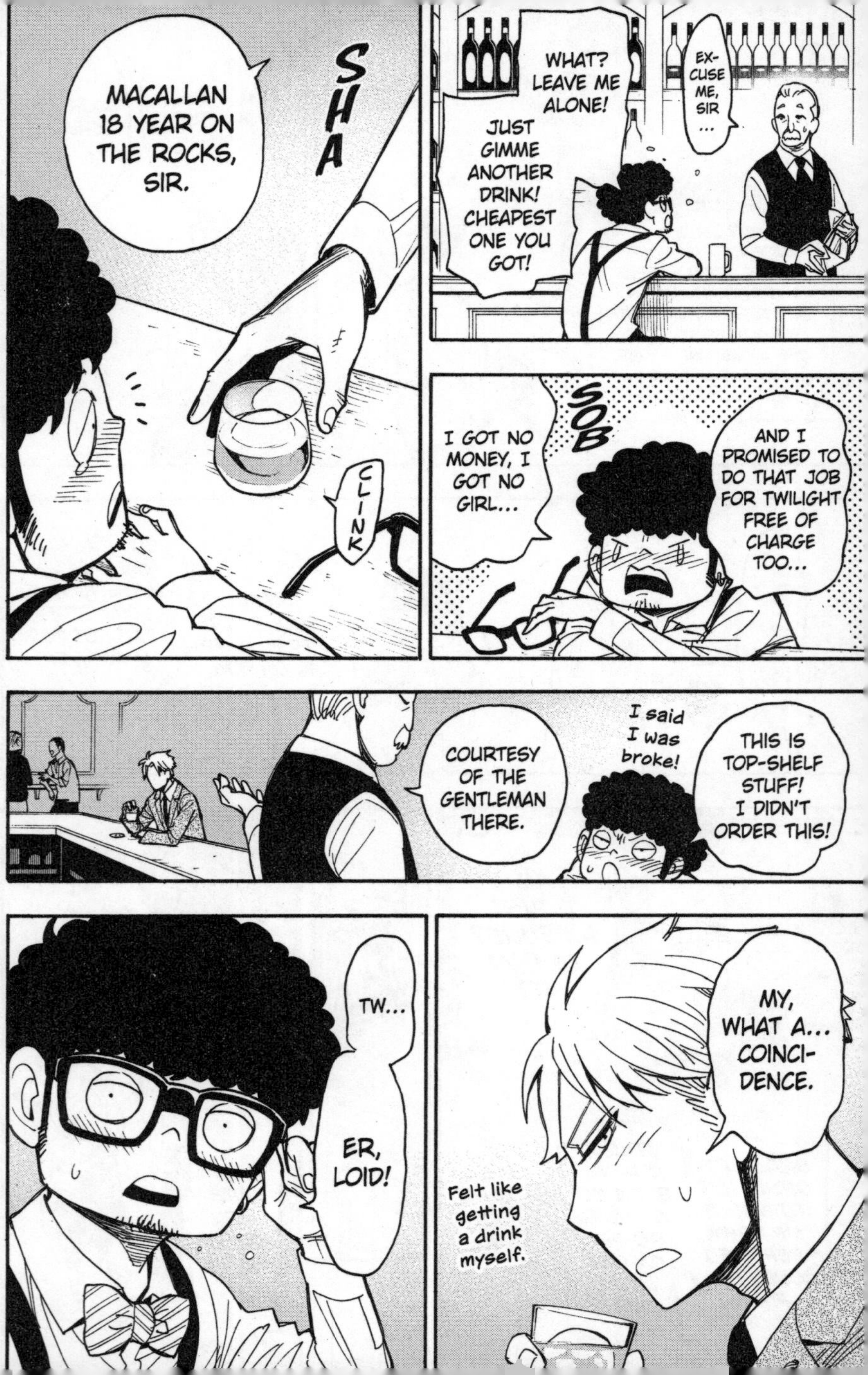
EX-CUSE ME, SIR...
WHAT? LEAVE ME ALONE!
JUST GIMME ANOTHER DRINK! CHEAPEST ONE YOU GOT!
SOB
I GOT NO MONEY, I GOT NO GIRL...
AND I PROMISED TO DO THAT JOB FOR TWILIGHT FREE OF CHARGE TOO...
MACALLAN 18 YEAR ON THE ROCKS, SIR.
SHA
CLINK
THIS IS TOP-SHELF STUFF! I DIDN'T ORDER THIS!
I said I was broke!
COURTESY OF THE GENTLEMAN THERE.
MY, WHAT A... COINCI-DENCE.
Felt like getting a drink myself.
TW...
ER, LOID!

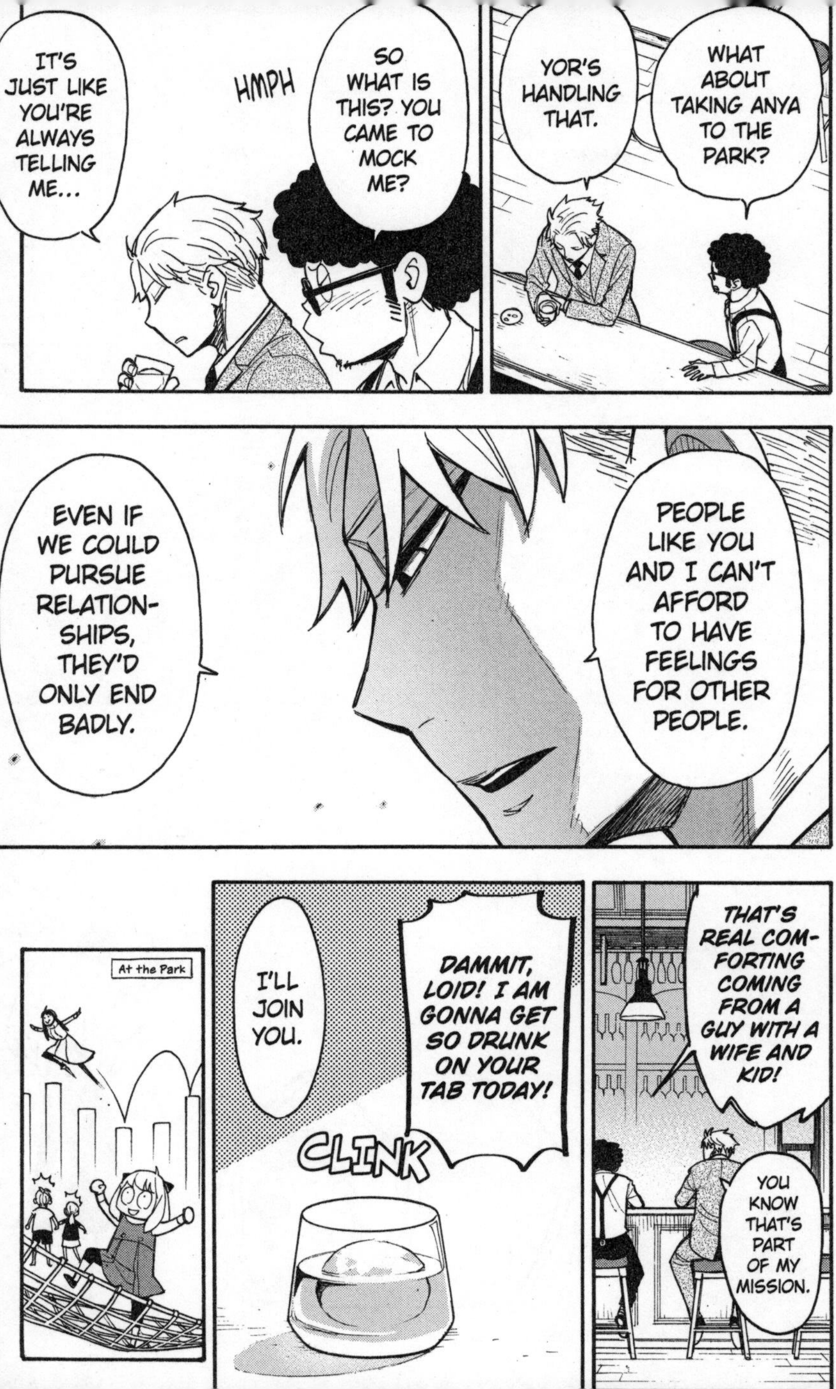

WHAT ABOUT TAKING ANYA TO THE PARK?
YOR'S HANDLING THAT.
SO WHAT IS THIS? YOU CAME TO MOCK ME?
HMPH
IT'S JUST LIKE YOU'RE ALWAYS TELLING ME...
PEOPLE LIKE YOU AND I CAN'T AFFORD TO HAVE FEELINGS FOR OTHER PEOPLE.
EVEN IF WE COULD PURSUE RELATION-SHIPS, THEY'D ONLY END BADLY.
THAT'S REAL COM-FORTING COMING FROM A GUY WITH A WIFE AND KID!
YOU KNOW THAT'S PART OF MY MISSION.
DAMMIT, LOID! I AM GONNA GET SO DRUNK ON YOUR TAB TODAY!
I'LL JOIN YOU.
CLINK
At the Park

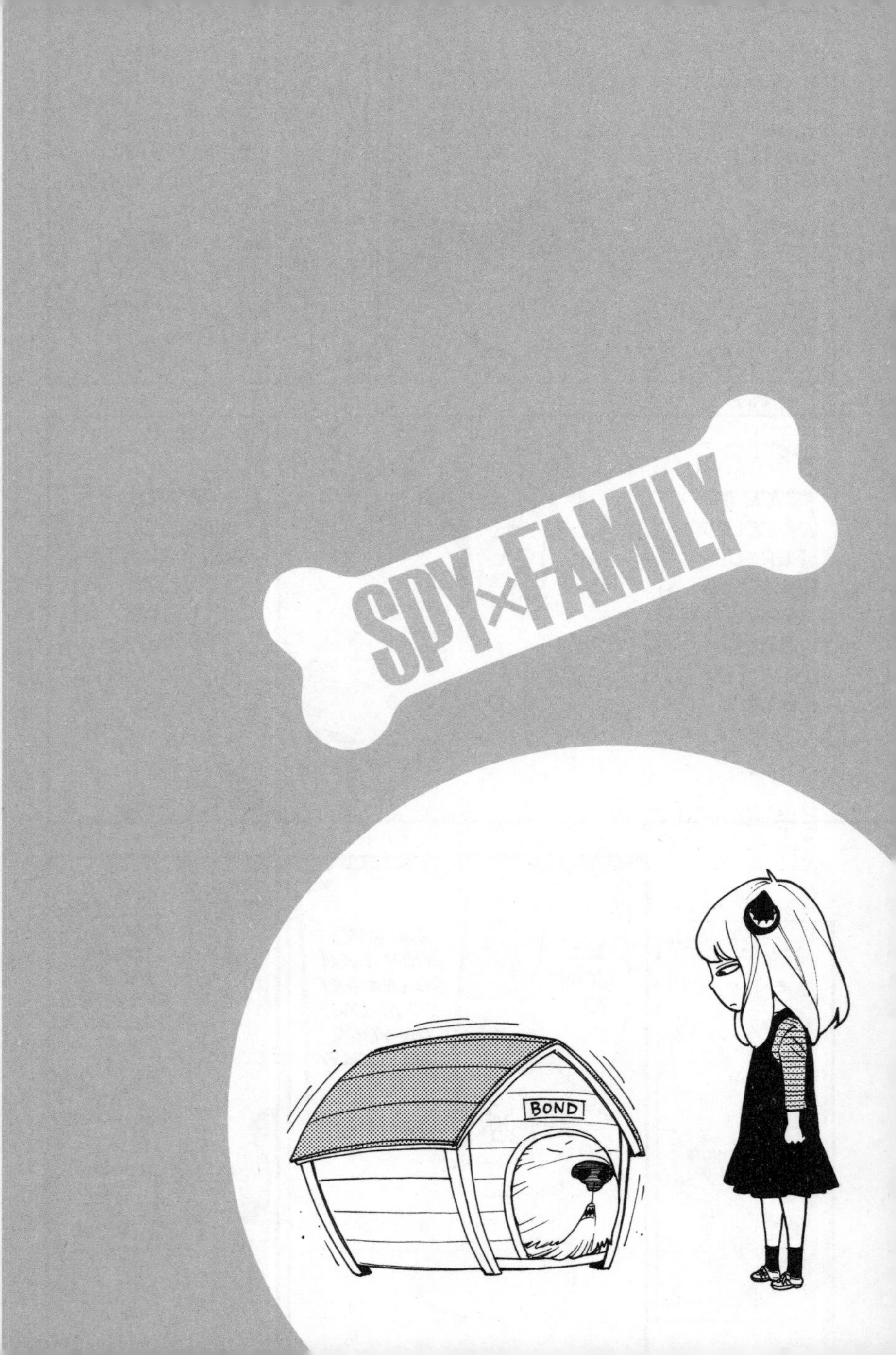
SPY×FAMILY
BOND

SPYxFAMILY VOL. 4
SPECIAL THANKS LIST

·CLASSIFIED·

ART ASSISTANCE

AMASHIMA	MAEHATA
SATOSHI KIMURA	YUICHI OZAKI
MIO AYATSUKA	MAFUYU KONISHI
KAZUKI NONAKA	KEISUKE HOSHINOYA
ERI HARADA	

GRAPHIC NOVEL DESIGN

HIDEAKI SHIMADA	ERI ARAKAWA

GRAPHIC NOVEL EDITOR

KANAKO YANAGIDA

MANAGING EDITOR

SHIHEI LIN

THANK YOU FOR PICKING UP VOLUME 4. IT'S A SILLY LITTLE MANGA, BUT I WOULD BE DELIGHTED IF IT MANAGES TO AMUSE YOU, EVEN IF ONLY JUST A LITTLE.

—TATSUYA ENDO

EYES ONLY   READ & ~~DESTROY~~   EYES ONLY

SPY×FAMILY

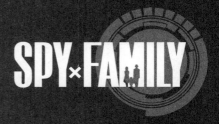

SPY×FAMILY

THE DOGGY CRISIS

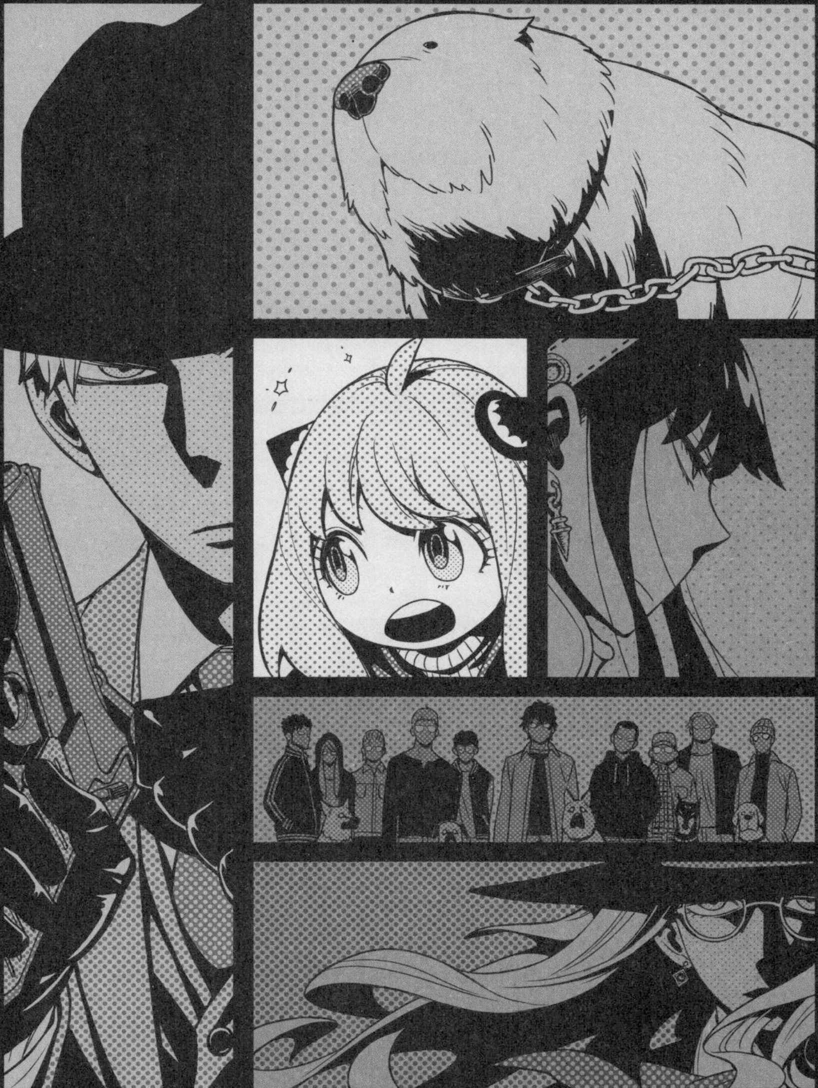

SPY×FAMILY

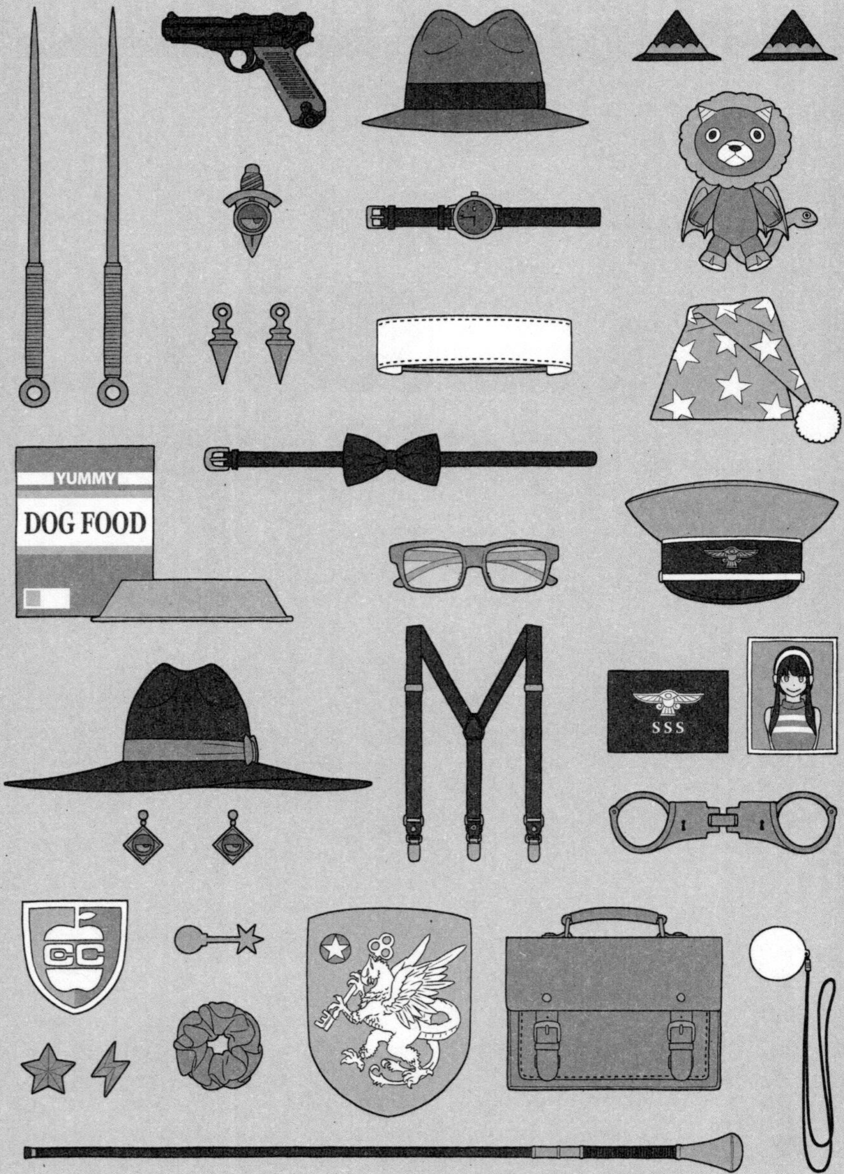
YUMMY
DOG FOOD
SSS
CC

THE DOG'S SECRET ORIGINS

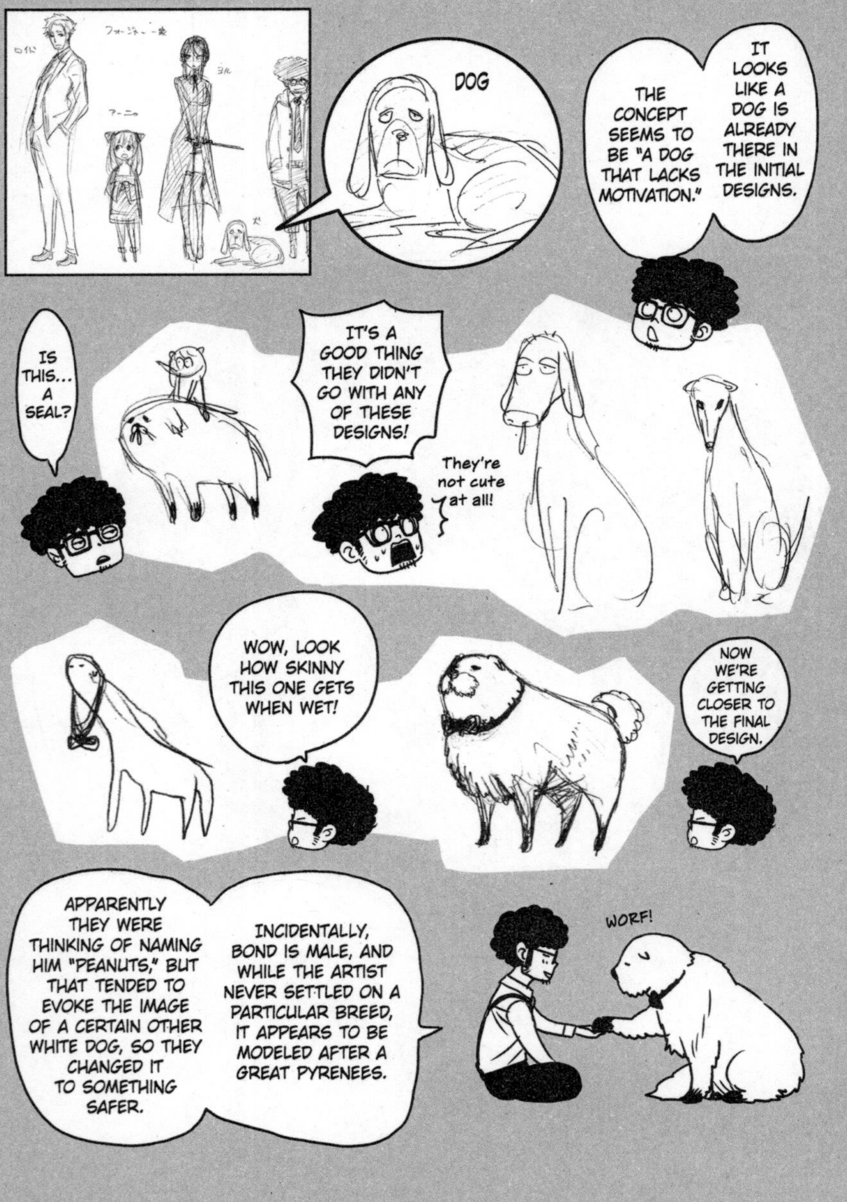
IT LOOKS LIKE A DOG IS ALREADY THERE IN THE INITIAL DESIGNS.
THE CONCEPT SEEMS TO BE "A DOG THAT LACKS MOTIVATION."
DOG
IT'S A GOOD THING THEY DIDN'T GO WITH ANY OF THESE DESIGNS!
They're not cute at all!
IS THIS... A SEAL?
NOW WE'RE GETTING CLOSER TO THE FINAL DESIGN.
WOW, LOOK HOW SKINNY THIS ONE GETS WHEN WET!
WORF!
INCIDENTALLY, BOND IS MALE, AND WHILE THE ARTIST NEVER SETTLED ON A PARTICULAR BREED, IT APPEARS TO BE MODELED AFTER A GREAT PYRENEES.
APPARENTLY THEY WERE THINKING OF NAMING HIM "PEANUTS," BUT THAT TENDED TO EVOKE THE IMAGE OF A CERTAIN OTHER WHITE DOG, SO THEY CHANGED IT TO SOMETHING SAFER.

I'm a cat person, but dogs are cute too.

—TATSUYA ENDO

Tatsuya Endo was born in Ibaraki Prefecture, Japan, on July 23, 1980. He debuted as a manga artist with the one-shot "Seibu Yugi" (Western Game), which ran in the Spring 2000 issue of *Akamaru Jump*. He is the author of *TISTA* and *Gekka Bijin* (Moon Flower Beauty). *Spy x Family* is his first work published in English.

SPY×FAMILY

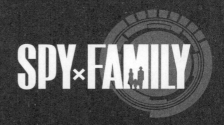